COURTS, CONSTITUTIONS AND KARMA

Although rarely acknowledged, Buddhist monastics are among the most active lawmakers and jurists in Asia, operating sophisticated networks of courts and constitutions while also navigating – and shaping – secular legal systems. This book provides the first in-depth study of Buddhist monastic law and its entanglements with state law in Sri Lanka from 1800 to the present. Rather than a top-down account of colliding legal orders, Schonthal draws on nearly a decade of archival, ethnographic and empirical research to document the ways that Buddhist monks, colonial officials and contemporary lawmakers reconcile the laws of the Buddha and the laws of the land using practices of legal pluralism. Comparative in outlook and accessible in style, this book not only offers a portrait of Buddhist monastic law in action, it also yields new insights into how societies manage multi-legality and why legal pluralism leads to conflict in some settings and to compromise in others.

BENJAMIN SCHONTHAL is Professor of Buddhist Studies and Affiliate Professor of Law at the University of Otago, where he also co-directs the Otago Centre for Law and Society.

CAMBRIDGE STUDIES IN LAW AND SOCIETY

Founded in 1997, Cambridge Studies in Law and Society is a hub for leading scholarship in socio-legal studies. Located at the intersection of law, the humanities, and the social sciences, it publishes empirically innovative and theoretically sophisticated work on law's manifestations in everyday life: from discourses to practices, and from institutions to cultures. The series editors have longstanding expertise in the interdisciplinary study of law, and welcome contributions that place legal phenomena in national, comparative, or international perspective. Series authors come from a range of disciplines, including anthropology, history, law, literature, political science, and sociology.

A list of books in the series can be found at the back of this book.

CAMBRIDGE
STUDIES IN
LAW AND SOCIETY

COURTS, CONSTITUTIONS AND KARMA

Buddhism, Law and the Practices of Legal Pluralism in Sri Lanka

Benjamin Schonthal

University of Otago

CAMBRIDGE
UNIVERSITY PRESS

CAMBRIDGE
UNIVERSITY PRESS

Shaftesbury Road, Cambridge CB2 8EA, United Kingdom

One Liberty Plaza, 20th Floor, New York, NY 10006, USA

477 Williamstown Road, Port Melbourne, VIC 3207, Australia

314–321, 3rd Floor, Plot 3, Splendor Forum, Jasola District Centre, New Delhi – 110025, India

103 Penang Road, #05–06/07, Visioncrest Commercial, Singapore 238467

Cambridge University Press is part of Cambridge University Press & Assessment, a department of the University of Cambridge.

We share the University's mission to contribute to society through the pursuit of education, learning and research at the highest international levels of excellence.

www.cambridge.org
Information on this title: www.cambridge.org/9781009706919

DOI: 10.1017/9781009706940

When citing this work, please include a reference to the DOI 10.1017/9781009706940

First published 2026

Cover image: Two monks walking at Pettah Bazar, Colombo, Sri Lanka / 2018 / Guido Cozzi / Atlantide Phototrave / Getty Images

A catalogue record for this publication is available from the British Library

A Cataloging-in-Publication data record for this book is available from the Library of Congress

ISBN 978-1-009-70691-9 Hardback

CONTENTS

FIGURES

TABLES

A NOTE ON LANGUAGES, NAMES AND CITATIONS

This book draws mostly on sources written in the languages of Sinhala, Pali and English. Sinhala is the dominant language spoken in Sri Lanka and the vernacular used by most Buddhists. Pali is the ancient, classical language associated with the sacred texts of Theravāda Buddhism, the variety of Buddhism that predominates in Sri Lanka. It is also a language in which many monastic legal texts are written.

Unless otherwise specified, the non-English words contained in this book come from Sinhala and are transliterated according to the standard conventions outlined in Gair and Karunatillake, with the exception that I tend to mark the conjoint consonants separately, for example, as *mb* rather than *m̆b*.[1] Pali transliteration follows standard practices used by the Pali Text Society. Where the reader might be confused about the source language of the non-English term, I use the following abbreviations to clarify: S: for Sinhala language terms and P: for Pali language terms.

Monastic legal texts often mix together Pali, Sinhala, Sanskrit and/or hybrid forms of the same word. For example, readers may encounter both *kamma* and *karma*, or *śāsana* and *sāsana*. In most cases, I have used the form of the word given in the original text. Where the Pali equivalent of Sinhala terms is not apparent, I have also included the Pali form in parentheses so that interested readers may make comparisons. Where a non-English term appears in the Oxford English Dictionary, I have used the OED spelling unitalicised (e.g. dharma, sangha, nirvana, bhikkhu, bhikkhunī). Following OED conventions, I do not italicise Vinaya Piṭaka, Sutta Piṭaka or Abhidhamma Piṭaka.

When referring to Buddhist monastics, I frequently use the standard convention of placing 'Ven.' before the name, meaning Venerable. In referring to monastic names, I do not include the many honorific prefixes and suffixes – indicating the education, rank and status of the

[1] James W. Gair and W. S. Karunatillake, *Literary Sinhala Inflected Forms with a Transliteration Guide* (Ithaca, NY: Cornell University, 1976).

person – that are often attached to such names in written sources. I have done this for purposes of clarity and consistency.

The name of the island that is now known as Sri Lanka has changed over time and is referred to differently across the authors and genres of texts examined in this book. The reader will encounter several names for the island in the chapters that follow. Monastic authors and Sinhala sources, particularly prior to the mid-twentieth century, refer to the island as Laṅkā and Lakdiva. Starting in the early nineteenth century, British colonial officials, political elites and others also referred to the island as Ceylon, the name given to the territory by the British. Ceylon served as the official name for the country until 1972, when it was changed to Sri Lanka. When speaking about the island, I follow two conventions: in most cases, I default to the name of the island used by the writers and speakers that I am examining; in other cases, so as not to confuse the reader, I use the official names of the island adapted by colonial and post-colonial governments, namely Ceylon prior to 1972 and Sri Lanka after that.

PREFACE: ACKNOWLEDGING KARMA

The odds are that somewhere, right now, a dispute is taking place between Buddhist monastics over the meaning and application of law. The disputants may be inside the walls of a temple and debating the meaning of disciplinary rules, with fraternity elders acting as judges. They may have travelled to a major city, such as Mandalay or Bangkok, to take part in a government-sponsored ecclesiastical court run by monastic officials whose decisions are enforceable by the police. Or perhaps they went to a local district court to resolve the matter in front of a magistrate, accompanied by lawyers carrying armloads of briefs explaining why their interpretation of Buddhist property law should be preferred over another. Wherever there are Buddhist monastics, there are laws – and debates about how to apply them.

This fact may surprise some readers. Buddhist monastics tend to be known for their spiritual rather than legal accomplishments. They are usually imagined as contemplatives, preachers and scholars, not litigants or jurists. Scholars of Buddhism have unwittingly reinforced this impression. While we frequently write about Buddhism's ancient code of monastic law, the Vinaya Piṭaka, we too often ignore the bustling universe of other laws and legal institutions – some authorised by the Buddha, others created by monastic fraternities and yet others promulgated by governments and local lay communities – that shape the lives of Buddhist clerics and their followers today.

And yet Buddhist monastic communities (called sanghas) comprise some of the most active lawmakers and jurists in Asia. In Southern Asia, approximately 1 out of every 200 Buddhists has been ordained as a monastic, submitting themselves to traditions of law that date back more than 2,000 years. This makes Buddhist sanghas not only some of the largest legal communities in Asia but also some of the longest-practising legal communities anywhere in the world. This book examines these legal communities in Sri Lanka.

LAW'S KARMAS

Sri Lanka's Buddhist monastics inhabit a complex legal landscape. As the title of the book suggests, they engage with multiple kinds of *courts* and *constitutions* – some authorised by the government, others by the Buddha, and yet others by the leaders of monastic fraternities. Monastics also engage with multiple kinds of *karma*, a phrase that, as readers will discover, has several important legal connotations.

At its broadest, karma refers to the cosmic laws of cause and effect that lie at the core of the Buddha's teachings. Karma aligns actions with consequences, linking a person's behaviour in the present with outcomes, or 'fruits', in the future. The logic of karma also holds that one's current life conditions are shaped by past behaviours, including actions done in one's previous rebirths. In this way, karma crosses the threshold of death, affecting beings across multiple lifetimes. To speak of law's karma in this frame of reference is to situate legal action in larger webs of cause and effect – to highlight the personal and cosmological stakes that accompany seemingly mundane acts of making or interpreting law.

A second, more technical connotation of karma is equally important for this book. In the context of monastic law, the word karma – which simply means 'action' – also refers to the most basic legal procedures used by a monastic community: the 'communal legal action,' or *saṅgha karma*. Like the legal procedures used in modern state courtrooms (e.g. opening a courtroom or taking an oath), *saṅgha karma*s involve carefully scripted collections of words and gestures that, when performed correctly, *enact* the law. *Saṅgha karma*s are the events that turn accused persons into guilty ones, buried stones into ritual boundaries and open questions into settled judgments. To speak of law's karma in this second sense is to point towards the formal, structured protocols, or 'actions,' that bring law to life.

A KARMIC APPROACH TO LAW

A third notion of karma also weighs on this book. Although implicit more than explicit, a karmic approach to law pervades my analysis, one which – like the doctrine of karma itself – focuses on actions and effects over time. This karma-informed approach treats laws not as fixed collections of artefacts – courts, codes and rules – but as shifting, unstable amalgams that humans define and redefine over time. It views today's laws as the products of previous legal actions, and it shows how contemporary legal activities condition law's content and conceptualisation in the future.

More specifically, this book treats accounts of legal pluralism as themselves the products of human action. Just as one action leads to another in karmic succession, so too do humans construe their multi-legal worlds in distinct but entangled ways: one rendering of legal pluralism elicits another, which elicits a third, and so on. I refer to this karma-like process of recurring and recursive actions as *practices of legal pluralism*.

The layout of this book echoes this karmic logic. It presents the multi-legal lives of Buddhist monastics as a chain of past actions, present conditions and future outcomes. Part I considers monastic law's nineteenth-century past, examining the inter-braiding of British colonial and monastic legal traditions. Part II offers a detailed ethnographic study of the contemporary monastic legal system as practised by one of Sri Lanka's largest monastic fraternities. Part III considers the consequences and ongoing challenges of balancing state and monastic legal authority in Sri Lanka, with a future-oriented lens.

KARMIC DEBTS

Chains of cause and effect also apply to the creation of this book. My own actions in writing this book were only made possible by the generosity of so many others.

A major debt of gratitude is owed to judges and judicial officials in the Rāmañña Nikāya for sharing their thoughts and time so generously with me. Special thanks go to Ven. Raluvē Padmasiri, Ven. Attanganē Ratanapāla and Ven. Makulāvē Vimala, who supported this project from the earliest moments. Ven. Padmasiri, in particular, has been a very generous friend and colleague, giving so much of his time and energy to help me understand the details here.

This project would never have happened were it not for the conversations and support of Professor Asanga Tilakaratne, whose insights, feedback and encouragement have been absolutely critical. It also would not have happened without the many conversations and translation sessions conducted with Bandara Herath, who helped me navigate the difficult language and scripts of many monastic legal texts.

Over the nearly ten years that I conducted research for this project in Sri Lanka, I was lucky to work with many wonderful researchers, without whose help none of this would have happened. Dinushka Peiris, Amali Priyadarshani, Gihani De Silva, Anushka Kahandagama, Dinithi Ranasinghe, Ven. Kahavaththē Amitha, Iromi Perera (and the Social Indicator team) and especially Tilak Jayatilaka supported and guided me through various phases of the project. Nilantha Indika helped locate and scan rare monastic legal texts, in many cases transcribing difficult-to-read images into transliterated typed script. The kind staff at the Sri Lankan National Archives (including the Kandy branch), JR Jayawardena Centre and National Museum Library made a major difference in this work.

At various stages during the writing process, I was blessed to have the support and insights of Alan Strathern, Alex McKinley, Alicia Turner, Andi Shubert, Anne Blackburn, Anne Mocko, Anushka Kahandagama, Asanga Welikala, Ben Berger, Berthe Jansen, Beth Hurd, Brenton Sullivan, Bui Ngoc Son, C.R. de Silva, Cuilan Liu, David Engel, Deane Galbraith, Dinesha Samararatne, Faisal Kamal, Farzana Haniffa, Fernanda Pirie, Gehan Gunatillake, Gihani De Silva, Greg Kourilsky, Ian Hurd, Iromi Perera, Iza Hussin, Jaclyn Neo, John Rogers, John Shaver, Jonathan Young, Justin Henry, K.D. Paranavitana, Kalana Senaratne, Kitsiri Malalgoda, Krishantha Fedricks, Levi McLaughlan, Lina Verchery, Masahiro Kitsudō, Martin Krieger, Matt Nelson, Matt Walton, Matthew Drew, Matthew Eerie, Melissa Crouch, Miguel Alvarez Ortega, Miranda Johnson, Mitra Sharafi, Mohammed El-Sayed Bushra, Neena Mahadev, Nick Cheesman, Nicole Roughan, Paride Stortini, Paul Halliday, Prabhath Sirisena, Prasantha Lal De Alwis, Rebecca French, Rohan Edrisinha, Sanjana Hattotuwa, Sanjayan Rajasingham, Shamara Wettimuny, Shayne Clarke, Steven Kemper, Steven Young, Sujit Sivasundaram, Tamir Moustafa, Tarun Khaitan, Theunis Roux, Tissa Jayatilleke, Tom Ginsburg, Tomas Larsson, Tom Borchert, Will Sweetman and Winnifred Sullivan. I also need to acknowledge the formative influence of John Holt, Udaya Meddegama, Uditha Egalahewa and Rohan Edrisinha, who saw the very early days of my interests in this area.

Asanga Tilakaratne, Petra Kieffer-Pülz and Christian Lammerts were extremely generous in reading these chapters and offering crucial feedback on Pali legal matters in particular. I am also very grateful to Bruno Shirley, who read an early draft of this manuscript and made many helpful interventions. I cannot thank them enough. Series editors, Mark Massoud and Rachel Stern, gave incisive feedback on chapters at critical stages in the process.

I am extremely grateful to the Marsden Fund of the Royal Society of New Zealand and the University of Otago for supporting this work.

This work builds upon scholarly actions undertaken in the past, including some revised and updated portions of published work. Chapter 4 draws some elements from 'Buddhist Law beyond the Vinaya: Monastic Constitutions (*Katikāvatas*) and Their Transformations in Colonial Sri Lanka' in *History of Religions*. Chapter 5 draws on and revises some content from 'Judging in the Buddha's Court: A Buddhist Judicial System in Contemporary Sri Lanka' in *Asian Journal of Law and Society*. Chapter 8 offers an entirely reconceived argument based on case studies appearing in 'Litigating Vinaya: Buddhist Law and Public Law in Contemporary Sri Lanka' in *Buddhism, Law & Society*.

As in all things in life, my biggest debts are owed to my family: Paula, Oliver and Henry. It is they that made this, and all things, possible. It is to them that I dedicate this book.

CHAPTER ONE

MONASTIC LAW, STATE LAW AND THE PLURALITY OF LEGAL PLURALISM IN SRI LANKA

Despite his gentle demeanour and frail frame, Venerable Dhammaratana was a formidable presence. For half a century, he had served as a judge in Sri Lanka, adjudicating disputes and writing decisions. Now in his seventies, his pace was slowing, yet he continued to hear cases, each one represented by a thick brown folder overflowing with files. A stack of these folders peeked out from a locked glass cabinet in the corner of his concrete-floored office. From his desk, Dhammaratana could see the whitewashed entrance of the small Buddhist temple where he resided. It was one of many temples he had lived at since becoming a monk in his youth, when he first shaved his head, donned saffron robes and began going by his monastic name, meaning 'Jewel of the Teaching'.[1]

Dhammaratana's legal work, like his life, was deeply rooted in Buddhist traditions. As a monastic judge, Dhammaratana rarely set foot in Sri Lanka's state courtrooms, where the architecture of bar and bench alerted visitors to the English-style common law that prevailed there. Instead, when he took the 'seat of judgment', he did so in temporary 'adjudication halls', rooms of temples, monasteries or monastic schools that were periodically set aside for the solemn task of judging. Although many of his cases were minor – petty disagreements among monastic peers – some were more serious, ranging from

[1] Dhammaratana is a common monastic name. Here I use it as a pseudonym.

conflicts over temple property to accusations of serious misconduct, like theft or inappropriate contact with women.

In judging these cases, Dhammaratana used sources and principles whose origins stretched across millennia: he consulted the ancient disciplinary instructions promulgated by the Buddha, known as *vinaya*; he reviewed the modern constitution of his monastic fraternity, known as a *katikāvata*; he read commentaries and handbooks on jurisprudence written by eminent monks; and he studied the legal opinions penned by other monastic judges. All of these he considered to be important parts of *bhikṣu nītiya* – a Sinhala phrase that I translate in this book as 'monastic law'.

Yet Dhammaratana dealt with more than just monastic law. His work also intertwined with the work of civil courts and government departments. In Sri Lanka, these institutions also make decisions about monastic law and 'Buddhist affairs'. From time to time, even Sri Lanka's Supreme Court gives opinions on *vinaya* – when monastic disputes appear to touch on constitutional rights or the government's legal obligations 'to protect and foster Buddhism'.[2]

The diversity and overlapping nature of these laws – some emanating from the monastery and others from the state – made Dhammaratana's job tricky. Although monks rarely questioned his expertise in *vinaya* or *katikāvata*, frustrated litigants occasionally challenged his verdicts in civil courts using civil law. In those courts, Dhammaratana's written opinions counted as evidence but not as binding judgments.

Dhammaratana knew that state courts regularly ignored the verdicts of monastic judges like himself, so he wrote his opinions carefully with an eye towards two audiences. For monastic litigants, he cited the words of the Buddha, passages from his fraternity's constitution and the opinions of famous monks. For civil judges, he documented evidence, provided witness names and stressed the regular, systematic nature of his inquiry.

Much depended on Dhammaratana's skill in composing judgments. When written well, Dhammaratana's opinions could construe monastic and civil law as an integrated whole, each law supporting the other. He could assure monastic litigants that they were treated fairly and that

[2] These obligations fall under Article 9 of Sri Lanka's Constitution. I discuss these obligations in greater detail later and in Chapters 2 and 8. Government of Sri Lanka, *Constitution of the Democratic Socialist Republic of Sri Lanka (Amended 2015)*, Chapter Two entitled 'Buddhism.'

appeals to the civil courts were unlikely to succeed. If not written with care, Dhammaratana's words might alienate readers of one type or another. Civil court judges might deem Dhammaratana's rationales to be irregular or inconsistent. Monastic litigants might see his words as too bureaucratic, too distant from *vinaya*.

Worse outcomes were also possible, given that the universal laws of karma also applied to Dhammaratana's work. According to karma, and its cosmic rules of cause and effect, Dhammaratana's judicial decisions impacted not only litigants' lives but also his own life and prospects for reincarnation. An unfair verdict delivered in this life could send a careless jurist to hell in the next rebirth.

I learnt about Dhammaratana's work during an interview that I conducted with him in 2019. It took place at his temple, a small compound of modest buildings hidden down a palm-fringed lane that meandered off the coastal highway between Colombo and the southern port city of Galle. We met on a shady veranda near his office. It was late in the morning and already quite hot.

Dhammaratana spoke for more than an hour about the multiple laws and interests that he navigated as a judge. Towards the end of the conversation, my mind was swimming in details. At one point, as though noticing my confusion, he looked up and said:

> You see, when we say *monk*, we are also talking about a *person*, someone with civil rights . . . someone with human rights. . . If I have a problem in the monastic system, I can also seek a solution in the civil courts. . . Therefore, monks have more responsibilities, more legal liabilities, more pressures than other people . . . we [monks] are bound by two laws: by state law (*rājya nītiya*) and by monastic law (*bhikṣu nītiya*).[3]

*

This book begins where Dhammaratana left off. What he intended as an answer, I approach instead as a series of questions. I ask: what does it mean to be 'bound' by more than one law, to be obliged to state law and monastic law together? How have Buddhist monastics, some of the world's largest and oldest clerical communities, come to acquire the complex web of 'responsibilities' and 'pressures' about which Dhammaratana speaks? Moreover, what can the experience of Buddhist monks tell us about

[3] Interview with senior monastic judge (*jyeṣṭhānuvijjaka*) 14 December 2019.

how human societies throughout the world manage the multiple traditions of law that shape their lives?

In posing these questions, I connect the study of Buddhism and law in Sri Lanka with broader scholarly conversations about *legal pluralism*, the phrase most commonly used to denote the coexistence of multiple laws in a given place.[4] Through examining the lives of Buddhist monastics – communities that have navigated legal multiplicity for more than 2,000 years – this book argues that legal pluralism implicates not one feature of human experience but two. Not only does legal pluralism encompass the complex pool of 'legal liabilities' that persons like Dhammaratana confront, it also implies a set of *practices* that one uses to bring structure and sense to those liabilities in the first place. More than just something one *encounters*, legal pluralism is something one *does*.[5]

This twofold character of legal pluralism has significant consequences for how scholars, lawmakers and jurists ought to approach situations like that of Dhammaratana. It implies that those who wrestle with legal pluralism in courts, parliaments or universities – those who create policies to address it, programmes to promote it or theories to describe it – ought to think of themselves as confronting two distinguishable phenomena. Firstly, they confront a diverse collection of normative *artefacts*, sources and standards that purport to be the 'stuff' of law: things like codes, customs, canons, obligations, expectations, tribunals, institutions, duties, principles, procedures and norms. Secondly, they confront a diverse set of *practices*, actions and enunciations that collate or divide those artefacts into categories, identify their essential features and coordinate their relative influence and authority over human communities.

This book demonstrates how one field of normative artefacts can sustain a multitude of different practices. Dhammaratana's experience of multi-legality changes depending on how one renders the various liabilities that he confronts: as 'discipline' or as 'law', as one system or two, as voluntary or obligatory, as human or more-than-human, as conflicting or aligning, as a collection of pure sources or a miscellany of hybrid ones. It depends on whether one treats imperatives (Judge

4 On this common usage see, among others, Marglin and Letteney, 'Legal Pluralism as a Category of Analysis.'

5 I explain this argument further in the section 'Theories and Practices of Legal Pluralism'.

fairly!) as emanating from the Buddha, or from his monastic fraternity, or from the state or the universe, or some combination thereof. Artefacts alone do not explain legal diversity. Equally vital are the ways that humans bring order and meaning to those artefacts by grouping and consolidating them, ranking and distinguishing them, reconciling and contrasting them – that is, by *practising legal pluralism*.

THE LAWS OF THE BUDDHA AND THE LAWS OF THE LAND

In 2018, hundreds of saffron-robed monks occupied the central transportation hub in downtown Colombo. They gathered to denounce the arrest and imprisonment of a famous Buddhist monk on charges of contempt of court. What they condemned was not the charge itself but the conditions of the monk's detainment, specifically the clothes he was made to wear. As with other convicts, prison officials required the monk to remove his saffron robes and wear the standard prison uniform of white pants and a jumper. At the time of his conviction, Sri Lanka's prisons held fifteen other Buddhist monks, all of them dressed that way.[6] Yet the monk was popular, and his supporters were adamant: this was an assault on monastic law.

Politicians appealed to the protesting monks. There was no malice intended, they stressed, only the routine application of a neutral ordinance. Some even pointed to *vinaya*, noting that the Buddha himself allowed monks to reside without robes under conditions of duress.[7] But the arguments had little effect. In the space of weeks, matters escalated into national demonstrations, with protestors alleging an all-out conflict between monastic law and state law. In their speeches and placards, protestors spoke about more than just clothes. They declared that 'jumper-gate'[8] – as the affair came to be known – was proof that monastic rules were not compatible with Sri Lanka's penal code. The sacred laws

[6] This statistic comes from a press release issued by the Sri Lankan Centre for Human Rights and Research, dated 19 June 2018, signed by Kirti Tennakōn, the executive officer. Document in possession of the author.

[7] *Gnānasāra Himigē Upasampadāva Naeti Karanna Kaṭavat Baeae – Tripiṭakācārya Talaṅgama Sudhīrānanda Himi* [Ven. Gnanasara Cannot Be Nullified by Anyone – Ven. Talagama Sudhiranandal]; Schonthal, 'Buddhist Law Against the State? Representing Religion, Law, and Conflict,' 672–73.

[8] Literally, 'the story of the jumper' (S: *jampara-kathāva*). This was a phrase frequently used in the media to cover the related events.

made by the Buddha could not function alongside criminal laws inherited from the British. They chanted slogans and carried banners, including one that read: 'Don't let a son of the Buddha, who is bound by the Buddha's law, be attacked by white persons' laws'.[9]

Jumper-gate cast a national spotlight on two opposing ways of practising legal pluralism in Sri Lanka today.[10] On the one end are those, like the politicians, who stress compatibility, harmony and banality in the relationship between monastic and state law. On the other end are those, like the protestors, who stress the antagonism of monastic and state law, and demand that the former be protected from the latter. In between are a variety of blended positions that make use of the same normative artefacts to offer differing visions of multi-legality.

Those who stress the separation of monastic law and state law point to certain historical precedents. Early Buddhist legal texts proclaim monastic law's distinctiveness from 'the laws of the world'.[11] These texts say that when persons like Dhammaratana join the community of monastics, the sangha, they commit to observing the Buddha's rules of monastic discipline (*vinaya*), as embodied in a text called the 'Basket of Discipline' or Vinaya Piṭaka.[12] That text (the Vinaya Piṭaka) and those disciplinary norms (*vinaya*) purposefully separate monastic behaviour and appearance from that of non-monastics, called laypersons, or 'householders'. The Pali-language version of the Vinaya Piṭaka, which is observed by monastics in South and Southeast Asia, including in Sri Lanka, requires that monastics shave their heads, wear saffron-coloured

[9] *'Buddha nītiyen bandunu budu putekuṭa suddāgē nītiyen pahara dennaṭa iḍa notabamu!'* Laṅkādīpa. *'Gnānasāra Himiṭa Set Patā Nuvaraeḷiyē Pāgamanak* [Procession in Nuwara Eliya to Bless Ven. Gnanasara].'

[10] I have written about this elsewhere, including in Schonthal, 'Buddhist Law Against the State? Representing Religion, Law, and Conflict.'

[11] Early monastic legal commentaries make an important distinction between conduct that offends against the normative standards of the world (P: *lokavajja*) and conduct that merely offends against the norms of monastic discipline (P: *paṇṇattivajja*). These terms first appear in the fourth- or fifth-century commentary on the Vinaya Piṭaka, the *Samantapāsādikā* discussed in Chapter 2 of this book. However, the origins of this distinction can be traced to earlier parts of the Vinaya, where other terms are used. For an investigation of these earlier terms and their application, see Kieffer-Pülz, *Verlorene Gaṇṭhipadas zum buddhistischen Ordensrecht*, I, 322. von Hinüber, 'Buddhist Law,' 16–18.

[12] On the distinctions between *vinaya* (as discipline) and Vinaya (as the shortened title of the Vinaya Piṭaka) see Chapter 2.

robes and live in monasteries set off from other human settlements. It instructs monastics to 'beg' for their food rather than prepare their own meals as householders do. A significant number of the Vinaya's 227 rules for monks and its 331 rules for nuns purport to preserve the moral and physical separation between monastics and laity.[13] These monastic rules include prohibitions against speaking deceptively, engaging in business or trade, congregating with laypersons, preaching to soldiers, using gold or silver, consuming intoxicants, and 'travelling by vehicle'.

Despite this ancient ideal of separation, monastic law and state law merge together in many ways in modern Sri Lanka. As with other 'semi-autonomous social fields', the field of Buddhist monastic law has, over the past two millennia, intermeshed with the laws of the kingdom, the colony or, for most of the past century, the modern nation-state.[14] This merger can be seen, among other places, in the modern lexicon of state law in Sinhala, the language spoken by three-quarters of Sri Lankans and the language in which most laws are drafted and interpreted.[15] A variety of modern Sinhala legal terms can be traced to Pali terms taken from the Vinaya Piṭaka. When jurist monks like Dhammaratana speak about courts (*adhikaraṇa*), accusations (*cōdana*) or adjudication (*viniścaya*), they use terms that are appropriate both to the Sinhala-language vocabulary of contemporary state law and to the Pali-language protocols of monastic law.

The merging of monastic and state law is also visible institutionally. Although conducted according to Vinaya standards, monastic ordinations must also be registered with government departments. Those who wear monastic robes must obtain government-issued ID cards and have proof of their monastic residence. Failing to do so, one can be charged with the crime of illegally 'hold[ing] [one]self out as a monk'.[16] Monastics must declare pious donations made to their temples and keep accounting records for periodic auditing by Sri Lanka's Department

[13] Seven of the 227 rules for monks and seven of the 331 rules for nuns concern methods of dispute settlement rather than injunctions. On the nature of these rules, see Chapter 2. On the status of Buddhist nuns (bhikkhunīs), see later in the chapter.

[14] Moore, 'Law and Social Change,' 720.

[15] Sri Lankan statutes are generally published in all three official languages: Sinhala, Tamil and English. But it is common that they will have a clause specifying that the Sinhala version of the bill takes priority if there are discrepancies in meaning among the three language versions.

[16] Buddhist Temporalities Ordinance (Act) (Sri Lanka), §42.

of Buddhist Affairs. That Department also administers a national statute relating to 'Buddhist property' (*bauddha dēpaḷa*) called the Buddhist Temporalities Ordinance. Alongside monastic courts, civil courts also adjudicate disputes among monks and produce common law doctrine concerning the rules of monastic succession or the nature of temple property. These doctrines, which build on the jurisprudence of British colonial courts, are known today as Buddhist Ecclesiastical Law – a body of law that, in many ways, epitomises the dynamics of integration and separation that characterise the relationship between the Buddhist sangha and the Sri Lankan state.

THEORIES AND PRACTICES OF LEGAL PLURALISM

No single portrait of legal pluralism perfectly captures this mixture of legal influences, even though almost everyone agrees about the major artefacts of law in play. (A broad list of these can be found in Table 1.1.) At times, Sri Lanka's monastics, state officials and everyday citizens treat these sources of law as distinct or in conflict. Other times, they treat them as interwoven and aligned.

This situation is not usual. Like Dhammaratana, people throughout the world navigate the multiple 'legal liabilities' and 'pressures' that they face in diverse and dynamic ways. This dynamism, however, remains submerged in many policy papers and scholarly articles on legal pluralism. That is because, in most cases, analysts approach legal pluralism as a stable construct, treating legal multiplicity as a structural condition within which humans operate. Analysts reflect on how a finite set of legal *systems* function and interact. They consider how such systems change over time and move across space, exchanging ideas, terminology and officials.[17] More recently, scholars have highlighted 'interlegal', 'hybrid' and 'entangled' forms of legality that, although built from legal systems, are not reducible to any one of them.[18]

[17] Among others, see Ginsburg, Chernykh, and Elkins, 'Commitment and Diffusion: How and Why National Constitutions Incorporate International Law'; Nelken and Feest, *Adapting Legal Cultures*; Stilt, 'Contextualizing Constitutional Islam: The Malayan Experience'; Watson, *Legal Transplants*.

[18] Among others, see Berman, 'Towards a Jurisprudence of Hybridity Symposium'; Klabbers and Palombella, *The Challenge of Inter-Legality*; Krisch, 'Framing Entangled Legalities beyond the State'; Peletz, 'Malaysia's Syariah Judiciary as Global Assemblage'; Santos, 'Law'; Visser and Harding, 'Monarchical Constitutional Guardianship and Legal Métissage in Asia.'

TABLE 1.1 Important sources of norms relating to monastic life

Associated with the Buddha	Written by legal experts	Produced by monastic fraternities and their officials	Authorised by state officials and lay persons
The Vinaya Piṭaka: the canonised record of the Buddha's instructions, preserved in writing	Commentaries on the Vinaya Piṭaka and other texts	Constitutions (*katikāvatas*)	Buddhist Ecclesiastical law: civil jurisprudence relating to monastic property, succession and other matters
Vinaya: the total body of monastic disciplinary norms, including but not limited to those contained in the Vinaya Piṭaka	Sub-commentaries	Bylaws	Buddhist Temporalities Ordinance: statute governing 'Buddhist properties'
Dharma: the Buddha's teachings about the nature of the cosmos, preserved in multiple textual sources and orally	Glossaries	Monastic court decisions	Orders from the Department of Buddhist Affairs
	Rulebooks consolidating important norms	Judicial manuals	Judicial orders from state courts
	Handbooks concerning monastic legal procedures	Executive orders	Constitutional clauses, including the Buddhism Chapter
	Treatises on *vinaya* jurisprudence and other matters		Expectations of lay donors
	Compendia of important legal decisions		

Tracing how legal systems change and evolve is a crucial part of understanding how legal pluralism manifests in the world. However, to focus only on these high-level dynamics is to miss the unstable and often competing ways that normative multiplicity is expressed on the ground. Where scholars speak about hybridity or borrowing across systems of law, legal actors frequently voice anxiety about protecting law's purity or fidelity to the past. They may worry that a tradition is vulnerable to outside influences that could distort or damage it. Where academics emphasise the inevitability of legal blending, many legal actors speak of 'their' laws as independent and autonomous.[19]

In this, scholarly debate and real-world legal reasoning mirror each other. As with academic accounts of legal pluralism, monks, judges, bureaucrats, officials and others living in Sri Lanka employ their own schemas to make sense of the legal diversity they all agree exists. Everyone accepts the presence of multiple laws, yet they carve up and characterise those laws in diverging ways, producing a plurality of legal pluralisms.

Sometimes, legal actors construe the island's laws as opposing systems whose integrity depends upon their separation. Other times, they celebrate laws' similarity and interweaving – or suggest their shared embodiment of some higher-order principle (such as due process or moral restraint). Yet other times, distinctions between bodies of law matter less than the internal distinctions within supposedly unified legal regimes. Frequently, legal multiplicity is regarded as unremarkable, a fact of life that requires little reflection at all.

Those who live in multi-legal worlds adopt many frames of classification and strategies of action – many *practices of legal pluralism* – for bringing order and meaning to their lives. Those practices communicate different messages about the boundaries, nature and essence of laws: their integrity or porousness, complementarity or incommensurability, purity or adulteration, and their endurance or transformation over time. I track each of these *relational pairs* in the chapters that follow.[20]

By centring the human dimension of legal pluralism – the importance of legal pluralism *as a practice* – I seek to bridge the gap between

[19] Such declarations of law's autonomy and defences of its purity appear frequently in the everyday negotiation of normative complexity in many parts of the world. For example, Pirie, 'Legal Autonomy as Political Engagement.'

[20] On these relational pairs, see section entitled 'Organisation of the Book'.

scholarly models of legal pluralism and the numerous, shifting paradigms expressed by legal actors themselves. Rather than giving a better high-level account of legal systems – one that 'gets the ontology right' – I call attention to the ways that *laws' users*, themselves, give structure and meaning to the 'stuff' of law.[21] I treat monks like Dhammaratana not merely as subjects of legal pluralism, but as theorists of it, agents who produce their own systemic accounts of laws and how they interact.

Such accounts are not just *interpretations* of an otherwise singular legal pluralism. They are *enactments*, consequential expressions of multi-legality that do things in the world. When pronounced by important people or in important contexts, practices of legal pluralism have power and authority. They shape events and influence others. They produce the realities of which they speak. They make things 'law'.

New insights about law and society emerge when one attends to practices of legal pluralism. A focus on practices reveals the numerous, overlapping paradigms of multi-legality that coexist at any one time, each carrying its own consequences for governance and coexistence – each implying its own calls to action (Protect! Reject! Recognise! Reconcile!). These practices may appear in written policies, such as the formalised 'tertiary rules' or 'inter-polity laws' designed to bridge legal regimes and sovereignties.[22] Yet, they can also be seen in informal and episodic practices, such as the protest marches described above.

Examining the multiple practices of legal pluralism operating in a given setting allows one to test academic theories while also acknowledging the significance of legal reasoning on the ground. It calls attention to the interests that underlie one view of legal multiplicity

[21] I do not want to overstate the originality of this approach. My interventions build on and share insights with the work of many other scholars. In its focus on the subjective experience and expression of normative complexity, it builds on the insights of Kleinhans and Macdonald, and their notion of 'critical legal pluralism'. In its focus on law as practice (rather than 'product'), it is informed by Taekema, and by Fuller's ideas about 'interactional law'. In my concern with written and verbal expression, I share Krisch's interest in 'entanglement' discourse. In my concern with examining human behaviour *in situ*, I share interests with anthropologists of law, many of whom appear in the pages that follow. Kleinhans and Macdonald, 'What Is a Critical Legal Pluralism'; Krisch, 'Entangled Legalities in the Postnational Space'; Merry, 'An Anthropological Perspective on Legal Pluralism'; Taekema, 'Between or Beyond Legal Orders.'

[22] Benton and Clulow, 'Interpolity Law and Jurisdictional Politics'; Michaels, 'Tertiary Rules.'

or another, along with the material stakes of purportedly neutral observations about law's nature and diversity. It makes clear that legal relations, like kinship, can be segmented or unified at different levels, such that same normative artefacts – a prohibition appearing in a *katikāvata*, an injunction in the Vinaya Piṭaka, a norm of ethical judging – can be treated as cosmic law or monastic law or fraternity law or Sri Lankan law, each of which entails its own possibilities for human action and communal autonomy.

Paying attention to practices of legal pluralism illuminates the relative (but not infinite) freedom of persons to influence and define their multi-normative worlds. Even where the normative artefacts seem fixed, or relatively so, humans nevertheless produce multiple scales of value and recognition, multiple acts of merger or opposition, and multiple projects for narrowing or widening the gaps between, in this case, the laws of the Buddha and the laws of the land.

BUDDHISM AND MONASTIC LAW IN CONTEMPORARY SRI LANKA

Practices of legal pluralism and debates about monastic law are not marginal events in Sri Lanka. Legal contests and protests like those described above occur regularly and often generate widespread publicity. This is because Buddhist monastic law is not just any form of law: it is the law that sits at the centre of the religion that sits at the centre of discussions about Sri Lankan national identity.[23]

Although one of several religions in Sri Lanka, Buddhism has tended to dominate Sri Lankan life demographically as well as politically. Over 70 per cent of Sri Lanka's population identify as Buddhist on national censuses, compared with 12.7 per cent, 9.7 per cent and 7.6 per cent identifying as Hindu, Muslim or Christian.[24] These religious identities overlap with ethnic and linguistic ones. Most Buddhists identify as ethnically Sinhalese (75% of the total population) and are Sinhalese-

[23] Other forms of religious and communal law also receive attention, especially the diverse legal institutions relating to Muslims and the state-recognised code of Jaffna Tamil customary law called the 'laws of the land' (in Tamil, *Tēsavaḻamai*). I consider both of these – and their function as foils in debates over monastic law – in Chapter 7.

[24] Roughly 81 per cent of Christians in Sri Lanka report to be Roman Catholic, leaving the estimated population of 'Other Christians' (which includes Protestant sects and other newer Christian groups) at approximately 1.5 per cent of the total national population.

speaking; most Hindus identify as ethnically Tamil (15% of the population) and speak Tamil;[25] most Muslims identify their ethnicity as 'Moor' or 'Malay' (9.3% and 0.2% of the population respectively) and speak Tamil, Sinhala or both.[26] Christianity alone crosscuts ethnic and linguistic backgrounds.

For more than a century, Sri Lankan politicians have made use of these demographic features to advance a particular vision of nationhood that privileges one religion (Buddhism), one ethnicity (Sinhalese) and one language (Sinhala). Politicians, artists and writers have portrayed Sri Lanka as an 'island of dharma' that joins Buddhism with Sinhalese-ness in a single civilisational vision.[27] Activists and entrepreneurs have drawn on this nationalist vision to shape politics and villainise minority groups, contributing to the island's three-decade-long civil war as well as to various other incidents of anti-Muslim, anti-Christian and anti-Tamil violence, which have occurred regularly since the Sri Lankan army's brutal military defeat of the Liberation Tigers of Tamil Eelam (LTTE) in 2009.

The political and cultural centrality of Buddhism in Sri Lanka means that Buddhist monks exert an influence on public life far greater than mere population numbers would suggest. Although there are only 42,000 registered monks (out of a general population of 22 million),[28] their status as protectors and embodiments of Buddhism endows monastic groups with special authority and prestige. This can be seen, among other places, in the honorific terms and deferential gestures used to address monks in daily life.[29] It can also be seen in monks' outsized

[25] The census separates ethnic Tamils into two categories: 'Up-Country' or 'Indian' Tamils (4%), which refers to those who claim descent from plantation labourers who came from India, and 'Ceylonese' or 'Sri Lankan' Tamils (11%), which refers to those who claim descent from the island's long history of Tamil inhabitants.

[26] The ethnic designation Moor usually applies to the descendants of Muslim traders from the Arabian Peninsula. Other important categories of ethnicity on the census include Burghers (descendants of the Dutch) and Veddas (indigenous Sri Lankans).

[27] Among others, see Kemper, *The Presence of the Past: Chronicles, Politics, and Culture in Sinhala Life*; Nissan, 'History in the Making: Anuradhapura and the Sinhala Buddhist Nation'; Rambukwella, *The Politics and Poetics of Authenticity*; Seneviratne, *The Work of Kings: The New Buddhism in Sri Lanka*; Rajasingham, 'Dilemmas of Defense and Deference: Buddhism and Constitutions in Sri Lanka and Thailand.'

[28] Weerasooriya, '180,458 Monks Registered with Department of Buddhist Affairs since 1930s.' This figure includes both novice monks and fully ordained bhikkhus. On that distinction, see the following section, 'Pluralism within 'the' Sangha.'

[29] When speaking with or about monks, people use special pronouns and verbs that convey an elevated air. For example, they refer to monks as carrying themselves

influence on national issues. As in other parts of Asia, Sri Lankan monks do more than just pursue nirvana. They play visible roles in politics, media and law, serving as lobbyists, campaigners and legal activists. Monks form pressure groups, hold press conferences and engage in what I've called 'Buddhist-interest litigation'.[30] When monks issue statements, politicians pay attention; when they organise protests, people show up. In recent decades, monks in Sri Lanka have even formed their own political parties, contesting – and sometimes winning – public office. In 2004, one such political party, consisting entirely of Buddhist monks, managed to win nine (of 225) seats in the island's parliament.[31]

The esteem given to Sri Lanka's monks comes, in no small part, from the important role they play in sustaining Buddhism on the island. Symbolically, monks evoke a direct link to the Buddha as part of an unbroken chain of ordinations beginning with the Buddha's first disciples. Through this chain, they pass down the Buddha's dharma, his teachings about the nature of the cosmos, and his advice for how living beings can escape the stressful cycles of rebirth that characterise normal human existence. (This escape, or 'extinguishing', is known as nirvana.) Monks are charged with disseminating this dharma, while also administering the key rituals of Buddhist life, such as donation (*dāna*), blessing (*pirit*), merit-making (*piṅkamma*) and funerary rites. As 'sons of the Buddha', monks are thought to guard the Buddha's textual, material and institutional legacies in the world, ensuring the continuity of artefacts that preserve the dharma: monasteries, shrines, relics, stories, instructions, manuscripts, ordination lineages and other things – a mass of physical treasures and cherished teachings collectively referred to as the *sāsana*.

The elevated status of Buddhism and Buddhist monks in Sri Lanka means that the topic of monastic law features regularly in the island's newspapers and political discussions. Buddhists care about monastic law because only a disciplined, law-abiding sangha can secure the religion

(*vaḍinavā*) rather than walking (*ävidinavā*) and consuming (*vaḷandanavā*) rather than eating (*kanavā*). Disānāyaka, *Encyclopaedia of Sinhala Language and Culture*, 205.

30 Schonthal, 'Securing the Sasana through Law: Buddhist Constitutionalism and Buddhist-Interest Litigation in Sri Lanka.'

31 Deegalle, 'Politics of the Jathika Hela Urumaya Monks: Buddhism and Ethnicity in Contemporary Sri Lanka'; DeVotta and Stone, 'Jathika Hela Urumaya and Ethno-Religious Politics in Sri Lanka.'

in its purest form. Sri Lankans care about monastic law because of its role in defining the parameters of monks' influence on public life. Unwanted forms of monastic activism are often blamed on the weakness or corruption of monastic law. In the 1940s and 1950s, for example, public voices pushed for the 'purification' of monastic law as a way to stop leftist activism among younger monks. In recent decades, critics have blamed laxity in *vinaya* standards for the rise of monk-led nationalist groups and political parties. Far from an arcane feature of Buddhist doctrine, then, it is fair to say that in Sri Lanka monastic law is a topic of national importance.

PLURALISM WITHIN 'THE' SANGHA

Although it is common to refer to 'the sangha' as a singular entity, in reality, Sri Lanka's monastics affiliate to multiple groups and subgroups, each with their own body of laws. These affiliations divide monastics by ordination status, fraternity, sub-fraternity, gender and a variety of other markers such as place of origin, caste or teacher lineage. Not every person can ordain into every monastic community.

As in other parts of the Buddhist world, Sri Lankan monasticism consists of two levels of ordination. A typical monastery contains both novice monastics, who tend to be younger than twenty years old, and fully ordained monastics who must be twenty years of age or older. Fully ordained men are called *bhikkhus*; fully ordained women are called *bhikkhunīs*. Novices undergo a simple form of ordination called 'going forth' during which they shave their heads, put on saffron robes and vow to observe ten basic precepts.[32] Fully ordained men and women undergo a more complex ordination rite called 'acceptance' (in Pali, *upasampadā*). During this, they formally take on a monastic teacher, gain admission to a fraternity and commit themselves to following the Buddha's instructions.

In Sri Lanka, most monastics belong to one of three major fraternities, or *nikāya*, each with its own lineages, hierarchies, ordination traditions, network of temples and legal customs. These major fraternities are the Siyam Nikāya, the Amarapura Nikāya and the Rāmañña

[32] The ten precepts followed by novice monks prohibit killing living beings, theft, sexual acts, incorrect speech (e.g., lying), consuming intoxicants, eating after noon, participating in entertainment such as singing or dancing, applying beauty products, using luxurious furniture and accepting money.

Nikāya.[33] The Siyam Nikāya, headquartered in the ancient royal capital of Kandy, is the oldest, largest and most influential fraternity, accounting for nearly half of the island's monks and most of its temples (~57%).[34] The Amarapura and Rāmañña Nikāyas make up roughly 28 per cent and 18 per cent of the island's monks and temples, respectively, and have headquarters located on the southwest coast, where the two fraternities first gained prominence during the nineteenth century.[35] In 2019, the Amarapura and Rāmañña Nikāyas formed a union called the 'United Sangha Council'.[36]

Undergirding these *nikāya* differences are other distinctions based on regional identity, teacher-student lineages, familial ties and caste. Current divisions among monastic fraternities first emerged during the eighteenth and nineteenth centuries, following the reintroduction of higher ordination traditions to the island after a period of absence.[37] Segmentation occurred for several reasons. Some fraternities arose to accommodate monks who were excluded from other fraternities because of their caste. Others evolved following disputes over ordination rituals, or temple property, or the interpretation of the Vinaya Piṭaka. These divisions endure not only across the Siyam, Amarapura

[33] Each fraternity is named for the place from which it traces its main ordination lineages: Siyam from Siam/Thailand; Amarapura and Rāmañña from regions in present-day Myanmar.

[34] Government of Sri Lanka, '*Vihārasthāna hā Bhikṣūn Vahansē Saṅgaṇanaya* [The Census of Bhikkhus and Temples].' Obtained by author from the Department of Buddhist Affairs in 2013.

[35] The case of the Amarapura Nikāya is somewhat more complex than the Rāmañña in that it developed from five ordination lineages, only three of which were rooted in Amarapura. See also Malalgoda, *Buddhism in Sinhalese Society*, 90–105.

[36] S: *amarapura-rāmañña sāmagrī mahā sangha sabhāva*. Although recognised by the government, the Department of Buddhist Affairs does not combine the two together as a single body in the reporting that I have read. Both major *nikāyas* continue to operate as independent institutions, but they have built a shared headquarters in Colombo. Communication with a senior lawyer and advisor to the monastic groups in Colombo, July 12, 2024. On the merger see Gamage, '*Amarapura Hā Rāmañña Nikāyan Deka Ek Nikāyak Bavaṭa Pat Karanavā* [The Two Fraternities of Amarapura and Rāmañña Are Becoming One Nikāya].'

[37] Historical sources recount that during the seventeenth century, Buddhist monasticism had degraded to the extent that there were no longer enough fully ordained monks on the island to hold a proper ordination ceremony. This meant that new ordination lineages had to be reintroduced from modern-day Thailand and Myanmar, which themselves had received ordination lineages from Sri Lanka in previous centuries. Blackburn, *Buddhist Learning and Textual Practice in Eighteenth-Century Lankan Monastic Culture*.

TABLE 1.2 Sri Lanka's officially recognised monastic fraternities

Siyam Nikāya (founded 1753)	Amarapura Nikāya (founded 1803)	Rāmañña Nikāya (founded 1864)
Largest, with eight recognised subgroups, including the important Malvatu and Asgiri Chapters, which are the oldest and largest	Second largest, with twenty-one recognised subgroups; since the 1950s run as a confederation organised around a single supreme great leader (*uttarītara mahānāyaka*)	Third largest, most of which functions as a single body, alongside a smaller group of highly ascetic, forest-dwelling monks
	Joined as Amarapura-Rāmañña United Sangha Council since August 2019	

and Rāmañña Nikāyas but also in the existence of sub-fraternities that have their own proper names, organisational structures and legal protocols.[38] According to official statistics,[39] the Siyam Nikāya contains eight subgroups, while the Amarapura Nikāya contains twenty-one.[40] Officially, the Rāmañña Nikāya is unitary, although it also includes a separate 'system' (*saṃsthāva*) of ascetic forest-dwelling monks, who have their own constitution and customs (Table 1.2).[41]

All fraternities register their members with the Department of Buddhist Affairs. Yet the total number of monastics and monastic groups on the island is likely larger than official statistics suggest for two reasons. Firstly, in addition to the registered monastic fraternities, Sri Lanka also has a small number of self-ordaining monks who do not affiliate directly with any of the three major *nikāyas* mentioned.[42]

38 The relationships among the subgroups, and the relative independence of each, vary. For example, some in Sri Lanka view the individual sub-fraternities within the Amarapura Nikāya as more independent from each other than the chapters of the Siyam Nikāya. Similarly, as will be seen later in the chapter, the leadership of a single monastery (such as the Dambulla Rangiri Vihāra, described in Chapter 8) may have, de facto, the autonomy of an independent subgroup.

39 *Vihārasthāna hā Bhikṣūn Vahansē Saṅgaṇanaya* [The Census of Bhikkhus and Temples], 3.

40 The Siyam Nikāya subgroups are called chapters (*pārśva*), while the Amarapura Nikāya ones are called, confusingly, fraternities (*nikāya*, I use the lower-case 'n' to distinguish the two).

41 Śrī Kalyāṇī Yogāśrama Saṃsthāva of the Rāmañña Nikāya.

42 Kahandagama, 'New Buddhist Trends in Post-War Sri Lanka.'

Secondly, and more importantly, official statistics do not fully record the levels of female monasticism on the island. Along with other governments in Southeast Asia, the Sri Lankan government does not recognise communities of fully ordained nuns (bhikkhunīs). The reasons for the government's position are complex and the topic of ongoing debates, some of which I explore in Chapter 8. Although not recognised by the government, Sri Lanka is home to an estimated 3,000 bhikkhunīs who trace their lineage to ordinations sponsored by Taiwanese nuns and Sri Lankan monks. There are also large, government-recognised communities of renunciant women called 'precept mothers', who lead lives very similar to bhikkhunīs but refuse that title.[43]

RESEARCH METHODS

The research for this book occurred between 2014 and 2024, a period of considerable social, economic and political change in Sri Lanka. It was also a time of renewed debates about monastic law, due, in part, to the rise of new monastic nationalist groups whose bellicose rhetoric and unruly protests raised questions about the vitality of monastic discipline on the island.[44] Newspapers printed stories about monastic law. Politicians introduced bills promising to buttress *katikāvata*s using state law. Talk shows hosted roundtables on the topic. Major academic institutions sponsored conferences. Some monks took to the streets.

It was in this context that I researched Dhammaratana's legal landscape, the tracks of which pointed in many directions at once: to ancient texts and modern ones, to colonial lawmakers and postcolonial politicians, to monastic jurists and ordinary monks who encountered the law as students and subjects of its discipline. Also important were non-monastic actors – judges, lawyers, bureaucrats, donors and ordinary citizens – whose interests and actions overlapped and intersected with monks like Dhammaratana.

43 De Silva, 'Vigilant Steps'; Salgado, 'Religious Identities of Buddhist Nuns: Training Precepts, Renunciant Attire, and Nomenclature in Theravada Buddhism'; Salgado, 'On the Question of 'Discipline' (Vinaya) and Nuns in Theravāda Buddhism.' See also Mrozik, 'We Love Our Nuns: Affective Dimensions of the Sri Lankan Bhikkhuni Revival.'

44 Haniffa, 'Who Gave These Fellows This Strength?'; Schonthal and Walton, 'The (New) Buddhist Nationalisms? Symmetries and Specificities in Sri Lanka and Myanmar'; Silva, 'Gossip, Rumor, and Propaganda in Anti-Muslim Campaigns of Bodu Bala Sena.'

Given the diversity of voices and sources, I adopted a research strategy designed to blend grounded detail and high-level overview while covering a broad historical period. For grounded details, I relied on archival work, ethnographies and interviews with monastic jurists. For the high-level overviews, I drew on broad institutional histories and codes written by monastic and state officials. I also conducted a large, national survey of 1,669 fully ordained monks drawn from across the country – the first of its kind to my knowledge.

Archival Research

Given the importance of written sources for the practice of monastic law, archival research played a large role in this book. The written sources that form the basis of the study were composed in the languages of English, Sinhala and Pali – and often in a mix of the latter two. Some sources came from personal and public collections.[45] Others came from university and national archives in Sri Lanka, the United States and the UK.[46] These texts, about which I will say much more in subsequent chapters, cover a long swathe of time as well as a wide variety of authors, formats and styles: some from the nineteenth century are written in the traditional form of *ola* manuscripts, composed on dried palm leaves with a metal stylus; others appear as handwritten letters or old-style block-print pamphlets; still others take the form of modern, bound, folio-style books printed by a commercial press. Further details appear in Table 1.3.

Locating these texts was not always easy. In some cases, it meant looking expectantly through large archival boxes with the goal of finding something relevant. More than once, I took to the strategy of investigating items that seemed *likely* to be monastic legal texts, submitting request-slips and waiting for archival files, in the hope that the designated 'order paper' or 'charge sheet' came from a monastic court.

45 These included the J.R. Jayawardene and N.M. Perera libraries in Colombo; the archive of the Young Men's Buddhist Association in Colombo; the filings and judgments of courts and litigants contained in court registries and lawyers' chambers; the libraries and archives of individual monastic jurists and monasteries, mostly in the regions near Colombo and Kandy; and many, many bookstores.

46 The Sri Lankan National Archives in Colombo as well as the regional branch of Kandy; the National Museum Library in Colombo; the British Library in London; the South Asia Manuscripts Collection at Cambridge University; the archives of Sinhala and English language newspapers at the Centre for Research Libraries and Haithi online archive.

TABLE 1.3 Texts consulted

Monastic legal texts: *Vinaya Piṭaka*; commentaries, condensations, rulebooks, handbooks, treatises, manuals and compendia of monastic law; constitutions (*katikāvatas*) of individual fraternities; decisions and orders written by monastic judges and executive councils An overview of these sources can be found in Chapter 2	**Colonial records**: communications, court decisions, administrative reports, commissions of inquiry (and associated evidence), gazetteers, diaries, Hansard transcripts **Post-independence records**: drafting documents, Hansard transcripts, committee reports, determinations and decisions from courts, legal submissions and other documents preserved at court registries, files from ministries and departments[47]	**Other written sources:** English and Sinhala newspapers, journals, pamphlets (issued by monastic and political bodies) written from early 19th century to the present **Multimedia texts**: television talk shows, recordings of press conferences, online news video clips

I found more recent monastic sources (those from the 1940s onwards) by speaking with monastic jurists, scholars, booksellers and colleagues. I also frequented shops (and sections of bookstores) that carry textbooks designed for monastic college students and asked monastic judges if I could see copies of (non-confidential) legal materials. To a lesser degree, I also searched for multimedia 'texts' about monastic law on Sinhala-language television shows and online sites.

Interviews and Ethnography – and Their Limits

To learn more about the contemporary, lived practices of monastic law, I engaged in observation and interviews with practitioners. For the

[47] The location and name of ministries and departments responsible for Buddhism and Buddhist monks varied over the course of the twentieth century. Prior to the emergence of the Department of Buddhist Affairs in 1981, relevant bodies included, especially, the Office of the Public Trustee and the Ministry of Cultural Affairs. From 1981, the name of the ministry overseeing the Department of Buddhist Affairs changed multiple times. In 2024, it came to be called the Ministry of Buddhasāsana, Religious and Cultural Affairs.

TABLE 1.4 Specialist monks who were interviewed, in addition to ordinary bhikkhus, lay lawyers and state officials

Legal specialist roles	Other leadership positions
Ordinary judge – *anuvijjaka*	Great leader (top position in a fraternity) – *mahānāyaka*
Senior judge – *jyeṣṭhānuvijjaka*	Deputy leader – *anunāyaka*
Judge in monastic Supreme Court – *uparimānuvijjaka*	Executive council (top governing body) – *kāraka sabhāva*
Chief Judicial Registrar – *adhikaraṇa lekhakādhikari*	Chief incumbent of a temple – *vihārādhipati*
Judicial Chief – *adhikaraṇa nāyaka*	Provincial head – *palāt nāyaka*
Specialist in monastic law – *vinayadhara*	Local or district head – *nāyaka*, *loku hamduruvo*

most part, this meant speaking with Buddhist monks who had a degree of expertise in monastic law and occupied the positions described in Table 1.4. I also interviewed ordinary monks who encountered monastic law as part of their education or life in a monastery. In total, I conducted sixty individual interviews and three focus groups, mostly with bhikkhus but also a small number of precept mothers and bhikkhunīs (about which more will be said below). I asked respondents about the various institutions, texts and practices they used to guide behaviour, resolve disputes, regulate decision-making, assess proper comportment, sanction poor conduct and establish hierarchies of authority and control. The *Vinaya Piṭaka* featured prominently in many discussions, as did other features of monastic law: the use and drafting of monastic constitutions (*katikāvatas*), the powers of regional and national monastic councils (*saṅgha sabhās*) and the protocols and standards observed by judges (*anuvijjakas*) and litigants in monastic courts (*sanghādhikaraṇa*). While part of my questioning focussed on the mechanics (How do these things work in practice?), I also inquired into respondents' own understandings, experiences and opinions about the monastic legal system and its connections to state law.

Alongside interviews with monastics, I conducted another series of interviews with lawyers and government officials who represented monks in court or oversaw monastic activities as part of their bureaucratic roles. These conversations were helpful in gaining a better understanding of the ways that government offices and courts understand and address questions of monastic law in their work. Discussants also offered insights into the ways that laws such as the Buddhist Temporalities Ordinance operate in practice. The interviews with both monks and non-monks ran between one and three hours. Most were conducted and transcribed with the help of research assistants. For longer interviews, research assistants also prepared preliminary translations based on the transcripts. All quotes used in this book are my own translations from the Sinhala transcript.

My engagement with monastic legal practice was not without limitations. Generally speaking, non-monks are prohibited from attending monastic legal procedures. To understand these activities without ordaining as a monk, one must rely on the second-hand accounts of participants and/or the written records left by them. As a layperson, this limitation applied to me. Certain opportunities for direct observation did arise, however. Thanks to the generosity of leaders in the Rāmañña Nikāya, I was invited to attend a series of semi-annual judicial trainings, which brought together monastic judges from around the island to discuss the processes, sources and meanings of monastic law. Over the years of this project, I attended six of these day-long sessions.

Survey Research

This book also draws on a third method of research, which does not feature commonly in studies of Buddhism in Southern Asia: a large-scale survey of Buddhist monastics. The survey gathered substantial responses across several categories, including age, monastery location and fraternity. Responses came from 1,669 bhikkhus, comprising approximately 9.5 per cent of the total population of fully ordained monks. The survey itself contained eight open-answer questions and seventy-six closed-answer questions, which were honed through three focus groups and two pilots (of twenty and a hundred monks, respectively). Surveys were distributed and collected in all provinces between July and October 2017, with data entry running from November 2017 to March 2018. All of this was done with the help of an experienced survey team located in Colombo, members of which also helped with coding the open-answer questions and cleaning data.[48]

[48] Several team meetings and training sessions were held in 2017. Survey enumerators distributed and received the questionnaires in person, in sealed envelopes.

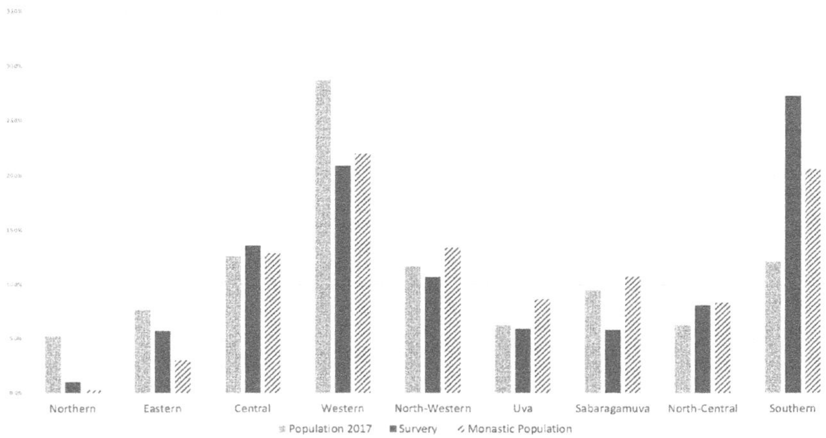

Figure 1.1 Survey sampling percentage ($n = 1669$) by province (black), compared with total population percentage (grey) and monastic population percentage (patterned) in 2017.

In addition to general information about a respondent's age, education and other things, questions in the survey covered five main areas. One group of questions was about the types of legal texts that monks used and with what frequency. A second group queried respondents' opinions about the nature and purpose of monastic law, rendered in Sinhala as '*vinaya* laws and traditions' (*vinaya nīti saha sampradāya*). A third set of questions examined monks' attitudes towards particular issues of monastic comportment, such as 'is it appropriate for monks to prepare horoscopes for lay persons?' The last two groups of questions queried bhikkhus' feelings about the relationship between Buddhist legal traditions and state law and the challenges facing Buddhism at that time. Data and findings from this survey appear throughout the chapters that follow. Although not forming the core of my analyses, survey findings provide an important feature of this study, helping to contextualise and confirm at scale many of the dynamics I observed on the ground (Figure 1.1).

ORGANISATION OF THE BOOK

In the chapters that follow, I examine the diverse practices of law employed by Buddhist monastics, colonial officials and contemporary lawmakers in Sri Lanka. I highlight developments and clashes among those practices, while also casting light on the social, political, economic and other factors connected to one practice or another – such as caste dynamics, colonisation, nationalism, civil war, party politics, property concerns, technological innovations and other things. Through all of it, I draw on, while holding lightly, the categories of state law, monastic law, Buddhist law and *vinaya*, treating them, on the one hand, as important rubrics used by actors to engage their normative worlds and, on the other hand, as unstable categories that artificially freeze law in context, producing a rhetorical unity that obscures underlying multiplicities.[49]

The book unfolds in three parts, each tackling a different time period. Part I (Chapters 2 to 4) focuses on the premodern and colonial periods, examining practices of legal pluralism evident in two bodies of sources: monastic legal texts compiled in ancient and modern periods; and monastic and colonial legal sources composed during the nineteenth century. Chapter 2 covers nearly 2,000 years of history, introducing readers to the key principles and sources of monastic law, while posing a question: how and why has this diverse collection come to be treated as a single system? Chapter 3 turns to the period of British colonial control (1798–1948) to consider colonial practices of legal pluralism as expressed in attempts to define and preserve 'Buddhist law', while also isolating it from the 'secular' laws of state. Chapter 4 also examines the colonial period, but using an alternative archive of Sinhala- and Pali-language sources written by Buddhist monks. Those sources suggest an entirely different way of practising legal pluralism: one that purposefully aligns the laws of the Buddha with the laws of the sovereign.

Part II of the book, Chapters 5 and 6, considers the situation of monastic law in Sri Lanka today, focusing especially on the institutions, texts and present-day opinions of monks in the island's third-largest monastic fraternity, the Rāmañña Nikāya. These chapters look closely at the practices of legal pluralism operating within a modern monastic institution. Chapter 5 draws on archival and ethnographic research to explore how monastic judges like Dhammaratana practise legal pluralism in ways that enhance the autonomy and efficacy of the Rāmañña legal system. It considers the subtle kinds of legal 'double

[49] On the idea of 'holding lightly', see Oraby and Sullivan, 'Law and Religion.' See also the important work of Ananda Abeysekara on the instability and discursive production of Buddhism as a category. Abeysekara, *Colors of the Robe*.

speak' that jurists use to simultaneously acknowledge and reject the commensurability of monastic law and state law. Drawing on similar sources, but emphasising a set of sixty interviews with specialist monastic judges, Chapter 6 investigates a second practice of legal pluralism visible among Rāmañña Nikāya jurists, one that contrasts the regulatory dimensions of monastic law with its larger soteriological mission of protecting the *sāsana* and facilitating the attainment of nirvana.

Part III, Chapters 7 and 8, considers a period running from the 1940s to the present, examining the impacts of government policies on the way that monks, politicians, lawyers and judges practise legal pluralism. Chapter 7 tracks a significant (and ongoing) series of attempts made by Sri Lanka's leading intellectuals, educators, monks and legislators to 'legalise' monastic law (S: *nītigata kirīma*) by creating some form of statute, tribunal or bureaucratic body that could blend monastic and state-legal authority. Chapter 8 focuses on several recent attempts to practice legal pluralism using constitutional law and litigation relating to Chapter II of the Sri Lankan Constitution, which obligates the state to 'protect and foster the Buddha Sāsana'.

The practices of legal pluralism visible in these chapters, although differently expressed, draw disproportionately on four sets of attributions, four *relational pairs*, used to frame encounters with legal multiplicity. The actors examined in Part I stress the importance of laws' *separation* or *integration* and the pluralism that emerges through processes of drawing or dissolving boundaries within and between monastic and state laws. The voices highlighted in Part II focus primarily on monastic law's *commensurability* or *incommensurability* with state law, its inherent compatibility or incompatibility with the legal rules and principles authorised by the government. The political, legal and monastic actors in Part III speak largely about laws' *purity* or *adulteration*, the refining or corruption of law that happens when one brings monastic and state authorities into proximity. Running throughout all chapters are claims about legal *continuity* or *rupture*, laws' links with the past and endurance over time. These four relational pairs – separation/integration, commensurability/incommensurability, purity/adulteration, and continuity/rupture – serve as leitmotifs in the practices of legal pluralism that I examine in this book. They are recurring pairs of qualifiers that shape the ways persons negotiate normative complexity.

THE GOALS OF THIS BOOK

Authors often write the books they want to read, and so it is with this one. It was during the end of the research for my first book on religion and constitutional law that I first came to appreciate the intricacies of monastic law in Sri Lanka and the normative richness of Dhammaratana's world. It is this richness and the diverse ways it is engaged that I aim to convey. Like Dhammaratana, I write for two audiences: the general reader, without special knowledge of Buddhism, Sri Lanka or legal theory; and the more expert audience, excited by the particularities of monastic law or analyses of legal pluralism. What follows, therefore, is a blend of big ideas and small details, English translations alongside Pali and Sinhala transliterations (in brackets or footnotes), technical footnotes for the specialist and broad framings designed to lead the general reader through unfamiliar terrain. I offer the account of monastic and state laws that I wished had existed when I began this project a decade ago.[50] In so doing, I hope to push Buddhist studies and socio-legal studies closer together. I suppose that I am also practising legal pluralism by trying to connect law-and-society scholarship with the perspectives of those who pursue justice and nirvana together.

*

An interesting thing happened at the very end of my interview with Dhammaratana, as we were packing up to leave. I had developed my own impressions about legal pluralism as I listened to him distinguish the Buddha's instructions for monks from other kinds of law. Hearing about all these norms and authorities, I started to practise legal pluralism myself. Putting the pieces together, I composed a portrait of

[50] Despite a substantial body of work on the Pali Vinaya and related commentaries, little work has been done on the history and practice of monastic law in Sri Lanka. A few important works examine temple epigraphy and monastic constitutions, but mainly for the premodern period. A somewhat larger body of work considers British legal policies towards Buddhism. There are also some lawyerly accounts of civil and statute laws relating to monks and monasteries. These sources appear in the footnotes of this book. I encountered no academic monographs surveying contemporary monastic legal practices, either in English or Sinhala. This has been part of my motivation for writing this book.

conflict and antagonism. After all, I had read about the protests at the transportation hub only six months earlier, with their placards pitting Buddhist law against state law.

To wrap things up, I offered what I assumed was an obvious summary of the matter. 'So the situation is one of conflict (*gäṭena avasthā*) between *vinaya* law and state law, right?' I was surprised when Dhammaratana disagreed:

> No there's no clashing. Monastic law embodies the instructions of the Buddha, the core rules[51] that a monk follows. Non-monks don't have something like that in civil society. . .. When monks commit an offence within monastic society, they face censure, shame and diminishment only within monastic society, not within civil society; these [consequences] do not emerge in civil law. It is when [a monk] transgresses civil law that he faces those things in civil society. There's no conflict in all of this.[52]

Dhammaratana described his normative universe as divided but not at odds. He spoke of the laws affecting him as distinct but not competing: monastic law was monastic law; civil law was civil law; karma was karma. What had been proclaimed as a monumental clash of laws on the streets of Colombo was, in Dhammaratana's opinion, an unremarkable state of affairs. Moreover, he pointed out, there was little chance of state law altering the laws of the Buddha: 'Governments may promulgate laws', he said, 'but we can never change the constitution (*vyavasthāva*) established by the Buddha'.[53]

It was these discussions with Dhammaratana that pointed me towards the plurality of legal pluralism. It was after speaking with him that I looked again at the many frames and categories that people used to engage their multi-legal worlds. And it was because of this that I conceded, somewhat reluctantly, that the book I had intended to write was not, in fact, possible: there was no big story – no master narrative – that summed up how monastic law and state law related. Instead, there were many laws and many frames of interpretation. There were multiple accounts of multiplicity, plural practices of legal pluralism. Each grew out of and called forth different kinds of actions: protest and conciliation, protection and repair, integration and separation, purification and recognition. Harmonious legal pluralism was not over

[51] Translating *prātimōkṣaya*. [52] Interview 14 December 2019. [53] Ibid.

the horizon. It was not to be found in sharper legal reasoning or a utopia of laws to come. Harmony existed already – alongside inveterate conflict – as two among many practices through which people brought order to and elicited action in their complex normative worlds. It is to these practices that I will now turn.

PART I

CHAPTER TWO

THE UNITY AND DIVERSITY OF BUDDHIST MONASTIC LAW

If you ask a Buddhist studies scholar about the sources of monastic law in Sri Lanka, they will almost certainly direct you towards a set of teachings compiled more than two millennia ago and attributed to the Buddha. Those teachings were shared orally at first, before being written down sometime around the turn of the Common Era in Pali, as well as in other languages.[1] Today, those teachings circulate as part of a text called the Basket of Discipline, or Vinaya Piṭaka (Vinaya for short), which is thought to contain the Buddha's original instructions on monastic behaviour and how to govern monastic communities.

As a text thought to contain the Buddha's words (*buddhavacana*), the *Vinaya* stands alongside two other 'baskets' of teachings that enjoy a similar canonical status: a Basket of Discourses, which contains sermons delivered by the Buddha, and a Basket of Further-Teachings,

[1] A royal chronicle written in Sri Lanka in the fifth century CE dates the first written version of the 'Three Baskets', including the Vinaya Piṭaka, around the first-century BCE in Sri Lanka. According to Kieffer-Pülz, the Pali Vinaya contains layers that were likely consolidated between the fourth or third centuries BCE and the first century BCE, with the third part of the Pali Vinaya, the *Parivāra* (described later in the chapter), consolidated later, perhaps in the first century CE. The oldest surviving manuscript copies of the Pali Vinaya were found in Nepal and are datable to the eighth or ninth centuries CE. On the dating of Vinaya elements, see: Kieffer-Pülz, 'Brief Summary of the Development of Buddhist Monastic Law Codes and Institutions.'

containing advanced philosophical reflections.[2] Yet even among these revered collections, the Vinaya Piṭaka stands out as especially significant for Buddhists in Sri Lanka. Historical sources proclaim that the Vinaya was the first of the 'three baskets' (in Pali, Tipiṭaka) to be compiled in the years following the Buddha's passing away.[3] Commentarial texts and contemporary monks – including many of my interviewees – declare the Vinaya Piṭaka to sit at the core of the Buddha's dispensation, constituting 'the very life of the *sāsana* itself'.[4] As one interviewee put it, 'the Vinaya and the *sāsana* are like the tree and its bark. The two things are one. The tree can't exist without its bark, and the bark can't exist without the tree. Each protects the other'.[5]

Given the special status of the Vinaya, it is unsurprising that those who go looking for monastic law in contemporary Sri Lanka, or other places, turn to the Vinaya Piṭaka first. Those who look more closely at the day-to-day management of monasteries, however, will eventually discover that, while the Vinaya Piṭaka might be the most exalted text of monastic law, it is not the only legal source with which monks engage. The Vinaya (in its various redactions) contains a diverse collection of materials that, by virtue of their organisation and sheer size, do not lend themselves easily to practical governance.[6] In virtually all places and times, therefore, monks have administered and studied monastic law using a wide variety of other texts that purport to clarify, explain, summarise or augment the contents of the Vinaya Piṭaka.

[2] Sutta Piṭaka and Abhidhamma Piṭaka, respectively. Collectively these sources are referred to as 'the Three Baskets' or Tipiṭaka. In English, scholars sometimes refer to them as constituting a 'Buddhist canon'. On the problems with the term 'canon' for Theravāda Buddhism, see Skilling, 'Nine Recitations and the Inclusive Tripiṭaka: Canon Formation in Pre-Modern Thailand.'

[3] Pali commentaries composed in Sri Lanka in the fifth century CE describe a series of councils that took place after the Buddha's death during which eminent monks compiled an authoritative record of his teachings. Disagreements at these councils led to divisions of the sangha into separate sects (*nikāya*), which preserved distinct versions of the Vinaya. Some of these various versions will be considered later in this chapter.

[4] All of these attributions appear, among other places, in the following survey of disciplinary literature, which is recommended reading at several monastic colleges in Colombo: Vajirajñāna Himi, *Lakdiva Vinaya Sāhityaya [Sri Lankan Vinaya Literature]*, 3–5.

[5] Interview with monastic judge (*anuvijjaka*), 17 December 2019, Moratuwa, Sri Lanka.

[6] Hallisey, 'Apropos the Pāli Vinaya as a Historical Document,' 206–7.

These sources, many of which will be examined below, tend to be shorter than the Vinaya Piṭaka and more directive in their form. They contain lists, glosses or summaries that help readers apply principles from the Vinaya Piṭaka to real-world scenarios. They also provide definitions and translations of the original text using the vernacular languages spoken by ordinary monks.

Although common to sanghas throughout history and across the world, these other monastic legal texts frequently escape the attention of scholars. Their omission derives, in part, from the overwhelming esteem conferred on the Vinaya Piṭaka in places like Sri Lanka. Even where monks have little direct contact with the full text, the Vinaya Piṭaka nevertheless looms over other monastic legal sources as 'the ultimate locus of interpretive authority', as Anne Blackburn has put it.[7]

The full diversity of monastic legal sources is also hidden by the polyvalence of the word *vinaya*, which – in addition to implicating the Vinaya Piṭaka – can also connote 'discipline' in a more general sense. This multivalence works in both Pali and Sinhala languages. When monastics speak about *vinaya* in Sri Lanka, therefore, they may have a range of referents in mind:

1. The 'root text' (P: *mūla*) of the Vinaya Piṭaka (a usage I distinguish in this book by using capital letters, unitalicised)
2. The major commentaries and sub-commentaries on the Vinaya Piṭaka that monks treat as indispensable tools for accessing the true meaning of the root text
3. The broader body of writing that purports to embody and/or explain features of 1 and 2
4. All institutions, practices and texts that deal with the issue of monastic discipline (*vinaya*)
5. Discipline (*vinaya*) as generic techniques for, or modes of, behavioural restraint, which can be found in many kinds of institutions and communities[8]

[7] Blackburn, 'Looking for the Vinaya.'

[8] An example of this usage can be seen in this quote from an interview with a senior jurist in Colombo: 'Without *vinaya* there can be no social institutions . . . not just this monastic order but any kind of social structure – a church, a house, a school . . . it is essential for the functioning of any social institution.' 14 December, 2019, Colombo (Pos. 1.22).

In many of the cases examined in this book, these multiple referents for *vinaya* seem to operate like a set of categorical nesting dolls, each incorporating the ones before it. No matter which level is intended (if one can determine intention at all), the Vinaya Piṭaka tends to be implicated. By using the term 'monastic law' in this book, therefore, I speak about many things at once: namely, all the texts, practices and institutions that purport to manage and administer monastic discipline (numbers 1 – 4 above, and, on occasion, 5).[9]

UNITY AND MULTIPLICITY IN LAW

The polyvalence of the word *vinaya* exemplifies the play of unity and multiplicity, coherence and diversity, which characterise many legal traditions. To the extent that one reads monastic legal texts as embodying a single set of instructions traceable to the Vinaya Piṭaka, they can be said to operate as a unitary body of law. At the same time, given the highly divergent contents and style of these texts – including the differing, sometimes contradicting, ways they render the core teachings of the Vinaya Piṭaka – these sources can also be said to represent multiple legal traditions. In this way, monastic law mirrors other presumptively singular bodies of law, such as *shari'a* or constitutional law. In each case, emphasis on a single legal wellspring, whether man-made or divine, both disguises and encourages the production of other legal texts.[10]

Although often overlooked, this dual aspect of monastic law – its focus on the Vinaya Piṭaka and its diversity across numerous legal sources – appears across the Buddhist world. In Tibet, for example,

[9] Other scholars have adopted other conventions for making sense of this play of unity and multiplicity, often with reference to criteria of 'canonicity'. Prebish, for example, has proposed a classification of 'vinaya literature' into the following three categories: canonical (reserved mainly for the Vinaya Piṭaka root text); para-canonical (reserved for two genres of text that I discuss later, called [in Pali] *Pātimokkhas* and *kammavācā* manuals, which contain lists of rules and legal formulas taken from the Vinaya Piṭaka); and non-canonical (which includes commentaries and other 'miscellaneous texts'). Prebish, *The Vinaya*; Prebish, *A Survey of Vinaya Literature*.

[10] The transcendent unity of Allah and his law, the divine *shari'a*, help to justify the existence of multiple schools of *fiqh*, which are understood to be imperfect human interpretations of a perfect divine law. Similarly, in many doctrines of constitutional interpretation, such as the 'basic structure' doctrine in South Asia, diverse elements of constitutional law are thought to evince a foundational unity of values. Jackson, *Islamic Law and the State*; Krishnaswamy, *Democracy and Constitutionalism in India*.

one sees this in the seeming contradiction that, despite widespread acceptance of the Vinaya's authority among jurist monks, the unglossed root text of the Vinaya Piṭaka plays little role in the monastic legal education or administration.[11] Instead, Tibetan monastics depend on commentaries on the Vinaya Piṭaka and various in-house constitutions (*chayik*) produced by monasteries.[12] This duality also helps explain why many East Asian monastic traditions have historically placed more emphasis on shorter collections of rules, such as pure rules and bodhisattva precepts, more so than the fuller Vinaya Piṭaka.[13] In fact, perceptions that the Vinaya Piṭaka did not play a sufficiently large role in monastic life motivated a variety of 'Vinaya revival' movements across East Asia in the twentieth and twenty-first centuries.[14]

UNITIES AND DIVERSITIES IN MONASTIC LAW

In this chapter, I introduce readers to the unities and diversities of monastic law in Sri Lanka. I start by focusing on several key principles from the Pali version of the Vinaya Piṭaka that undergird most monastic legal texts and practices on the island. These principles include the various categories of monastic rules, the protocols for classifying and handling legal cases, the procedures for conducting legal actions and the frameworks around penalties and sanctions. The first half of this

11 Tibetan monastics observe the Mūlasarvāstivāda version of the Vinaya Piṭaka, about which more will be said later in the chapter.

12 Particularly important is Guṇaprabha's *Vinaya-Sutra* along with its autocommentary. On the diversity of Tibetan monastic law, see: Dreyfus, *The Sound of Two Hands Clapping*; Finnegan, "For the Sake of Women, Too," 28; Jansen, *The Monastery Rules*; Nietupski, 'Guṇaprabha on Monastic Authority and Authoritative Doctrine'; Sullivan, 'Monastic Customaries and the Promotion of Dge Lugs Scholasticism in Amdo and Beydon.'

13 Most East Asian monastics observe the Dharmaguptaka version of the Vinaya Piṭaka, about which more will be said later in the chapter. On the status of bodhisattva precepts and pure rules, see: Chiu, 'An Overview of Buddhist Precepts in Taiwan and Mainland China'; Chiu, 'Bodhisattva Precepts and Their Compatibility with Vinaya in Contemporary Chinese Buddhism'; Lin, 'Bodhisattva Precepts in East Asian Perspectives and Beyond: Introduction'; Muller, *The Collected Works of Korean Buddhism, 11*; Poceski, *Rules of Engagement*; Yifa, *The Origins of Buddhist Monastic Codes in China.*

14 Bianchi and Campo, *Take the Vinaya as Your Master*; Campo, 'A Different Buddhist Revival: The Promotion of Vinaya (Jielü 戒律) in Republican China'; Kaplan, 'Updating the Vinaya.'

chapter explains these principles in some detail in order to give non-specialist readers a grounding that will prepare them for the chapters that follow.

The second (longer) half of this chapter introduces readers to the broader range of legal sources that constitute monastic law in contemporary Sri Lanka. Some of these sources are thought to be nearer to the Vinaya Piṭaka, closer to the centre of the categorical nesting dolls. These include the major commentaries and sub-commentaries on the Vinaya Piṭaka, as well as stand-alone compendia of rules (*Pātimokkhas*) and legal formulae (*kammavācā*) from the Vinaya Piṭaka that circulated alongside the root text. Other sources are regarded as being farther from the Vinaya Piṭaka root text on account of the novel rules they contain and/or as a result of the authorities responsible for creating and deploying them. This second collection of sources includes the various kinds of monastic constitutions (*katikāvatas*) promulgated by pre-colonial kings and modern monastic fraternities. It also includes the multiple forms of colonial and post-colonial law designed to govern the succession, property and behaviour of monks. Alongside these sources stands a wide variety of other legal texts – such as handbooks, didactic stories, compendia and manuals – which also play an important role in the education and application of monastic law.

This overview of Sri Lankan monastic legal sources is necessary not only as an introduction to the legal landscapes that will be considered in this book but also because, to my knowledge, no such overview exists. While scholars, mainly Buddhologists, have studied specific genres of monastic legal texts (especially those composed before the nineteenth century), I have found no overall survey of the various monastic legal sources visible in the contemporary period.

This absence may reflect inveterate biases built into the fields of Buddhist studies and legal studies, respectively. Buddhologists have exhibited a preference for older, written, philosophical sources, more than modern, legal and political ones. Scholars of law, for their part, have only occasionally welcomed ascetical and religious examples into the domain of the 'legal' – and rarely have they acknowledged the existence of religio-legal traditions outside the Abrahamic faiths. When it comes to Buddhist monastic law, these two disciplinary inclinations combine to doubly occlude the kinds of legal sources examined below – so much so that even one of the world's most prominent scholars of Buddhist law, Andrew Huxley, mistakenly speculated that 'after two hundred years of unsuccessful search for Sinhalese Buddhist legal literature, it would seem that it is non-existent'.[15]

VINAYAS AND THE VINAYA

Multiplicity exists even in the text presumed to unify the entire monastic legal corpus, the Vinaya Piṭaka. Although I have referred to it in the singular so far (as *the* Vinaya), in fact, multiple Vinayas have circulated from the earliest periods of Buddhism to the present. Each of these is considered authentic (i.e. *the* Vinaya) by the monastic fraternities that preserve them. Six more-or-less complete Vinayas, associated with distinct monastic groups, survive from earlier periods. Three of these Vinayas are still used today: Theravāda monastics, who predominate in South and Southeast Asia, use the Pali-language Vinaya Piṭaka; most East Asian Buddhist monastics use the Dharmaguptaka Vinaya preserved in Chinese; monastics in the Tibetan and Mongolian traditions of Buddhism, as well as those in some parts of Japan, affirm the authority of the Mūlasarvāstivāda Vinaya, which has been preserved in Chinese, Tibetan and Sanskrit.[16]

Rules in the Vinaya

In all its variants, the Vinaya Piṭaka contains at least two major parts, which together form the outlines of a monastic legal system. The first part, the 'Explanations of the Sutta' (P: *Sutta-vibhaṅga*),[17] lays out a list of rules that monks and nuns are expected to follow. The Pali version of the Vinaya, for example, contains 227 for monks and 331 for nuns;[18] other Vinayas contain different numbers of rules.[19] The second part,

[15] Huxley, 'Studying Theravada Legal Literature,' 65.

[16] For a general overview of the different Vinaya traditions, see: Clarke, 'Vinayas'; Heirman, 'Vinaya'; Prebish, *A Survey of Vinaya Literature*; Schopen, 'Vinaya.'

[17] 'Sutta' is the shorthand for the *Pātimokkha* [sutta], the list of rules that also circulates independently, as described later in the chapter.

[18] Included in the 227 and 331 rules are seven settlement procedures, explained later in the chapter.

[19] These recensions are not simply parallel translations of the same content. While Vinayas contain many similarities, they also show remarkable differences. For example, the Mūlasarvāstivāda Vinaya used by Tibetan monastics is much larger than the Pali variant and has a greater number of rules: 249 or 262 for monks, depending on the redaction, and 358 or 371 for nuns. The Dharmaguptaka Vinaya favoured in East Asia prescribes 250 for monks and 348 for nuns. Even the content and tone of the texts can differ. The Mūlasarvāstivāda stands out for its long, often

called the 'Chapters' (P: *Khandhaka*), focuses more on the history, rituals and institutional protocols of the Buddhist monkhood. This section includes, for example, instructions for how to conduct the fortnightly observance of *uposatha*, in which members of a monastic community gather to confess their offences. It also includes details about the annual practice of *vassa*, which requires monastics, some of whom may be itinerant, to reside at a monastery for three months during the rainy season. The Chapters section even contains a list of administrative positions that ought to be filled within every monastery, such as the 'keeper of the storeroom' or the 'distributor of robes'.[20] Kieffer-Pülz has referred to these two sections, respectively, as the 'penal and administrative law of the sangha'.[21] The Pali-language Vinaya also contains a third section, composed after the other two, which features prominently in the practice of law among Sri Lankan monks.[22] Called the 'Enclosing' (P: *Parivāra*), this section contains nineteen chapters, many of which summarise and analyse the other two parts.[23] Taken together, then, the Vinaya provides (1) a set of basic instructions (*sikkhāpada*) for monks, (2) a set of procedural rules describing how those instructions should be put into action and (3) a broader set of practices and administrative protocols designed to facilitate the running of a monastic residence.

humorous, stories about monastic conduct. The Pali Vinaya, although containing plenty of humour, tends to employ a less verbose style. Rules that appear in one version do not always appear in others. Schopen, 'Vinaya'; Clarke, 'Monks Who Have Sex: Pārājika Penance in Indian Buddhist Monasticisms.'

20 On these administrative roles, see Kieffer-Pülz, 'Officials: Buddhist'; Kieffer-Pülz, 'Review of Silk, Jonathan A., Managing Monks. Administrators and Administrative Roles in Indian Buddhist Monasticism (Oxford University Press, 2008)'; Silk, *Managing Monks*.

21 Kieffer-Pülz, 'Brief Summary of the Development of Buddhist Monastic Law Codes and Institutions,' 149.

22 The Mūlasarvāstivāda Vinaya also has a section beyond the first two. Clarke, 'Vinayas,' 60.

23 Hinüber, *A Handbook of Pāli Literature*, 21–22, §41–42. It is important to note that, although this three-fold division is acknowledged by Sri Lankan commentators and Vinaya scholars, when it comes to the physical copying of the Vinaya Piṭaka, a different sectioning is often used. Sri Lankan monks refer to different 'books' (*grantha* or *pāḷi*) of the Vinaya. As one monastic jurist put in the foreword to a volume on *vinaya* literature: 'The Vinaya Piṭaka that was preached by the Tathāgata contains five books (*grantha*): namely, *pārājika pāḷi*, *pācittiya pāḷi* [both part of the Explanations section] *mahāvagga pāḷi*, *cullavagga pāli* [both part of the chapters section] and *parivāra pāḷi*.' Vajirajñāna Himi, *Lakdiva Vinaya Sāhityaya [Sri Lankan Vinaya Literature]*, v.

Generally speaking, the Explanations section of the Vinaya Piṭaka breaks down the primary rules of monastic life into seven categories, corresponding with the penalties incurred from violating them. This is followed by an eighth category relating to legal disputes. As it relates to the rules for monks, the categories are as follows:

(i) **4 x defeat offences** (*pārājika*): The first four prohibitions (against sex, murder, theft and claiming non-existent supernatural powers) result in one's 'defeat', meaning disrobing and/or expulsion from a monastic community.[24]

(ii) **13 x penance offences** (*saṅghādisesa*): Violating these thirteen rules (e.g., making sexual innuendos, touching women, creating schisms in the sangha) requires special periods of penance and probation as well as formal meetings of the monastic order.

(iii) **2 x undetermined offences** (*aniyata*): Violation of these two 'undetermined' rules (dealing with uncertainty around contact with women) results in a variety of penalties, including *saṅghādisesa*.[25]

(iv) **30 x forfeiture and confession offences** (*nissaggiya pācittiya*): Breaking these rules (largely related to the inappropriate acquisition or use of property) requires monks to give up possessions and confess their guilt in front of the group.

(v) **92 x confession offences** (*pācittiya*): This broad and varied category of prohibitions, which covers everything from drinking alcohol to eavesdropping, requires only confession to the monastic community.

(vi) **4 x acknowledgement offences** (*pāṭidesanīya*): These four rules relating to accepting and eating food require only a simple acknowledgement of commission.

[24] Despite some uncertainty about the origin of the term *pārājika*, most scholars gloss it as 'defeat'. When speaking about this category of offence with monastics and laity in Sri Lanka, it is assumed that the term indicates the 'defeat' of a person's status as a monastic and their expulsion from the monastery. Clarke, however, has shown that in variants of Vinaya Piṭaka other than the Pali version, those who commit *pārjājikas* are permitted to remain within the sangha and reside at monasteries, albeit with a special probationary status. Clarke, 'Monks Who Have Sex: Pārājika Penance in Indian Buddhist Monasticisms.'

[25] Namely, *pārājika*, *saṅghādisesa* or *pācittiya*. On this class of offences, see Borgland, 'Undetermined Matters: On the Use of Lay Witnesses in Buddhist Monastic Procedural Law.'

(vii) **75 x training rules** (*sekhiya*): This section provides a long list of detailed instructions concerning how monks are supposed to conduct themselves while eating, walking, preaching and other everyday activities. Transgression of these norms, which is acknowledged to be unavoidable for most monks, requires no formal confession.

(viii) **7 x rules for settling legal cases** (*adhikaraṇa samatha*): This section provides a list of procedures to be employed for resolving disputes among monastics. (I examine these procedures in further detail below.)

As laid out in the Explanations section, these rules are not presented as a bare list. Rather, they appear alongside a larger body of stories and analyses, which, although varying in length, employ a similar format.[26] The passages begin with a backstory explaining why the Buddha promulgated a given rule.[27] Next comes a formulation of the basic regulation (*paññatti*) in the Buddha's own words,[28] along with a word-by-word clarification of the key terms and phrases used in the rule. Following that comes a list of possible conditions that affect the application of the rule, such as the value of a stolen item or the intention of the perpetrator. (Scholars often refer to this section as a 'casuistry'.) Then comes a list of exceptions that could nullify a person's guilt if they, for example, committed the offence while ill, insane, in mortal danger or unaware of what they were doing.[29] Further permission to bend or ignore rules is sometimes extended to monks who live in 'border regions', far away from major population centres.[30] Similar

[26] Kieffer-Pülz, 'What the Vinayas Can Tell Us about Law'; Kieffer-Pülz, 'Brief Summary of the Development of Buddhist Monastic Law Codes and Institutions.' These categories, which appear to apply more or less to the structure of rules in all Vinayas, are drawn from the Pali commentarial tradition. On the terms and their origins, see Hinüber, *A Handbook of Pāli Literature*, 13–14, §22–23.

[27] For certain rules, there can be more than one introductory story.

[28] Occasionally the text includes supplementary prescriptions (*anupaññatti*) as well, further refining the basic rule – either loosening or strengthening it.

[29] Also exempted are 'first offenders', the ancient monks who transgressed a primary rule before the Buddha made that rule known. Kieffer-Pülz sees this exemption as upholding the legal principle of *nullum crimen, nulla poena sine lege*, 'no crime or penalty without a law'. Kieffer-Pülz, 'What the Vinayas Can Tell Us about Law,' 53.

[30] Horner, *The Book of Discipline (Vinaya Piṭaka)*, vol. iv, 266–67; Oldenberg, *The Vinaya Piṭakaṃ*, vol i, 197.

leniency applies to rules that might conflict with a royal edict.[31] For the first nine rules (the four defeat rules and the first five penance rules), the Vinaya also includes a set of instructional cases (*vinītavatthu*) designed to clarify the application and meaning of the regulation.[32]

Consider, for example, the rule against drinking alcohol, which will be discussed in further detail below. This rule falls under one of the ninety-two confession rules in the Explanations section.[33] The framing of the rule begins with the story of a monk who, having been given alcohol by lay donors, falls ill and passes out at the town gate. (The lay donors had offered him alcohol because a group of six mischievous monks, who appear as the comic villains throughout the Vinaya, insisted that it was a suitable gift.) The monk is then brought, unconscious, to the Buddha, who uses the event to warn his gathered disciples about the hazards of drinking alcohol. According to the story, the Buddha declares that drinking alcohol causes one to behave in ways that are 'unbecoming, unsuitable, unflattering, not proper, and not to be done'[34] and that such behaviour will neither impress the laity nor increase their faith in the *sāsana* – which are described elsewhere as major goals of monastic law. The Buddha then promulgates the formal regulation that drinking spirits or wine will, from then on, be an offence that requires confession to the group.

The text then shifts from a narrative mode to a commentarial one and provides a list of definitions for various terms used in the rule: 'spirits', 'wine' and 'should drink'. This is followed by a casuistry clarifying the penalties that should apply depending on whether or not the offender knows the substance is alcohol and whether or not he drinks all of it. The instructions conclude with a list of circumstances that qualify as non-offences: if the liquid looks, smells or tastes like alcohol but is not; if the drink is not distilled or only very weakly distilled; if the monk is temporarily insane; or if he is the first wrong-doer.

31 Kieffer-Pülz, 'What the *Vinayas* Can Tell Us about Law,' 56.

32 Kieffer-Pülz, 'The Law of Theft: Regulations in the Theravāda Vinaya and the Law Commentaries'; Huxley, 'Buddhist Case Law on Theft: The Vinītavatthu on the Second Pārājika.'

33 Confession rule (*pācittiya*) number 51. Pali in Oldenberg, *The Vinaya Piṭakaṃ*, vol iv, 108–10. an English translation of passage appears in Horner, *The Book of Discipline (Vinaya Piṭaka)*, vol. ii, 382.

34 *Ananucchaviyaṃ, ananulomikaṃ, appaṭirūpaṃ, assāmaṇakaṃ akappiyaṃ akaranīyaṃ.* Oldenberg, *Vinaya Texts (Sacred Books of the East Vols. 13, 17, 20)*, vol. iv, 110.

Legal Cases (*adhikaraṇa*) and Settlements (*samatha*) in the Vinaya

In the Pali Vinaya, the Explanations section concludes with a short list of seven types of 'settlement' (*samatha*) that can be used to address 'legal cases' (*adhikaraṇa*), which are further clarified in the Chapters section:

1. A ***verdict in the presence of*** (*sammukhā-vinaya*) requires that parties settle their case in a face-to-face manner, in front of their fellow monks, while also being in the figurative 'presence' of the Buddha's teaching and the Vinaya.
2. A ***verdict of innocence*** (*sati-vinaya*) involves the accused recalling exactly what happened and clearing his name.[35]
3. A ***verdict of past insanity*** (*amūḷha-vinaya*) occurs when a monk is declared to have been temporarily delusional while committing offences.
4. ***[A settlement] by making a confession*** [of guilt] (*paṭiññāya kāretabba*) involves an accused monk acknowledging that he offended.
5. ***[A settlement] by the majority*** (*yebhuyyasikā*) takes place when the above measures do not work and the gathered monks, having disagreed about how to resolve the case, engage in a majority vote.
6. ***[A settlement] of obstinate wrongness*** (*tassapāpiyyasikā*) is one in which the accused initially denies committing an offence and is later found guilty.
7. ***[A settlement] of covering with grass*** (*tiṇavatthārako*) is one in which monks on all sides agree to collectively ignore and move past the dispute.

As presented, the list appears to contain discrete legal procedures that monks can use to resolve disagreements or determine guilt. Somewhat confusingly, the term 'settlement' seems to imply both a mode of adjudication (a type of trial) and a type of determination (a verdict). For this reason, while it is tempting to think of these legal settlements as different types of court protocols, this is not quite the case. Instead, one might think of them as different techniques for addressing a dispute, which can be used together or separately.[36]

[35] This verdict is said to apply to *arahants*, 'worthy ones' who, through their observance of the Buddha's teachings, have become fully awakened.

[36] The technical language given by the Vinaya Piṭaka to classify these settlements does not help disambiguate. The text classifies the first three settlements using the term *vinaya*, a polyvalent word that, as indicated above, may refer to the act of disciplining generally. However, the word also has a broader set of connotations, including 'removal' (e.g., of an issue) or 'ruling' (in the sense of discerning or judging). For

In the Chapters section, one finds that each of the settlements is associated with one (or more) of four different types of legal cases (*adhikaraṇa*):

1. ***Dispute cases*** (*vivādādhikaraṇa*) relate to disagreements among monks concerning the content and meaning of the Buddha's teaching.
2. ***Accusation cases*** (*anuvādādhikaraṇa*) arise when someone accuses a monk of violating a Vinaya rule.
3. ***Offence cases*** (*āpattādhikaraṇa*) involve debates about the nature and severity of an offence that a monk committed.
4. ***Action cases*** (*kiccādhikaraṇa*) involve disagreements over whether a particular legal action (*saṅghakamma*, discussed below) has been properly conducted.

For each of these types of cases, the Vinaya prescribes a particular set of settlement procedures. For example, dispute cases should be settled by two settlement procedures: *verdict in the presence of*, or *verdict by the majority*. Accusation cases, by contrast, are to be settled by four procedures (*verdict in the presence of*; *a verdict of remembering*; *a verdict of past insanity*; or *a settlement of obstinate wrongness*). A complete scheme is as follows:

1. Dispute cases are to be resolved by *verdict in the presence of*, and, if needed, *by the majority*;
2. Accusation cases are to be resolved by *verdict in the presence of*, and possibly a *verdict of remembering* or *past insanity* or *obstinate wrongness*;
3. Offence cases are to be resolved by *verdict in the presence of* and possibly *by making a confession* or *covering with grass*;
4. Action cases are to be handled through *verdict in the presence of*, only.[37]

As can be seen, the various settlements are implied as working in overlapping, even modular ways. First, one settlement is applied and

consistency, I have followed the convention of most scholars by translating *vinaya* in the first three terms as 'verdicts' – although 'discernment' might better convey the processes of adjudication (rather than decision-making) that seem to be implied. For a thorough technical analysis of these terms, see Nolot, 'Studies in Vinaya Technical Terms I–III,' 99–115.

[37] Adapted from Dutt, *Early Buddhist Monachism*, 163.

then, if necessary, another. In all cases, the first settlement to be tried is *verdict in the presence of*, which involves a technique similar to that used in contemporary state courtrooms. As described in the Chapters section, this technique takes the form of a hearing in the 'presence' of several things: an accuser and an accused (plaintiff and defendant); a set of rules against which the accused's actions will be assessed (in this case, particular instructions given by the Buddha); and the larger monastic community within which the offender resides.[38] This method, or a variation of it, was used to resolve virtually all of the monastic legal cases I learnt about during my research.

In spite of all these precise details, the Explanations and Chapters sections of the Vinaya offer little direct information about how to conduct a legal procedure, from start to finish. The most detailed accounts can be found in the Enclosing section of the Vinaya. In this section, one finds certain protocols concerning how, when and where one may accuse another monk of committing an offence. These passages indicate that an accuser should confront the accused with humility, a purposeful attitude, a mind committed to removing impurities,[39] an attitude of kindness, consideration and compassion, as well as a focus on rehabilitation (from offences) and devotion to monastic discipline.[40] These sections also describe the role of a jurist (*anuvijjaka*), who is responsible for examining legal cases – a term and a role visible in contemporary monastic law in Sri Lanka. As with the rules for accusers, the text recommends certain attitudes and approaches for judges: they should not speak hastily or heatedly, confrontationally or aimlessly, or in a way that causes resentment.[41] The text even provides a list of questions that can illuminate the mindset and motivations of the litigants and witnesses who are involved in the case.[42]

[38] The Vinaya does not explain the settlements in equal detail. Some settlements, such as those involving *verdicts of remembering* or *past insanity*, receive only very brief descriptions, focusing particularly on the communal action carried out at the end. Others, such as *verdicts in the presence of* and *by the majority*, are described in great detail.

[39] This refers to the impurities within one's own mind. Horner, *The Book of Discipline (Vinaya Piṭaka)*, Vol. vi, 264; Oldenberg, *The Vinaya Piṭakaṃ*, Vol. v, 163.

[40] This comes from the Chapters section, with the Pali reading: *kāruññatā*, *hitesitā*, *anukampatā*, *āpattivuṭṭhānatā vinayapurekkhāratā*. Oldenberg, *The Vinaya Piṭakaṃ*, Vol. ii, 250.

[41] Horner, *The Book of Discipline (Vinaya Piṭaka)*, Vol. 6, 255–56; Oldenberg, *The Vinaya Piṭakaṃ*, Vol. v, 158.

[42] Schonthal, 'Buddhist Rules About Rules,' 560–63.

'Legal Actions' in the Vinaya Piṭaka

According to the Vinaya Piṭaka, the conclusion of any settlement requires the performance of a 'legal action' (P: *saṅghakamma*, or simply *kamma* [*karma* in Sinhala]), a collective procedure undertaken by a community of monks with the goal of altering the status of persons and objects. Legal actions transform a layperson into a monk or declare a set of stones to be a ritual boundary; they may certify that an accused monk is now a guilty monk or that a guilty monk is now rehabilitated from his offence.

For legal actions to be valid according to the Vinaya, they must satisfy several conditions. Participating monks must congregate inside an official monastic boundary (*sīmā*), sitting or standing within arm's reach of one another. There must be a quorum of participants (between four and twenty monastics, depending on the procedure). Most importantly, those undertaking the legal action must closely follow a prescribed sequence of utterances and silences that create a ritual and illocutionary structure similar to that of modern secular courtrooms: in the same way that contemporary legal decisions or oaths are made effective through the use of prescribed formulas (e.g., 'I hereby swear') and carrying out specific actions (e.g., banging a gavel), so too do *saṅghakammas* mobilise a suite of actions and utterances to turn spoken words into finalised, official decisions.[43]

According to the Vinaya Piṭaka, legal settlements ought to conclude with legal actions that change the status of the legal case from one that is ongoing to one that has been 'put down'.[44] Three features of these actions are worth noting. First, these actions require the participation of all monks staying within the same residence area unless those monks are too ill to attend, undergoing penance (and thus ineligible to participate) or have otherwise been given permission not to attend and to communicate their consent by proxy.[45] Despite these exemptions, there still must be a minimum number of monks for the legal

43 Hinüber, 'Buddhist Law and the Phonetics of Pāli (Das Buddhistische Recht Und Die Phonetik Des Pāli)'; Winn, 'Legal Ritual.'

44 P: *nihatādhikaraṇaṃ*

45 The idea here is that monks who cannot attend the proceedings for legitimate reasons can send their consent (*chanda*) with another monk. The question of what counts as a residence area (*āvāsa*) and its relationship with ritual boundaries (*sīmā*) is complex. On the topic, see: Kieffer-Pülz, *Die Sīmā. Vorschriften Zur Regelung Der Buddhistischen Gemeindegrenze in Älteren Buddhistischen Texten*, 42–52. On the complex and variable use of *sīmās* as 'both boundaries and the places that are made by the creation of those boundaries', see also: Carbine and Davis, 'Introduction,' 2;

action to be valid.[46] Second, settlement actions that 'put down' legal cases require that the settlement be proposed in the form of a formal motion (*ñatti*) which the gathered group of monks (serving as a jury of sorts) has the opportunity to contest. Third, settlement actions – like other communal actions – must be followed by the *verbatim* uttering of standard formulas (*kammavācā*, literally, 'words for the legal action') taken from the Vinaya Piṭaka and other texts.[47] These formulas, which function like 'declarative questions' in other judicial settings,[48] name the monks involved, clarify the action to be taken, and ask the community to agree to the proposed action by remaining silent. For example, the formula that declares a monk rehabilitated from a period of penance includes the following phrases:

> Venerable sirs, may the [monastic] Community listen to me. This Bhikkhu (name) has fallen into [a specific offence]. He asked the Community for [a particular penance] for [a particular offence or set of offences]. The Community granted him [that penance for that offence] . . . He – having undergone penance – asks the Community for rehabilitation. If the Community is ready, it should rehabilitate Bhikkhu (name). This is the motion.
>
> Venerable sirs, may the Community listen to me. This Bhikkhu (name) has fallen into [a specific offence]. He asked the Community for [that penance] for [that/those offences]. The Community granted him [that penance] . . . He – having undergone penance – asks the Community for rehabilitation. The Community is rehabilitating Bhikkhu (name). He to whom the rehabilitation of Bhikkhu (name)

Carbine, 'How King Ramadhipati Handled His Boundary Case: Sima, Sasana, and Buddhist Law.'

46 A sangha of four monks can conduct all legal actions except for higher ordination, the group confession at the end of the rainy-season retreat (*pavāraṇa*) and rehabilitation or reintegration into the order after a serious offence (*abbhāna*). A sangha of five can conduct *pavāraṇa* and higher ordination in remote areas. A sangha of ten can ordain anywhere. A sangha of twenty can conduct rehabilitation (*abbhāna*). For more information regarding quorums and who is permitted to participate in *saṅghakammas* see Borgland, 'A Study of the Adhikaraṇavastu: Legal Settlement Procedures of the Mūlasarvāstivāda Vinaya,' 450, fn 876; Kieffer-Pülz, 'Brief Summary of the Development of Buddhist Monastic Law Codes and Institutions,' 170; Nolot, 'Studies in Vinaya Technical Terms I–III,' 75–77.

47 While the Vinaya contains a number of *kammavācā*, new ones were also developed in different places and at different times. *Kammavācā* also circulated independently of the Vinaya in the form of special collections or as part of broader sets of guidelines and rulebooks, as described later.

48 Danet, 'Language in the Legal Process.'

> is agreeable should remain silent. He to whom it is not agreeable should speak.
>
> A second time . . . A third time I speak about this matter. . .
>
> Bhikkhu (name) has been rehabilitated by the Community. This is agreeable to the Community, therefore it is silent. Thus do I hold it.[49]

One can see in this excerpt the patterns and repetition that characterise action words. The formula begins with a motion regarding the penitent monk, which is then followed by three proclamations from the gathered community that look virtually identical to the motion, aside from the verb tense; this is then followed by a concluding agreement.[50] Both in the content of the formula and in the performative requirements of the legal action, the Vinaya communicates the idea that the decision comes not from a particular monastic judge but from the entire monastic community. In fact, the Vinaya states specifically that, for communal action to be legitimate, the monks must come together not only as a physical group, but they must be in unified agreement as well.[51]

Penalties and Rehabilitation

Although the format of the Explanations section implies a one-to-one correlation between particular transgressions and particular penalties, the relationship between rules and sanctions in the Vinaya is relatively complex. For example, in order for one of the first four rules to warrant the full penalty of 'defeat', a number of conditions have to be met: the monk has to have intent, make a concerted effort, and carry out the act completely. Short of this, the penalties associated with the act will not be removal but milder penalties, such as temporary suspension and probation. Similar considerations of intention and action also apply to other kinds of offences that are deemed to be *sacittaka* ([improper when done] with intent).[52]

[49] The final sentence is considered to be the agreement, for which there is no technical term. Translation in Ṭhānissaro Bhikkhu, *The Buddhist Monastic Code*, Vol ii, 1146.

[50] Motions (*ñatti*) appear in the optative, while proclamations (*anussāvanā* or *kammavācā*) appear in the indicative. I am grateful to Petra Kieffer-Pülz for pointing this out.

[51] The key Pali term here is *sāmaggi*, which denotes not only the physical completeness of the sangha, but the overall harmony or unanimity of the monks as well. This will be discussed in greater detail in Part II of this book.

[52] In the case of 'intent-less' (*acittaka*) rules, one transgresses the rule whether intentionally or negligently. See Kieffer-Pülz, *Verlorene Gaṇṭhipadas zum buddhistischen*

Although they are not the most severe type of offence, punishments associated with penance offences (*saṅghādisesa*) receive the most explanation in Vinaya. Only thirteen primary rules are categorised as penance offences. Yet penance offences also apply to monks who commit defeat-worthy offences to which mitigating circumstances apply, such as killing or stealing without intending to do so.

All penance offences require observing periods of penance (*mānatta*) and, in some cases, a period of probation (*parivāsa*). During the penance, which runs for a period of six days and six nights, monks must observe ninety-four restrictions that limit their ability to participate in monastic life. These restrictions prohibit things like travelling, sitting or conversing with other monks, receiving gestures of respect or practical assistance from peers and participating fully in communal meals and rituals (including legal actions). Monks undergoing penance ought to announce their penitent state to any monk that they meet. Any transgression of these restrictions results in the monks starting the penance period all over again.[53] In cases where monks conceal their offences deliberately for a period of time, the Vinaya advises that, prior to commencing the penance, monks should observe a period of probation for a number of days equal to the length of time the offence was concealed.[54] At the conclusion of the probation-penance period, the monk is declared 'fit for re-admission' and freed from all restrictions.[55] Each step of the process – from the confession of guilt, to the application of penance procedures, to the process of rehabilitation – requires legal actions, with the final reinstatement action considered so important that a full quorum of twenty monks is required.

The Vinaya pays close attention to the procedures through which monks are rehabilitated from their offences, restored to full status and

Ordensrecht, Vol. i, §Z15 and §Z25. For example, whether or not one does so intentionally, it is an offence to act as a messenger between lovers (penance rule [*saṅghādisesa*] number 5). Norman, Kieffer-Pülz, and Pruitt, *Overcoming Doubts (Kaṅkhāvitaraṇī): Vol. I The Bhikkhu-Pātimokkha Commentary*, Vol. i, 143.

[53] Nolot, 'Studies in Vinaya Technical Terms I–III,' 116–136; Ṭhānissaro Bhikkhu, *The Buddhist Monastic Code* Vol. ii, 358–96.

[54] During that probation, monks must observe virtually the same restrictions as during *mānatta*, without the requirement of making daily reports. Unlike the *mānatta* penance, if a monk violates the restrictions given during the probation period, he is not required to start again from the beginning of the sentence but only to extend the period by an additional day.

[55] Nolot, 'Studies in Vinaya Technical Terms I–III,' 133.

reintegrated into the community.[56] In fact, one phrase used by the Vinaya to characterise the nature of these sanctions is that they are ways of setting a monk upright after he has fallen down.[57] In other words, the Vinaya presents probation and penance not as payback for misdeeds but as correctives designed to remind monks of their shared discipline and guide them back to the community. The text construes transgressions as temporary lapses, rather than as evidence of wilful defiance. In this way, Vinaya sanctions appear more concerned with restoring discipline than penalising or deterring transgressions.[58]

MONASTIC LAW BEYOND THE VINAYA

The practice of monastic law in Sri Lanka draws heavily on the ideas and terms from the Vinaya Piṭaka described above.[59] Beyond the Vinaya, however, monks also rely on a variety of other sources that purport to summarise, condense, explain and supplement the root text. This wider body of monastic legal texts can be classified into different genres. Certain genres adhere closely to the Vinaya Piṭaka, presenting themselves as precise summaries, glosses or distillations of its component parts. These include commentaries, sub-commentaries, lists of rules (called *Pātimokkhas*) and collections of 'words for legal actions' (*kammavācā*). (Indeed, it is not unusual for commentaries and the *Pātimokkhas* to be treated as foundationally connected to the body of

[56] According to Nolot, in parts of the Vinaya, as well as in the *Samantapāsādikā* commentary, the reintegration (*abbhāna*) is a subtype of a more general category of 'restoration' (*osāraṇā*) procedures; the punitive actions, along with *mānatta* and *parivāsa*, are subsets of a broader category of 'dismissal' (*nissāraṇa*) procedures. Nolot, 'Studies in Vinaya Technical Terms IV–X,' 39–57.

[57] P: *āpattiyā vuṭṭhānā*. Ṭhānissaro Bhikkhu, *The Buddhist Monastic Code*, Vol. ii, 358–59. For an example, see Oldenberg, *The Vinaya Piṭakaṃ*, Vol. i, 64.

[58] Voyce, 'Ideas of Transgression and Buddhist Monks.'

[59] It is important to note that these ideas and terms represent only part of the entire Vinaya Piṭaka. Taken as a whole, the Vinaya is a large and complex text containing more than just rules and protocols. Central to the Vinaya are also humorous stories, histories of the *sāsana*, complex collections of aphorisms and much more. Moreover, as preserved in manuscript collections and contemporary bookstores, the Vinaya has not always been transmitted as a single unit. When asked about the most significant sources of monastic law, many of the bhikkhus whom I surveyed and interviewed routinely referred not to the Vinaya in general but to sections of it, most often the sections describing the four most severe offences (*pārājika pāḷi*) of the Explanations Section, which itself constitutes a portion of the entire Vinaya Piṭaka.

the Vinaya Piṭaka such that each implies the other.[60]) Other genres exhibit a greater degree of authorial flexibility, emphasising practical guidance over verbatim citation and explanation of the root text. These texts – including handbooks, manuals, compendia and constitutions – focus on applying monastic discipline to daily administration. A third category comprises case law, legislation and regulations, which connect to the Vinaya Piṭaka indirectly. These 'hybrid laws'[61] are authorised by the state but specifically govern Buddhist monastic conduct and property, using modern administrative techniques to (in the eyes of lawmakers) uphold the Vinaya and regulate monastic life.

The remainder of this chapter examines these various forms of monastic law, providing a broad overview of the sources that shape the way *vinaya* is taught, understood and applied in Sri Lanka.

(Early) Commentaries and Glossaries of the Vinaya Piṭaka

By far, the most significant source of monastic law outside of the Vinaya root text is the Pali Vinaya Piṭaka commentary entitled *Samantapāsādikā (All Pleasing)*.[62] The text is attributed to the fifth-century CE monk Buddhaghosa, but likely compiled by a committee of authors.[63] It is difficult to overstate the significance of this text for the transmission and interpretation of monastic law among Theravāda monks, who trace their lineage to the Mahāvihāra monastery in Sri Lanka, where Buddhaghosa reputedly lived. Some Theravādins consider the *Samantapāsādikā* to be similar in status to the Vinaya itself, the two even forming a single unit.[64] Indeed, monks' understandings of the

[60] Vinaya scholars might take this analysis one step further by pointing to the 'internal commentary' in the Vinaya itself, evident in the word analysis and casuistry in the Sutta Vibhanga itself. Kieffer-Pülz, 'Vinaya Commentarial Literature in Pali,' 430.

[61] Liu, 'Hybrid Courts and Hybrid Laws.'

[62] The Pali term for commentary is *aṭṭhakathā*, literally 'explanation of the meaning'.

[63] As Heim puts it, 'the proper name Buddhaghosa has more than one signification, only one of them the flesh-and-blood individual we imagine who actually sat down, translated, and edited some or all of these texts. The name Buddhaghosa also designates the authorship of a systematic corpus of material recognised and celebrated by the Mahāvihāra scholars'. Heim, *The Forerunner of All Things*, 10 and ff.

[64] The fifth-century Great Chronicle of Sri Lanka (*Mahāvaṃsa*) claims that the monks of the Mahāvihāra monastery treated the commentaries authored by Buddhaghosa, including the *Samantapāsādikā*, "as if they were the canonical texts [*piṭakas*] themselves". Heim, 8. Lammerts (in personal communication) confirms an even stronger association in early modern and contemporary Burma, where, according to him, the term *vinaya* almost always seems to refer to a category of texts (which includes the

root text frequently rely on glosses and analyses taken from this cornerstone commentary. As one indication of its importance, 35 per cent of the monks I surveyed reported referring to the *Samantapāsādikā* at least within the last six months.[65]

Since Buddhaghosa's time, Pali commentarial literature has expanded to include a wide span of other sub-commentaries and glossaries,[66] which attempt a similar task to that of Buddhaghosa's text: synthesising earlier materials, especially the Vinaya, and clarifying the meaning of difficult passages.[67] These Pali sources represent the most scholarly and specialised types of texts within Southern Asian Buddhist legal literature, traditionally accessible only to those with advanced training and language skills (although recent Sinhala translations of the *Samantapāsādikā* and other commentaries may broaden their accessibility).[68] Commentaries and sub-commentaries on the Vinaya Piṭaka,

root text and commentaries), rather than simply the root text. Evidence of this can be seen, for example, in the cataloguing practices of Burmese manuscript collections. See, for example, Luce and Htway, 'A Fifteenth Century Inscription and Library at Pagan,' 218–219. This differs slightly from practices in Sri Lanka, where, the *Samantapāsāikā*, even though acknowledged as essential for engaging the Vinaya Piṭaka, is also singled out as a separate text in analyses and discussions among monastic jurists.

65 Question 3.2(a)

66 A variety of sub-commentaries (P: *ṭīkās*) exist. They were written in reference not only to the Vinaya Piṭaka and *Samantapāsādikā*, but to other important texts such as the *Pātimokkha* and *Kuddhasikkhā*, both of which are discussed in this chapter. There is evidence of glossaries (S: *gäṭapada* P: *gaṇṭihpada*) pre-dating the *Samantapāsādikā*, to which Buddhaghosa refers. On all of these matters, readers are strongly urged to consult the work of Petra Kieffer-Pülz: 'Vinaya Commentarial Literature in Pali'; and *Verlorene Gaṇṭhipadas zum buddhistischen Ordensrecht*.

67 In my research, two sub-commentaries (*ṭīkās*) appeared to be cited most frequently. Both were composed around the twelfth century in Poḷonnaruva, Sri Lanka. They are the Illumination of Essential Meaning (*Sāratthadīpanī*, also known as *Līnasāratthadīpanī*) attributed to Sāriputta; and the slightly later, *Elimination of Doubts* (*Vimativinodanī*) attributed to Coḷiya Kassapa, also referred to as Mahākassapa. The second of these two presents itself as a polemic against the first, saying that it reflects the views of the rival monastery to the Mahāvihāra. When it comes to the production of Buddhist texts, including commentaries, twelfth–thirteenth-century Polonnaruva is particularly important. On this period, Gornall, *Rewriting Buddhism*; Kieffer-Pülz, 'Reuse of Text in Pāli Legal Commentaries'; Shirley, 'Constructing Buddhist Sovereignties: Text and Landscape in a Medieval Lankan Kingdom.'

68 Ambalaṅgoḍa Dhammakusala, *Samantapāsādikā Vinayaṭṭhakathā*.

while presented as explanations of the root text, serve mainly as expert reference works rather than general guides for the day-to-day administration of monasteries. Their main function is to help specialists clarify ambiguous terms or phrases in the Vinaya – a role evident in the judicial decisions of contemporary monastic courts (discussed further in Chapters 4, 5 and 6 of this book).

More practically oriented are *Pātimokkhas*, or bare lists of rules that are meant to be chanted fortnightly by monastics.[69] Although these rules are embedded and defined within the Explanations section of the Vinaya, *Pātimokkhas* have circulated independently since the earliest periods of Buddhism and function practically as stand-alone texts.[70] A survey of training materials across fifteen monastic schools (*pirivenas*) in the Colombo area turned up a variety of Sinhala adaptations and explanations of the Pali *Pātimokkha*, most of which were composed by contemporary scholar monks.[71] Rather than containing only lists of rules, these contemporary *Pātimokkha* manuals also include introductions, overviews, Sinhala translations and reflections on the meaning and implications of the rules in modern life. One of the most frequently used books of this type even makes a case for the unique importance of the Pātimokkha, as compared with the Vinaya root text itself. At the end of his preface, the author, Ven. Bujjampola Dhammaparāyana Tissa opines that although monastic law is based on the morality and precepts (*sīla hā śikṣāpada*) of the Vinaya Piṭaka, it is, in the final analysis, 'made secure under the *Pātimokkha*'.[72]

[69] Separate *Pātimokkhas* exist for male and female monastics (bhikkhus and bhikkhunīs). It is important to note that the *Pātimokkhas* that circulated independently were substantially the same as the content of the Vinaya Piṭaka, with the difference being that the *Pātimokkhas* only contain the final version of the rule, whereas the Vinaya describes the backstory and progressive fine-tuning of the rules over time. Ingo Strauch refers to *Pātimokkhas* and *kammavācā* manuals as 'practical' texts. Strauch, 'Lost in Translation?'

[70] This is demonstrated, in part, by the existence of a separate commentary on the *Pātimokkhas*, called *Kaṅkhāvitaraṇī (Overcoming Doubts)*. Norman, Kieffer-Pülz, and Pruitt, *Overcoming Doubts (Kaṅkhāvitaraṇī): Vol. I The Bhikkhu-Pātimokkha Commentary*; Hinüber, *A Handbook of Pāli Literature*, 109, §221–225.

[71] This survey was conducted in July and August 2019 with the help of Ven. Kahavaththē Amitha. The surveyed group includes *pirivenas* belonging to each of the three major divisions of Sri Lanka's monastic fraternity: the Siyam, Amarapura and Rāmañña Nikāyas.

[72] Dhammaparāyanatissa, *Prātimokṣa Vivaraṇaya*, 30.

Works like this – which present the *Pātimokkha* as an object of commentary and reflection – have a long history and ongoing relevance. Some of the earliest available Pali commentarial works take the *Pātimokkha*, rather than the Vinaya, as their object of commentary. The most important of these is the fifth- or sixth-century commentary *Overcoming Doubts*, or *Kaṅkhāvitaraṇī*, which itself became the object of multiple sub-commentaries.[73] Two thousand years later, *Pātimokkha* commentaries continue to arise throughout the world. In some cases, authors, such as the famous Vietnamese Zen monk Thích Nhất Hạnh, have even tried to 'update' the *Pātimokkha* rules to suit modern monastic life by, for example, elaborating new rules about cell phones or driving automobiles.[74]

Similar observations could be made about *kammavācā* manuals, compendia of 'words for legal actions'. These texts collect together the essential verbal formulas that monastic communities must use to perform their required legal actions.[75] Like the rules contained in the *Pātimokkha*, these verbal formulas appear in the Vinaya Piṭaka, alongside much longer explanations and stories concerning the procedural rules of monastic life. Yet the condensed format of *kammavācā* manuals makes them more accessible for undertaking legal actions within monasteries.

Consider, for example, the presentation of *kammavācā* formulas in one modern compendium, which combines the *Pātimokkha* rules and *kammavācā* words together. This contemporary Sinhala text, called the *Bhikṣu Prātimokṣa and Vinaya Karma together with Sinhala Instructions*, classifies *kammavācā* according to the events for which they are required: ordination, fortnightly *uposatha* rites, probation, etc. Alongside these lists, it provides detailed step-by-step instructions for how and when to recite these phrases, along with the correct gestures and body positions to use. The following excerpt summarises the words and actions for the full- and new-moon confession days

[73] Kieffer-Pülz, 'Vinaya Commentarial Literature in Pali.'

[74] Borgland, 'Some Reflections on Thích Nhất Hạnh's Monastic Code for the Twenty-First Century.'

[75] Clauson, 'A New Kammavācā;' Baynes, 'A Collection of Kammavācās;' Dickson, 'The Upasampadā-Kammavācā: Being the Buddhist Manual of the Form and Manner of Ordering of Priests and Deacons. The Pāli Text, with a Translation and Notes;' Kieffer-Pülz, 'Kammavācā Manuscripts as Written Artefacts for Ordination (Upasampadā) as a Buddhist Monk or Nun?;' Peters, 'Die Birmanischen Kammavācā-Sammlungen Mit Neun Abschnitten.'

called *uposathas*, when monks come together to chant the *Pātimokkha* and to confess any offences:

The Method for Conducting a Basic *Uposatha*[76]

[S:] Having done the previous actions [that is, 'duties such as setting the ritual area which has to be done before the *uposatha* action'], a monk who is known to be learned and strong, having explained the offences and indicated the suitable year, season and phase of the moon, [that monk] should offer salutation by laying down the [following] formal motion:

[P:] *Suṇantu me āyasmantā ajjuposatho (paṇṇaraso/cātuddaso). yadāyasmantānaṃ pattakallam mayaṃ aññamaññaṃ pārisuddhi uposathaṃ kareyyām'* [Listen to me, venerable monks, today is the *uposatha* (fifteenth day/fourteenth day). If now is a suitable time (it seems right) for the venerable monks, let us carry out/perform the observance with one another by [declaring our] purity.

[S:] Then the [following] salutation should be offered three times by the elder monks who are squatting together

[P:] *Parisuddho ahaṃ āvusō*! [I am pure O' brothers]...[77]

Here, as well as in other parts of the text, the author draws together important rules, phrases and procedural instructions from the Vinaya Piṭaka into a handy set of directions that can be used by monks. Sometimes the directions are intended for all Buddhist monks; other times they address a specific kind of community, such as a monastery or monastic fraternity. (This particular text was written by monks from a forest monastery and drafted with those monks in mind.) Books like this are extremely popular, appearing on the syllabi of most monastic schools and occupying visible positions in monastic bookstores.

[76] There are several different types of *uposatha* ceremony described in the Vinaya Piṭaka. These types vary according to the number of monks attending, and other factors. This example comes from a shortened *uposatha*. Unlike the full version of the *uposatha* ritual, this abbreviated version does not require that monks recite the full *Pātimokkha* but only confess their purity to the others. Personal communication from Petra Kieffer-Pülz.

[77] Araṇya Sēnāsanaya, *Bhikṣu Prātimōkṣaya Saha Vinaya Karuṇu (Siṁhala Anuvāda Sahitayi)*, 120.

Condensations and Rulebooks

Pātimokkhas, *kammavācā* manuals and *vinaya*-specific commentarial texts emphasise their faithful adherence to the Vinaya root text, presenting themselves as direct explanations or extracts of it. In contrast, other genres of monastic legal literature take a more interpretive approach. Anne Blackburn, for example, has documented how eighteenth-century monastic education in Kandy relied heavily on didactic narratives taken from another 'basket' of the Tipiṭaka, namely the Sutta Piṭaka, or Basket of Discourses. These discourses – which go by titles such as 'The Ten Things to Reflect On', 'Judgment' and 'The Duty of Kindness' – communicate Vinaya concepts in the form of stories about the Buddha and and his teachings. While they do not claim to directly summarise the Vinaya Piṭaka, they nevertheless contain sermons and lists of qualities that communicate Vinaya principles in simple terms that may appeal to students. These same stories are still used in monastic education today.

Alongside didactic stories like these, one also finds other, more obviously legalistic texts that claim to condense key principles from the Vinaya in the form of prescriptive rules. These generally take the form of rulebooks based on precepts contained in the Vinaya but organised in new formats. Some of the earliest Pali examples of these kinds of texts are the *Mūlasikkhā (The Foundational Rules)* and the *Khuddasikkhā (The Minor Rules)*, which date to the second half of the first millennium, and whose use is attested in Sri Lanka and other parts of Southern Asia since at least the twelfth century.[78] As with the *Pātimokkha*, these texts have also become the source of their own glossaries and commentarial literature.[79] *Mūlasikkhā* and

[78] Ratnapala, *Katikāvatas*, 130 (§§7–8). Antecedents to these texts can be found as early as the late sixth century, roughly around the time of the *Samantapāsādikā*. The *Assessment of Vinaya* (*Vinayavinicchaya*) and the *Further Assessment* (*Uttaravinicchaya*), both ascribed to the Sri Lankan monk Buddhadatta, are Pali 'versified manuals' designed, in the words of the author, to serve as a 'ship' to help monastics navigate 'the sea of the Vinaya'. Kieffer-Pülz, 'Vinaya Commentarial Literature in Pali,' 435; Hinüber, *A Handbook of Pāli Literature*, 154–157 (§§324–331). The ship analogy appears at the beginning of the *Viniyavinicchaya*: P: *apāraṃ otarantānaṃ, sāraṃ vinayasāgaraṃ, bhikkhūnaṃ bhikkhunīnañca, nāvābhūtaṃ manoramaṃ* Buddhadatta, *Buddhadatta's Manuals*, 2:1 (§4). This is commented on in Vajirajñāna Himi, *Lakdiva Vinaya Sāhityaya [Sri Lankan Vinaya Literature]*, 100–101.

[79] Kieffer-Pülz, 'Vinaya Commentarial Literature in Pali,' 435.

Khuddasikkhā are relatively short texts (being roughly 8 pages and 32 pages in modern print, respectively), which group together various sets of precepts in versified form, ostensibly for the purpose of memorisation. The *Mūlasikkhā*, for example, is divided into six sets of lists that the author considers to be important: the defeat-worthy offences, the seven serious offences, the forfeiture offences, the confession offences, the varieties of bad speech and the types of purification.[80]

In Sri Lanka, the *Mūlasikkhā* and *Khuddasikkhā* texts served as the bases for Sinhalese translations, adaptations and commentaries, which are still used today.[81] One of the oldest and most important condensations of this type, composed sometime between the sixth and tenth centuries CE, is the *Heraṇasikha* (*Rules for Novices*), a Sinhala text that contains concise lists of numbered precepts taken from various parts of the Vinaya.[82] Monastic constitutions (*katikāvatas*) written in the twelfth and thirteenth centuries attest to the importance of this text, instructing readers to memorise the verses alongside other important sources.[83]

Contemporary versions of the *Heraṇasikha* still circulate today, along with its standard commentary (*Heraṇasikkha-vinisa*), and are featured in the syllabi of monastic schools. One modern edition of the *Heraṇasikha* and commentary breaks down the text into four main sections covering the ten precepts (*dasasil*), the ten types of defeats (S: *pariji*; P: *pārājika*), the ten types of behaviour that lead to exclusion from the monastery (*nāsanā*) and the ten punishments (*daṇḍuvama*).[84] While the lists of ten serve as effective mnemonic devices, they also create numbered sets that differ from those listed in the Vinaya Piṭaka. Where the Explanations section declares four

80 Müller, 'Khuddasikkhā and Mūlasikkhā'; Hinüber, *A Handbook of Pāli Literature*, 157 (§§332–333).

81 Kitsudō, *Pāli Texts Printed in Sri Lanka in Sinhalese Characters with Supplementary Information on Related Texts*, 12–14 (§§5–6).

82 Godakumbura dates the *Heraṇasikha* 'a century or two' after the compilation of the Sinhala translation of the *Mūlasikkhā*, called the *(Mūl)sikhavaḷan̆da*, and the commentary *Sikhavaḷan̆da-vinisa*, which he attributes to sometime between the sixth and tenth centuries CE. That would place *Heraṇasikha* somewhere before the twelfth century. In any event, the *terminus ante quem* for the text is the twelfth century, given that it is mentioned in the *Mahā-Parākramabāhu Katikāvata*. *The Sinhalese literature*, 17–19; Ratnapala, *Katikāvatas*, 39 (§8).

83 Ratnapala, *Katikāvatas*, 49 (§17), 50 (§19, §22).

84 Vijitananda, *Heraṇa Sikha hā Heraṇasikha vinisa*.

types of 'defeat', or *pārājika*, for example, the *Heraṇasikha* lists ten 'defeat' behaviours:

What are the ten pārājikas for a novice?

1. It is a *pārājika* to knowingly take the life of animals.
2. It is a *pārājika* to knowingly take even a thread that belongs to someone with the intent to steal it.
3. It is a *pārājika* to knowingly engage in sexual activity even with an animal one encounters along the road.
4. It is a *pārājika* to knowingly speak falsehoods even while joking around.
5. It is a *pārājika* to knowingly imbibe a small amount of alcohol even if you are thirsty.
6. It is a *pārājika* to speak poorly about the Buddha.
7. It is a *pārājika* to speak poorly about the dharma.
8. It is a *pārājika* to speak poorly about the sangha.
9. It is a *pārājika* to engage in sexual activity even with a virtuous nun.
10. It is a *pārājika* to have various wrong-views.

The above are the ten pārājikas for a novice.

While some of the novice *pārājikas* are familiar (e.g. the prohibitions on killing and stealing), others are not part of the *pārājika* section of the Vinaya for fully ordained bhikkhus (such as the prohibitions on slandering the Buddha, dharma and sangha). Indeed, the broader *Heraṇasikha* seems less like a collection of *verbatim* rules (such as the *Pātimokkha* and *kammavācā* manuals above) and more like a summary designed to amplify and explain the essence of the rules for a particular audience—in this case, novices.[85] The *Heraṇasikha* and its commentary establish foundational guidelines for current and prospective monastics, outlining the requirements for admission into the order and the activities that could result in expulsion from it.

Texts such as the *Heraṇasikha* may be the inspiration for another type of text which has become especially widespread among Sri Lankan monastic groups. This text appears, in various editions and imprints, in

[85] In the Chapters section of the Vinaya (Vin i, 85,19–26), one finds a list of ten actions that will lead to novices' expulsion (P: *nāseti*) from the monastery. They do not appear in the Explanations section, however. On these lists and the expansion of categories from the Vinaya, see Kieffer-Pülz, *Verlorene Gaṇṭhipadas zum buddhistischen Ordensrecht*, Vol. ii, 1764–1772 (Z290–Z291).

virtually every *pirivena* and monastery around the country: *Preaching and Dharma Book for Novices* (*Sāmaṇera Baṇa Daham Pota*).[86] As the name suggests, the work serves as something of a training manual for novices who are joining the monkhood. The chapters generally cover a variety of topics, including the precepts, routines, offerings and chants a novice monk is supposed to know.

One popular edition of the text, first published in 1980 and reprinted since, contains within it a copy of the *Heraṇasikha* along with other abbreviated lists of rules, such as:

- The four types of virtuous conduct that restrain [monks] (S: *satara saṃvara śīlaya*):[87]
- The seventy-five training rules (*sekhiyā*)
- The places that one should not go to for alms
- The relatives from whom you may request the four requisites
- The rules for using the four requisites (robes, food, dwelling places and medicines)[88]
- The thirty-two types of talk (*kathā*) that are prohibited for bhikkhus
- The twenty-one kinds of wrongdoing that a monk might use to win over the laity (*anēsanas*).[89]
- The forty types of people who are unsuitable for renunciation

In compiling these lists, the author draws from multiple sources. Some rules are taken directly from the Vinaya and *Samantapāsādikā*, while others seem to be drawn from Sutta literature, monastic constitutions and the Sinhalese translation of the *Mūlasikkhā*, the *Sikhavaḷaňda*, and its commentary, the *Sikhavaḷaňda-vinisa*. Vanaratna's edition even includes a constitution (*katikāvata*) used at a well-known contemporary monastic school, which lays out in minute detail the

86 Although a variety of books (containing similar sorts of material) circulate with this same title, the edition by Vanaratna, explored here, appears to be particularly widespread.

87 Namely: virtuous conduct in behaviour; virtuous conduct in the senses; virtuous conduct with respect to having a pure lifestyle (S: *ājīva pāriśuddhi*); virtuous conduct with respect to the four requisites.

88 Other lists of requisites also exist. Later on in the same text, the author lists the eight requisites (S: *aṭapirikara*), namely the 'three robes' (the one-part, two-part and inner robes) and belt, the bowl, razor, sewing needle and the water strainer. Vanaratna, *Theravādī Sāmaṇera Baṇadaham Pota*, 68–69.

89 This includes giving to laity things that have been donated to the monastery, such as fruit, flowers, betel nuts, palm leaves. A complete list in English can be found in Carter and Palihawadana, *The Dhammapada*, 450 fn. 7.

ideal day-to-day routine for novice monks, including waking up before dawn, contemplating the triple gem, chanting sacred verses, cleaning the temple grounds, making offerings to the Buddha, studying, meditating, lighting lamps at night and many other things.[90] As presented by the author, the book collects together 'all those things that are essential for going forth and becoming disciplined, and which have come down through the lineage of the Mahāvihāra [monastery], and which should be memorised by sons-of-good-families (*kula putrayan*) who want to become ordained into the *sāsana*'.[91]

Handbooks, Treatises, Manuals and Compendia

If novice monks rely heavily on the *Heraṇasikha* and the *Preaching and Dharma Book for Novices*, fully ordained monks also employ a variety of other texts that consolidate and summarise important rules for the life of a bhikkhu. Often these texts are referred to as 'handbooks' (S: *atpot*), and any visitor to a bookstore in Sri Lanka is sure to be impressed by the sheer number and range of books in this category. Among the 1669 bhikkhus surveyed for this research, 35 per cent responded that they had 'referred to' (*pariśīlanaya karanavā*) a handbook at least once within the last month.[92] The largest and most famous series of handbooks was written by Ven. Rērukānē Candavimala (1897–1999), a scholar monk from the Shwegyin sub-fraternity of the Amarapura Nikāya, which developed a reputation for strict adherence to monastic discipline. Candavimala's books are widely used in *pirivenas* and appear in most bookshops containing Buddhist literature, often taking up an entire bookshelf (see Figure 2.1). When invited to write down the name of any handbook they had consulted in the last six months, many respondents to my survey wrote Candavimala's books by name: 22 per cent wrote down his *Book of Vinaya Karmas* (*Vinaya Karma Pota*), 9 per cent mentioned his *Virtuous Conduct for Fully Ordained Monastics*

[90] This author notes that the *katikāvata* was provided by Ven. Ahungallē Vimalanandi Tissa (1925–2005), who would eventually become the Supreme Great Leader (*uttarītara mahānāyaka*) of the Amarapura Nikāya. The rules in this *katikāvata* – which, according to the excerpt, were promulgated in 1878 – appear to be based on those visible in the thirteenth-century *Dambadeṇi Katikāvata* and then repeated in the eighteenth-century *katikāvata* of Kīrti Śrī Rājasiṃha. Ratnapala, *Katikāvatas*, 158 (§96–§98). For related passages in the commentaries see, von Hinüber, 'Everyday Life in an Ancient Indian Buddhist Monastery,' 26–29.

[91] Vanaratna, *Theravādī Sāmaṇera Baṇadaham Pota*, 5. [92] Question 3.4

Figure 2.1 Bookshelf of handbooks by Ven. Rērukānē Candavimala, Colombo, July 2024.

(*Upasampadā Śīlaya*), and 7.5 per cent listed his *Entrance into the Sāsana* (*Śāsanāvataraṇaya*).[93]

Like other texts of this type, Candavimala's handbooks bring together quotations from primary texts in Pali along with explanations and translations in Sinhala, all around a general theme, such as legal actions or ordination. For example, his popular book on legal actions, *Book of Vinaya Karmas*, breaks down the various types of actions (referred to in Sinhala as *vinaya karmas*) into twenty-eight different categories of actions based on how they are used, including renunciation (as a novice), higher ordination, confessing offences, full- and new-moon (*uposatha*) actions, rains retreat (*vassa*) actions and so on. (A complete list of chapter headings can be found in the appendix.)

93 Question 3.4(a).

Under each of these headings, the author provides further subcategories, breaking down the overall action into separate steps, each of which receives an explanation. For example, under the heading of penance (S: *vat mānata*, P: *mānatta*), he includes the following topics, prefaced by a general introduction to the concept of penance:

Penance

Penance for Unconcealed Offence
The Words for Requesting Penance
The 'Legal Action Words' Given for Penance
The Words for Begging for one's Rehabilitation
Concealed Offences[94]

Given that these rules may be scattered throughout different sections of the Vinaya and, especially for non-specialists, difficult to understand, handbooks like these can be extremely useful for Sri Lankan monks.

Beyond these general handbooks, monastic writers have also produced a variety of treatises organised around specific legal topics, often those that have been the focus of debate. One topic that has been important and contentious in the history of Buddhism is the process of measuring and establishing *sīmā*s, or monastic boundaries. As described earlier in the chapter, a correctly reckoned *sīmā* is essential for monastic life because legal actions, including ordination, will be invalid if the *sīmā* has not been properly established.[95] For this reason, monastic jurists have produced numerous treatises on the topic of *sīmā*s. Those treatises bring together excerpts on the topic (taken from the Vinaya Piṭaka and related commentaries), the decisions made by monastic judges, and other sources, presenting them in a form that can be consulted by specialists when disputes arise.

Authors sometimes write treatises like these to vindicate (or impugn) the correctness of a legal decision undertaken by a particular group of monks. Many such texts were produced in Sri Lanka in the nineteenth century during a period of growing schisms and segmentation among the island's monastic fraternities. These texts – which bear titles such as the *Removal of Confusion about Sīmā*s (*Sīmā Saṅkara Vinodanī*) or *Clarification of the Concealed Meaning* (*Līnārttha Dīpanī*) – mix together elements of monastic law relating to *sīmā*s with records of

94 Candavimala, *Vinaya Karma Pota [Book of Vinaya Acts]*, 118–25.
95 Carbine and Davis, 'Introduction.'

famous judgments issued by jurist monks in a particular case.[96] In addition to treatises on *sīmā*s, monks in Sri Lanka also created treatises on the proper reckoning of ritual calendars, the rules around donations to the monastery and the permissibility of worshipping deities.[97]

In Burma, an entire textual genre emerged starting in the seventeenth century, with the ostensible aim of collating and collecting legal decisions made by judges, both real and mythical.[98] This diverse genre, which came to be known as *pyatton*, contained a body of 'judgment tales' culled from Buddhist story literature and the work of historical judges, interspersed with commentary from the author. According to Andrew Huxley, such texts reflected the strong emphasis in Burmese culture on litigation over legislation, fostering an atmosphere of legal practice he characterises as 'common law Buddhist'.[99] This characterisation is misleading, however, given that such records probably did not function as precedents in the modern juridical sense but served other purposes: as apocryphal tales of wise judges (some non-human) designed to convey moral messages; as stories designed to affirm a particular understanding of inheritance, property or some other legal principle; or simply as entertaining stories designed to amuse audiences.[100]

Building on these traditions of jurisprudential writing, twentieth-century monks have developed new manuals aimed at the needs of jurist monks tasked with resolving disputes. As I discuss in the chapters that follow, Sri Lankan monks have developed what might be called manuals of monastic legal practice. Some of these are publicly available, while others circulate within fraternities themselves. One of the most significant publications, which was recommended to me by

96 Malalgoda, *Buddhism in Sinhalese Society*, 155–72; Kieffer-Pülz, 'Translocal Debates and Legal Hermeneutics.' *Sīmā* treatises can be found well before the nineteenth century. For an excellent study and translation of one such text, from the early thirteenth century, see: Kieffer-Pülz, *A Manual of the Adornment of the Monastic Boundary*.

97 Malalgoda, *Buddhism in Sinhalese Society*, 131–44, 169–70.

98 While the oldest surviving manuscripts date to the seventeenth century, according to Lammerts, other written versions are likely to have existed earlier. Lammerts, 'Genres and Jurisdictions: Laws Governing Monastic Inheritance in Seventeenth-Century Burma.'

99 Huxley, 'Studying Theravada Legal Literature,' 72, 78–81; Huxley, 'Lord Kyaw Thu's Precedent.'

100 Personal communication from Christian Lammerts.

several monastic jurists, goes by the simple title *Adjudication* (*Adhikaraṇa Viniścaya*).[101] Published in 1954 by an eminent jurist monk in the Rāmañña Nikāya, Ven. Nitalavē Śrī Gñāṇissara, the book was designed as a short, synoptic aid for monastic judges responsible for hearing legal disputes. It contains three clearly structured chapters, each of which collates and explicates passages from the Vinaya and related commentaries on the topics of legal cases (*adhikaraṇa*), modes of settlement (*samatha*) and methods of adjudication (*viniścaya*). In his introduction to the text, Gñāṇissara explains that he wrote the book with the goal of providing 'for precept-abiding monks and *sāsana*-loving laity ... a single book that would allow them to understand readily the mass of facts about the process of adjudication which are [normally] scattered across various *vinaya* books'.[102]

In the decades following Gñāṇissara's handbook, other compendia and collections of writings[103] have been published with similar goals.[104] More than just explanations of the Vinaya and its procedures, such as

[101] According to the preface, the volume had been written at the invitation of Prime Minister D.S. Senanayake, who served as a president of the 'Rāmañña Nikāya Committee' at the time but who died in 1952 before the book was published. Senanayake presumably welcomed the work as part of his broader effort to encourage greater internal discipline and autonomy for monastic groups, especially the Rāmañña Nikāya for whom he had acted as a special patron. A short letter from Senanayake, prefaced to the main text, calls the volume 'a valuable aid to the flourishing of the sangha and the stability of the *sāsana*'. The context of Senanayake's comments will be considered in Chapter 7 of this book. Gñāṇissara, *Adhikaraṇa Viniścaya*.

[102] Nitalavē Gñāṇissara, ii. It is unclear whether he is referring to the Vinaya or to *vinaya* books as a broader genre of texts about monastic discipline.

[103] S: *saṅgarā*, *lekhanasammucaya*.

[104] This is not to say that these are the first texts to anthologise or 'digest' *vinaya* materials. Kieffer-Pülz has written about the range 'Vinayapiṭaka digests' (*saṅgahas*) and their commentaries. One of these is cited with some frequency in contemporary *vinaya* literature: the massive *Vinayasaṅgaha* (*Vinaya Compendium*), or *Pali Muttakavinayavinicchaya* (*Compendium of Vinaya Rulings Independent of the Canonical Text*), attributed to Sāriputta in Poḷonnaruva in the twelfth century. A commentary to this work, the seventeenth-century *Vinayālaṅkāraṭīkā*, composed in Burma, is also well used. According to Kieffer-Pülz, the Vinaya Compendium 'consists of rearranged, reused text mainly from the *Samantapāsādikā* and the *Vinayapiṭaka*, but also from the *Kaṅkhāvitaraṇī* and *Sumaṅgalavilāsinī* [Buddhaghosa's commentary on the *Dīghanikāya* of the Sutta Piṭaka]. It is arranged in thirty-four chapters, dealing with topics of the monks' daily life and with issues affecting the community as a whole. Although it does not contain original text, it is an important document because it illuminates the topics considered important to monastics in 12th-century Sri Lanka.' Kieffer-Pülz, 'Vinaya Commentarial

those provided in the handbooks described above, these works collect together monastic and scholarly writings that will be useful for contemporary monastic judges and other legal specialists. In addition to condensing and summarising relevant portions of the Vinaya and its commentaries, these texts also consider the practical administration of monastic courts as well as monastic law's similarities to and relationship with state law. For example, in one important collection of more than 300 pages, called *Illumination of Legal Issues*, the author, a senior jurist monk named Ven. Mirissē Dhammasiri, included the following sections:

1. **Section on the Sangha** containing chapters on the 'origin', 'spread', 'organisation' and 'evolution' of the monastic community.
2. **Section on [monastic] Necessities** (P: *paccaya*) containing chapters on the development of monastic possessions in India and in Sri Lanka and 'the categories of Buddhist property'.
3. **Section on the Rules/Precepts** (*śikṣāpada*) containing chapters on the era of law before, during and after the Buddha promulgated the Vinaya precepts.
4. **Section on Legal Cases** (*adhikaraṇa*) containing chapters on: the nature of legal cases, their analysis, their resolution, the associated legal actions, an analysis of legal conventions or expressions (*adhikaraṇa vōhāra*), an analysis of conflict, how to write legal judgments, things to consider when re-opening a legal case (*ukkōṭana*), decisions made about previous legal cases, the meanings of key words, the sangha organisation in Thailand, the Buddhist Temporalities Ordinance, collections of previous (monastic) court cases, lists of related books and other addenda.

As seen in its table of contents, the volume includes a considerable range of topics and sources, covering everything from why the Buddha created monastic rules in the first place, to the different categories of monastic property, to examinations of important concepts from the Vinaya Piṭaka and related commentarial texts. Unlike other condensations discussed above, Ven. Dhammasiri's book also includes a mixture of contemporary monastic and state-legal sources: decisions made by monastic jurists from the Rāmañña Nikāya, judgments from civil court cases, passages from relevant state laws like the Buddhist Temporalities

Literature in Pali,' 438. See also: Crosby, 'Sāriputta's Three Works on the Samantapāsādikā.'

Ordinance and details about the Sangha Acts that govern monastic life in Thailand. The book even begins with an introduction written by the Chief Justice of Sri Lanka's Supreme Court, who praises the book's value for both lay and monastic readers – offering lay legal professionals insight into monastic law and jurisprudence while providing monks an overview of 'the common law of the country'.

The book's dual approach can be seen, particularly, in its section on 'decisions made in previous cases'.[105] This section begins by introducing the idea of *stare decisis* (spelt out phonetically in Sinhala), which the author describes as a key principle from common law that also applies to monastic jurisprudence. He then goes on to categorise the various kinds of already-decided cases that one might consider as precedents for monastic legal disputes. Building on categories contained in a twelfth-century sub-commentary on the Vinaya and commentary on the *Samantapāsādikā*,[106] he offers his own list of possible sources for monastic *stare decisis* including:

(1) the instructional cases from the Vinaya which demonstrate the jurisprudential logic of the Buddha (*vinītavatthu*);
(2) the truthful decisions made by eminent monks within in Theravāda sangha in accordance with the *Pātimokkha* and the fourfold Vinaya;[107]
(3) the decisions made by opposing groups of people,[108] including those from other kingdoms, fraternities or *nikāyas*, who do not

[105] Dhammasiri, *Saṅghādhikaraṇa Jotikā [Elucidations of the Monastic Court]*, 197 and ff.
[106] *Vimativinodanīṭīkā*. The reason for preferring this may have to do with the fact that the author comes from a fraternity, the Ramañña Nikāya, that traces its origins to a part of modern-day Myanmar, where the seventeenth-century Vinaya sub-commentary called *Vinayālaṅkāraṭīkā* (attributed to Tipiṭakālaṅkāra) was very influential. That commentary draws on all three Vinaya sub-commentaries – the twelfth–thirteenth-century *Sāratthadīpanīṭīkā* and *Vimativinodanīṭīkā* and the earlier, undated *Vajirabuddhiṭīkā* – but prefers the *Vimativinodanīṭīkā*. Personal communication from Petra Kieffer-Pülz.
[107] The author refers particularly to decisions made by Mahā Paduma Thera, Mahā Summa Thera, Ābhidhammika Godadatta Thero and other notable monks whose opinions are recorded by name in the early commentaries. In some ways, this list of names represents a standard set of early monastic elders whose authority is also affirmed in other *vinaya* literature, from a very early date. This particular version differs slightly, however, in that nearly all commentaries present and reject the opinion of Mahāpaduma in contradiction to that of Mahāsumma. Kieffer-Pülz, 'Stretching the Vinaya Rules and Getting Away with It,' 41–44.
[108] *paravādī tīndu*.

understand things correctly and whose opinions can be used as an example of poor jurisprudence;

(4) legal decisions that are 'taken from commentaries such as the *Samantapāsādikā* and the *Dhammapada* commentary';

(5) decisions coming from contemporary sangha courts; and

(6) 'the collections of decisions and orders coming from civil courts in accordance with the [Administration of Justice] Act No. 44 of 1973 and coming from the criminal courts under the Code of Criminal Procedure Act No. 15 of 1979.'

As presented in this compendium, then, monastic jurists are invited to base their decisions not just on the Vinaya but on multiple bodies of case law taken from the Vinaya and its commentaries as well as from contemporary monastic and civil courts.

The categories of legal text that I have outlined above – the *Pātimokkhas*, *kammavācā* manuals, condensations, rulebooks, handbook, treatises, manuals and compendia – are meant to be indicative rather than comprehensive. Indeed, many of the works I referred to could be classified differently. For instance, in his extremely useful overview of Pali sources in Sri Lanka, Masahiro Kitsudō consolidates several of the sources above (including *Pātimokkhas*, *kammavācā* manuals *Khuddasikkhā* and others) under the single heading of 'Vinaya manuals'.[109]

Nor are the categories above exhaustive. The following chapters will examine additional types of legal sources, with Parts I and II of the book giving attention to two other forms of legal writing: written judicial decisions (*tīndu*) issued by monastic jurists (Chapter 4), and the internal workbooks and handouts prepared for and circulated among monastic judges in the Rāmañña Nikāya (Chapters 5 and 6).

Monastic Constitutions (*katikāvatas*)

Monastic constitutions – collections of administrative rules and guidelines clarifying the core norms, offices and procedures of monastic life – are among the most important legal sources shaping monastic life. In Sri Lanka, these kinds of texts are generally referred to as *katikāvatas*.[110]

[109] Kitsudō, *Pāli Texts Printed in Sri Lanka in Sinhalese Characters with Supplementary Information on Related Texts*, 11–24.

[110] The term derives from the word *katikā*, which (as well as its cognates *katikasaṇṭhāna* and *katikāvatta*) can be found in early Pali sources, including the Vinaya Piṭaka, to refer to agreements created by monks and laypersons to bring order and regularity

Katikāvatas cover a variety of topics, including ordination, education, ritual obligations, daily duties, meditation, apprenticeship (*nissaya*), property, dispute resolution, administrative offices and protocols for legal actions. Like the other types of law mentioned above, *katikāvatas* also bring together rules from a variety of sources: the Vinaya root text, commentaries, sub-commentaries, the *Mūlasikkhā* and a variety of other Pali and Sinhala texts.[111] The five complete *katikāvatas* that survive from the premodern period were drafted by monastic elites and promulgated in the name of kings, for the purpose of governing all monks within the realm.[112] From the nineteenth century, monastic fraternities took control of *katikāvatas*, drafting them through executive committees and applying them to their members.

Monastic constitutions continue to play a significant role in the governance of fraternities in Sri Lanka today. Most fraternities – as well as sub-fraternities, chapters or sangha councils[113] – have drafted *katikāvatas*, which range in size from several pages to several hundred pages. Recently, a constitution has also been drafted by the island's 'precept mothers' (*silmātā*), renunciant women who lead monastic lives but do not call themselves bhikkhunīs for reasons that will be explained in Chapter 8 of this book.[114] Like earlier *katikāvatas*, contemporary group *katikāvatas* draw from a variety of texts, borrowing their style,

to various matters – from agreements among merchants in market towns, to regulations used by monasteries to manage water use and waste disposal. The term *katikāvata* becomes more standardly applied to the laws governing monasteries, fraternities and sanghas from the early first millennium. In contemporary Sri Lanka, other words are sometimes used as well, such as *vyavasthāva*. On the category see: Kieffer-Pülz, *Verlorene Gaṇṭhipadas zum buddhistischen Ordensrecht*, Vol I, 261–64; Shirley, 'Constructing Buddhist Sovereignties: Text and Landscape in a Medieval Lankan Kingdom,' 58–59; Suraweera, *Siṁhala Katikāvat Hā Bhikṣu Samājaya [Sinhala Katikāvata-s and Monastic Society]*, 163.

111 Ratnapala, *Katikāvatas*, 233–54.

112 Scholars refer to these early texts, which can be dated between the twelfth to the eighteenth centuries, as *sāsana katikāvatas* because they address themselves to the entire *sāsana*, rather than to residents of a single monastery. These are distinguished from another genre of texts, which scholars refer to as *vihāra katikāvatas*, which applied only to particular monasteries (*vihāra*). Inscriptions and manuscripts also refer to *vihāra katikāvatas* using other terms, including customs (*sirit*, *vatsirit*), constitutions (*vävasthā*, *vyavasthā*) or standards (*niyama*). On this history, see Schonthal, 'Buddhist Law beyond the Vinaya,' 295–296.

113 S: *nikāyas*, *pārśvayas*, *sangha sabhāvas*.

114 De Silva, 'Vigilant Steps'.

structure and substance from earlier Pali and Sinhala sources as well as contemporary state laws.[115]

Rāmañña Nikāya Katikāvata

Consider, for example, the constitution of the monastic fraternity that will be examined most closely in this book, the *katikāvata* of the Rāmañña Nikāya. As refined by the group over the past 150 years, the Rāmañña Nikāya katikāvata has adopted striking similarities to Sri Lanka's national constitution.[116] Like the national constitution, the Rāmañña constitution is divided into chapters, sections and numbered clauses, using the same conventions (of numbers, Roman numerals and letters) as the national law. The Rāmañña *katikāvata* consists of fourteen chapters:

1. Basic Principles
2. [Rules for] Novice and Full ordination
3. Conduct for Ordinary Monks
4. The Appointment of Chief Incumbent Monks and the Control of Monastery Property
5. Regional Monastic Councils
6. The Governing Monastic Council
7. The Executive Monastic Council and the Board of Special Authorities
8. Development Councils
9. The Qualification Assessment Council
10. [Protocols for] Holding Meetings and Advancing Proposals
11. The Appointment of Chief Authorities and Officials
12. The Positions of District Judge and Judicial Councils and their Organisation of Duties

[115] This is not to say that all *katikāvatas* are directed towards entire chapters or *nikāyas*. *Katikāvata* for individual monasteries (*vihāra*) continue to exist. Consider for example these two manuscripts located in the Sri Lankan National Archives: '*Tittavela Vihāraya Vävasthā Patraya* [The Constitution of the Tittavela Temple]' (June 3, 1874), SLNA 5/63/178/2 filed as '*vyavasthā patriyak*'; '*Paramadhammachetiyārāmaya Katikāvata* [The Constitution for the Paramadhamma Monastery]' (B.V. 2421 1878), SLNA 5/63/6/25 filed as '*katikāvata*.'

[116] The first Rāmañña Nikāya *katikāvata* was drafted in 1871.

13. The Fraternity Protection Council
14. Forest Hermitages and Practice Centres

Ten of the fourteen chapters deal directly with the activities, responsibilities and appointment procedures relevant to the key offices of monastic administration. The remaining four chapters (Chapters 1–3, 10) clarify the core responsibilities, expectations and procedures important for all ordinary Rāmañña monks.

The first chapter, concerning 'Basic Principles', refers to the *katikāvata* as an 'administrative framework' and 'behavioural code' for the fraternity, clarifying its 'ultimate purpose' as being 'the endurance, protection, development and administration of the existing lineage of monks in the Rāmañña fraternity'.[117] Also notable in the first chapter is a six-page-long 'Definitions' section that glosses fifty-two technical terms taken both from the Vinaya Piṭaka and from the administrative lexicon of contemporary Sri Lankan law, including terms such as 'petition' (*petsama*) and 'charge sheet' (*cōdanā patraya*).[118]

Similar to the Sri Lankan state, the administrative structure laid out by the Rāmañña *katikāvata* entails a threefold division of executive, legislative and judicial councils. The executive council (*kāraka saṅgha sabhāva)* consists of the fraternity's highest-ranking monastic officials (*adhikārīn vahansēlā*), such as the twenty senior preceptors who supervise ordinations and eight provincial chiefs who serve as the administrative heads of Rāmañña fraternity for each province.[119] Overseeing the council is a steering committee presided over by the fraternity's highest-ranking monk, the great leader (*mahānāyaka*), along with seven deputy leaders (*anunāyakas*) and the judicial chief (*adhikaraṇanāyaka*). Legislative power is vested in a governing monastic council (*pālaka saṅgha sabhāva*), which, like parliament, has primary duties consisting of drafting and amending regulations consistent with the *katikāvata*.[120] The Rāmañña constitution currently provides for 226 members (compared with the 225 MPs in Sri Lanka's parliament), who are elected from regional constituencies through a process of majority vote by Rāmañña monks living in that

117 Rāmañña Nikāya, *Śrī Laṅkā Rāmañña Mahā Nikāya katikāvata*, 1.
118 The term *codana* also appears in Pali *vinaya* literature as a technical term for 'objection'.
119 All provinces in Sri Lanka are represented except the Northern (where the group has no monasteries).
120 Rāmañña Nikāya, *Śrī Laṅkā Rāmañña Mahā Nikāya Katikāvata*, 48, §64, §65.

region.[121] The entire body is reconstituted every seven years, at which point all members must be re-elected.

The third branch of monastic government laid out in the Rāmañña constitution are the institutions of the judiciary, which will be discussed in detail in Part II of the book. For now, it is enough to observe that, as laid out in the *katikāvata*, the structure of the Rāmañña judiciary parallels that of state courts, in its threefold structure of District, Senior and Supreme Courts. Like the national Supreme Court, the Rāmañña Supreme Court even has the power to review some of the actions of the governing and executive councils.[122]

The rights and obligations of individuals are at the heart of the third chapter in both the Sri Lankan constitution and the Rāmañña *katikāvata*. In the case of the former, Chapter 3 provides a list of fundamental rights for citizens; in the case of the latter, it contains a list of twenty 'behaviours (*pratipatti*) that must be observed'. Roughly a quarter of the behaviours pertain to the daily duties of monks. For example,

- Every single monk should ask himself daily 'Have I protected my monasticism (*bhikṣūtvaya*)?'
- [Monks] should engage in the four postures [of walking, sitting, standing and lying down] mindfully and in a manner that is suitable for a monk.
- [Monks] should meditate at the prescribed time daily at a meditation site that is chosen according to their own disposition.
- [Monks] should make offerings three times per day. In addition to praising the triple gem [the Buddha, his teaching and the monks], in the evenings they should chant protective verses, following the tradition of the fraternity.

[121] Ties are settled through lottery, with ballots counted in front of the candidates. Most regions send three monks to the governing council. However, more populated regions send more representatives: areas with more than sixty temples and eighty bhikkhus can elect six, while areas with more than forty-five temples and sixty-one bhikkhus elect four. There are also ten supplementary members (*atirēka sāmājikayan*) whom that the executive council appoints to the governing council. In addition to these groups, all monks who have served in the highest leadership positions in the fraternity – such as the mahānāyaka or judicial chief – are entitled to serve as honorary lifetime members with voting rights. Rāmañña Nikāya, 43, §56(i)–(ii).

[122] Rāmañña Nikāya, 96, §145.

- [Monks] should attend daily to the *dagoba*, the bodhi tree and the statues as well as make sure the temple treasures, the temple premises and the areas nearby are cleaned.[123]

This list of duties draws upon and consolidates lists of daily tasks for monks taken from older monastic handbooks and constitutions dating from the twelfth to nineteenth centuries, such as the one appearing in the *Preaching and Dharma Book for Novices*, mentioned above. Yet it does so in a language and form reminiscent of modern national constitutions. A similar combination of ancient content and contemporary style can also be seen in seven (of the twenty) rules that refer directly to procedures, protocols and penalties from the Vinaya Piṭaka, such as the admonishments to monks to confess disciplinary offences immediately to monastic superiors so that they can undergo an appropriate penance.[124] In all cases, the Rāmañña *katikāvata* reframes these complex Vinaya rules as general principles and succinct directives.

The last set of prescribed behaviours relates to the appearance and conduct of monks in public, a matter that has concerned Buddhist monks from the earliest eras. Here, too, the Rāmañña constitution appears to have drawn from and repurposed older injunctions to update them for the modern world. Three prescriptions involve the proper appearance and use of monastic robes, umbrellas and bowls, which, the *katikāvata* insists, ought to have the official colours and insignia agreed upon by the fraternity.[125] Other prescriptions relate to how a monk ought to behave outside the monastery, for example:

- [Monks] should not be in unsuitable (*agōcara*) places [a category glossed in the 'Definitions' section of the *katikāvata* as 'places that defile the respectability of a monk' such as bars, restaurants, dance and musical performances, sporting events, abattoirs].[126]
- As it would lead to the decline of monasticism (*bhikṣutvaya*), [monks] should not participate in party politics nor be members of

[123] Rāmañña Nikāya, 14–15, §23: (i), (ii), (iv), (vii), (viii).
[124] Ibid., 14–15, §23: (iii)–(v), (xiv)–(xv)–(xvii).
[125] Ibid., 14–15, §23: (ix), (x), (xx).
[126] The term *agocara* literally means an 'improper pasture', or land that cannot be grazed. In monastic legal contexts, *gocara* refers to a village to which monks go to collect alms while *agocara* refers to those places that monks should not go to collect food. Here, the Rāmañña lawmakers use the term more widely, as places monks should not spend time for any reason. The constitution's definition can be found at Rāmañña Nikāya, 1,§3(1).

> a political party; nor should they hold a membership in things such as a provincial council, or city council, or local council, or state council; nor should they go forward as a candidate for one [of those].[127]

While earlier *katikāvatas* do not discuss bars, political parties or city councils, they do contain admonitions against inappropriate types of interactions with laypersons, such as sitting privately with women or wandering around villages without a purpose. Although not displacing these regulations, the current Rāmañña constitution selectively underscores certain types of moral behaviour as being uniquely important and worthy of entrenching. Similar decisions have been made as part of the processes of amending and updating the *katikāvata* in 1901, 1925, 1950, 1964, 1973, 1989, 2003 and 2014.[128]

State Law and Hybrid Laws

In spite of the multiple genres of law described above, in most parts of Asia, including Sri Lanka, monastics do not have total autonomy over the regulation of monastic life. A variety of national ordinances, statutes and even national constitutions also claim to govern the conduct, institutions and behaviour of Buddhist monastics. As one monk put,

> [Monastery administration] is not like it was in the past. Today temples are not the same. Now, temples are legal entities. They are connected to the law of the state. It's not like it was. They can't just be some little [temple] in the forest. That's because they are legally connected to the laws of the state. Their governance is linked with that.[129]

This merger of monastic and state-legal authority has a long history in Asia. It can be seen, among other places, in the premodern *katikāvatas* of Sri Lanka, the royal orders of Burma and the long history

[127] Rāmañña Nikāya, 14–15, §23: (xii), (xiii).

[128] In most cases, when amending constitutions, monastic lawmakers edit and broaden the text by revising existing provisions and adding new ones. As one monastic interviewee remarked when I asked him about these amendments, 'as things change and new situations arise, monks get together and make the necessary additions.' Interview with abbot of Rāmañña Nikāya branch monastery in Kandy, 28 July 2019 (Pos. 141).

[129] Interview with senior judge (*jyeṣṭhānuvijjaka*) near Colombo December 14, 2019.

of imperial regulation of monks in China.[130] In the contemporary period, one sees similar (if more state-centric) forms of regulation in Thailand's Sangha Acts or Myanmar's Laws Relating to the Sangha Organization.[131] I refer to these kinds of laws, following the work of Cuilan Liu, as 'hybrid laws' because they join together principles and categories from monastic legal sources with the instruments and structures of state law.[132]

Compared with other countries in Southeast Asia, Sri Lanka exercises relatively little direct authority over the administration of monastic fraternities. Unlike Thailand or Myanmar, there is no official state-recognised monastic bureaucracy whose orders are backed by the courts or police. Although the Sri Lankan government maintains membership registers for the island's monastic fraternities, the *katikāvatas* and courts of those fraternities operate without any formal legal recognition. This means that monastic groups must enforce their own laws independently, without any government support – an important fact whose consequences will be explored in detail in Part II of this book.

To say that the Sri Lankan state has not created an official monastic hierarchy is not to say that it does not regulate monks in other ways. For historical reasons, which will be explored in Chapter 3, Sri Lanka has developed two bodies of law that govern the use, control and administration of monastic property as well as succession to important monastic offices. The first is a body of civil court case law that has come to be called Buddhist Ecclesiastical Law. The second is a statute and associated regulations referred to as the Buddhist Temporalities Ordinance. These two bodies sit alongside a national constitution that further empowers the government to 'protect and foster' Buddhism itself.

Buddhist Ecclesiastical Law and Buddhist Temporalities

Buddhist Ecclesiastical Law is a large and diverse body of decisions covering a range of sangha-related topics: from categories of monastic property to the question of whether Buddhist monasteries are 'juristic persons' in the eyes of the state. The most significant issues in Buddhist

130 Tun, *The Royal Orders of Burma, AD 1598–1885*; Liu, *Buddhism in Court: Religion, Law and Jurisdiction in China*.
131 On these laws and related regulations in Southern Asia, see: Schonthal and Ginsburg, 'Breaking the Saffron Wave?.'
132 Liu, 'Hybrid Courts and Hybrid Laws.'

Ecclesiastical Law relate to a particular monastic office, the office of 'chief incumbent of the monastery' (*vihārādhipati*). Since the British colonial period, monastic and state-legal systems have recognised this office as having trustee-like control over the assets and property associated with a monastery. These assets are significant. Buddhist monasteries often possess large amounts of agricultural lands and leased properties, giving considerable power and influence to the chief incumbent monk. When a chief incumbent dies, therefore, there may be competition for the role. This scenario (and related issues) has formed the core of Buddhist Ecclesiastical Law over the past two hundred years, producing a massive body of case law with important precedents numbering into the hundreds.[133]

Starting in 1889, Buddhist Ecclesiastical Law came to be augmented by a particular ordinance (and later parliamentary act) concerned specifically with the rules that chief incumbent monks must follow when administering a given monastery or other Buddhist site (*vihārasthāna*). The law, called the Buddhist Temporalities Ordinance, applies to every 'temple' on the island, defined as including 'any place of Buddhist worship', including monasteries and pilgrimage sites.[134] The law permits the chief incumbent to serve as the 'trustee' of Buddhist sites and, in that capacity, to manage its properties, collect income (e.g. from donations, leases or ritual services), sue and be sued in its name. The Ordinance also establishes a set of rules concerning how temple income may be used. (Permissible expenditures include undertaking repairs, maintaining resident monks, paying for rituals, educating monks and laity, or engaging in charity.)

Although the Ordinance gives significant power to the chief incumbent, it gives ultimate authority to the government which, through the

[133] In the estimation of one lawyer with whom I spoke in 2014, and who specialises in such matters, approximately forty cases relating to Buddhist Ecclesiastical Law will be reviewed in the courts in any given year. As one indication of the scope and complexity of this body of law, one of the most important recent textbooks on the topic runs more than 800 pages. Weerasooria, *Buddhist Ecclesiastical Law*.

[134] The statutory definition encompasses all monasteries (*vihāra*), pagodas (*dāgäba*), deity shrines (*dēvāla*), Hindu temples (*kōvil*), monastic hermitages (*āvāsa*) or 'any place of Buddhist worship'. Including the temple housing the island's most sacred relic (the Temple of the Tooth), the important pilgrimage site associated with the Buddha's footprint (Śrīpada or Adam's Peak) and the eight sacred sites located in the vicinity of Sri Lanka's ancient capital of Anuradhapura.

Office of the Commissioner of Buddhist Affairs,[135] has powers of 'general supervision', including the right to audit the income, expenses and use of temple assets and to make various regulations relating to these topics.[136] (According to those familiar with this office, Commissioners tend to exercise these powers lightly, rarely undertaking intensive audits of temples.[137]) The Commissioner of Buddhist Affairs is also charged with maintaining a 'Register of Bhikkhus' for the entire country, using 'ordination registration forms' which fraternities are required to fill out and submit whenever they ordain new novices or bhikkhus.[138] A final section of the law makes it an offence for any person whose name is not on the register to 'hold himself out to be' a monk.[139]

The 'Buddhism Chapter' of Sri Lanka's Constitution

Since 1972, Sri Lankan lawmakers have extended the influence of government officials over monastic life through special protections for Buddhism in the island's constitution. These protections appear in Chapter 2 (Article 9):

> The Republic of Sri Lanka shall give to Buddhism the foremost place and accordingly it shall be the duty of the State to protect and foster the Buddha Sasana, while assuring to all religions the rights granted by Articles 10 and 14(l)(e) [namely, 'freedom of thought, conscience and religion' and freedom 'to manifest one's religion or belief in worship, observance, practice and teaching'].

135 Buddhist Temporalities Ordinance (Act) (Sri Lanka), §5. This office was created in 1981. Prior to that the supervisory powers were given to the office of the Public Trustee, who had similar administrative authority over other religious and charitable trusts.

136 Buddhist Temporalities Ordinance (Act) (Sri Lanka), §43.

137 Interview with Assistant Secretary to the Ministry of Buddhist Affairs, Colombo, 2 July 2016.

138 §41. These forms contain, in addition to general biographical information about the person who is ordaining, key details that may be important in adjudicating disputes over succession. These include information about the date and time of the event, as well as the names of the robing tutor (*ācārya bhikṣuva*) presiding over the events. The ordinance describes the creation, maintenance and protection of the registers in enormous detail. This indicates how important it is, legally and organisationally, for the state and the fraternities to have an authoritative and clear chart of monastic lineages.

139 §42.

Since its inception, the 'Buddhism Chapter' has been invoked by courts and parliaments to regulate the behaviours of monks and challenge the validity of legislation that might adversely affect monastic life. Under this constitutional provision, petitioners have contested a monk's right to become a lawyer and to obtain a driving licence. They have called for and contested draft bills that would create a national sangha court and grant statutory recognition to *katikāvatas*. All of this will be explored in Part III of this book.

The Sri Lankan state's importance in matters of monastic law can be seen in the fact that many of the contemporary manuals and handbooks described above make a point of explaining state laws to readers. The *Illumination of Legal Issues*, for example, includes multiple pages of case lists and explanations designed to inform monastic jurists of terms and topics that might be salient if a monastic dispute enters the civil courts. This includes terms such as monastic status (*bhikṣu bhāvaya*) and topics such as monastery incumbency.[140] Although the judicial trainings that I observed focussed primarily on *vinaya* literature and *katikāvata*, speakers also referred to important cases appearing in the civil courts as part of Buddhist Ecclesiastical Law. As one jurist put it at a judicial training that I attended: 'In our [legal] situation we [monastic jurists] have a serious responsibility to understand not only [our] constitution (*katikāvata*) and the Vinaya but also, in most cases, the Buddhist Temporalities Act as well. These are the three kinds of legal understanding one needs [i.e., Vinaya, *katikāvata* and the Buddhist Temporalities Act] . . . all three of these things must be studied.'[141]

Non-Textual Vinaya

A considerable body of written laws – from *vinaya* literature, to *katikāvatas* to hybrid laws – govern Buddhist monastic life in Sri Lanka. By focusing on written law, however, I do not mean to suggest that the norms shaping monastic behaviour come from texts alone. When it comes to monastic discipline, two other non-textual sources must also be mentioned. The first are the daily practices of monastery life, through which monastics, particularly novices, learn to embody disciplined ways of being. The second are the expectations and social pressures coming from lay Buddhists on whom monastics rely for support.

[140] Dhammasiri, *Saṅghādhikaraṇa Jotikā [Elucidations of the Monastic Court]*, 219 and ff.

[141] Address given by senior jurist at a training workshop for monastic judges, in Colombo, 14 December 2018.

Vinaya through Doing

The important role of physical behaviours in shaping monastic discipline has been examined closely by Jeffrey Samuels in an ethnography of Rāmañña Nikāya monastics in Sri Lanka. Samuels argues that novice monks learn about monastic law not by reading the rules contained in the *Heraṇasikha* or the *Preaching and Dharma Book for Novices* but by actually behaving 'like a monk' – which is to say by walking, eating, chanting and cleaning in ways that emulate the style and comportment of more senior monks.[142] According to this 'action-oriented pedagogy', *vinaya* norms gain salience in the lives of monastics not only through texts but through behaviours impressed onto the body by habits of moving, speaking and conducting oneself in space.

My own research has confirmed Samuels' findings. Many of the monks I interviewed commented on the importance of habituated behaviours for creating the kinds of attitudes (*ākalpa*) and decorum (*hikmīma*) that are the goal of the Buddha's disciplinary precepts. Important in this regard is the practice of learning to embody the seventy-five 'training rules' (*sekhiyā*) contained in the last part of the Explanations section of the Vinaya Piṭaka. In one focus group, with three monks in their mid-twenties, the following reflections were offered:

Speaker 1: The first [Vinaya lesson] is the *sekhiya* rules instructing us how one is supposed to eat, walk and speak like a monk – how one is supposed to *be*. Thus, to my mind, the *sekhiyas* are the best of the Vinaya. [For example, in Pali] '*Na capucapukārakaṃ bhuñjissāmīti*' ['I will not eat making noise'] which means don't make noise while eating. That's a good lesson to learn. . .

Speaker 2: There's no more important idea than this one: taking supreme attention with eating. Our head monk also used to say, 'don't lick your hands while eating', 'don't lick your bowl', 'don't take too much alms food', 'don't make any noise while eating' – those are actually the things that come to mind. Even now, when I get alms, I think 'don't take too much!' This kind of approach is

142 Samuels, 'Toward an Action-Oriented Pedagogy: Buddhist Texts and Monastic Education in Contemporary Sri Lanka'; Samuels, *Attracting the Heart*. See also the work of Salgado for similar observations in the contexts of female renunciants in Sri Lanka. Salgado, *Buddhist Nuns and Gendered Practice: In Search of the Female Renunciant*; Salgado, 'On the Question of 'Discipline' (Vinaya) and Nuns in Theravāda Buddhism.'

> still something I try to uphold. I very much appreciate [those rules]: that's the thing I remember most about the Vinaya.[143]

Here, as in other conversations, interviewees insisted that creating new behaviours ultimately transformed the way they thought about monastic life and the Vinaya Piṭaka itself. From imagining the Vinaya as a set of regulations that were imposed on monks, they came to see the principles of monastic discipline as a kind of recipe for reforming and remaking themselves from the inside out. Embodying these behaviours, they explained, ensured not only that one understood the Vinaya principles but that they transformed themselves into 'a person who is truly tamed'.[144]

Lay Expectations

The second non-textual source of *vinaya* norms comes from interactions with laity, who are essential contributors to monastic life. Although some monastics have alternative sources of income – for example, rental incomes from monastic estates – most monastic communities rely, to a greater or lesser extent, on the beneficence of lay donors. This reliance on lay donors figures centrally in the Buddha's teachings about monastic life. The word for fully ordained monastics is bhikkhu, meaning beggar. The word for a devout layperson is *upāsaka*, meaning 'one who attends to [the sangha]'. At the core of the monastic vocation in the Vinaya and other texts, therefore, stands the image of an alms-person who relies on donors for their material well-being.

Monks' dependence on lay support, both actual and ideal, shapes monastic behaviour. The risk of losing lay patronage is repeatedly warned against in the Vinaya Piṭaka, which admonishes monks not to alienate or aggravate the laity. Throughout the Vinaya – including after the promulgation of each new rule in the Explanations section – the Buddha explains to his followers that legal rules are designed to 'bring faith (*pasāda*) to those who do not believe [in the dharma] and to increase the faith of those who already have it'. This call to inspire lay Buddhists appears frequently in *vinaya* literature. It was also repeated to me regularly by monastic jurists, who understand the phrase to mean that monks must maintain a disciplined image to would-be

143 Focus group interview with monks from Rāmañña, Malvatu and Asgiri fraternities, Kandy, July 26, 2016.

144 *Manuśyayāṭa honda hikmīmak äti karanavā.*

supporters.[145] Of the nearly 1,700 monks that I surveyed, 66 per cent agreed that 'a fundamental goal' of *vinaya* rules and traditions was to 'impress and inspire the laity' in the manner indicated above.[146]

In some accounts of monastic life, the expectations of laity even supersede the Vinaya Piṭaka in significance. In his ethnography of monastic communities in northern Thailand, Michael Chladek found that despite studying and knowing the Vinaya Piṭaka well, Thai monks did not see the Vinaya as 'the main instrument for deciding how to enact their monastic role in their everyday lives'.[147] Instead, what seemed to shape their behaviour, in Chladek's estimation, were the explicit or imagined expectations of laity concerning how pious monks

[145] For example, one jurist explained the matter on a television talk show as follows: 'the Buddha preached that, when one becomes a monk, [they should observe the maxim] '*appasannānam vā pasādāya, pasannānam vā bhiyyobhāvāya*' which means that one must behave in such a way that further increases the confidence of Buddhist people. Not only that, but if monks are behaving in a way that actually damages the minds of Buddhists or diminishes their faith or devotion (*śraddhāvak bhaktiyak*), the sangha councils have to take steps to deal with that.' Ven. Mahagalkadavalē on 'Television Broadcast: Theravādī Bauddha Saṅghādhikaraṇaya [The Monastic Court in Theravāda Buddhism].'

[146] Question 5.2. Although it is not a feature of monastic law, according to my definition, it is worthwhile observing that, from an early period, Pali sources spoke about an analogous 'discipline of the laity' (*gihi vinaya*). This idea gained prominence in Sri Lanka in the form of collections of disciplinary rules for laity. A medieval Pali text, called the *Ornament of Lay Followers* (*Upāsakajanālaṅkāra*), was likely produced in the thirteenth century, based on a tenth-century source (*Patipaṭṭisangaha, Compendium of Practice*). This was popularised and translated into Sinhala by an elite Siyam Nikāya monk, Moratoṭa Dhammakkhandha, in the late eighteenth century. At least since that time, rulebooks for virtuous laity have become a popular genre in Sri Lanka, with multiple books being published under the title *gihi vinaya*, including one by Anagarika Dharmapala in 1898. Although perhaps influenced by the Pali and Sinhala texts described above, most books on *gihi vinaya* take the form of commentaries on the *Sīgalovāda Sutta*, a story from the Sutta Piṭaka regarding the proper standards of behaviour for laity. Most Buddhist bookstores in Sri Lanka carry some version of this. On *gihi vinaya* see: Agostini, *The Ornament of Lay Followers*; Crosby, 'A Theravāda Code of Conduct for Good Buddhists: The 'Upāsakamanussavinaya"; Gombrich and Obeyesekere, *Buddhism Transformed: Religious Change in Sri Lanka*, Chapter 6; Ortega, 'Gihi, Sangha, Raja'; Seneviratne, *The Work of Kings: The New Buddhism in Sri Lanka*, Chapter 3; Young, 'Adornments of Virtue: The Production of Lay Buddhist Virtuosity in the Upāsakajanālaṅkāra.'

[147] Chladek, 'Imagined Laity and the Performance of Monasticism in Northern Thailand,' 185.

should behave. It was lay idealisations of monks, and not the Vinaya standards themselves, that were more influential. This idea – that lay actors help define the disciplinary norms of monks – has also been confirmed in the work of Borchert and Darlington, also in Thailand. Their work offers stories of powerful lay authorities, such as policemen and politicians, imposing their own interpretations of Vinaya rules on monks in ways that deviate from the root text. In one instance, policemen disrobed monks who were found drinking alcohol – in spite of the fact that consuming alcohol is a relatively minor offence in the Vinaya Piṭaka, requiring only confession. Although unorthodox, Borchert and Darlington explain that these popular interpretations of Vinaya (i.e. that drinking alcohol is a defeat-worthy offence) nevertheless find their way back to monastic communities themselves, leading to new interpretations of the Vinaya rules concerning alcohol.[148] Here, too, then, one finds a powerful merger of monastic legal texts and other normative orders: in addition to monastic laws entangling with forms of state legality, one also finds them merging with notions of proper monastic comportment circulating among the laity.

CONCLUSION

This chapter has offered a broad overview of principles, categories and legal sources that shape monastic life. The diversity and complexity of these sources are vast. (It can even be overwhelming for scholars of Buddhism.) Nevertheless, an awareness of this legal landscape helps one understand the many kinds of legal ideas and artefacts that inform legal pluralism in Sri Lanka and other places.

Despite the many changes and innovations in monastic law over the centuries, procedures and principles from the Vinaya Piṭaka continue to play an important role. This includes the Vinaya's primary instructions; its protocols for legal actions (P: *kamma, saṅghakamma,* S: *karma*, *vinaya karma*); its categories and procedures for analysing and resolving legal issues (P:/S: *adhikaraṇa*); and the range of sanctions ('defeat', penance, etc.) that the Vinaya applies to monastics who have committed offences. These Vinaya principles appear not only in the technical analyses of Pali commentarial texts but also in the more practically oriented vernacular texts used by monks to study, administer and

[148] Borchert and Darlington, 'Political Disrobing in Thailand.'

interpret monastic law in their everyday lives. They also appear in the context of narratives, instructions, summaries and lists, such as those that appear in the *Preaching and Dharma Book for Novices* or the modern handbooks of Ven. Rērukānē Candavimala. Terms and ideas from the Vinaya feature centrally in the post-nineteenth-century constitutions (*katikāvatas*) produced by the island's growing number of monastic sects, although often in the form of more simplified, direct injunctions. They also impress themselves on the bodies and minds of Buddhist monks as part of 'action-oriented pedagogies' and behavioural adjustments calculated to satisfy the disciplinary expectations of lay supporters.

In addition to introducing readers to these important legal principles and artefacts, this chapter has also encouraged readers to consider the dynamics of unity and multiplicity that crosscut monastic legal traditions – and which lend themselves to differing practices of legal pluralism. Depending on one's perspective, one can engage the sources and principles examined above as unified or distinct, collapsable or separable, hierarchical or autonomous. To look closely at these sources is to confront monastic law's simultaneous singularity and multiplicity and its coincident potentials for integration and subdivision.

How Sri Lanka's lawmakers, judges and monastic communities manage these potentials for unity and diversity – how they construe their multi-legal milieu and practice legal pluralism – differs across contexts and environments, as the following chapters of this book will show. While most monks do not treat hybrid laws as expressions of the Vinaya Piṭaka, a large number of secular lawmakers and civil court judges do (as will be seen in Chapters 3 and 7). While many monks treat commentaries, *Pātimokkhas* and *kammavācā* manuals as close to or coextensive with the Vinaya root text, other monks insist that they are separate bodies of law (as will be seen in Chapter 8). While most monastics acknowledge the symmetry between *katikāvatas* and state law, they are often reluctant to treat them as commensurable (as will be seen in Chapters 5 and 6). Diverging claims can also be found about *katikāvatas*' relationship to the Vinaya Piṭaka and the importance of 'updating' its rules to suit the needs of modern technology, education and administration (as will be seen in Chapters 4 and 7).[149]

[149] For example, Buddhist monks and laity regularly pointed out in the contexts of interviews that the modern administration of monastic fraternities, organised around the figure of the great leader (*mahānāyaka*) and his deputies, was novel. 'The Buddha never spoke about *mahānāyakas*' I was told with some frequency.

Although united in their influence on monastic law, the legal principles and artefacts examined in this chapter have, over the past two hundred years, been configured in multiple ways – yielding multiple expressions of legal pluralism. Over the next two chapters, Part I of this book, I introduce readers to the configurations that arose during the nineteenth century, when British officials and monastic jurists came into contact, each side attempting to make sense and bring order to the legal tradition of the other.

Appendix

CHAPTER TITLES AND LIST OF LEGAL ACTIONS CONTAINED IN VEN. RĒRUKĀNĒ CANDAVIMALA'S BOOK, *VINAYA KARMA POTA (BOOK OF VINAYA ACTS)*[150]

1. Novice Ordination (*pabbajjā*)
2. Full Ordination (*upasampadā*)
3. Confessing Offences (*āpatti desana*)
4. Bimonthly confessions rites (*uposatha*)
5. Protocols for the annual rainy-season retreat (*vassa*)
6. Procedure of inviting admonishment at the end of Vassa (*pavāraṇā*)
7. Robe offering procedure, also at the end of Vassa (*kaṭhina*)
8. Penance (*mānatta*)
9. Probation for a monk who has committed multiple probation-worthy offences and concealed them for multiple days (*agghasamodhāna parivāsa*)
10. Probation given for a monk who does not remember the number of offences he committed or the number of days he has concealed those offences (*suddhanta parivāsa*)
11. Probation (*parivāsa*) given to monastics who come from another sect or tradition, generally for four months
12. Action for confessing unauthorised property in one's monastic cell (*kuṭivatthu desana kamma*)
13. Action for admonishing a monk (*samanubhāsana kamma*)
14. Action for expelling a monk (*pabbājanīya kamma*)

[150] Note there are no numbers in the original text. I have also added Pali equivalents in parentheses.

15. Action taken against one who sows discord in the sangha (*anuvādakāropana kamma*)
16. Action taken against one who sows strife in the sangha (*vihesakāropana kamma*)
17. Restoring a monk to the community after a period of penance and/or probation (*osāraṇa*)
18. Ex-communication of a monk (*brahma daṇda*)
19. Action taken against a monk who sows delusion within the community (*mohāropana kamma*)
20. Censure action through which a monk is temporarily deprived of privileges (*tajjanīya kamma*)
21. Action that places a monk under a period of supervision by a senior monk (*nissaya kamma*)
22. Reconciliation with a lay donor after a monk has offended them (*paṭisāraṇīya kamma*)
23. Turning over the bowls [procedure for excommunicating the laity] (*pattanikkujjana kamma*)
24. Suspension action (*ukkhepaṇīya kamma*) for monks who do not acknowledge their offences
25. Suspension action (*ukkhepaṇīya kamma*) for monks who do not want to repair their offences
26. Suspension action (*ukkhepaṇīya kamma*) for monks who do not want to revise their evil views.
27. Agreements (*sammuti*)
28. Vinaya actions relating to *sīmā*s
29. Action words (*kammavācā*) relating to the act of nullifying and agreeing upon *sīmās*

CHAPTER THREE

JURISDICTIONALISING BUDDHISM IN COLONIAL CEYLON

When pressed, definitions of law seep out from accounts of legal pluralism like water from a sponge. To speak of legal pluralism is, after all, to assume something about the nature of law and its diverse expressions. It is to classify certain human artefacts as examples of law (e.g., those concerned with 'institutionalised norm enforcement'[1]), while excluding others (e.g., doctrines of rebirth or principles of cosmic order). Like so many other social constructs, what counts as law is all too often in the eye of the beholder.[2]

To study legal pluralism historically is to confront this fact over and over again, and perhaps nowhere more so than in the history of the British Empire. In South and Southeast Asia, British officials 'beheld' many different kinds of law, drawing on familiar prototypes to establish the laws that would support indirect rule.[3] Under the pretence of merely recognising local laws, British jurists confected new ones, grouping together disparate traditions and authorities into a set of broad legal unities – Kandyan Law, Mohammedan Law, the Laws of the Gentoo – conceived roughly in the image of English law. Where indigenous norms did not fit common-law sensibilities, colonial jurists

1 Tamanaha, 'A Reconstruction of Transnational Legal Pluralism and Law's Foundations,' 11.
2 Tamanaha, 'A Non-Essentialist Version of Legal Pluralism.'
3 This is particularly true after the late eighteenth century. See, for example: Burset, *An Empire of Laws*.

reshaped them to conform to 'English ideas and standards'.[4] They treated local, variegated practices as though they were stable systems the rules of which could be codified in writing and distilled through judicial reasoning.

The colonial recognition of law, however, entailed a fundamental misrecognition of how things worked on the ground. In most cases, no one text or body of jurists claimed ultimate authority over what came to be known as Mohammedan or Kandyan law. In consolidating local laws, British jurists in fact inserted their own authority, acting as though they were indigenous jurists. Prioritising some sources and authorities over others, they entrenched new versions of orthodoxy as if they were locally produced.[5]

*

This chapter investigates these dynamics – these practices of legal pluralism – as used by British colonists during the nineteenth century to govern an island that they referred to as Ceylon and that most Sinhala speakers referred to as Laṅkā. The British colonisation of Ceylon/Laṅkā was neither the first nor the longest period of European occupation on the island. The Portuguese and Dutch both controlled parts of the island's littoral 'lowlands' from 1505 to 1658 and 1658 to 1796, respectively. Yet the period of British control, which ran from 1796 until 1948, was decisive for the transformations of law and Buddhism that took place. This was especially true for the decades following 1815, when the British annexed the last independent kingdom of Kandy and, for the first time, projected their power across the entire island.

This chapter is one of two that consider this period of British control, each focussing on a different set of actors and legal sources. Chapter 4 draws on *monastic* legal archives preserved in Pali and Sinhala languages to examine the practices of legal pluralism undertaken by Buddhist monks. This chapter considers British *colonial* practices of legal pluralism, relying mainly on an English-language legal archive of colonial correspondence, court decisions, draft laws, government

4 Warren Hastings as quoted in Cohen, 'Law and the Colonial State in India,' 136.
5 Kugle, 'Framed, Blamed and Renamed: The Recasting of Islamic Jurisprudence in Colonial South Asia'; Anderson, 'Islamic Law and the Colonial Encounter in British India'; Demian, 'Dislocating Custom,' 92.

transcripts, and newspaper reports. Colonial practices resulted in the creation of new common law categories, such as 'ecclesiastical succession', 'Buddhist temporalities' and 'temple lands', while also generating new bodies of law: in particular, a body of civil-court case law governing monks called Buddhist Ecclesiastical Law and an influential ordinance regulating the use and administration of 'Buddhist properties', called the Buddhist Temporalities Ordinance.

KING OF ENGLAND AS PROTECTOR OF BUDDHISM

To some degree, the practices of legal pluralism in colonial Ceylon mirror those of other colonies. In colonial India, Malaya, Egypt and Burma, the British also created new laws relating to religious communities and properties. In these cases, as in Ceylon, colonial attempts to concretise religious law overlapped with a variety of imperial goals: the signing of treaties, the extraction of revenue, the recruitment of local elites, and, eventually, the imperial requirement that colonial states not 'interfere' with local religions.[6]

Ceylon differs from most of these cases, however, when it comes to the instruments used to communicate British sovereignty. In contrast to the treaties signed at Allahabad in 1765 or Pangkor in 1874, the bilingual Kandyan Convention (Figure 3.1) that proclaimed British sovereignty over the entire island of Ceylon in 1815 did not devolve authority over religious matters to local elites. Rather, Article 5 of the English version of that convention announced that the King of England would ensure that:

[6] Among others, see: Adcock, *The Limits of Tolerance Indian Secularism and the Politics of Religious Freedom*; Appadurai, *Worship and Conflict under Colonial Rule*; Acevedo, 'Divine Sovereignty, Indian Property Law, and the Dispute over the Padmanabhaswamy Temple'; Chatterjee, *The Making of Indian Secularism*; Crouch, 'Promiscuity, Polygyny, and the Power of Revenge: The Past and Future of Burmese Buddhist Law in Myanmar'; Hussin, *The Politics of Islamic Law: Local Elites, Colonial Authority, and the Making of the Muslim State*; Huxley, 'Positivists and Buddhists: The Rise and Fall of Anglo-Burmese Ecclesiastical Law'; Ikeya, *Refiguring Women, Colonialism, and Modernity in Burma*; Kamal, 'A Theory of Religious Sovereignty Private Law Disputes and State-Religion Relations in Bangladesh and Pakistan'; Kozlowski, *Muslim Endowments and Society in British India*; Lammerts, *Buddhist Law in Burma*; Lhost, *Everyday Islamic Law and the Making of Modern South Asia*; Moustafa, *Constituting Religion*; Presler, *Religion under Bureaucracy*; Stephens, *Governing Islam*; Redding, *A Secular Need*; Whitaker, *Amiable Incoherence*.

> The Religion of Boodhoo professed by the chiefs and inhabitants of these provinces is declared inviolable, and its Rites, Ministers and Places of worship are to be maintained and protected.

The Sinhala version of the text, signed by assembled 'Kandyan Chiefs', was even more explicit. It named as objects of Crown protection not only the Buddha *sāsana* but also the important traditions of deity worship that had become central to the Kandyan tradition:

> The Buddha *sāsana* and the religion of the gods (*devāgama*), which are worshipped by nobles and inhabitants living in these districts (*raṭaval*) may never be broken and the duties (*kaṭayutu*) to them as well as to the sangha, the [Buddhist] temples and places of worship (*vihārasthāna*) and the deity shrines (*dēvāla*) must also be maintained and protected.

Rather than colonising Ceylon as a neutral power, the treaty signed in Kandy presented King George III as the successor to the last king of Kandy and the guarantor of its ancient traditions, holy places, clerics and practices – particularly those associated with Buddhism.

In the years following 1815, colonial officers effectively acted as though they *were* Kandyan kings. The British Resident in Kandy stood in for the deposed monarch in public parades and rituals. He issued official letters of appointment to monastic hierarchs. He made public offerings of food and financial support to Kandyan monasteries and commanded Crown soldiers to guard the island's holiest Buddhist treasure, the tooth relic of the Buddha.[7] Even after they discontinued these symbolic acts of patronage, British officials continued to write about the Kandyan Convention as binding on colonial policies, a source of ongoing obligations to Buddhism.

The Jurisdictions of Buddhism

The special promises made during the annexation of Kandy led to special methods of recognising Buddhism in law. Unlike in India, where British jurists produced regimes of Muslim or Hindu personal law to govern disputes concerning marriage, inheritance, divorce and property among presumptively distinct populations, in Ceylon they promised to secure the integrity of an entire 'Religion' along with its 'Rites, Ministers and Places of worship'. Rather than one among many

[7] Sivasundaram, *Islanded: Britain, Sri Lanka, and the Bounds of an Indian Ocean Colony*; Obeyesekere, *The Doomed King*.

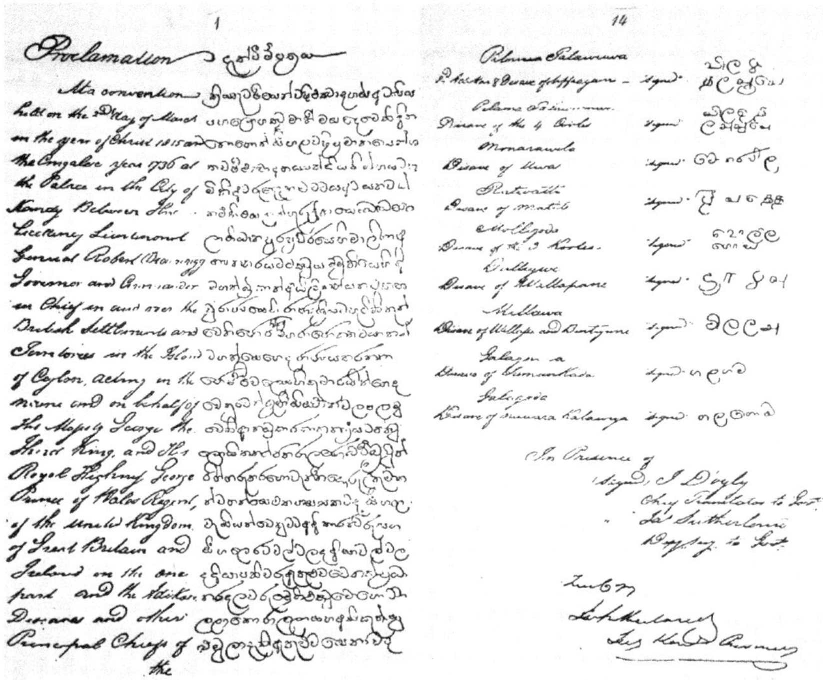
1

Proclamation

At a convention held on the 2nd day of March in the year of Christ 1815 and the Cingalese year 1736 at the Palace in the City of Kandy Between His Excellency Lieutenant General Robert Brownrigg Governor and Commander in Chief in and over the British Settlements and Territories in the Island of Ceylon, acting in the name and on behalf of His Majesty George the Third King, and His Royal Highness George Prince of Wales Regent of the United Kingdom of Great Britain and Ireland on the one part and the Adikars Dissaves and other Principal Chiefs of the

14

In Presence of
(Signed) J. D'Oyly
Chief Translator to Govt.

Figure 3.1 The first and last pages of the Kandyan Convention, with English and Sinhala versions.
Image courtesy of the Government Archives of Sri Lanka, Photographed by MediaJet, Public domain, via Wikimedia Commons.

religions, colonial officials treated Buddhism as a uniquely important object of legal protection.

The idea of jurisdiction – of laws having discrete domains of authority – was central to the colonial government's practices of legal pluralism with respect to Buddhism.[8] Initially, the dominant frame of jurisdiction was territorial: the protections promised to Buddhism were construed as a subset of a larger set of concessions made to preserve Kandy's 'laws, institutions, and customs'.[9] This changed over the course of the nineteenth century, as colonists tried to centralise and unify the legal system.

[8] This is also true in other colonies. See, for example: Benton and Ross, *Legal Pluralism and Empires, 1500–1850*; Benton, 'Colonial Law and Cultural Difference.'

[9] §4 Kandyan Convention of 1815.

From a territorial body of laws, Kandyan law came to be conceived as a species of personal law applying to descendants of Kandyan residents. At the same time, laws pertaining to Buddhism's 'Rites, Ministers and Places of worship' were carved off from the broader body of Kandyan customs and subjected to a more precise set of limits. Buddhist law's 'civil' elements were distinguished from its 'spiritual' elements – the first being justiciable in colonial courts, the second being 'legally indifferent'.[10] Jurists also worked to prise apart those features of Buddhism that the governors (as successors to the Kandyan king) were required to protect, from those that they (as representatives of a Christian monarch and purportedly non-religious parliament) ought not to touch for fear of unwittingly endorsing or interfering with it.

Over time and in response to these imperatives, colonial jurists came to map Buddhism onto particular spaces, issues and communities, such that 'the Religion of the Boodhoo' acquired at least three different types of jurisdictions. It took on a *territorial jurisdiction*, defined in narrower or broader ways: as the boundaries of monasteries or monastic land, as the borders of the Kandyan kingdom, or even the watery perimeter of the entire island. It gained a *subject-matter jurisdiction*, consisting of Buddhist 'civil' matters, on the one hand, and Buddhist 'spiritual' affairs on the other. Finally, it acquired a *personal jurisdiction*: a discrete community – of monks, lay leaders and/or unmarked 'Buddhists' – who were treated as Buddhism's subjects and/or authorities.

THE 'TERRITORIAL JURISDICTION' OF BUDDHISM

To say that colonists gave Buddhism a territorial jurisdiction is not to say that analogous ideas were absent from Buddhist history. The idea that there is a territory appropriate to the Buddha's dispensation (the *sāsana*) or his monastic community can be found well before the nineteenth century. One finds claims about the geographical spread of the *sāsana*, including its expansion during the reign of particular rulers, in epigraphy dating back before the Common Era. The notion that monastic groups ought to reside in their own space appears, among other places, in the Vinaya Piṭaka and its rules about ritual boundaries, or *sīmā*s (discussed in Chapter 2). While the binaries of 'public' and

[10] 'Legally indifferent' comes from the work of Lemons, who examines similar bifurcations in colonial India. Lemons, *Divorcing Traditions*.

'private' or 'religious' and 'secular' land do not map neatly onto Buddhist history, the idea that Buddhist monasteries *had* boundaries and *had* land was clearly well established.[11]

Well before the British arrived, Laṅkan kings took an interest in the territories associated with Buddhist monasteries (*vihāras*). These kings conducted their own surveys and accounting to determine *vihāra* boundaries and assets.[12] Although Laṅkan monarchs exempted monastery lands from most forms of taxation, they also imposed special regulations on them. Those regulations specified that revenues and rents gained from tax-free lands should support activities such as feeding resident monks, conducting rituals and maintaining buildings.

The importance of these *vihāra* estates grew over time in Laṅkā, as they did in other parts of Southern Asia. This is particularly true under the reign of Kandan kings (1590–1815), who expanded the scope of *vihāra* donations considerably. In addition to endowing *vihāras*, Kandyan monarchs also donated land to the kingdom's major deity shrines – called *dēvālas* – which played an important role in expressing and securing royal rule.[13] Because *vihāra* and *dēvāla* grants claimed to be valid 'for as long as the sun and moon endure', the properties donated to these institutions accrued over time, such that, by the

[11] These endowed areas were generally defined by grant documents issued by kings and prosperous lay patrons and, in some cases, even monks. Gunawardana, *Robe and Plough*, 60 and passim; Milligan, 'Monastic Buddhist Asset Capitalization in Ancient Sri Lanka'; Schopen, 'Monastic Law Meets the Real World'; Schopen, *Buddhist Monks and Business Matters: Still More Papers on Monastic Buddhism in India*; Schopen, 'On the Legal and Economic Activities of Buddhist Nuns.'

[12] Abeyawardhana, *Boundary Divisions*, 6–7; Friedrich, 'Merchants, Ministers, and Monks'; Gunawardana, *Robe and Plough*, 181–200; Meyer, 'Lekam miti.'

[13] The history and role of *dēvālas* is complex and beyond the scope of this chapter. The network of *dēvālas* during the Kandyan period consisted of four major temples located near the capital and a network of dozens of other shrines located in each of the major divisions of the kingdom. The larger of these had lay trustees (*basnāyaka nilame*) attached to them. Those officials oversaw the regular rites and offerings for those shrines – presided over by a ritual specialist called a *kapurāla* – while also supervising the use and revenue associated with estate lands. The position of trustee was lucrative and was usually given to a noble lord chosen by the king, in exchange for an annual payment of tribute (*däkum*) by him. On *dēvālas* see, Dewaraja, *A Study of the Political, Administrative, and Social Structure of the Kandyan Kingdom of Ceylon, 1707–1760*; Holt, *The Buddhist Visnu*; McKinley, 'Mountain at a Center of the World'; Meegama, 'From Kôvils to Devâles.'

1840s, one colonial officer estimated that nearly one-third of all paddy land in the Kandyan kingdom fell under estates of this type.[14]

Onto these Buddhist and Kandyan notions of territory, British officials layered further cartographic techniques and imperatives. As the British expanded their footprint of influence on the island – from the coastal areas ceded to them by the Dutch in 1796, to the newly conquered Kandyan interior – they expanded their maps, overlaying the marks indicating roads and rivers with fresh lines formalising new legal-administrative regions.[15] After the Kandyan Convention was signed in 1815, revised surveys and maps followed almost immediately. When a 'new and correct' map of the island appeared in 1822, the recently annexed Kandyan Kingdom appeared neatly bounded as the 'Kandyan Provinces'.[16] More cartographic adjustments followed in the ensuing decades, as the island's diverse landscapes were made to align with the circuits of colonial courts.

In crafting their maps and laws, British officials treated the protection of *vihāra* and *dēvāla* properties – which they referred to collectively as 'temple lands' – as essential for ensuring the allegiance of its new Kandyan subjects. Less than three years after signing the Kandyan Convention, one British official recollected that, during the treaty negotiations, the issue of temple lands had been 'one most anxiously pressed by the Kandyan Chiefs'. In the same correspondence, the official urged the government to quickly 'ascertain the extent of landed property and annual revenue' of *vihāras* and *dēvālas*, so that the government might cordon off those lands and funds from other use.[17]

The Crown's failure to adequately protect temple lands was even identified as the major cause for a rebellion of Kandyan chiefs that nearly dislodged colonial control in that same year. In the proclamation that reasserted British sovereignty after the rebellion, the

[14] 'One third of all the paddy lands in the Kandyan provinces are ostensibly in the possession of temples, together with large tracts of adjoining forests, numerous villages, and a large population who do them suit and service for their lands.' C. Pridham, as quoted in Evers, 'Buddhism and British Colonial Policy,' 324. Evers estimates that even in the 1960s, 10 per cent of all paddy land was held by temples. 'Monastic Landlordism' in Ceylon, 688.

[15] Sivasundaram, *Islanded: Britain, Sri Lanka, and the Bounds of an Indian Ocean Colony*, 218–19.

[16] Barrow, 'Surveying in Ceylon during the Nineteenth Century,' 84.

[17] 'Minute by His Excellency the Governor, 21 January, 1818' in Government of Ceylon, *Report of the Commissioners*, 42.

governor affirmed the importance of those lands. He declared that 'all lands which now are Property of Temples . . . [would be free from] all Taxation whatever'. This, he announced, demonstrated 'the adherence of [his] Government to its stipulation [in the Kandyan Convention] in favour of the Religion of the People'.[18] In addition, he confirmed clerical control of those lands, by guaranteeing that tenants living on donated estates would be made to perform their traditional duties of 'royal service' to the relevant *vihāra* or *dēvāla* – requiring them to provide food, resources and ritual support for their local monasteries and deity shrines.

Mapping 'Temple Lands'

Colonial protections for *vihāra* and *dēvāla* lands were embedded within a larger legal sleight-of-hand. The British practised legal pluralism in a way that promised to replace the deposed Kandyan king while continuing to administer his laws 'in accordance with the Ancient and established usages of the Country'.[19] Yet, marking off 'temple lands' for special protection was not simply an act of maintaining ancient laws; it was an economic gambit. In ruling *out vihāra* and *dēvāla* lands from colonial taxes, British officials were also ruling *in* other lands as legitimate areas for extraction and development. Specifying the territories of 'religious establishments'[20] also meant defining the non-religious territories that could be used for commerce and revenue. Thus, when, in 1819, the governor formally proclaimed the need to determine the precise boundaries of temple lands, he declared that the project would not only guarantee the continuity of 'Ancient and established usages' but 'the security of His Majesty's Revenue'.[21]

18 Proclamation of 21 November 1818 §16 and §21. Government of Ceylon, *Record of Legislative Acts of the Ceylon Government from 1798 to 1833*, 1:223–28. For a list of royal services (*rājakāriyas*), see Evers, *Monks, Priests and Peasants: A Study of Buddhism and Social Structure in Central Ceylon*, Chapter Four.

19 Proclamation §7. See also Hayley, *Laws and Customs of the Sinhalese; Or, Kandyan Law*, 534.

20 'Minute by His Excellency the Governor, 21 January, 1818' reproduced in Government of Ceylon, *Report of the Commissioners*, 42.

21 Proclamation of the 19 September 1819 in Government of Ceylon, *Legislative Acts 1796–1833*, 268. Another legislation from the period is also instructive: Ordinance No. 12 of 1840 not only established one-sided legal procedures for disputes over the boundaries of Crown land, it also declared that 'all forest, waste, unoccupied or uncultivated lands shall be presumed to be the property of the Crown until the contrary is proved'.

Dreams of a complete map outlining the divisions between religious establishments and taxable land motivated an astounding amount of colonial activity in the middle decades of the nineteenth century. From 1819 to 1870, colonial officials undertook a series of commissions designed to compile a 'List of all Lands, of all descriptions' belonging to *vihāras* and *dēvālas*. Two separate projects were undertaken (and eventually abandoned) in 1819 and 1831, before a third attempt would be inaugurated as part of the 1857 'Temple Lands Ordinance'.

Over the following two decades, the newly formed Temple Lands Commission crisscrossed the Kandyan region, seeking to verify the boundaries of *vihāra* and *dēvāla* estates using 'documentary evidence which could not be impeached'.[22] For more than a decade, two full-time commissioners, along with a small army of labourers and assistants, undertook the mammoth task of mapping temple lands throughout the rugged Kandyan highlands. In all, hundreds of thousands of acres of land were investigated, documented and divided, with 376,000 acres being officially certified as 'temple lands'.[23]

In determining the boundaries of *vihāra* and *dēvāla* lands, the Temple Lands Commission not only surveyed the territory of Kandyan 'religious establishments', they also aimed to distinguish between those parcels of land that had been donated in good faith and those that had been donated 'as a mere pretext for escaping tax'.[24] Multiple deceptions were alleged. Commissioners accused landowners of establishing sham temples to use as their own personal tax havens, allowing them to pass off 'small, scattered portions of land' as private dedications to village *vihāras*.[25] Defining the scope of temple lands, it seems, required that officials also investigate the hearts of Kandyan donors.

[22] Government of Ceylon, *Report of the Temple Land Commissioners on the Progress and Results of the Commission from Its Constitution, in February 1857, to the End of 1858*, 8, 14. The list of acceptable evidence included proof of written dedication by a king, noble or another 'private party with the written consent of the King or Dissawe' in the form of sannas or 'authenticated Tudepat' (palm leaf land grant), or other 'satisfactory evidence of possession free of tax or service, in the Kandian time, including in all cases distinct proof of the boundaries of the lands claimed'. Ibid., 14.

[23] Government of Ceylon, *Report of the Commissioners*, iii.

[24] Government of Ceylon, *Report of the Temple Land Commissioners on the Progress and Results of the Commission from Its Constitution, in February 1857, to the End of 1858*, 11.

[25] Government of Ceylon, 13.

In its first eighteen months of operation, commissioners rejected nearly 45 per cent of the claimed paddy lands and nearly 85 per cent of forest areas.[26] Reports issued in the following years record similar rates of rejecting claims, along with a growing candour that – in the absence of solid documentary evidence – decisions about the boundaries of temple lands would rely considerably on the (often suspicious) instincts of government assessors.[27] Accredited temple lands were recognised through the issuing of government certificates: *vihāra* lands would be placed under the control of the chief incumbent monk (*vihārādhipati*) of the associated temple, while *dēvāla* lands were vested with a lay official called the *basnāyake nilame*. Rejected lands were either reverted (as taxable acres) to the purportedly deceptive landowners or to the government itself.

Commissioners' reports are studded with accounts of alleged malfeasance. Consider, for example, the description of an entire 'class of [fraudulent] claims' contained in a report from 1859:

> A strange priest finds out the site of an abandoned Temple, and takes possession of the *Wihare watte* [monastery estate], which is seldom appropriated by the lay villagers, further than taking the fruits of areka and coconut trees.... The people who have been cultivating the lands are too glad to acknowledge themselves tenants and thus escape taxation. The priest only asks them to put up a small *Pansele* [temple], the old Bo tree is still standing, and probably a number of old stone pillars, and when a small *Pilimege* or *Malesunge* [image and offering houses] covered with old tiles has been put up, there is nothing to lead one to suppose, at first sight, that a place with so many remnants of antiquity about it, has not been in almost the same state for centuries.[28]

Cautioning their fellow commissioners against schemes like this, the Temple Lands Commission carved up the territorial boundaries of Buddhism in Kandy through a double act of division. Firstly, they distinguished temple lands from taxable lands using the evidence gathered from inscriptions, deeds and the testimonies of donors, monks

[26] Government of Ceylon, 25–52.

[27] These sentiments are visible throughout many reports and journals left by the Temple Lands Commission, many of which are preserved in the Sri Lankan National Archives.

[28] Government of Ceylon, *Report of the Temple Land Commissioners on the Progress and Results of the Commission from Its Constitution, in February 1857, to the End of 1858*, 11–12.

and lay trustees. Secondly, they divided up those temple lands into those gifted through genuine expressions of piety and those used as instrumental acts of tax dodging. Finding the territorial jurisdiction of Buddhism, in other words, required not just locating land grants and *sīmā* stones but scrutinising the inner motives of landholders.

THE 'SUBJECT-MATTER JURISDICTION' OF BUDDHISM

As the nineteenth century wore on, one practice of legal pluralism gave way to another. The act of clarifying the physical boundaries of temple lands only accentuated questions about the laws used to govern those lands. Under the obligation to honour the 'Ancient laws and usages of the Country', the British promised to uphold traditional land tenure practices. As noted already, this included enforcing the royal service obligations (*rājakāriya*) of tenants – even after the British had abolished similar kinds of obligations on other forms of property based on caste. This also included responsibilities to ensure that the correct individuals controlled those lands. Of particular concern was the question of how to identify and appoint the chief incumbent monks of monasteries. Which principles and rules governed succession to these powerful clerical positions?

Although British officials understood the importance of appointing chief incumbents and resolving disputes relating to the role, they did not always welcome the task.[29] Ruling on such issues meant intervening in disputes between robed clerics on questions of proper monastic practice – an activity that seemed to flout the Crown's claims not to interfere in the practice of local religions.[30] In the earliest phases, officers skirted the intricacies of intra-monastic disputes, in part, by affirming the decisions made by sangha councils and endorsing *their* appointments to high clerical offices. Evasion was more difficult when

29 Some of the earliest records of the judicial commissioners in Kandy comment on the fact that succession disputes, particularly among the Asgiri fraternity, had been regular features of judicial life for Kandyan monarchs. So much so that the king had even 'appointed a special officer, Hantiya Nilame, to hear and report on all cases regarding land belonging to the [Asgiri] Vihāra'. Judicial Commission, *28 Aug 1817* as reported in Lawrie, *A Gazetteer of the Central Province of Ceylon (Excluding Walapane)*, vol I, page 69.

30 For example, *Report from Mr. F. Rogers to the Right Hon. W.E. Gladstone* on June 25, 1846.

disputes involved multiple monks or monastic sects, each with its own versions of orthodoxy and claims to authority.

These issues became more acute over the course of the nineteenth century. The decades following 1800 were not only a period of rapid colonial expansion but a period of rapid segmentation among the island's monastic groups. Between 1800 and 1900, the number of monastic groups holding their own independent ordination ceremonies grew from two to more than fifteen.[31] Where Laṅkan monks had once been notionally governed by the Malvatu and Asgiri chapters of the Siyam Nikāya, whose headquarters were in Kandy, monks in the late nineteenth century lived in an atmosphere of dispersed and contested sangha authority.[32] (I describe this further in Chapter 4.) These new groups challenged the dominance of the Siyam Nikāya, proclaiming their own doctrines of clerical succession and their own bodies of monastic law.

Cartographic practices of legal pluralism purported to clarify the territorial boundaries of temple lands, presenting them as separate spaces to be governed. In the eyes of colonial officials, those separate spaces required clarity on the legal sources and authorities that should govern them. Practising legal pluralism in this second way required Ceylon's courts to do some juristic fancy footwork. On the one hand, the laws governing temple lands had to be intelligible to and consonant with the English legal principles employed by judges. On the other hand, those laws had to be sufficiently grounded in 'Ancient and established usages' so as to plausibly support the idea that colonial courts were not threatening the 'inviolability' of the *sāsana* (as spelt out in the Kandyan Convention) nor 'interfering' with religion (as mandated by Crown policy).

It is in this context that notions of subject-matter jurisdiction came to be applied to Buddhism. The norms governing *vihāras* and *dēvālas*,

[31] Department of Buddhist Affairs, *Śrī Laṅkāvē Nikāyayan Pilibaňda Toraturu [Report on the Nikayas in Sri Lanka]*.

[32] One should be careful not to project this unified version too far back in time. Prior to the eighteenth century, Laṅkan monks did *not* reside continuously under a hierarchically organised Siyam Nikāya. The Siyam Nikāya itself was only formally incorporated in the mid-eighteenth century, when a delegation of monks came from Siam (modern-day Thailand) to 'restore' ordination to the island. According to Laṅkan written sources, the island, at the time, did not have enough fully ordained monks to conduct a proper ceremony. On the organisation of the sangha in this and earlier periods, see Ilangasinha, *Buddhism in Medieval Sri Lanka*; Gunawardana, *Robe and Plough*.

which were initially understood as twin elements of Kandyan Law, came to be framed as distinct bodies of case law and categorised in mid-century court reporting under a number of headings: the Laws of Buddhist Priests, the Laws of Temple Lands, Buddhist Temporalities and, eventually, Buddhist Ecclesiastical Law.[33] A key feature uniting the collected cases was an assumption that the colonial courts only intervened in the 'civil' dimensions of Buddhism, while avoiding its 'purely spiritual' or 'ecclesiastical' features. Thus, in a manner similar to the cartographic division of space into taxable versus temple lands (which were further subdivided into *bona fide* and illegitimately donated parcels), colonial judges and lawmakers sought to recognise a distinctive arena of Buddhist monastic law, while at the same time drawing a line between its justiciable and non-justiciable elements – separating those that were properly civil in nature from those that were properly ecclesiastical.

Civil and 'Purely Ecclesiastical' Matters

Separating the civil from the ecclesiastical was not something unfamiliar to British jurists, nor was it something unique to matters of Buddhism. Similar practices of legal pluralism appear in legal judgments in England, and in other colonial jurisdictions from at least the 1700s.[34] The earliest expression of this idea in the courts of British-controlled Ceylon emerged not in relation to Buddhism but in response to a dispute between rival Muslim groups over the 'customary rights' to hold an annual festival. In that case, the island's Supreme Court refused to intervene on the basis that no 'civil injuries' were at stake because the matter was 'purely ecclesiastical'.[35]

[33] In some cases, court reporters and jurists separated the rules regarding monks and *vihāras* from those regarding *kapurālas*, *basnayake nilames* and *dēvālas*. In other cases, they did not. This can be seen in the collected judgments of Charles Marshall, the first island-wide Chief Justice under the 1833 judicial reform. Marshall, *Judgments and Other Decisions and Directions of the Supreme Court of the Island of Ceylon, from the Promulgation of the New Charter, 1st Oct. 1833 to March 1836.*

[34] See, in particular, the case of *Middleton v Crofts*. On this important court case, see Harris, 'Secularizing a Religious Legal System.' Hayley, in particular, was struck by the deep similarities between church-state history in England and Ceylon. Hayley, *Laws and Customs of the Sinhalese; Or, Kandyan Law* Introduction, p. 533 . For comparative perspective see, Sullivan, *The Church State Corporation* Ch 1, p. 90.

[35] Marshall, *Judgments and Other Decisions and Directions of the Supreme Court of the Island of Ceylon, from the Promulgation of the New Charter, 1st Oct. 1833 to March 1836*, 657–8. According to the judges, this was 'a dispute between parties

While colonial courts studiously dodged disputes they considered to be 'purely ecclesiastical' within Muslim (and, later, Hindu) communities,[36] they found disentangling the civil and religious elements of monastic disputes somewhat trickier, given the nature of Laṅkan Buddhism and the Crown's obligations to it. As mentioned above, colonial jurists could not entirely avoid intervening in Buddhist monastic matters because the Crown had officially committed itself – in the Kandyan Convention and subsequent laws – to protect and maintain Buddhism's 'Rites, Ministers and Places of worship'.[37] It was under these conditions that colonial courts made their first forays into recognising the rules relating to the succession of incumbency from one monk to another.

In determining the succession practices of Buddhist monks, judicial officials consoled themselves that, although related to monastic life, such practices were – unlike the Muslim ritual prerogatives mentioned above – not purely ecclesiastical in nature. As the Chief Justice of the Supreme Court put it in the late 1830s, although 'the tenets of the Buddhist religion [held] that a man, on becoming a Priest, resigns all worldly wealth . . . [t]his entire abnegation of earthly possessions . . . seems not less difficult to be put in practice in Ceylon than

of the Mohamedan creed' touching on matters 'altogether of an Ecclesiastical nature and therefore not a matter for the civil courts'. Therefore, the judges opined, any action taken by the court would commit 'the very offence of injury which . . . we are bound by our oaths to prevent[:] that of interference with the people, in the free and peaceable exercise of their religious rites and ceremonies'. See also: Norris, J. DC Calutara 12,348 (1835) in Morgan, *A Digest of the Decisions of the Supreme Court Sitting at Colombo, Since the Promulgation of the Charter of 1833*, 51–52.

36 This supposedly clear line between 'ecclesiastical' and 'civil' matters was affirmed in various other cases over the course of the nineteenth century. See, for example, Modder, 'The Principles of Buddhist Ecclesiastical Law: Being a Manual of the Customary Law, Decided Cases, and the Statute Law of the Buddhist Church of Ceylon [Unpublished Manuscript in Mimeograph] (SLNA 25.98/19-20),' 54–56. In 1892, in a widely cited opinion, the Supreme Court refused to adjudicate a disagreement between two Brahmin priests over donations at a famous Hindu temple, underscoring the court's obligation not to 'interfere in the concerns of religious communities' unless 'a civil element enters, which brings it within the sphere of the Court's civil jurisdiction'. *Kurkukel v Kurukel* in Pereira and Fernando, *The Supreme Court Reports*, 348.

37 As one District Judge would put it in 1918, 'startling though the proposition might appear, at the present time, the King of England is the head of the Buddhist Church in Ceylon'. Woodhouse, 'Sissiyanu Sissiya Paramparawa and Other Laws Relating to the Buddhist Priesthood (Part I),' 175.

elsewhere'.[38] To the extent that the rules of monastic succession implicated the control of 'earthly possessions', therefore, they could be considered customary practices and civil matters, rather than 'religious tenets'. To learn about these Buddhist civil practices, therefore, British jurists relied not on sacred scriptures but on testimonial accounts offered by senior monks or written land-transfer documents, such as copper-plate *sannas* and lithic inscriptions. In fact, despite references to the Vinaya in early legal petitions made by Buddhist monks,[39] and despite explicit discussions of the Vinaya in mid-century accounts of Buddhism,[40] citations of the translated text of the Vinaya do not appear in the determinations of Ceylonese judges until the early 1900s.[41]

To determine the rules of monastic succession, early-nineteenth-century judges prioritised accounts given by the senior-most monks from the two oldest and largest monastic fraternities, the Malvatu and Asgiri Chapters of the Siyam Nikāya. A key moment came in 1829 when, as a way to resolve a dispute over control of a wealthy temple, the judicial commissioners in Kandy ordered prelates from these two chapters to write separate statements defining what they understood to be the two major forms of succession that applied to Kandyan monasteries: 'succession by students' (S: *śiṣya paramparāva*, later referred to as 'student-after-student succession' *śiṣyānu śiṣya paramparāva*) in which incumbency was passed to the students of a deceased incumbent; and 'succession by robes' (S: *sivuru paramparāva)* according to which incumbency must remain with monks who were members of a particular noble family, so as to keep the temple property within that bloodline.[42] Four years later, in a subsequent case, the judicial commissioners presented those accounts to an assembly of Kandyan chiefs who, according to

[38] Marshall, *Judgments and Other Decisions and Directions of the Supreme Court of the Island of Ceylon, from the Promulgation of the New Charter, 1st Oct. 1833 to March 1836*, 649–50.

[39] See, for example, Pieris, *Tri Sinhala*, 166–9.

[40] Gogerly, 'On Buddhism'; Gogerly, 'On Buddhism, No. 2.'

[41] The earliest judicial references to the Vinaya appear in *Sumangala Unnanse v. Dhammarakkita et al.* DC Colombo no. 23,208 (1908) as reported in 11 NLR (New Law Reports) 360. This possibly follows the practices in Burma at the time. It also may follow the popularisation of partial and full translations of the Pali Vinaya by Oldenberg and Horner: Oldenberg, *Vinaya Texts (Sacred Books of the East Vols. 13, 17, 20)*; Horner, *The Book of Discipline (Vinaya Piṭaka)*.

[42] *Dantura v Government of Ceylon* (1829) as reported in Vanderstraaten, *The Decisions of the Supreme Court of Ceylon Sitting in Appeal* Appendix D.

court reports, declared that the 'succession by students' rule advocated by the Malvatu was 'more correct' and should be considered the default rule for determining incumbency for all monks.[43] This same Malvatu-based standard is upheld by Sri Lanka's civil courts today, even in cases involving non-Malvatu monks – a fact that continues to frustrate some contemporary monks.

From this early stratum of cases, judges in Ceylon developed an elaborate jurisprudence relating to monastic succession and the use of temple properties. Although carefully framed as civil matters, implicating the customary practices of Buddhist monks (rather than 'matters purely ecclesiastical'), colonial judges nevertheless touched on a wide variety of issues that tested the limits of that binary. Courts ruled on the complex permutations of the succession-by-students model.[44] They determined which assets should be considered as the property of the *vihāra* or monastic fraternity (P: *sanghika*) and which should be considered as the property of individual monks (P: *puggalika*). They developed protocols for dealing with monks who took over control of abandoned property, or who disrobed and re-robed, or who moved among multiple temples.[45] They even ruled on the ritual elements required for establishing a valid clerical ordination and pupillage.[46]

In many of these cases, judges made an effort to distinguish for monks the 'tenet[s] of their religion' from the 'practices' of Ceylon's monastic community. In 1835, for example, the Supreme Court upheld the conviction of a Buddhist monk who refused to give evidence against an alleged offender, claiming that he did not want to violate 'the doctrines of the Buddhist religion'.[47] In deciding the matter, the court pointed out that, despite the monks' pleas, 'scarcely a criminal session passes without one or more priests giving evidence against prisoners

[43] *Eriminne Unnanse v Senabowe Unnanse and Parekumbure Unnanse* (1832) as reported in Vanderstraaten Appendix D.

[44] For example, what happens if the monk's chief student dies or the monk has no chief students or the chief student abandons the chief monk while he is still alive?

[45] Woodhouse, 'Sissiyanu Sissiya Paramparawa and Other Laws Relating to the Buddhist Priesthood (Part I)'; Woodhouse, 'Sissiyanu Sissiya Paramparawa and Other Laws Relating to the Buddhist Priesthood (Part II).'

[46] *Parusselle Dhammajotyi* Unnanse *v Tikiri Banda Paranatale and others* DC Kandy no. 81,630 (1881) as reported in SCC. Vol. IV., No. 31, 121.

[47] DC Ambalangoda No. 41, 10 June (1835) as reported in Marshall, *Judgments and Other Decisions and Directions of the Supreme Court of the Island of Ceylon, from the Promulgation of the New Charter, 1st Oct. 1833 to March 1836*, 128.

without objection'. Therefore, while the monk might consider it part of his 'religious scruples', refusing testimony was certainly not part of 'the constant practice' of Laṅkan monks.[48]

Similar distinctions between religious and civil law were also used by higher courts to correct lower ones. In 1863, the Court of Request in Kegalle dismissed the case of a monk who was trying to collect an unpaid loan because, the judge insisted, Buddhist monks ought not to engage in trade. On appeal, the Supreme Court overturned the decision, warning the lower-court judge that it was not his prerogative to 'enter into the religious scruples of Buddhist Priests'. Regardless of what the Buddha's teachings might say about a monk engaging in business, the higher court admonished, when it came to civil matters such as loans, 'in the Courts of the Island he [the monk] is a layman'.[49] In these, as in other cases, colonial judges practised legal pluralism in a way that stressed the court's distance from Buddhism and its laws while at the same time confirming its powers to act as an arbiter of monastic orthodoxy.

Separating the ecclesiastical from the civil proved particularly thorny when monastic courts were implicated alongside civil courts. This occurred when disputes over temple lands involved claims of significant misbehaviour that might lead to a monk's removal from the sangha (a class of offences referred to in the Vinaya as 'defeat worthy,' or *pārājika*). On those occasions, civil courts were required to either ignore or uphold the decisions made by monastic courts (e.g. removing temple incumbents who had been declared *pārājika*).[50] In so doing,

48 DC Ambalangoda No. 41, 10 June (1835) as reported in Marshall, 128–30. Interestingly the court also engaged in its own analysis of Buddhist 'doctrines' based on the testimony given by the defendant. The court came to the conclusion that the monk's own analysis of 'Buddhist lore' was erroneous: giving incriminating evidence was not a severe infringement of monastic discipline but a minor offence for which they could be forgiven.

49 *Sumana Unnanse v. Kira* in Court of Request Kegalle no. 2743 (1863) as reported in Solomons, *Decisions of the Supreme Court on Appeals from Courts of Requests, 1861–67*, 10. See also *Appuhami v Ratnapala Unnanse* in DC Kandy no. 59,921 (1874) as reported in Modder, 'The Principles of Buddhist Ecclesiastical Law,' 327.

50 In 1870, for example, the Supreme Court upheld a decision by the District Court of Galle to remove an incumbent monk from office on the grounds that the relevant sangha court had declared the monk to be guilty of a *pārājika* offence, thereby expelling him from the community and nullifying any claims he had to the position. Galle 29,056 as reported in Woodhouse, 'Sissiyanu Sissiya Paramparawa and Other Laws Relating to the Buddhist Priesthood (Part I),' 186. In the case of *Terunanse v*

judges struggled to mark the distance between their authority and that of the monastic jurists.

One of the most significant cases of this type concerned the incumbency of a key pilgrimage site, Adam's Peak, which the Supreme Court decided in 1872.[51] In its judgment, the Court took pains to point out that, although it was effectively upholding the decision made by one monastic council (to oust a misbehaving incumbent and install another), it was not pronouncing on the issue of 'a High Priest's Budhist [*sic*] orthodoxy' nor was it recognising the decision of the monastic tribunal per se. The judgment carefully distinguished between the 'Buddhist Ecclesiastical Tribunal' convened by the monks of the Malvatu monastery that ousted the incumbent for 'ecclesiastical reasons' and the Supreme Court's own, separate powers and justifications to oust the monk. Those powers and rationales, the court stressed, were entirely different in nature because they were restricted to civil matters only: matters of property, embezzlement and the misuse of funds, rather than the ecclesiastical matters of 'apostasy or heresy'.[52]

As with secular power in other settings, practices of legal pluralism that aimed to separate the civil and ecclesiastical elements of Buddhism only further entangled colonial officials with monastic life. The conundrums created by one practice of legal pluralism were addressed through further practices, which expanded rather than narrowed the ambit of colonial authority.[53] Although the courts were careful not to claim ecclesiastical

Abeyanaike et al., the requirement that the monk not be a *pārājika* was spelt out in the deed granted by the donor. The court even applied standards from Gogerly to see if the *sangha kamma* was regular. See report in Modder, 'The Principles of Buddhist Ecclesiastical Law,' 314 and ff.

51 DC Ratnapura no. 9353 as reported in Vanderstraaten, *The Decisions of the Supreme Court of Ceylon Sitting in Appeal*, 215 and ff. See also: Blackburn, *Locations of Buddhism: Colonialism and Modernity in Sri Lanka*, 18–33; de Silva, Premakumara, 'Colonial Governmentality: Legal and Administrative Technologies of the Governance of Sri Pada Temple in Sri Lanka.'

52 Similar contortions are visible in the original District Court decision, which made considerable effort to distinguish between the ecclesiastical authority of the sangha's executive council, or *kāraka sabhāva*, which had no power of enforcement, and the legal power of the courts, which had no authority over the *kāraka sabhāva*. Modder, 'The Principles of Buddhist Ecclesiastical Law,' 254. See also *Terunanse v. Abeyanaike et al.* 1 Matara 21 (1908) as reported in De Kretser, *Matara Cases, Being a Collection of Hitherto Unpublished Decisions by the Supreme Court of Ceylon, on Appeal from the District Court of Matara*. i, 21.

53 See, for example: Agrama, *Questioning Secularism: Islam, Sovereignty, and the Rule of Law in Modern Egypt*.

power for themselves, they nevertheless reflected on the degree to which individual monks and monastic councils were acting properly according to the Buddhist disciplinary standards that had been encoded into colonial case law. They pronounced on whether monastic legal actions (*sangha karmas*) were correctly performed.[54] They offered their own interpretations of monastic 'vows'.[55] They occasionally justified the relative powers of colonial courts and monastic incumbents by reading *katikāvata*s (which one judge referred to as monks' 'ancient ecclesiastical law'[56]). After 1900, judges sometimes referred to the Vinaya Piṭaka.

By the early 1900s, colonial judges displayed a seeming degree of comfort in assessing the procedures and rationales of monastic courts. In several instances, civil court judges pronounced on which determination – that of monastic authority A or that of monastic authority B – was the correct one according to monastic law. In so doing, they drew on a mixture of case law precedents, translated Pali and Sinhalese legal

[54] DC Galle 29,059 as reported in Modder, 'The Principles of Buddhist Ecclesiastical Law,' 314. See also: *Gooneratne Terunanse v Ratnapala Terunanse* (1899) as reported in De Kretser, *Matara Cases, Being a Collection of Hitherto Unpublished Decisions by the Supreme Court of Ceylon, on Appeal from the District Court of Matara*. i, 227.

[55] *Appuhamy* vs. *Ratnapāla Unnānse, D. C. Kandy, 59,921*, S. C. Civ. Min., 22 Dec. (1874) as reported in Modder, 'The Principles of Buddhist Ecclesiastical Law,' 325–26. Archibald CJ opined, 'I think it is of the highest importance that the Courts of law established by the Crown in this Island should pay regard to the religious feelings of the inhabitants, and that their decisions should not ignore or be at variance with the vows, which the law permits to be taken up by priests or laymen. I can imagine nothing more hurtful to the morality of the people than that Courts should assist and encourage Buddhist priests to violate with impunity the sacred obligations of poverty or celibacy, which they undertake at the ordination. In deciding that all property which a priest acquires during his incumbency is acquired for his vihare [*vihāra*, monastery] and does not belong to himself individually and absolutely, I think I not only affirm an undoubted rule of Kandyan law and an essential tenet of the Buddhist religion, but also a rule which may prevent and check maladministration of office by priests and the improper and fraudulent secularisation of temple property. I do not think that this decision unduly recognises religious doctrines, with which a Court of law has no concern. I think I am as much bound to pronounce on it as I would be to affirm in deciding that it was illegal for . . . Catholic priest to have wine with children'.

[56] DC Ratnapura no. 9353 as reported in Vanderstraaten, *The Decisions of the Supreme Court of Ceylon Sitting in Appeal*, 216–17.

sources and notions of due process taken from British common law.[57] Thus, when, in 1913, the Ceylon Supreme Court was called on to assess accusations that a monk had been ejected unfairly from an Amarapura monastery, the court was able to assert, with apparent confidence, that not only did sangha councils have standards of due process (including the right of an accused party to know and defend against such accusations) but that those standards had been met by the Amarapura prelates in the case at hand.[58]

In the process of policing the supposedly clear boundary between civil and ecclesiastical matters, then, colonial courts further demonstrated the ways in which the two were, in practice, intertwined. Sangha property had 'spiritual' dimensions, especially for donors who sought a karmic return on their donations.[59] Similarly, monks who transgressed the 'tenets of Buddhism' could be expected to face material consequences in the form of disrobing or ejection from a monastery. As will be seen in Chapter 4 of this book, some of the monastic practices at the centre of civil court disputes (such as the writing of succession deeds) came to be prohibited by monastic fraternities around the same time.

This de facto intertwining of civil and ecclesiastical matters appears even in the inconsistent nomenclature used to try to prise them apart. Phrases such as 'Buddhist Ecclesiastical Law' or 'Buddhist Law' were used to connote both colonial law and monastic law,

[57] For example, *Terunanse v. Abeyanaike et al.* 1 Matara 21 (1908) as reported in De Kretser, *Matara Cases, Being a Collection of Hitherto Unpublished Decisions by the Supreme Court of Ceylon, on Appeal from the District Court of Matara.* i, 21. *Sumangala Unnanse v. Dhammarakkita et al.* DC Colombo no. 23,208 (1908) as reported in 11 NLR 360; *Dharmarama Unanse v. Wimalaratna Unanse CR* Panadura no. 10,247 S.C.Civ. Min. Feb (1913) as reported in Modder, 'The Principles of Buddhist Ecclesiastical Law,' 227, §II.5.i.; *Attadassi Unnanse v. Rewata Unnanse* DC Kurunegala no. 8,665 (1928) as reported in 29 NLR (New Law Reports) 361.

[58] *Dharmarama Unanse v. Wimalaratna Unanse CR* Panadura no. 10,247 S.C.Civ. Min. Feb (1913) as reported in Modder, 'The Principles of Buddhist Ecclesiastical Law,' 227, §II.5.i.; *Attadassi Unnanse v. Rewata Unnanse* DC Kurunegala no. 8,665 (1928) as reported in 29 NLR (New Law Reports) 361.

[59] Those who donated to Buddhist monasteries often did so with an expectation of 'earning merit' (*puñña*), which would lead to a better rebirth. The amount of merit earned depended both on the virtuousness of the monks residing at the monastery and on the endurance of the monastery itself.

judicial decisions and *katikāvata*s, customary 'usages' and textual ideals.[60] All the while, legally minded Buddhist monks and laity made use of the imagined boundary between civil and ecclesiastical matters, justiciable and non-justiciable elements of Buddhism, to categorise the world around them in ways that invited or resisted a particular kind of judicial action.

'PERSONAL JURISDICTION' AND THE COMMUNITY OF BUDDHIST LAW

In affirming the jurisdictional boundaries between temple and taxable lands and between ecclesiastical and civil matters, colonial practices of legal pluralism not only purported to address the interests of local Buddhists, they also responded to the concerns of Christian missionaries and colonial bureaucrats in Ceylon and London. When speaking to Buddhists, officials could point to the Temple Lands Commission or decisions handed down by the civil courts as proof that the Crown was upholding its commitments to Buddhism under the Kandyan Convention. When speaking with Christian missionaries and lawmakers in London, they could point to the same practices as evidence that they were neither supporting nor interfering with a foreign faith. Reliant, as they were, on drawing new cartographic and conceptual boundaries, British administrators worked hard in their written correspondence to express a tenable balance between their obligations to protect and maintain Buddhism while at the same time eschewing any substantive 'connexion with it'.[61] Nevertheless, from the moment the Kandyan Convention was signed, Ceylon's governors faced pressure from politicians, lobbyists and, especially, evangelical leaders in both the colony and the metropole to withdraw from all involvement with the 'idolatry' of Buddhism.[62]

[60] *Henepolle Pansalle Sumangana Unanse v. Hennepolle Pansalle Sobite Unanse*, DC Kurunegala no. 21,217 as reported in Supreme Court of Ceylon, *The Supreme Court Circular* v, 235 [28 December 1883]. As another examplec see the contempt of court case relating to Ven. Tibbotuwewa Siddhartha Sumaṅgala as reported in the newspaper *The Ceylon Observer*, July 6, 1908, p. 977.

[61] House of Commons, 'Hansard Reports for the House of Commons Vol. 123,' 713–14.

[62] Hardy, *British Government and the Idolatry of Ceylon*. 'Report from Rogers to Gladstone,' 25 June 1846, as reproduced in Government of Ceylon, *Correspondences*

Whether motivated personally or politically to do so, governors considered various practices to 'withdraw from direct interference' in Buddhism over the course of the nineteenth century. Most chose a similar strategy: they would create a 'constitution' for Buddhists which they could then use to 'hand over Buddhism to its professors'.[63] By constitution, colonial officials meant an ordinance designed to incorporate Buddhism as a legal entity – a 'church' or corporation – that could assume control over its civil *and* ecclesiastical aspects.[64] From the 1840s to the 1870s, although various plans were drafted, no comprehensive constitution was ratified.[65] Instead, governors and

Relating to the Buddhist Temporalities Ordinance (Sessional Paper IV of 1907), 15–17. Ceylon was not alone in this pressure. Similar pressure from London was also being felt by the British East India Company around the same time. In 1833, the Court of Directors of the East India Company ordered servants of the Company in Calcutta to 'withdraw from all arrangements which implicate the Government, be it in a greater or lesser degree, in the ministrations of the local superstitions of the Natives', on the basis that they 'exhibit the British power in such intimate connexion with the unhappy and debasing superstitions' as quoted in Arvind, 'Religious Endowments and Trusts Law in Colonial India,' 14, 8.

63 'Report from Rogers to Gladstone,' 25 June 1846, as reproduced in Government of Ceylon, *Correspondences Relating to the Buddhist Temporalities Ordinance (Sessional Paper IV of 1907)*, 15–17. This idea of a 'constitution' for Buddhists appears regularly throughout colonial documents from the second half of the nineteenth century.

64 Governor Colin Campbell drafted one of the earliest and most comprehensive versions of such a plan in 1846. His draft ordinance created a 'Central Committee' – consisting of 'Chiefs and Priests' from Kandy – that could take over 'all the rights, powers and privileges which by virtue of the Convention of 2 March 1815 were vested in the Governor ... [relating] to the appointment or removal of Priests and Chiefs of Temples and to the internal discipline of the Ministers of the Buddhist Religion'. Committee members would be empowered to survey temple lands, monitor and commute *rājakāriya* services and adjudicate disputes involving temple property. The ordinance even mandated that the Committee would take over the jurisdiction of the District Courts on these matters. *Despatch of April 13, 1847, Lord Grey to Governor Viscount Torrington* in Government of Ceylon, 19. See also: 'Ordinance enacted by the Governor of Ceylon with the advice and consent of the Legislative Council thereof' No. 2 as reprinted in *The State and Religion in Ceylon since 1815*, 247.

65 For example, the plan described in the footnote 64 was rejected by the colonial secretary on the grounds that it gave 'a dangerous organization to the Buddhist hierarchy'. *Extracts of an Address of His Excellency the Governor on Opening the Sessions of the Legislative Council for 1888*, in Government of Ceylon, *Correspondences Relating to the Buddhist Temporalities Ordinance (Sessional Paper IV of 1907)*, 12.

colonial courts appeared to work incrementally to 'hand over' whatever elements they could.

The most consequential policy change emerged in early 1853, following a public inquiry in the House of Commons about 'the connexion between the Queen's Government in Ceylon, and the idolatry of any part of Her Majesty's subjects'.[66] Promising the House that he would ensure 'an entire cessation of interference in Buddhist affairs',[67] the colonial secretary in London directed the governor to make two changes to existing policy that, in his estimation, would extricate the Crown from Buddhist affairs without giving the impression that colonists were reneging on their promises in the Kandyan Convention. Firstly, the governor should stop issuing formal legal instruments (warrants, certificates or diplomas) to appoint monks to high clerical offices, such as the great leader or *mahānāyaka* positions of fraternities. From then on, those positions would be filled by means of majority voting through a 'regular electoral body' consisting entirely of monks within a given fraternity.[68] Secondly, the governor would hand over guardianship of the tooth relic to a committee headed by heads of the Asgiri and Malvatu Chapters,[69] who would therein be responsible for protecting the sacred item on behalf of the country.

66 House of Commons, 'Hansard Reports for the House of Commons Vol. 123,' 715.

67 As quoted in De Silva, *Social Policy and Missionary Organizations in Ceylon: 1840–1855*, 128.

68 As quoted in De Silva, 126. This was no small matter for monks. The governor's refusal to sign an Act of Appointment for a *mahānāyaka* or *anunāyaka* position, as Governor Campbell did in 1840, was perceived by many as depriving those positions of legitimacy and legality. According to Kariyawasam, Kandyan monks vehemently opposed the refusal of appointments by holding processions and making petitions to the government to reconsider. Kariyawasam, *Religious Activities and the Development of a New Poetical Tradition in Sinhalese 1852–1906*, 11–13. Such a reconsideration was made by Governor G.W. Anderson, who, between 1851 and 1853, reinstated the practice of issuing legal warrants for monastic appointments, with the unanimous support of his Executive Council; that is, until it was abolished. De Silva, *Social Policy and Missionary Organizations in Ceylon: 1840–1855*, 116–17.

69 In taking these half-step measures, Pakington was nonetheless cautious and, not wanting to rouse resentment, assured Buddhists in the published version of his despatch that these measures would not amount to 'any withdrawal of the protection or any infringement of the immunities granted to the Buddhist religion by the Convention of 1815'. De Silva, *Social Policy and Missionary Organizations in Ceylon: 1840–1855*, 126–27.

Visible in the Crown's practices of legal pluralism was a foundational irony. In its efforts to hand over Buddhism to Buddhists, colonial laws highlighted and, in many cases, helped amplify the diversity of interests and organisations that comprised the island's monastic and lay communities–thereby making it more difficult to form a single, unified body of Buddhists. Who ought to have jurisdiction over Buddhist matters? Nobles? Monks? And if monks, which ones?

Over the course of the nineteenth century, the practices undertaken by colonial officials and judges helped undermine many of the structures of power and authority that governed monks during the previous Kandyan period, leading to the segmentation of the sangha into a variety of monastic groups. Where it was once plausible to treat the Kandyan (Asgiri and Malvatu) prelates and sangha councils as the accepted centres of Buddhist authority on the island,[70] by the mid-nineteenth century, multiple new monastic fraternities flourished outside of the Kandyan region especially in the 'low country' maritime areas, the leaders of which began to challenge the Kandyan monks' claims to authority.

Citing their commitments not to intervene in ecclesiastical matters, colonial jurists largely accepted the assertions of independence made by these new monastic groups.[71] At the same time, they seemed to treat the Kandyan prelates, who still controlled the majority of temples and properties, as the de facto spokespersons for Buddhism. All of this meant that at the same time that colonial officials and Christian missionaries were urging that Buddhism be handed over to the Buddhist 'church', colonial policies were making such a handover increasingly impossible. Practices of clarifying the geographic and subject-matter jurisdictions of Buddhist law, in other words, provoked

[70] Memorialists to Arthur Gordon refer to the Asgiri and Malvatu Vihāras as 'the Oxford and Cambridge of Laṅkā.' Government of Ceylon, *Memorial of the Buddhists of the Kandyan Provinces (Sessional Paper XIII of 1888)*.

[71] In disputes over succession, courts could intervene to ensure that *vihāra* property would be controlled by a particular *nikāya* but not a subdivision of the *nikāya*. Woodhouse, 'Sissiyanu Sissiya Paramparawa and Other Laws Relating to the Buddhist Priesthood (Part I),' 179. See *also Crown v. Rambukwella Unnanse* DC Kandy 8,950 (1838) Lawrie, A *Gazetteer of the Central Province of Ceylon (Excluding Walapane)*, 362 and ff.

further questions about who, exactly, were the authorities who should speak for Buddhist laws and lands? And who, exactly, were the 'Buddhists' over whom that authority was presumed to apply?

Buddhist Temporalities

Debates about the personal jurisdiction of Buddhism became especially important with the 1876 appointment of a new special commission designed to 'enquire into the administration of Buddhist temporalities' and to stem the 'mis-management' thereof. That phrase, Buddhist temporalities, although visible in correspondence between London and Colombo as early as the 1840s, gained widespread prominence in the late nineteenth century, as a replacement for the phrase 'temple lands'.

This new phrase carried with it new frames of reference. By referring to the lands as temporalities, the commissioners (and others) made a comparison with the administration of Christian church lands, also called temporalities, for which the governor had introduced similar ordinances starting in the 1840s.[72] In referring to the temporalities as Buddhist, the commissioners no longer concentrated their attention on the local tenants or 'Ancient usages' that applied to those lands under the Kandyan kings. Instead, they focussed on a particular human community – the Buddhist analogue to the Anglican or Catholic communion – who were presumed to have rightful interests in those lands. The purpose of the commission was therefore summarised as ensuring that 'the revenues derivable from [temple] lands are expended to the advantage of the majority of the Buddhist community'.[73]

It is worth noting that this focus on a 'Buddhist community' consisting of individual, undifferentiated 'Buddhists' appears to be relatively new one in nineteenth-century Ceylon, at least lexically speaking. While one can find a variety of terms in older epigraphical and textual sources to refer to persons who follow the dharma and support the

[72] For example, ordinances pertaining to Episcopal Church Temporalities (1846), Presbyterian Church Temporalities (1846), Episcopal Churches Temporalities (1855) as documented in Government of Ceylon, *Record of Legislative Acts of the Ceylon Government from 1796: Distinguishing Those Now in Force, Vol II, Containing Ordinances, Orders in Council and Letters Patent from 1833 to 1852.*

[73] Government of Ceylon, *Report of the Commissioners*, v.

sāsana, the emphasis on a clear, bounded human group that self-identified simply as 'Buddhists' (S: *bauddhayo*) – rather than as bhikkhu, *upāsika*, *dāyaka*, etc. – does not appear widely in Sinhala-language sources (at least those investigated in Chapter 4) until the mid-to-late-nineteenth century. The popularisation of the phrase 'Buddhists' likely coincides with the popularisation of the term 'Buddhism' (*buddhāgama*), which gained currency in Sinhala in the later nineteenth century.[74] That it was not a widespread term used by legally minded monastic writers may perhaps be seen in the fact that, to the extent that they use the term at all, the authors of *katikāvata* and monastic court decisions seem to use the term 'Buddhist(s)' (*bauddhayā/o*) less frequently than other terms such as 'devotees [of the *sāsana*]' (*sähādavan*) or Buddhism-adherents (*bauddhāgama adahannāvū minissu*).[75]

As with the practices that established the geographical and subject-matter jurisdictions of Buddhist law, the practices for identifying its personal jurisdiction – that is, the 'Buddhists' who spoke for and were subject to it – required interventions in the lives of monks and laity that the Crown was keen to disavow. Instructions given to the newly appointed Buddhist Temporalities Commissioners reminded officers that:

> it is not the intention of Government in any way to *interfere* with the Buddhist church *as a church*, or either now or hereafter to involve itself in any question connected with *the Buddhist religion*. It will thus be beyond the scope of the Commission to enquire into the manner of conducting religious ceremonies, or into kindred matters, whether of discipline or doctrine, and great care must taken to avoid giving any ground for any misconstruction of the intentions of the Government in this regard. The Government wishes to deal with the question solely as one of administration.[76]

[74] On this see: Carter, 'The Origin and Development of 'Buddhism' and 'Religion' in the Study of Theravada Buddhism'; Malalgoda, 'Concepts and Confrontations: A Case Study of Agama'; Scott, 'Religion in Colonial Civil Society: Buddhism and Modernity in 19th-Century Sri Lanka'; Houtman, 'How a Foreigner Invented Buddhendom in Burmese: From Tha-Tha-Na-to to Bok-Da Ba-Tha.'

[75] 'Legal Decision (*adhikaraṇa viniścaya*) Number 133,' dated April 5, 1911. SLNA 5/63/51. See Chapter 4 for a discussion of this document.

[76] Government of Ceylon, *Report of the Commissioners*, v, italics mine.

Evident in the instructions are the kinds of line-drawing described at the outset of this chapter. Commissioners were ordered, firstly, to distinguish between 'religion' and 'administration', focussing on the latter while eschewing the former. Secondly, they were enjoined to distinguish between 'the Buddhist church', which ought not to be interfered with, and 'the Buddhist community', which was the beneficiary of the new administrative measures. Thus, just as colonial agents attempted to carve off temple land from taxable land and distinguish Buddhism's ecclesiastical elements from its civil ones, they also attempted to identify Buddhist persons who could act in the interests of the 'Buddhist community' without encroaching on the 'Buddhist church'.

The topic of Buddhist temporalities dominated a great deal of colonial law and policy from the 1870s to the 1930s, leading to multiple government commissions and no fewer than *seven* versions of a Buddhist Temporalities Ordinance drafted between 1889 and 1931.[77] These practices of legal pluralism activated at least two different visions of Buddhist law's human embodiments, generating debates that continue to shape Sri Lankan society today (as examined in Parts II and III of this book).

The earliest versions of the Buddhist Temporalities Ordinance, ratified in 1889 and 1905 respectively, vested primary authority in committees of laymen who 'profess[ed] the Buddhist religion'.[78] Those laymen would serve as the trustees of *vihāras* and *dēvālas*, where they would oversee the use of property and the 'temporal' conduct of resident monks. Laymen, particularly wealthy landowners, were also eligible to serve on district-level or provincial-level committees that supervised the activities of trustees in a given area.[79] With the creation of the 1931 ordinance, however, lawmakers shifted the location of Buddhist authority away from the laity and towards the monastic community, vesting special power in the chief incumbent monks of

[77] Buddhist Temporalities Ordinance No. 3 of 1889; Buddhist Temporalities (Amendment) Ordinance No. 17 of 1895; Buddhist Temporalities Ordinance No. 3 of 1901 (withdrawn); Buddhist Temporalities Ordinance No. 8 of 1905; Buddhist Temporalities (Amendment) Ordinance no. 27 of 1912; Buddhist Temporalities (Amendment) Ordinance No. 15 of 1919; Buddhist Temporalities Ordinance No. 19 of 1931.

[78] §7 Buddhist Temporalities Ordinance No. 8 of 1905.

[79] Under the 1889 version, two committees existed. In 1905, the Provincial Committees were abolished.

temples, who were empowered to serve as the temple's trustees.[80] These developments are examined below.

The Earlier Ordinances: Buddhist Authority as Lay Authority

A monarchical and lay-led vision of Buddhist authority and community emerges clearly in the Report of the 1876 Commission as well as in the first two versions (from 1889 and 1905) of the Buddhist Temporalities Ordinance. According to this schema, authority over monastic property and (to some degree) monks themselves ultimately resided in the hands of the sovereign, a lay person, rather than the hands of sangha. In its Report, the 1876 Commission put the matter in no uncertain terms. According to the 'ancient Kandyan system', the report asserts,

> the priests were not allowed to have any control over the lands, which were managed for them by laymen under the directions of the king, who exercised absolute authority over the priests as well as the laity.[81]

Lay control, the authors go on to say, was not simply a matter of royal practice but a norm established in 'Buddhist law' in the form of three monastic constitutions, or *katikāvatas*, written between the thirteenth and eighteenth centuries, translations of which they appended to the report as evidence. Those *katikāvatas*, the authors stressed, contained a set of royal orders concerning the administration of the sangha, which monks were obliged to follow. The British government, as 'succe[ssor] to all the rights of the Kandy kings', therefore possessed a similar authority to impose its own scheme for 'giv[ing] to Buddhism an honest working constitution for the proper management of its temporal affairs'.[82] Authority over Buddhism, in other words, passed from Kandyan kings to the British Crown to the ordinances of colonial lawmakers; and those lawmakers had the authority to appoint lay trustees as the rightful custodians of Buddhist temporalities for the benefit of 'the Buddhist community'.

Invitations to act on this royally endorsed, lay-led vision of the Buddhist authority appeared throughout the various evidence submitted to the 1876 Committee as well as in subsequent debates about the Buddhist Temporalities Ordinance in newspapers and legislative

[80] While the 1931 Ordinance retained the idea of having a separate trustee for temple property, lawmakers permitted the chief incumbent to assume that position for himself – an option that nearly all incumbents took up.
[81] §15. [82] §10.

councils. In the minutes of evidence attached to the 1876 report, for example, one finds numerous witnesses – both lay and monastic (including the Asgiri *mahānāyaka* and members of the Malvatu sangha council) – alleging that the island's current chief incumbent monks had misused temple property to enrich themselves, through selling off temple assets and unrightfully profiting off leases. While the structure of the commissioners' questions was designed to elicit these complaints,[83] the totality of the evidence presented in the report gives the impression that, as one monastic witness put it, 'priests are too much occupied with the temporal affairs of the *vihāra* to devote themselves to education and study'.[84] What was needed, therefore, was a restoration of the 'ancient system' of lay-led, governmental control.[85]

This lay-led vision of Buddhist authority appeared widely in submissions made to the colonial government. Consider, for example, the text of an 1888 'Memorial from Kandyan nobles and 631 others to the Governor', which protested that

> [t]he majority of these [Kandyan monks] are ... lead[ing] lives quite inconsistent with the rules laid down by Buddha. Many of these [monks] have families and engage their time, as laymen do, bringing up their families and attending to secular work.[86]

In this account, and others from the period, groups of laypersons (and sometimes monks) invite the Crown to 'interfere' with the practices and spaces of temple property in order to restore a more pristine practice of Buddhism. By (re)asserting royal authority over Buddhism, the logic goes, the colonial state could repair corruptions that had been introduced into the Buddhist community following the end of the Kandyan monarchy.[87]

[83] For example, in questioning one *ratēmahatmayā*, the commissioners asked: 'There is a general impression that the Buddhist priests of endowed vihāra enrich their relations at the expense of the vihāra of which they are the incumbents. Is this the case?' Government of Ceylon, *Report of the Commissioners*, 2.

[84] Paruswelle Unnanse quoted in Government of Ceylon, 7.

[85] Government of Ceylon, 9, 12, 32.

[86] Government of Ceylon, *Memorial of the Buddhists of the Kandyan Provinces (Sessional Paper XIII of 1888)*.

[87] As the Buddhist Temporalities Commissioner put it in a letter to the colonial secretary in 1905: 'The *lay* administration of temporalities is compulsory under the Buddhist religion ... for priests to handle money, to bring actions in court, or in fact to interfere in any way with mundane matters is abhorrent to the spirit of Buddhism'. Emphasis added. *HL Crawford CCS to Colonial Secretary on Feb 8,*

The Later Ordinances: Buddhist Authority as Monastic Authority

Monks had a lot to lose in the lay-led visions of Buddhist authority that influenced colonial practices of legal pluralism from the 1870s to the 1920s, and none more so than the head monks of the Malvatu and Asgiri Chapters in Kandy. Handing over their 'temporalities' to laymen meant transferring control of many thousands of acres of land to non-monastics who, in some cases, had little reverence for the authority of the *mahānāyakas*.[88] Unsurprisingly, therefore, the sangha councils of Malvatu and Asgiri, together with a team of legal experts and amanuenses, actively challenged the jurisdictional vision embodied in the 1889 and 1905 Ordinances, engaging in their own practices of legal pluralism. From the late 1880s through the early 1900s, Kandyan monks issued no fewer than five memorials to the Crown, offering a radically different vision of Buddhist authority and community.

Central to the Kandyan monks' claims was the idea that the lay-led policies endorsed by the government violated multiple systems of law. A memorial from 1888, for example, criticised the draft ordinance for transgressing not only 'the laws of Buddhism' but also the conventions of ancient kings, the customary practices of temples, 'the intent and meaning' of land grants, Section 5 of the Kandyan Convention and even the 'constitutional laws of England'.[89] Drawing on legal arguments that were, by that time, well known to both monks and judges on the island, the memorialists also pointed out that legislation on monastic property was 'outside the function of a Christian legislative assembly' and

1905 on 'Memorial of the Sangha' in Government of Ceylon, *Correspondences Relating to the Buddhist Temporalities Ordinance (Sessional Paper IV of 1907)*, 1–2. Similar sentiments would be expressed in the lead up to the 1931 Ordinance, with future president JR Jayawardene warning the public in a newspaper editorial that, by returning control of temporalities back to the incumbent monks, lawmakers would be opening the door to more monastic involvement in litigation, and thereby more transgressions of the Vinaya. Jayewardene, J.R. 'The Buddhist Temporalities: Flaws to be Remedied in the New Ordinance' *Ceylon Daily News*, Mar 14, 1931, 1–3.

[88] Premakumara de Silva, 'Colonial Governmentality: Legal and Administrative Technologies of the Governance of Sri Pada Temple in Sri Lanka.'

[89] 'Petition to the President and Members of the Legislative Council of Ceylon from the High Priests, Anunāyaka Priests and other Officiating Priests of the Malwatta and Asgiriya Vihāras of Kandy' in Government of Ceylon, *The Buddhist Temporalities Bill, Petitions (Sessional Paper No. IX of 1889)*, 5–6.

involved 'purely religious' issues that 'seriously interfere[d] with the faith and practice of Buddhists'.[90]

When the governor failed to issue a favourable reply to the memorial, the Siyam Nikāya monks wrote directly to King Edward VII. This letter protested that the lay-led policies of the colonial government misunderstood Buddhism and the role of monks therein, confusing local religious traditions with those of Christianity:

> [It is] a false analogy to imagine that there is a Buddhist Church in Ceylon constituted on a basis similar to that of the established Church in England; and that the laity form a part of that Church, and consequently must have a voice in the management of its temples and endowments.[91]

In Europe, the monks pointed out, the church and its property are owned by 'all worshippers'; and priests are 'paid servants' of the church. In Buddhism, by contrast, 'the temples (vihares) are not built for, or dedicated to, the worship of any supernatural being'. When a temple is built and gifted to 'the Buddhist religion', they argued, it becomes 'the absolute property of the Sangha, who are the only living representatives of Buddhism on earth'.[92] Therefore, they insisted

> [B]y the laws of the Buddha, the laity form no part of the religion, they have no proprietary rights in the temples or in the religious endowments. They were never allowed to interfere in either the internal discipline of the Sangha or in the management of its temporalities. The Sangha has a perfect organisation within itself to manage all its concerns, including the endowments.[93]

[90] Ibid., §20, 6. A further petition from the Malvatu and Asgiri *mahānāyakas* was published in the newspaper in October 1891 repudiating the idea of vesting of temple property with laymen 'most of whom are nominal Buddhists'. To do so, they argued, would be to allow laymen to 'sit in judgment on the actions of priests, to decide their property or impropriety' which was totally prohibited by 'Buddhist ecclesiastical law'. 'The Legislative Council' *in The Overland Ceylon Observer* Oct 29, 1891, p. 1170.

[91] 'Petition to King Edward VII from the Mahanayakas, Nayakas, and Sthaviras, presenting the Sangha of Ceylon' 29 December 1904 [but signed by monks from the Malvatu, Asgiri and Dambula Chapters of the Siyam Nikāya]' in Government of Ceylon, *Correspondences Relating to the Buddhist Temporalities Ordinance (Sessional Paper IV of 1907)*, 7.

[92] Ibid., §26, 7. [93] Ibid.

With this emphatic repudiation of lay authority, the Kandyan monks protested to the King that the two Buddhist Temporalities Ordinances, implemented by his majesty's government in 1889 and 1905, constituted not a protection of Buddhism but an 'inversion of the natural order of things'.[94]

Although presented on behalf of 'the Sangha in Ceylon', the Kandyan monks' memorial clearly acted on the interests and experiences of the Siyam Nikāya more than those of the new monastic sects in the coastal areas. Those groups, for the most part, had a closer dependency on lay supporters (discussed in Chapter 4).[95] At the same time, the Siyam Nikāya authors framed monks' grievances using common law legal terms and concepts that could support a variety of claims and interests. Indeed, by the 1920s, the concerns raised by the Kandyan *mahānāyakas* were being articulated by a variety of other critics (monastic and lay) as violations of 'monks' rights' (*ayitivāsikam*) and 'autonomy' (*ātma balaya*).

These accusations appeared prominently in one Sinhala language pamphlet written by the incumbent monk of a small temple in Gampaha. Reacting against the by-then decades-long history of the 1889 and 1905 Buddhist Temporalities Ordinances, he writes,

> Buddhism (*buddhāgama*) and its properties aren't new things. They are old things dating back thousands of years. Therefore, the powers over Buddhism and religious properties (*āgamē dēpaḷavala*), its protection and development, continue [to be vested] with Buddhist monks. Things like religious books, merit ledgers and constitutions (*katikāvata*) clarify

94 Ibid., §26(d), 8. Rather than being 'mere priests who officiate for the benefit of laity at the worship of a god or gods in the temples built for that purpose', the sangha ought to be treated as 'part and parcel of the [Buddhist] religion itself . . . an integral portion of the Buddhist religion'. Moreover, given that the 'other two inseparable units of the Buddhist trinity', the Buddha and the dharma, were 'invisible and impersonal entities', the sangha's role should be seen as even more significant: monks alone were 'the visible representatives of Buddhism and the accredited guardians and exponents of its teaching in the world' Ibid., §9, 3.
Supporting these claims, the writers appended a series of annexes to their memorial, offering English and Pali quotations from the Vinaya, Sutta Piṭaka and Mahāvaṃsa along with passages from *Eastern Monarchism*, a (critical) account of Buddhism written by a former Bishop of Colombo.

95 Kariyawasam, *Religious Activities and the Development of a New Poetical Tradition in Sinhalese 1852–1906*; Jayawardena, *Nobodies to Somebodies*; Malalgoda, *Buddhism in Sinhalese Society*.

> completely how monks should administer the property belonging to Buddhism. It's agreed under the dharma, that Buddhist property is a right and a possession (*bhuktiyak*) of Buddhist monks. … By separating monks from properties, and giving ownership and control to lay people … [the Buddhist Temporalities Ordinance] not only opposed the Buddha dharma it has been a cause for the destruction of the customs and practices (*sirit virit*) of the [Buddhist] religion.[96]

Here, and throughout his pamphlet, the author refers to his fellow monks as the rightful possessors and trustees (*bhāradhāris*) of the *sāsana*. Just as those who donated lands to temples 'transferred the right, control and protection of those properties to [the sangha]', so too did the Buddha transfer guardianship of the *sāsana* to monks. If monks lose control of temple properties, he warns, they will also lose control of the *sāsana* such that they can no longer protect it. Rather than hand over control of Buddhism to Buddhists, therefore, the 1889 and 1905 Buddhist Temporalities Ordinances had done exactly what the British had promised not to do since the Kandyan Convention: perpetuate a pernicious 'interference' (*mädahatkamak*) in the *sāsana* itself.

Other Visions of Buddhist Community and Authority

These arguments about the Buddhist Temporalities Ordinance amplified the profile and salience of long-standing debates about the characteristics of Laṅkan Buddhism. Although disagreements between lay-led and monk-led visions of Buddhist authority were most visible, the issue of Buddhist temporalities also provided opportunities to advance other paradigms and practices of legal pluralism premised on other ideas about the ideal nature and structure of the 'Buddhist community'.

Earlier memorials from the Malvatu and Asgiri Chapters, for example, make efforts to distinguish the interests and status of Siyam Nikāya monks from those of the Amarapura and Rāmañña Nikāya fraternities on the grounds that the latter were not only newer to the

96 Kē Ñāṇavimala, *Bauddha Vihāra Devālaya Gam Ājñāpaṇata Hā ē Sambandha Guṇadrōṣa Sat Darśanaya [Buddhist Temporalities: The New Ordinance with a Critical Study of the Same]*, 61–62.

island, but they also had different financial incentives to support the Buddhist Temporalities Ordinance, given their lesser landholdings:

> There are several sects among the Buddhist priests of the present day, viz., the Siamese sect, the Amarapura sect, and a new sect called the Rāmañña, which has branched off from the Amarapura. The two latter are hostile to the former, to which the petitioners belong, because [the Siyam Nikāya] has existed from ancient times, has large endowments and was honoured by the Sinhalese kings and princes. Your Honourable Council must, as a matter of course, expect petitions from members of the two hostile sects in favour of a Bill which will deprive the petitioners [Siyam sets] of the premier position they hold, and place them in subjection to, and at the mercy of, laymen.[97]

In this statement, the Siyam Nikāya leaders cautioned the Crown not to see all monastics as equal. Rather than writing as a singular sangha, the Kandyan prelates – along with other authors writing at the time – defined Buddhist authority and community along economic and sectarian lines.[98]

Defining the nature and boundaries of the 'Buddhist community' in law also sparked debates about the status of *dēvāla*s and whether their lands and specialists, *kapurālas* and *basnāyaka nilames*, ought to be classified alongside *vihāras* in the greater mass of Buddhist temporalities. As with their admonishments against confusing the role of Buddhist monks with that of Christian priests, Siyam Nikāya memorialists

[97] 'Petition to the President and Members of the Legislative Council of Ceylon from the High Priests, Anunāyaka Priests and other Officiating Priests of the Malwatta and Asgiriya Vihāras of Kandy' in Government of Ceylon, *The Buddhist Temporalities Bill, Petitions (Sessional Paper No. IX of 1889)*, §14, 6.

[98] Some monks and lay patrons from temples without large endowments requested exemptions from the Buddhist Temporalities Ordinance altogether. They argued that, because they relied on lay donations rather than rents from property, lay donors would ensure that temple assets were used properly. As one government report from 1903 put it, 'in the low-country the laity have the remedy [for misappropriation] in their hands for, if they find the priests neglectful of their duties they can cut off supplies'. 'Final Report on the Working of the Buddhist Temporalities Ordinance, North-Western Province' in Government of Ceylon, *Papers Relating to the Proposed Amendment of the Buddhist Temporalities Ordinance, No. 3 of 1899 (Sessional Paper XXXIII of 1904)*, 23. See also 'The Petition to the President of the Legislative Council from Rēvata Anunāyaka Unnanse and other Buddhist Priests and Laymen of the Four Kōrālēs in the Kēgalla District' in Government of Ceylon, *The Buddhist Temporalities Bill, Petitions (Sessional Paper No. IX of 1889)*, 1–2.

criticised British colonial officials for failing to adequately distinguish *vihāras* from *dēvālas*. These two institutions, the Kandyan monks argued, had 'nothing in common except the English word "temple" which was promiscuously employed by persons unacquainted with Buddhism'. *Dēvālas*, they corrected, were run by lay ritual specialists (*kapurālas*) and trustees; and instead of honouring the Buddha, they were 'dedicated to aboriginal spirit worship and to Hindu gods and goddesses'.[99]

CONCLUSION

As they did in other settings, British colonists in Ceylon helped produce the legal pluralism that they claimed to manage. In so doing, they assigned to 'the Religion of the Boodhoo' discernible spaces, topics and persons – that is, to particular jurisdictions. Through practices such as mapping temple lands, defining the rules of monastic succession and enacting a legislative scheme to administer Buddhist temporalities, colonial lawmakers and judges established a body of Buddhist law separate from state law but also protected by it. These acts of separation and protection depended upon further categorical bifurcations: temple lands had to be separated from taxable lands, the laws governing Buddhist monks had to be set off from the laws governing others, the 'Buddhist community' and the 'Buddhist church' had to be distinguished from the population at large. Such categorical bifurcations themselves relied on a series of other distinctions: between civil matters and ecclesiastical or 'purely spiritual' ones, between the 'religious tenets' of Buddhism and the customary practices of Buddhist monks, between lay authority and monastic authority, and so on. One practice of legal pluralism gave way to the next, each producing unities that exposed multiplicities, which themselves need to be managed.

Rather than simply responding to an already-given condition of legal pluralism – a natural ecology of multi-legality against which colonial

[99] 'Petition to King Edward VII from 'the Mahanayakas, Nayakas, and Sthaviras, presenting the Sangha of Ceylon' 29 December 1904 in Government of Ceylon, *Correspondences Relating to the Buddhist Temporalities Ordinance (Sessional Paper IV of 1907)*, §14, 4. On the longer history of these kinds of debates, see Rogers, 'Religious Belief, Economic Interest and Social Policy: Temple Endowments in Sri Lanka during the Governorship of William Gregory, 1872–1877'; Malalgoda, *Buddhism in Sinhalese Society*.

policies could be tuned – colonial lawmakers, judges, lawyers and others clustered Buddhist legal authority around geographic, thematic and communal nodes. Yet they did not codify that authority in a statute (as they did for Mohammedan Law), nor as a system of Buddhist personal law (as the British did in Burma), nor as a unified principle of Buddhist charitable trusts (as the British did with Hindu temples and wakfs in India). The result is that in 1900, Ceylon's Supreme Court justices could speak of 'Buddhist law' in their decisions, and court reporters could classify 'Buddhist law' in their headnotes without referring to the same thing.[100]

Despite promises made in the Kandyan Convention, British commitments to Buddhism were also an apparent source of discomfort for many colonial officials. Giving Buddhism discrete jurisdictions was not simply a way to secure its 'Rites, Ministers and Places of worship'. It was also a way to separate colonial law from concepts, norms and institutions that were, at best, alien to it and, at worst, idolatrous or diabolical in the eyes of lawmakers and evangelicals in London. In this way, jurisdictionalising Buddhism also reflected (and enacted) the presumed incompatibility of English law and local law, common law and religious customs. Colonial practices of legal pluralism drew on two of the four relational pairs described in Chapter 1 of this book: they underscored the *separation* (rather than integration) of Buddhist normative practices and colonial ones, while at times stressing the *incommensurability* between the two. Thus, when it came to Buddhism in Ceylon, British officials concretised a form of legal pluralism similar to that which Julia Stephens has observed in India: 'an exaggerated colonial parody of secular governance, in which religious and secular spheres were cast not just as separate, but mutually antagonistic'.[101]

Yet, there is more to this story than the colonial legal archive suggests. In the next chapter, Chapter 4, readers will see that Buddhist monks were also mobilising their own practices of legal pluralism, which divided life up in very different ways.

[100] It is worth noting that in the same way that the label 'Buddhist law' gave an air of solidity, coherence and historicity to a diverse and changing collections of monastic and royal practice, so too did the idea of 'the Crown' (which crystallised alongside it) artificially smooth over and unify the internal contradictions and tensions among colonial legal texts, actors and institutions.

[101] Stephens, *Governing Islam*, 10.

CHAPTER FOUR

PRACTISING LEGAL PLURALISM IN THE MONASTERY

Wherever they went, colonial officials reshaped and reimagined religious laws. In India, British jurists transformed a handful of elite Sanskrit texts into the basis for 'Anglo-Hindu law', a system of personal law based on a 'homogenous, unitary conception of Hinduism' unreflective of the diverse populations it purported to govern.[1] A similar process unfolded with the creation of 'Anglo-Mohammedan' law in Malaya and India. There, colonial lawmakers converted fluid bodies of Islamic legal practice into a fixed set of codes and court precedents, creating a 'reified and static entity' that had never previously existed.[2]

Nor was Buddhism exempt. In Burma, the British devised a novel system of 'Burmese Buddhist Law', to regulate marriage, inheritance and divorce among Burman Buddhists. Claiming to recover older legal

1 Davis and Lubin, 'Hinduism and Colonial Law,' 97. See also Fleming, *Ownership and Inheritance in Sanskrit Jurisprudence*, 14, Ch 4; Lariviere, 'Justices and Paṇḍitas'; Rocher, 'The Creation of Anglo-Hindu Law'; Rudolph and Rudolph, 'Barristers and Brahmans in India: Legal Cultures and Social Change'; Srikantan, *Identifying and Regulating Religion in India*; Sturman, 'Marriage and Family in Colonial Hindu Law.'

2 Kugle, 'Framed, Blamed and Renamed: The Recasting of Islamic Jurisprudence in Colonial South Asia,' 258–59. See also: Anderson, 'Islamic Law and the Colonial Encounter in British India'; Buskens, 'Sharia and the Colonial State'; Crouch, 'Islamic Law and Society in Southeast Asia'; Hussin, *The Politics of Islamic Law: Local Elites, Colonial Authority, and the Making of the Muslim State*; Lemons, *Divorcing Traditions*; Lhost, *Everyday Islamic Law and the Making of Modern South Asia*; Moustafa and Sachs, 'Islamic Law, Society and the State'; Redding, *A Secular Need*; Stephens, *Governing Islam*.

traditions, British jurists, in reality, produced new ones – taking a small set of 'haphazardly excavated' legal texts and redeploying them as the official 'customary law' of an entire people.[3]

Given the case studies in Chapter 3 of this book, Ceylon/Laṅkā's legal history could easily be read in a similar light. Colonial archives attest to the creation of novel forms of law in Ceylon, such as the Buddhist Temporalities Ordinance and Buddhist Ecclesiastical Law. There, as in India or Burma, British jurists forged new orthodoxies and new rules for religious life. While the British were not the first ruling regime to create laws for the island's monks (pre-colonial monarchs did so as well), they nevertheless deployed their laws in unprecedentedly far-reaching ways, drawing on modern tools of communication and administration.

Jurispathesis and Colonial Law

Focusing on the transformative effects of colonial law is one way of examining legal multiplicity in the nineteenth century – one way of studying legal pluralism. This approach frames the encounters between colonial rule and local laws as acts of domination and displacement, in which the new supplants and weakens the old in a process that Robert Cover calls 'jurispathesis', or legal destruction.[4] Understanding this jurispathic history is important because it helps to correct apologetic or naïve accounts of colonial legality that view Anglo-Muhammadan or Anglo-Hindu law as simply formalising what was already there, faithful translations of existing orders.

Yet, jurispathesis is only part of the story and focusing too narrowly on these dynamics carries its own unintended hazards. At the extreme, a fixation on legal destruction overlooks the agency of local actors who, even if absent from official accounts, played crucial roles in reforming and revitalising law. As Iza Hussin points out in colonial Malaya, the construction of 'Islamic law' did not so much dismantle local legal practices as it did provide 'a central arena for ... struggle [in which]

[3] Lammerts, *Buddhist Law in Burma*, 181.Lammerts, p.181. See also: Crouch, 'Promiscuity, Polygyny, and the Power of Revenge: The Past and Future of Burmese Buddhist Law in Myanmar'; Ikeya, *Refiguring Women, Colonialism, and Modernity in Burma*.

[4] Cover, 'Foreword: Nomos and Narrative.'

colonial officials and local elites conditioned each other's expectations' about the role, nature, and status of religious law.[5]

A narrow concentration on 'jurispathesis' concedes too quickly empires' own claims of societal transformation. As Benton has pointed out, empires did not change local societies in whole cloth. Rather, the coverage of imperial law was 'lumpy' and uneven.[6] Imperial governments were themselves divided, incomplete, polycentric and inconsistent, penetrating deeply into certain domains of life while sitting lightly on others.[7]

Looking beyond jurispathesis, however, requires more than just a shift in perspective. It poses a methodological challenge. To give an account of local legal production, one must have access to a body of sources that testifies to that creativity – a suitable counter-archive that permits one to stray beyond the lamplight of colonial legal records.

COUNTER-ARCHIVES OF LAW

Fortunately, Buddhist monastic communities provide just such an archive. For centuries, both before and during colonialism, the island's monks have produced and preserved a wide variety of legal texts. In the nineteenth century, as with centuries in the past, Buddhist monks copied and edited versions of the Vinaya Piṭaka, the ancient code of monastic discipline, understood to contain the rules of monastic life as expressed in the Buddha's own words. They wrote commentaries, handbooks, procedural codes, admonitions (*anuśāsanas*) and legal judgments (*vinicchayas*, *tīnduvas*). Importantly, they also composed a great number of monastic constitutions (*katikāvatas*) that served as administrative charters for the monks affiliated with a particular fraternity or monastery, including the many new fraternities that were created between 1800 and 1900. When it comes to the legal history of nineteenth-century Laṅkā then, British legal documents may be the largest

5 Hussin, *The Politics of Islamic Law: Local Elites, Colonial Authority, and the Making of the Muslim State*, 5.

6 Benton, 'Colonial Law and Cultural Difference.'

7 Benton and Ford, *Rage for Order*; Wheatley, *The Life and Death of States*. This fragmented view of imperial power conflicts with the self-image cultivated by the legal archives of empires. Mindful of this, Premo and Yannakakis have cautioned scholars to treat the judgments, reports and transcripts left behind by colonists not as general evidence of past events but as historical materials shaped and pruned to fit the 'imperial logic of the archive'. Premo and Yannakakis, 'A Court of Sticks and Branches,' 29, 33.

and best-preserved body of texts, but they are not the only historical witnesses.

This is not to say that the monastic legal archive is complete or perfectly representative of all monks. The palm-leaf, paper and pamphlet texts held in archives located in Sri Lanka and the UK were acquired through the selective collecting of monastic exegetes, academics, government civil servants and colonial officials. This means that the total collection of monastic legal texts is neither as expansive nor as evenly distributed as one would like.[8] The preserved texts generally contain the perspective of monastic elites from a small set of fraternities rather than the experiences of ordinary monks distant from the levers of power. Moreover, as with other legal texts, the contents of many monastic laws are normative rather than descriptive. They often describe *what should be*, rather than *what is*; and therefore cannot be read as faithful accounts of everyday life.

Nevertheless, a substantial archive exists, providing alternative possibilities for examining Laṅkan legal history. Viewed through these sources, rather than colonial legal archives, one can see the nineteenth-century history of monastic law in a new light. Colonial legal instruments certainly influenced the outlook of monastic lawmakers and jurists. Yet, as read through the monastic archive, this influence looks far less dominating, less determinative, than the impressions given in Chapter 3 of this book.

Jurisgenesis and the Shapes of Monastic Legal Pluralism

In fact, monastic legal texts express entirely different schemes of legal pluralism than those of their colonial analogues. Instead of highlighting disruptions with the past, monastic legal texts stress continuity with the era of pre-colonial kings. Instead of communicating a sense of powerlessness, these texts offer new frames of authority and new mandates for monastic action. Read through monastic legal sources,

[8] In addition to archives kept by individual monastic fraternities, there are two public archives that contain a significant number of these sources: Ceylon's 'Historical Manuscripts Collection' (herein HMC) housed in the Sri Lankan National Archives and the vast archives of the colonial civil servant Hugh Nevill (1847–1897) housed in the British Library. The index for the HMC appears in mimeograph at the Sri Lankan National Archives. An index and catalogue for the Nevill collection can be found in: Sōmadāsa, *Catalogue of the Hugh Nevill Collection of Sinhalese Manuscripts in the British Library*.

the nineteenth century appears less like a jurispathic era, in which monastic law was damaged or destroyed, and more as a time of profound jurisgenesis – widespread production and expansion in the field of monastic law.

Those who wrote monastic legal sources practised legal pluralism in their own way. Rather than imposing legal boundaries between monastic and colonial laws, or stressing the incompatibility between sanghas and the state, monastic jurists highlight dynamics of integration, borrowing and exchange between local and imported laws. Rather than merging monastic legal practices into a broader notion of 'Buddhist law' (to be cordoned off from colonial law), these authors underscore the important divisions that distinguish the laws of one monastic fraternity from those of another.

In many cases, monastic lawmakers underplay the disjunctions between new and old laws, presenting the King of England as the latest in a long line of monarchs on the island. In fact, monastic lawmakers frequently wrote that they were not changing laws but simply updating monastic rules 'in accordance with the times'. Accommodating and integrating aspects of colonial law was, in this frame of reference, unsurprising – a continuation of what earlier monastic lawmakers did under previous Laṅkan kings.

Reading nineteenth-century history through monastic legal archives, one recognises that, in the words of Alexey Kirichenko, colonisation stands as 'the *background* not the root cause' of changes to monastic law.[9] What, through colonial legal records, looks like the top-down displacement of local law by colonial ones, appears, through the monastic record, to be *yet another* moment in a much longer legal evolution – yet another occasion of monastic jurists renewing their legal traditions.

MONASTIC CONSTITUTIONS IN THE EARLY NINETEENTH CENTURY

Attempts to blend monastic and imperial laws date back well before the nineteenth century. Buddhist history is filled with documents claiming to harmonise monastic norms and royal orders, cosmic laws and human rulings. One precedent for such practices (which was cited by many of

[9] Kirichenko, 'The Thathanabaing Project: Monastic Hierarchies and Colonialism in Burma,' 155.

my interviewees) comes from the Vinaya Pitaka. In a passage explaining the monastic interdiction against theft, the Vinaya presents the Buddha as modelling his law on the laws of a local king, by purposefully aligning his definition of theft with that of the monarch. A similar alignment, albeit in the other direction, can be seen in premodern royal edicts – the quintessential form of positive law in ancient Southern Asia. Edicts, such as those issued by the ancient emperor Aśoka, reconcile Buddhist norms and royal rule by presenting the monarch as an epitome of dharma and implying that royal laws come from the same ultimate source as monastic law.[10]

Efforts to align royal and monastic law appear clearly in *katikāvatas*, or monastic constitutions from the early first millennium onwards. The lawmakers who composed these important texts (or at least those versions that endure from the twelfth to the eighteenth century) describe their purpose as bringing order, purity and unity to all monks living in the kingdom.[11] With the end of Laṅkan monarchy in the nineteenth century, *katikāvatas* came to be promulgated by monastic groups themselves, usually in the name of the chief monks or executive councils of a given fraternity. Like earlier *katikāvatas*, these new constitutions summarised the major rules of conduct, structures of authority and protocols for managing misbehaviour.[12] They also placed these intra-fraternity rules in relation to the rules of the government and other monastic groups.

Rather than diminishing in significance over the course of the nineteenth century, as the jurispathic paradigm would suggest, the genre of monastic constitutions flourished. During my research, I located at least twenty new *katikāvatas* drafted between 1800 and 1948. Many more almost certainly exist. While most of these new constitutions draw content from the royal variants promulgated before the fall of Kandy, they also show important differences: rather than applying to all monks in a given polity, nineteenth-century *katikāvatas* assert the independence of an individual monastic fraternity

[10] In some cases, scribes legitimise rulers' authority in even more dramatic ways. They describe monarchs as genealogical descendants of the Buddha and/or embodiments of a future Buddha themselves. Collins and Huxley, 'The Post-Canonical Adventures of Mahasammata'; Holt, *Buddha in the Crown: Avalokitesvara in the Buddhist Traditions of Sri Lanka*; Tambiah, 'King Mahasammata: The First King in the Buddhist Story of Creation, and His Persisting Relevance'; Walters, 'Buddhist History: The Sri Lankan Pāli Vaṃsas and Their Commentary.'

[11] Ratnapala, *Katikāvatas*. [12] Schonthal, 'Buddhist Law beyond the Vinaya.'

or sub-fraternity. Rather than being imposed *on* monks by an external political authority, they are promulgated *by monks themselves*, sometimes in collaboration with influential lay patrons. Although clearly distinct from earlier royal *katikāvatas*, these new constitutions nevertheless present themselves as part of an ancient tradition of lawmaking that continues into the present.

The Constitution of Ven. Galgiriyāvē Srī Dhammarakkhita

Consider, for example, a monastic constitution from 1829 promulgated by Ven. Galgiriyāvē Srī Dhammarakkhita Sumaṅgala, the head of the largest monastic group on the island, the Malvatu fraternity of the Siyam Nikāya, at the beginning of his twenty-one years at the head. At a time when monks throughout the island were breaking away from his fraternity,[13] Galgiriyāvē drafted a constitution that would, in his words, ensure that Malvatu monks remained unified, disciplined and harmonious. Like earlier constitutions, Galgiriyāvē's law contains a long list of specific rules, using a mixture of Pali phrases and vernacular Sinhala explanations. Also, like earlier variants, it stresses the importance of unity and warns against creating divisions in the sangha, while also touching on a range of other topics: admonitions against farming or business activities; rules against practising astrology, exorcism or medicine; prohibitions against grazing cows on the temple grounds; instructions to be polite around laity and to treat temple property with care. The law concludes with instructions to its audience to recite the text aloud every fortnight during the regular confessional ceremonies (*uposathas*) required of Buddhist monastics.

Although Galgiryāvē had had recent troubles with colonial courts, his text does not repudiate colonial law. Rather, it enacts a

[13] In the lead-up to its drafting, Galgiriyāve and his associates in Kandy had struggled to assert control over monks who were forming their own break-away factions in the island's southern and western coasts. Three times between 1802 and 1815, Siyam monks travelled to Burma to obtain their own fresh ordinations so that they could create new fraternities in Ceylon. In 1812, the deputy leader of the Malvatu Chapter, Karatoṭa Dhammārāma, challenged Kandyan authority when he refused to renounce his office as chief monk in the low country after being instructed to do so. Adding injury to insult, in 1827, the Malvatu hierarchy even failed to regain control of one of its wealthiest temples when colonial commissioners decided it should vest with Karatoṭa and his followers. Malalgoda, *Buddhism in Sinhalese Society*, 85–86.

paradigm of legal pluralism that interweaves British rule and monastic authority:

> From his eminence, the governor, who now rules this island of Laṅkā, and by the order of the king that [awarded] us the positions of *mahānāyaka* and *anunāyaka* of the Pōyamaḷu Vihāra, we have acquired the authority to purify the religion (*āgama*) by correcting those mistakes that have been done by those bad (*pāpa*) individuals who misbehave in their monasticism[.] [In doing this, the governor] is among the previous kings who ruled over Śri Laṅkā as protectors of the Buddha's dispensation and who similarly purified the *sāsana* by removing from the monkhood and returning to householder-ship those individuals who, having become monks, began misbehaving and [acting in] shameless or immoral ways. Therefore, this *katikāvata* is enacted on the basis of the command of the king (*rājajñāva*) as well as for the preservation of the Buddha's commandments (*buddhājñāva*).[14]

To one familiar with earlier *katikāvata*s, as the drafter would have been, the preface is striking not in its novelty but in its stylistic and expressed continuity with monastic constitutions of the past: the rules are presented as embodying both royal and monastic authority. They are described, as with earlier variants, as being both the 'order of the king' and 'the commandments of the Buddha'. Only this time, the king was not the Kandyan monarch but the King of England, who ruled the island through his governor (the English term being transliterated into Sinhala).

As with earlier *katikāvata*s, monastic lawmakers projected the new charter as complementary with, even a facet of, the ruling regime – a legal pluralism characterised by the integration rather than separation of the sangha and the colonial state. In fact, the instruction portion of the text begins not with an order from the head monk, but with the caveat that before considering the rules, readers should 'firstly trust in the fact that they are living under an [English] government which is [now] supreme'. The document itself even concludes with a phrase that, like earlier royal *katikāvata*, aligns the legal authority of the sangha with that of the new king:

> Those who do not heed the above-mentioned injunctions (*avavāda*) must have their admission in the *sāsana* [that is, their status as a bhikkhu] nullified because they have transgressed both the king's

[14] Two versions of the *Galgiriyāvē Katikāvata* were consulted: SLNA 5/62/162 and National Museum Library HCP Bell Collection, file no. 63.

> commandment (*rajājñāva*) as well as the commandments of the Buddha (*buddhājñā*). If there are people like this, write to [the monks in] Kandy about it.... This *katikāvata* has been written in order to protect both the royal commandments and the commandments of the Buddha.... Having heard this commandment (*ājñāpatraya*), no monk – whether senior, novice or middle-ranking – should neglect or forget it. Keep this firmly in your mind.

The Constitution of Parakum̆burē Srī Vipassī

Monastic constitutions, like that of Galigirāvē, responded to and reflected changing patterns of colonial governance. They also construed their own legal authority in ways that both echoed and integrated it. The constitution I just described was, in its own way, the photo negative of the 1815 Kandyan Convention, in which the British had promised to protect and maintain 'the religion of the Boodhoo'[15]: it appeared to contain a corresponding commitment given by monks to protect the laws of the British sovereign.

As the British began to alter their policies towards Buddhism, so too did monastic elites seem to shift the practices of legal pluralism visible in their constitutions. Changes appeared particularly following mid-century attempts by the British to 'hand over Buddhism to its professors' (described in Chapter 3). When, in 1853, the governor announced that he would no longer issue Acts of Appointment for high-ranking monks and that he intended to hand over the Buddha's tooth relic to local leaders, including the Asgiri and Malvatu prelates, the Malvatu chapter responded with a new constitution for itself. This new constitution was drafted by the successor to Galgirāvē, Parakum̆burē Srī Vipassī, in 1853.

This new constitution, called the *Illumination of the Essence of the Teaching* (*Sārōvāda Dīpanīya*), shared many of the regulations with the previous text written by Galgiriyāvē. Yet it contained new provisions as well. Among these were exhortations to monks that they 'protect [the tooth relic] carefully as though it were our own lives'.[16] Tellingly, the text acknowledged the growing importance of colonial courts for

[15] For more on this, see Chapter 3.

[16] Wijetunga, 'Sārōvāda Dīpaniya,' 8. The monastic lawmakers chose to present the events in a more positive light, as the British entrusting the tooth relic to them on account of their virtue and competence.

managing disputes over temple property and incumbency, albeit in a rather surprising way:

> [We] must totally trust the noble English government for all time as a good partner (*supakṣa*), possessed of eminence, resplendence, dignity and glory. When summoned by the district police to do something such as be a litigant (*naḍukiyaman*) or to give witness statements in a courtroom, [we] must prepare [our] statements in a way that accords with the dharma and *vinaya*[;] and [we] must undertake all actions upholding the Buddha's teachings, including responding to court orders and judging offences, so as to be mindful of the four undesirable rebirths and to be in accord with dharma and *vinaya* and with attributes of loving-kindness.[17]

In this text, monastic authors confronted head-on the challenges posed by the new governmental order: if the King of England was cast as the new sovereign of Laṅkā under the previous constitution, the 'English government' was presented in this one as a 'partner', but not a patron of Buddhism. Paeans of praise, which had previously been attributed to kings in earlier constitutions, were now, in this iteration, reserved for the Buddha and members of the sangha.

Drafters of this new constitution practised legal pluralism in ways that stressed continuity in the form and function of these texts while also rooting the text within the new legal-political reality: the Malvatu was to be (by necessity) independent of state patronage but nevertheless responsible to a new, but still glorious, king. This was a document claiming to discipline monks and protect the *sāsana*, but in a new era of split authority – one in which the sovereign no longer had direct jurisdiction over Buddhism, as it did in the past, but nevertheless commanded monks' obedience.[18]

The Supreme Dhamma Constitution of the Asgiri Chapter

The kinds of legal updates and adaptations that were taking place among the Malvatu monks were also taking place among monks in other fraternities. Shortly after Parakum̆burē introduced his constitution, the island's second-largest monastic group, the Asgiri Chapter of

[17] Wijetunga, 9.

[18] Contrast this with a contradictory injunction found in the last royally sponsored *sāsana katikāvata* drafted by Kandyan king Rājādhi-Rājasiṃha, warning that monks 'must not go to the residences of *radala* chiefs with lawsuits (*naḍu habu*) connected with anyone, whether relatives or not'. Ratnapala, *Katikāvatas*, 124, §15.

the Siyam Nikāya (which in the previous century broke with the Malvatu Chapter), wrote its own updated *katikāvata* that shared many features with the Malvatu version. The Asgiri constitution is a much longer document, which calls itself the *Supreme Dhamma Constitution*.[19]

Like the Malvatu version, the 1858 *Supreme Dhamma Constitution* is rich in details and fascinating rules. It also contains extended references to British colonial policies on the island, ostensibly attempting to reconcile monastic law with the practices of the new regime. In one passage of the *katikāvata*, for example, the authors quote a passage from the *Samantapāsādikā*, the major commentary on the Pali Vinaya, that clarifies the meaning of an instruction attributed to the Buddha in the Vinaya root text. The instruction requires monks to pay attention to the ritual calendar declared by a local king, even if the monks disagree with the king's astronomical reckoning.[20] To explain the passage, the commentary broadens the implications of the instruction. Rather than a rule about calendars, the commentary explains, the passage conveys a more general injunction relating to the relationship between monks and political rulers: just as the Buddha required those monks to obey the declaration of *that* king, so too did the Buddha intend for monks to follow the orders of all kings.

Referring to this part of the commentary in the new *Supreme Dhamma Constitution*, the Asgiri monastic lawmakers take the injunction one step further, updating the norm to fit their new political circumstances. Quoting the excerpt from Vinaya root text in abbreviation, they go on in Sinhala to analogise the ancient king mentioned in the commentary with the English king who now rules over the island:

> *Anujānāmi bhikkhave dhammikānaṃ rājāṇaṃ anuvattituṃ* [Pali quote from the commentary, meaning: O'monks I allow [you] to follow kings who adhere to dharma.]
>
> [In Sinhala] Because [the commentary] says this, it is advisable to abide by the orders of a dharmic king (*dähämi rāja*)[;] it means that out of

[19] *Paramadharma Katikāvata*. This document exists as a palm leaf manuscript held by the Sri Lankan National Archives SLNA 5/63/178/1. It is a long document, running seventy-six leaves. I am grateful to Prof. K D Paranavitana, who sent me a transcription of this document that he completed some years ago while working at the National Archives. All translations come from this document. Page numbers refer to the PDF file in my possession.

[20] Takakusu and Nagai, *Samantapāsādikā*, Vol. V, p. 1068, 3–7.

> obedience to the noble English government that exists today[,] one must abide by royal orders which accord with the dharma and are given in good faith.[21]

In this and other passages, Asgiri lawmakers practise legal pluralism in ways that integrate monastic and colonial laws while also presenting that integration as deeply traditional – a mode of reconciliation recommended by the Vinaya, its commentators and even the Buddha himself. For those who wrote and read (or listened to) the *Supreme Dhamma Constitution*, the authors' textual allusions would likely have been clear, as would their contemporary implications. Asgiri monks were to conform to the new legal status quo and adjust monastic regulations accordingly. Imperial laws and courts were to be treated no differently than the royal laws and courts encountered by monks in the time of the Buddha. Monks should respect colonial law, provided there was no obvious violation of the Buddha's teachings.

MONASTIC CONSTITUTIONS FROM THE LATE NINETEENTH CENTURY

The monastic constitutions described above embody practices of legal pluralism very different from those of the British colonial officials examined in Chapter 3. Rather than an alien or competing normative order, monastic lawmakers present colonial law as a legitimate and complementary one – yet another royal system that they were obliged to accommodate. Rather than dismissing British policies, post-1815 these *katikāvata* drafters appeared to treat those policies as invitations to reinterpret and rewrite their own laws.

Later-nineteenth and early-twentieth-century *katikāvata*s continue these trends while innovating in other ways. One important innovation was the use of print technologies and textual features visible in colonial legal documents. Whereas *katikāvata*s had once been inscribed on palm leaves, monastic groups in the 1880s increasingly published their constitutions in the form of printed pamphlets and books. These new print materials integrated the conventions of colonial print culture, using subtitles, section numbers and indented lists that look very similar to the format of

[21] *Paramadharma Katikāvata*, page 22 in transcription.

ordinances, draft papers and committee reports coming from the colonial government.[22]

The Constitution of the Amarapura Sirisaddhammavaṃsika Nikāya

A good example of this new style of *katikāvata* is a text, published in 1904, that calls itself *The Constitution of the Amarapura Sirisaddhammavaṃsika Nikāya of the Lineage of the Mahāvihāra.*[23] Even from the title, one gets a sense of the style and purpose of this charter. The name announces the rules of a new sub-fraternity within one of the island's three major fraternities: the Lineage of the Resplendent and True Dhamma (*sirisaddhammavaṃsika*) sub-fraternity in the Amarapura Nikāya lineage. It positions that new sub-fraternity as the modern inheritor of the traditions introduced by the Mahāvihāra, the ancient Sri Lankan institution considered to be the wellspring of orthodox Laṅkan Buddhism. Visible here, as in other *katikāvata*s from the period, are dual strategies of legitimation and individuation: the production of a new *katikāvata* expresses the autonomy of the new group while also placing that group in a monastic lineage deemed to be pure and correct.

Even more can be gleaned from the title page. Immediately under the title, the pamphlet clarifies that the *katikāvata* was written at the invitation of Vijaya Guṇaratna Rājapakṣa, a wealthy layperson, who not only funded the process but urged the constitution's drafting in the first place. Also visible is the role played by another layperson, with the title of secretary to the True-Dhamma Protecting Council (*sudharmadhāra sabhāva*). That person is credited with printing the pamphlet 'with the permission' of the chief monk (*mahānāyaka*).

These details attest to the growing role and influence of non-monks, laypersons, in the creation and dissemination of monastic law. As with the formation of new monastic sects, this new, empowered role for lay Buddhists grew out of the social and economic changes catalysed by colonialisation. Growing export and trade economies in

[22] Such material and typographical influences also became evident in the various catechism-like collections of Buddhist doctrinal principles and instructional manuals that evolved in Sri Lanka around the same time. On this trend, see: Malalgoda, 'New Manuals for New Times: A Comparative History of Buddha Ädahilla and A Buddhist Catechism'; Anderson, 'Constituting Communities.'

[23] Amarapura Sirisaddhammavaṃsika Nikāya, *Sirisaddhammavaṃsika Katikāvata (1904)*. I am grateful to Petra Kieffer-Pulz for sharing a scan of this rare document with me.

British-controlled Ceylon gave rise to a new, wealthy middle class. That middle class provided monastic groups with alternative sources of patronage beyond the traditional landed nobility that had donated to monasteries in previous centuries.

These changes were particularly visible in the coastal areas most affected by colonial trade.[24] There, a new bourgeoisie emerged, drawing its membership from castes and classes beyond the elite land-holding groups, such as the Goyigama cultivators of Kandy, who, for decades, if not centuries, had dominated the ranks of temple trustees and monastic hierarchies. In fact, it was not until the formation of the Amarapura Nikāya in 1800 that Sri Lankan monastic orders explicitly invited non-Goyigama men to join.

Historians of Sri Lanka credit this new donor class with stimulating a revival of Buddhism in the late nineteenth century, of which *katikāvata* drafting was a part. Lay donors funded new monastic sects, temples and schools; they built printing presses and formed scholarly societies. They funded campaigns and debates designed to resist the influences of Christian missionaries and Western lifestyles, including habits such as eating meat and consuming alcohol. Influenced by trends in other parts of the world, they advocated for 'modernist' forms of religiosity that encouraged all Buddhists, including non-monks, to read and interpret sacred texts. With the spread of this style of Buddhism, laity gained new platforms to speak for the religion and new opportunities to influence its monastic institutions.[25]

Turn-of-the-century *katikāvata*s reflect changing attitudes towards lay authority and caste in the sangha. In addition to mentioning the importance of lay patronage, constitutions also list the multiple administrative roles played by donors, such as the various lay-led councils (*sabhā*) that contributed to the leadership of a fraternity or chapter. Several *katikāvata*s contain passages that criticise caste exclusivism in more or less explicit ways.

[24] Jayawardena, *Nobodies to Somebodies*.

[25] Bond, *The Buddhist Revival in Sri Lanka*; Dharmapala, *Return to Righteousness*; Deegalle, 'The First Sinhala Tripiṭakaya Translation'; Gombrich and Obeyesekere, *Buddhism Transformed: Religious Change in Sri Lanka*; Kariyawasam, *Religious Activities and the Development of a New Poetical Tradition in Sinhalese 1852–1906*; Malalgoda, *Buddhism in Sinhalese Society*; Prothero, 'Henry Steel Olcott, Anagarika Dharmapala and the Maha Bodhi Society'; Seneviratne, *The Work of Kings: The New Buddhism in Sri Lanka*; Young and Somaratna, *Vain Debates: Buddhist-Christian Controversies of Nineteenth-Century Ceylon*.

Apparent criticism of caste can be seen, among other places, in the ways that monastic lawmakers chose to interpret Vinaya Piṭaka passages. For example, the authors of one 1842 constitution interpreted a well-known Vinaya provision referring to the process of 'examining' prospective monks, which in other cases had been used to justify caste exclusivity, as a rule about education and a candidate's parents[26]:

> [Pali passage from the Vinaya] *pabbājentā sodhetvā pabbajjaṃ detha upasampādentā sodhetvā upasampadaṃ detha.* [Meaning: having examined the ordinand, give lower ordination; having examined [the novice monk] you should give higher ordination.]
>
> [Sinhala explanation] Because this is said, children of good families (*kula daruvan*) must not be ordained without the permission of their parents[.] Even those who have ordained with their parents' permission, if they become a monk hundreds of times, because again and again they keep giving up robes and going back to the life of a householder, for each of those hundred separate times, the person may only be ordained when the permission of his parents is obtained by the teacher-monk who is admitting him. Everyone who receives lower ordination [does so] via examination (*suddhiyen*)[;] therefore, those children-of-good-families should be ordained only after they understand clearly, in the same manner as higher-ordained monks, the letters written by [their] teachers, including all ten types of consonants.[27]

In contrast to other interpreters who defined the Pali term *sodhetvā* (having examined or purified) as referring to the process of examining the ordinand's caste and family, these monastic lawmakers treated the phrase as referring to examining the ordinand's education and whether he has received his parents' permission (one of several important criteria for ordination according to the Vinaya).

Further interpretations of this Pali passage appear in other post-1800s *katikāvatas*. For example, one monastic constitution published in 1926, but written earlier, interprets the phrase as advising monks to 'clear' (*śudha koṭa*) ordinands by making sure that they are 'free from those bad marks/qualities (*ariṣṭa lakṣaṇa*) and other impure things' in addition to confirming that the prospective monks know how to write, read, and speak well and that they understand the duties of monastic life.[28]

[26] The caste-specific interpretation can be found here: Schonthal, 'Buddhist Law beyond the Vinaya,' 310–11.

[27] De Soysā, 'Amarapura Samāgamē Katikāvata,' 125.

[28] *Syāmopālinikāyika Śri Kalyāṇī Sāmagrīdharma Katikāvata (1926)*, 6, §1.

The need to update monastic constitutions to reflect changes in society is discussed with striking candour in the introduction to a 1925 *katikāvata* for the Rāmañña Nikāya. The authors, monastic members of that fraternity's 'Śrī Sugata Sāsana Protection Council', declare that the word *katikāvata*, itself, comes from the conjunction of the Pali terms *katikā* and *vatta*: *katikā*, which, they argue, refers to a regulation put in place concerning 'things that are to be done' (*kaṭayutuvū dē*), while *vatta* connotes facts or conditions (*karuṇu*) that must be acknowledged in order to maintain the suitability or virtuousness (*yahapat*) of those regulations. As rendered by the authors, then, monastic constitutions were, at their core, charters that revised the essential rules of monastic life to accommodate new circumstances.[29]

INNOVATION AS CONSERVATION

Over the course of the nineteenth century, monastic lawmakers gradually reoriented the genre of *katikāvata* from a royally endorsed form of public law that structured the relationship between the government and the sangha-at-large (as it was under Kandyan kings) to a community-based form of private law that laid out the internal rules of individual monastic groups, as issued *by* and *for* those groups themselves. Monastic legislators also reshaped the purpose of that law. Rather than an instrument for uniting multiple sangha groups into a single community, nineteenth-century *katikāvata* drafters justified and rationalised the individuation and independence of new monastic chapters, fraternities, or sangha councils. As opposed to stressing the unitary nature of monastic law, as British jurists tended to do, the authors of new *katikāvatas* practised legal pluralism in ways that highlighted the multiplicity of monastic constitutions used by the island's growing number of fraternities, even pointing to the disagreements among them.

This practice of distinguishing and assessing the laws of monastic groups can be seen, among other places, in the preambles of turn-of-the-century *katikāvatas*. These sections often contain genealogies that establish the group's continuity with the past while also offering more proximate reasons for the group's creation. One good example is the 'agreement' (*sammataya*) of the Jayavardhanapura Kōṭṭē Śrī Kalyāṇi

29 Rāmañña Nikāya, *Śri Rāmañña Nikāyē Katikākavata (1925)*, xi.

Sāmagrīdharma Saṅgha Council, the first low-country branch of the Siyam Nikāya. Published in 1893, the constitution begins with a historical justification for group's formation:

> In the year of the Buddha 2290 [1747], with the tremendous help of Kīrti Śrī Rajasiṅha, the king who ruled over Śri Pada, the ten-fold bhikkhu sangha came to our island of Laṅkā under the leadership of the elder monk Upāli of the lineage of the Mahāvihāra from Siam. Higher ordination was established by that group along with twenty-five bhikkhus at the Pushpārāma Uposathagāra in Kandy, [thus] ensuring [the *sāsana*'s] continuity for the future. Our monk Välivīṭa Saraṇaṅkara was the sangha king and guided the sangha at that time[.] [Yet] the conventions (*katikādharma*) that he created to suit the times (*kālānurūpa*) broke and the sangha had to survive the splintering [groups][.] Things like distributing food, receiving robes, putting on robes, keeping the monastery storehouse, [duties] which are in the Vinaya, [these practices have] also receded among monks.... Because the rule of royal law degenerated, there was also a decline in the quality (*guṇa*) of the monks relating to bad behaviour and legal settlements (*adhikaraṇa samatha*)[;] and this was visible in the respect that was given to them[.] We recognise that these things are increasing in our current environment in which there is no king who can reform the *sāsana*[.] For this reason, we need a place [the authors' monastery] for helping the *sāsana* as quickly as possible and for training each of the virtuous monks who live there.[30]

The above passage is a masterpiece of innovation presented under the sign of conservation. The text begins with a standard history (echoing that of other Kandyan-era *katikāvatas*), which describes the process through which higher ordination was restored in Sri Lanka under the leadership of King Kīrti Śrī Rājasiṃha (r. 1747–1782) and the founding monk of the Siyam Nikāya, Välivīṭa Saraṇaṅkara. It frames this story as a glorious past, which would fade following the demise of Saraṇaṅkara and the end of Kandyan royalty. The story then presents the formation of the new Kalyāṇi Chapter, to which the authors of the text belonged, as the restoration of that glorious past. Throughout the narrative, the authors ingeniously mix together a standard account of the Kandyan sangha (which was familiar to most

[30] As cited in Jayavardhanapura Kōṭṭē Śrī Kalyāṇī Sāmagrīdharma Mahāsaṅghasabhāva, *Jayavardhanapura Kōṭṭē Śrī Kalyāṇi Sāmagrīdharma Mahāsaṅghasabhāva*, 26.

monks at the time) with novel elements that justify the creation of a new sub-fraternity of the Kandyan lineage in the low-country, all the while voicing 'appreciation for the unity (*sāmagrī*) of all ascetics who come to the *sāsana* in order to pursue nirvana'.[31]

Similar narrative strategies can be seen in other *katikāvatas* from the late nineteenth and early twentieth centuries, including the revised and updated *katikāvatas* of the oldest monastic groups. In 1921, the Malvatu Chapter of the Siyam Nikāya published its own 'brand new' (*abhinava*) *katikāvata*, which contained a preface that, like the constitution of the Kalyāṇi Chapter, justified the independence and authority of the group according to its own historical reasoning. In this case, the authors shift back the timeline of the narrative. They start with the Buddha's discovery of the dharma in the fifth century BCE and end with the founding of the Siyam Nikāya in the eighteenth century CE, under the *katikāvata* promulgated by the Kandyan King Kīrtī Śrī Rājasiṃha. The authors then characterise that *katikāvata* as the last constitution to be authorised by the island's 'Buddhist kings'.[32] However, the authors go on,

> with the disappearance of Buddhist kings and the loss of devout nobles and ministers there was a gradual decline in the acceptance of the above-mentioned constitutions [i.e., *katikāvatas*] (*vyavasthāvanhi*). These days, one can see and hear some monks who are living without the unified, complete dharma and who, through being associated with various fraternities and serving only themselves, have rejected the ascetic life and are living without composure, ethics and other things [.] Because of this, we [the authors] have published this brand-new *katikāvata*, which has been agreed to by all the monks in our order's great sangha council[.] [We have done this] in order to prevent the above-mentioned crisis and in order to develop the complete dharma among monks of our monastic chapter[;] [we have done this] in order to preserve our connection with the true body of the dharma by not confusing [our dharma] with that of other fraternities and in order to protect the reputation of our sangha.[33]

As with the above for the Śrī Kalyāṇi sangha council, the brand-new *katikāvata* of the Malvatu Chapter presents the new law and its authors

[31] Jayavardhanapura Kōṭṭē Śrī Kalyāṇī Sāmagrīdharma Mahāsaṅghasabhāva, 27.
[32] *rājabalaya hā saṅgha balayat ätuva*. Malvatu Chapter of the Siyam Nikāya, *Malvatu Katikāvata Saha Baṇadaham Pota (1921)*, iv.
[33] Malvatu Chapter of the Siyam Nikāya, iv.

as successors to, and interveners in, the history of the *sāsana*. Practices of legal pluralism that stress the distinctiveness and special authority of the Malvatu law (vis-à-vis other forms of monastic law) also stress its continuity and integration with earlier traditions of authorised law, extending all the way back to the Buddha. The Malvatu authors also present the new constitution as updating monastic laws 'in accordance with the times (*kālānurūpa sē*)'.[34] Yet, they add an element of narrative one-upmanship to the Kalyāṇi variant. While the Malvatu authors acknowledge the decline in monastic orthopraxy that followed the era of Buddhist kings, they present the solution not as founding a new, reform-minded sangha council but as the reconfirmation of the complete and true dharma coming from a single, original monastic group: the Malvatu.

PROHIBITIONS ON MONASTIC MIXING

The above-mentioned narratives of decline and reform parallel those of pre-colonial royal *katikāvatas*, which also claimed to 'purify' monastic law by restoring its fidelity to the Buddha's ancient teachings. Yet nineteenth-century *katikāvatas* differ from the royal variants in an important way: rather than glorifying the reunification of the sangha – a project that authors claimed to be impossible in the absence of a Buddhist king – they work to establish the purity and virtuosity of a single sangha group. That is, they practise legal pluralism in a way that separates, rather than aggregates, the laws and customs of the island's disparate monastic groups, presenting them, in many cases, as a hierarchy of more-or-less orthodox variants based on their imputed continuity with ancient monastic sects and the Buddha's original teachings. The Malvatu *katikāvata*, for example, cautions against association with impious monks who associate with other fraternities (*nikāya*). The *Śrī Kalyāṇi* preamble makes similar claims to establish a separate, pure tradition that stands apart from others.[35]

[34] The *Mahā-Parākramabāhu Katikāvata*, for example, contains a rule that prohibits a monk from a different group (*gaṇa*) from staying at one's monastic residence if the visitor does not have an introduction card confirming his good standing with the group from which he came. Ratnapala, *Katikāvatas*, 40, §11; 55, §42. The *Daṁbadeṇi Katikāvata* includes a very similar rule, specifying further that the host monk must see either an agreement (*sammatayak*) or an invitation card before letting the visitor stay.

[35] Śri Kalyāṇī Sāmagrīdharma Mahāsaṅghasabhāva, *Syāmopālinikāyika Śri Kalyāṇī Sāmagrīdharma Katikāvata (1926)*, 4, §7.

Attempts to distinguish the laws of monastic groups can be seen, among other places, in *katikāvatas*' regulations designed to limit the mixing of monks from different groups. While rules of this type are not unknown in earlier pre-colonial *katikāvatas*,[36] norms of inclusion and exclusion gained prominence after 1800, leaving no doubt that monks from one group may not participate in the rituals or legal actions of another group.

These limitations on inter-group mingling build upon rules contained in the Vinaya Piṭaka. The Vinaya requires that monks who participate in legal actions must be free from outstanding disciplinary offences, and they must congregate in a state of concord and unanimity (*sāmaggi*). Allowing strange monks to participate in these events can have negative consequences: it might give the inappropriate appearance that those monks are part of one's own lineage and tradition, and it risks undermining the disciplinary purity and *sāmaggi* of the communion and thereby invalidating the legal action.[37]

Unlike older royal *katikāvatas*, which purported to unify all monks into a single fraternity, turn-of-the-century group *katikāvatas* treated the merger of monastic traditions as potentially hazardous and an area for vigilance. The 1926 *katikāvata* of the Śrī Kalyāṇi Saṅgha Council admonishes that 'anyone who has received high ordination in a suspicious (*sāsaṅka*) ritual boundary or in a way that was not completely in keeping with the Vinaya must not participate in important legal actions (*vinaya karmas*)'.[38] The 1901 Rāmañña Nikāya *katikāvata* offers an even more strident prohibition:

> By saying '*vinayampatvā garuke ṭhātabbaṃ* [having reached (an understanding of) the Vinaya one should stick to it]',[39] it means that a bhikkhu who shares in the dhamma and material resources (*dharmāmiṣa*) of another *nikāya*, and who does not observe the constitution and legal

[36] Malvatu Chapter of the Siyam Nikāya, *Malvatu Katikāvata Saha Baṇadaham Pota (1921)*, iv–v.

[37] On monastic legal actions, see Chapter 2 of this book.

[38] Śri Kalyāṇī Sāmagrīdharma Mahāsaṅghasabhāva, *Syāmopālinikāyika Śri Kalyāṇī Sāmagrīdharma Katikāvata (1926)*, 4, §7.

[39] The phrase *vinayaṃ patvā garuke ṭhātabban* is likely taken from Dharmapāla's 'old sub-commentary' on Buddhaghosa's commentary on the *Dīgha Nikāya* called *Sumaṅgalavilāsinī*. Slightly differing statements can be found elsewhere, namely: *vinayapariyāyaṃ patvā garuke ṭhātabbato, vinayavinicchaye hi āgate garuke ṭhātabbaṃ*, etc. For a discussion of this sequence, see Kieffer-Pülz, *Verlorene Gaṇṭhipadas zum buddhistischen Ordensrecht*, Vol. 3, [Z 345], p. 2027, 2029–2030, and n. 20.

> actions (*karmas*) from this *nikāya*, including the legal actions relating to higher ordination, should not participate in the legal actions of this *nikāya*.[40]

With rules like these, monastic lawmakers shored up the ritual, legal and geographical boundaries of monastic groups. They practised legal pluralism in ways that emphasised the separation of individual fraternities. They prohibited the involvement of out-group monks in higher ordination ceremonies and other legal actions, while underscoring the in-group structures of monastic hierarchy and seniority. They restricted the ability of monastics to move across fraternity boundaries while also confirming the location and importance of monastic residences and ritual boundaries (*sīmās*).[41]

Some nineteenth- and twentieth-century *katikāvatas* even urged monks to observe the boundaries dividing villages that historically supported one monastic group from villages that historically supported another. The Malvatu constitution of 1921, for example, advises that

> One should not engage in any religious activities (*āgama piḷiba[n]da kisi kaṭayuttak*) for a 'prey village' (*goduru gama*) that has been dedicated to a particular monastery by a king and his ministers or by a donor who built that *vihāra* or *ārāma*, without the permission of the headquarters or chief monk of the nearby *vihāra*. If there are religious activities that must be done urgently such as [administering] last rites (*āsanna dharmadeśana*), or if [a monk] comes to a place in an emergency out of a need to conduct those sorts of activities, [then, in those cases], he should perform those [rites] with compassion, [and] having come to the nearby *vihāra* and being aware of the situation there, he should perform the appropriate customs (*sirit pävätviyayutu*).[42]

Embedded in this admonition is the idea – a long-standing one within Sri Lankan Buddhism – that monasteries have special relationships with local communities who ensure that monks from that *vihāra* have adequate food, clothes and ritual provisions. Visible in this rule

40 Rāmañña Nikāya, *Rāmaññanikāyē Katikāvata (1901)*, 12, §9.

41 The purity and integrity of monastic ritual boundaries were the topics of considerable disagreement in the nineteenth century and a common reason given for the creation (or discrediting) of new monastic groups. Malalgoda, *Buddhism in Sinhalese Society*, 153–68; Kieffer-Pülz, 'Translocal Debates.'

42 Malvatu Chapter of the Siyam Nikāya, *Malvatu Katikāvata Saha Baṇadaham Pota (1921)*, 7, §6.

(and similar ones from other groups[43]) is the idea that borders extend not just to monasteries but to lay communities as well.

With these rules, as with the rules mentioned above, monastic lawmakers practised legal pluralism differently to colonial officials. Where colonial practices of legal pluralism produced a unified ideal of Buddhist law in order to separate it from purportedly neutral common law practices and institutions, monastic jurists stressed the distinctions among monastic groups, while often underplaying the frictions between monastic and colonial law. If colonial practices of legal pluralism claimed to prevent the Crown's interference or 'connexion' with Buddhism, monastic practices guarded against other kinds of threatening interference: local donors supporting another monastic fraternity, fellow monks re-ordaining in other *nikāya*, or forming their own schismatic sects. Where British judges and lawmakers claimed to pronounce on monastic customs rather than 'the tenets of Buddhism', monastic lawmakers underscored the doctrinal purity of their fraternity's laws, highlighting that they were, in fact, aligned with the original words of the Buddha.

WRITTEN DECISIONS FROM MONASTIC COURTS

The monastic archive is not limited to *katikāvatas*. One also finds records, however sporadic, of legal orders and decisions issued by monastic courts and executive councils. As with monastic constitutions, these orders attest to a vibrant and expansive legal culture that blends colonial with monastic legal idioms, styles and structures. They, too, construe colonial law less as an opposing system to monastic legal forms than as a set of institutions and technologies that might be aligned or even blended with monastic law.

A particularly interesting archive can be traced to the head of the Malvatu chapter, Ven. Parakuṁburē, discussed above. Not long after Parakuṁburē promulgated his constitution in 1853, he issued a number of legal decisions[44] from his executive council based in Kandy. The text

[43] Consider, for example, the following rule: 'One should not persuade and influence laypeople living near another *vihāra* or *ārama* [in order to] take for oneself the donations (requisites, *pasaya*) that are from a 'prey village' (*godurugama*) belonging to those *vihāras* and *āramas*'. *Syāmopālinikāyika Śri Kalyāṇī Sāmagrīdharma Katikāvata (1926)*, 12, §28.

[44] Variously written as *tīṇḍū* or *tīndū*.

of these decisions has been preserved in manuscript collections held by the British Library with dates ranging from 1856 to 1859.

The legal decisions relate to a dispute over the possession of two Buddhist sites, a monastery and a Buddhist temple, in rural areas outside of the ancient capital of Anuradhapura. The properties in question had been controlled by a senior monk, Ven. Tōruvavē; but when Tōruvavē died, his teacher, Ven Payimaḍuvē, took control of the properties, rather than the deceased monk's disciples (*gōlayō*) who, in the eyes of senior monks in Kandy, should have been the proper recipients.

The dispute, and Parakum̆burē's orders, blend together colonial and monastic legal authorities and expressions in striking ways. According to the sources, litigation took place both at the Anuradhapura District Court and in the monastic courts of the Malvatu at roughly the same time. While the precise timing of the two trials is not clear, the reader is told that in addition to being heard by a magistrate, the matter was also adjudicated at the Ruvanvälisāyē temple in front of a 'sangha council of 27 monks, along with the chiefs (*disāves*) of the districts (*satkōralē*) and several provinces'.[45] At that hearing, the gathered monks and lay leaders conducted their own examination, assessing evidence and reviewing the reports made to the district court. Eventually, the monastic and aristocratic adjudicators came to their own decision, concurring with the district court that the properties should be given to the students, not the teacher – and insisting that their verdict was 'totally proper both according to the path of the courts (*nadumārgē*) and according to the sermons and dharma [of the buddha] (*banē dharmē*)'.[46]

The language of Parakum̆burē's orders suggests a style of legal action that blends monastic and colonial idioms: Parakum̆burē speaks of plaintiffs and defendants, complaints and orders, often blending together terms derived from the vocabulary of the Vinaya with those taken from colonial legal jargon – so much so that it is sometimes difficult to discern whether he is referring to the monastic legal case or the case in the colonial courts, or if he even wants to treat the two as rigidly separable. What is clear is that the consequences of the order have both material and religious implications. 'If Ven. Payirmaduvē does not

45 Order 2, 1857, from *Parakumburē Saraṇaṅkara Mahānāyakayan dun Vihāra Naḍu Tīnduvak* [A Monastery Legal Decision given by Mahānāyaka Parakumburē Saraṇaṅkara], BL Or. 6607(21).

46 Ibid.

accept this order', one of the orders warns, 'he should be excluded from performing any sort of religious activity at all (*āgamē monayam kaṭayuttakatavat*)', clarifying that the consequences extended not only to civil sanctions but 'religious punishment' (*āgamē daṇḍuhan*).[47]

This interweaving and implied complementarity of monastic and colonial law goes even further. The copies of the orders held at the British Archives are addressed not to the disputing monks but to a variety of other monastic and political leaders in the region. Looking at the addresses on the documents, it seems that the Malvatu leadership in Kandy sought to execute their directives not only through their monastic subordinates, such as the deputy leader monk resident in Habarana,[48] but also through local rulers, such as the headmen (*mahatmayā*) of the districts. Parakuṁburē's order invites these grandees to apply the appropriate pressure to monks and lay Buddhists in the region as part of an expression of their 'love of the Buddha *sāsana*' and also to ensure that they will be 'protected by the gods'.[49] Thus, the mechanism of enforcement insinuated by these texts blends together colonial, monastic and other local practices of justice – a combination that upholds not only working of civil law but also dharma, while also 'ensur[ing] that there is unanimity (P: *sāmaggi*) within the monasteries'.[50]

Orders from Monastic Courts at Mid-Century

As the century progressed, the format and language of monastic orders also adapted new forms which, like that of monastic constitutions, echoed colonial methods. Several decisions made by sangha courts from the early 1900s – referred to variously as court orders (*naḍu tīndū/tīṇḍū*) and sangha judgments (*saṅgha viniścaya*) or legal-case resolutions (*adhikaraṇa samatha*) – provide examples of monastic judges recording their decisions in ways that align stylistically and schematically with those of the island's civil courts.

47 Order 1, 1856, from *Parakumburē Saraṇaṅkara Mahānāyakayan dun Vihāra Naḍu Tīnduvak.*

48 Order 2, 1857, also cautions readers that, if the accused does not observe the orders, the instructions would be sent to monks around the country.

49 Order 1, from *Parakumburē Saraṇaṅkara Mahānāyakayan dun Vihāra Naḍu Tīnduvak.*

50 Order 3, 1859, from *Parakumburē Saraṇaṅkara Mahānāyakayan dun Vihāra Naḍu Tīnduvak.*

Consider, for example, the text of an 1896 'legal case resolution' written by a monastic judge (*anuvijjaka*) in Galle, which declares an accused monk to be 'defeated' (*pārājika*) and therefore excluded from communion[51]:

> As proved by the plaintiffs and the witnesses who appeared on their behalf, [Ven] Muditakāsīlakkandha has committed offences, including quite serious ones, and it appears that they even shade into *pārājikas*. Therefore, because he has not received the consent of the plaintiff and also because a complaint has come before the sangha regarding some property that has been stolen, the settlement (*samatha*) to this is as follows:
>
> [Pali quote from the *Samantapāsādikā*] *[If] having been accused thusly by a careful [monk], a shameless [monk] does not give [his] acknowledgment with regards to the many issues that have arisen, he [the shameless monk] should neither be called pure nor impure. But he is one whose life is extinguished, one who is rotting away while still unripe. But if any other such matter arises for him, that is not to be judged. In that way, he will indeed become one who is 'destroyed' [i.e. excluded from the community].*[52]
>
> According to this, it seems that [Ven.] Muditakā must be excluded from the community; and, therefore, considering this judgment (*viniścaya*), I, as the monastic judge in this case – together with the executive council – declare that from now on the above-mentioned Muditakā is to be prevented from associating with the dharma or the material gifts (*dharmāmisa*) of the sangha;[53] this is accepted and declared for the entire sangha and confirmed by the undersigned in the year of the Buddha 2439.
>
> Resident of the Gāllē Paramānandārāma [monastery] Kogalla Sirisaṅghatissa Sthavira.

51 '*Adhikaraṇa Samathak* [Legal Case Resolution] SLNA 5/63/162/4.

52 This passage comes from the commentary on the eighth penance offense (*saṅghādisesa*). [In Pali:] *evaṃ lajjinā codiyamāno alajjī bahūsupi vatthūsu uppannesu paṭiññaṃ na deti, so neva 'suddho'ti vattabbo na 'asuddho'ti. Jīvamatako nāma āmakapūtiko nāma cesa. Sace panassa aññampi tādisaṃ vatthu uppajjati, na vinicchinitabbaṃ. Tathā nāsitakova bhavissati.* The passage deals with the case of a corrupted monk who accuses another monk of an unfounded *pārājika* offence. Takakusu and Nagai, *Samantapāsādikā*, Vol. iii, 591, 27–29.

53 Added in handwriting in the margin: 'and because he has committed *kuladūsana* [the offense of corrupting families] in a way that is unsuitable and [unreadable word] he will be removed from the monastic compound through a legal action of expulsion [*pabbājanīya* karma]'. The term *kuladūsana* comes from the Vinaya, and generally refers to those acts that damage the faith of lay supporters.

As with the mid-century orders described above, the author of this order invokes colonial and monastic legal terminology, using words for complainants (*cōdanāvarun*) and witnesses (*sākśivarun*) that could be thought to apply to both regimes. The author, Ven. Sirisaṅghatissa, also uses a formal style and format similar to that of civil court decisions. He writes on paper, rather than palm leaves, with his signature and date of declaration prominently displayed.

The above decision was written at a time, after the introduction of the Buddhist Temporalities Ordinance, when the colonial government sought to 'hand back' legal authority over Buddhist property to Buddhists themselves (see Chapter 3). It is likely, therefore, that the author wrote his judgment for a complex audience of monastics and laity, state officials and local donors. It might have been read not only by monastic judges and litigants but also by judges in the civil courts, who would treat such documents as evidence. Monastic legal decisions like this might also be reviewed by newly formed district committees that had been given state-legal authority to resolve disputes over monastic lands. It is likely, therefore, that monastic judgments written this way would demonstrate both fidelity to the Vinaya and fidelity to colonial legal standards of reasoning, justice and evidence – not just aligning colonial and monastic legality but appealing to them together.

The conjoint style and multiplex audience of early-1900s monastic legal orders can be seen clearly in a printed document from the Sri Lankan National Archives titled 'Legal Decision (*adhikaraṇa viniścaya*) Number 133', dated 5 April 1911.[54] The very look of the document bears a striking resemblance to the published decisions of colonial civil courts: it is a formally written, typed document complete with numbered paragraphs and subtitles, and signed both by an English-language stamp of the jurist's name, 'A. Sumangala', and by the jurist's own hand. At the top of the document are the basic details of the case, resembling the form of a headnote – a common feature of colonial law reports – containing the location, parties, judges, date and nature of the dispute:

> In the great sangha council, under the leadership of the great leader, Śrī Siddārtha Sumaṅgala Tibbaṭuvāvē, chief incumbent of the Malvatu monastery in Kandy that was convened at the Ätakanda Vihāra in Kurunegala on the 5 of April 1911 of the Christian Era.

[54] 'Legal Decision (*adhikaraṇa viniścaya*) Number 133,' dated 5 April 1911. SLNA 5/63/51.

Judges (*anuvijjakas*)[:] Pahamuṇē Srī Saraṇaṅkara Sumaṅgala, Principle Leader of the Northwest District.

Secretary: Ambanvällē Sumaṅgala

In Villihatpattuvē in the Northwest District

Nine Buddhists, including Kogalla Guruge Udēnis, who were staying in the shops near the train station on the way from Neliyāgo[da] to Kurunegala, along with forty persons, including Pusvällē Kalubaṇḍā, of Hēvāvissa in the Seven Kōrales, the local chief of the Kaḍihāgama area.

Plaintiffs (*pämiṇili kārayō*)

Vs.

Resident of Jayakaḍu Vihāra in the same Hēvāvissē Kōralēs Pusvällē Dhammapāla, **Defendant** (*vittikārayā*)

This headnote, written in the style of civil court judgments, frames the case as a contest between certain plaintiffs versus (S: *ediriva*) an accused monk, Ven. Pusvällē Dhammapāla, all of whose names are highlighted and separated at the top of the page. Following the headnote, the authors give a summary of the case, commenting, for example, that the hearing had to be held in Kurunegala because the accused monk had refused to come to Kandy.

The bulk of the document is presented as the 'method that was used by the great monastic committee to come to an agreement on the facts of the case according to the evidence that was presented during the examination'. The jurist explains this method over sixteen numbered paragraphs, which document the evidence given by the plaintiffs and witnesses. As spelt out by the jurist Sumaṅgala, the case against the Dhammapāla is severe. Witnesses are said to have given 'especially reliable evidence' that the monk had been seen drinking alcohol in the street and that he had undertaken a series of amorous affairs with women, including keeping secret wives somewhere in the region. Evidence was given that the accused had been hunting and killing animals, cutting down trees, gambling, and 'constantly, almost daily', drinking alcohol with toddy tappers. Fourteen of the sixteen paragraphs describe witness evidence of a highly immoral person whose actions might be considered criminal 'according to the methods of both the law of the Buddha's dharma and the law of the state'.[55] One witness was said to have testified that:

> now no one worships the Buddha [at the Jayakaḍu Vihāra] no one offers lamps or flowers or offerings; no Buddhists who live in the [nearby]

[55] *Buddha dharma nītikramayaṭada rājanītikramayaṭada.*

> village go to the *vihāra* at all; the only persons who go there are the bunch of thieves who are friendly with the accused... And if a moral person (*sīlācārakenek*) or monk does go to the temple, or if [people] ask 'why would such a person do that?' he [the accused] will threaten them, and insult them[;] not only that, he will even have them beaten up. And, because of that, laity and monks will not go anywhere near there.

In contrast to these harrowing allegations, the judgment characterises the main plaintiffs as devoted Buddhists (*bauddhayō*) who follow the dharma and have no connection whatsoever with the accused.

The last few paragraphs of the document contain a separate statement clarifying the terms and rationales of the monastic court's judgment. This portion begins with a clarification that the monk is guilty not only of the alleged offences but also of disregarding the order (*āñāva*) issued by the monastic court. It then lays out in great detail the terms of its decision according to the dharma, quoting extensively from the Vinaya and its commentaries:

> [In Sinhala] The accused Pusvällē Dhammapāla, because he is without any ascetical qualities (*śramaṇa guṇayak näti*) that a renouncer should have, and because he is shameless (*alajji*) and of low morals (*dussīlayek*)...
>
> [Pali quote from the Vinaya:] *[For one who has committed a defeat-worthy, pārājika offence] it is as though that person has had their head cut off and, being unable to reattach it, is incapable of living; in that same way O'monks, one who engages in sex, is a non-monk; he is not a son of the Buddha.*[56]
>
> [In Sinhala] According to this judgement, the Buddha preaches that, in the same way that it is completely impossible to restore the life of a man who has [lost] his head ... the renunciant who indulges in sexual activity becomes a reprobate (*dussīlayek*) who is not a true renunciant (*aśramaṇa*) and is no longer a son of the Buddha[;] and by means of this [principle] the accused has become an offender (*varadakārayā*). Looking at the harms and damages he committed on laypeople by doing things like killing stolen cows etc., he is, from now on, guilty of *pārājika*[;] and taking into consideration the many other harms he did, it is certain that everyone will easily treat him as a guilty person. Because he is now considered guilty, by way of his entering into offences such as *pārājika*s in this way,

[56] *Seyyathāpi nāma puriso sīsacchinno abhabbo tena sarīrabandhanena jīvituṃ, evameva bhikkhu methunaṃ dhammaṃ paṭisevitvā assamaṇo hoti asakyaputtiyo*. Oldenberg, *The Vinaya Piṭakaṃ*, Vol i, 96, 7–11.

[In Pali, quote from the *Vimativinodanī-ṭīka*, a Vinaya sub-commentary]: *Even one who has been fully ordained, having become a pārājika, that person is one who has destroyed his existence even as a sāmaṇera who goes [to the sangha] as a refuge; he has given up residence in a monastery; it should be known that, for him, the benefits of the sangha are not obtained.*[57]]

[In Sinhala] According to the teaching stated here, by means of the *pājājika* offence committed by the fully ordained monk, one cannot even accept that person for a rainy-season retreat (*vassa*), because of the fact that he has caused his status even as a novice – as someone who has gone forth and takes refuge, etc. – to be destroyed. An immoral renunciant is one who cannot partake at all in the dharma and material benefits of the sangha.

Because of this and what is [also] said in subcommentaries (*ṭīkā*) such as the *Paramattha Mañjūsā*,[58] and because the accused Pusvällē Dhammapāla is completely unfit to wear the garb of a renunciant (*śramaṇa*) and to attend any monastic legal action[59] and to partake of any of the (material) benefits belonging to the *sāsana*, we declare that he [Ven. Dhammapāla] should turn over his robe and take on the clothes of a lay person and that he should be made to leave Jayakaḍu Vihāra.

In contrast to the civil-law format and style of the document until then, the judgment (*viniścaya*) portion grounds the decision in statements from the section on major offences (*pārājikas*) in the Vinaya and the late-twelfth-century sub-commentary the *Dispelling of Confusion*, or *Vimatividanī-ṭīkā*. The author chooses quotations that, in addition to containing the finer points of *vinaya* law regarding how a *pārājika* is to be treated, also demonstrate the familiarity with the broader passages and literature from which they are taken. The author glosses the phrases in ways that explain and justify the punishments being prescribed. He also clarifies that the judgment was written in 'full agreement of all members of the adjudication committee' and with the endorsement of the great leader of the Malvatu chapter.

At the very end of the order, however, the author returns to addressing and evoking the colonial-legal aspects and implications of his order.

[57] *Uppasampannānampi pārājikasamāpattiyā saraṇagamanādisāmaṇerabhāvassāpi vinassanato senāsanaggāho ca paṭippassambhati, saṅghalābhampi te na labhantīti veditabbaṃ. Vimativinodanī of Kassapa: Chaṭṭhasaṅgāyana* CD-ROM, Version 3.0. Igatpuri: Vipassana Research Institute, 1999, v, 108.

[58] *Treasure Chest of the True Meaning*, Buddhaghosa's commentary on the *Visuddhimagga*.

[59] *śāsanika saṅghakamma*.

He declares that the guilty monk should be stripped of his role as temple authority (*adhikāri*), a state-recognised office that, under the terms of the 1905 Buddhist Temporalities Ordinance, had powers to oversee the day-to-day affairs of resident monks. Moreover, he clarifies that 'according to the powers regarding Buddhist places of worship under the current state laws', he had 'issued an order to the district committee' (which had ultimate control over Buddhist places of worship under the 1905 Ordinance) to remove the monk from his post. Copies of this judgment, the author points out, were also sent to senior government figures in the North-western Province.

Taken together, what is particularly striking about this legal judgment, and its practices of legal pluralism, is the way it harmonises and integrates colonial and monastic legal terms and formats in a way that could persuade multiple audiences using multiple legal sensibilities. On the one hand, the document appears to be formatted and written to suit the expectations and tastes of those who held official positions and political power: colonial judges, civil servants and district committee members in the government. For this audience of lay officials, the author includes a clear summary of parties, methods and evidence used to arrive at the decision. He also included a clearly marked declaration and 'order' (*āñāva*) to be actioned.

On the other hand, the author also addresses an audience of Buddhist monastics and laity (including lay Buddhists on the district committee) whom he sought to persuade both of the judgment's dharmic validity and of the discipline, purity and erudition of the monastic jurists who adjudicated the matter – along with the discipline of the broader Malvatu sangha itself. Evidence of this audience can be seen at the end of the copy of the judgment contained in the Sri Lankan National Archives, which contains a handwritten note scribbled in the margins of the text from a plaintiff in the case. That note praises the work of adjudicators and the Malvatu sangha, suggesting that, because of them, 'the up-county *śāsana* has not been lost'.

CONCLUSION

To examine monastic practices of legal pluralism, this chapter draws on a body of monastic constitutions and legal decisions that represent only part of a larger Sinhala- and Pali-language legal archive from the nineteenth century. In addition to these sources, one can also find a body of legal polemics written by monastic jurists in order to justify or defend the creation of new fraternities and sub-fraternities. These polemics, which have been examined by Kitsiri Malalgoda, left their own collections of legal treatises and decisions on topics such as how to calculate the lunar calendar properly, how to wear the monastic robe, or whether it is acceptable for monks to worship deities.[60] Similarly, Petra Kieffer-Pülz has analysed the legal texts and correspondences associated with disputes about the proper reckoning of monastic boundaries called *sīmā*s.

Both bodies of academic work, that of Malalgoda and Kieffer-Pülz, speak further to the volume and vitality of legal production by monks in Sri Lanka during the nineteenth century. They, too, demonstrate that monastic jurists and lawmakers wrote for more than just a local or island-wide audience.[61] They also wrote legal texts for a 'transnational' audience of monastic jurists and royal officials living in modern-day Myanmar and Thailand – sending their legal texts to the chief prelates and kings of Siam and Burma and requesting them to take action.[62] Together with the materials examined in this chapter, these sources testify to a state of legal vitality that challenges the narratives of legal destruction, or jurispathesis, discussed in the introduction. Far from being sidelined by colonial law, monastic legal activities continued and expanded in the nineteenth century.

More than just producing laws, nineteenth-century monks practised legal pluralism in entirely different ways to British officials. They presented the coincidence of monastic and colonial law as complementary (rather than contradictory). They appeared to integrate alternative sources of normativity (rather than eliminate them). They wrote laws and drafted decisions that aligned the laws of the Buddha with the laws of the British, while treating these alignments as, themselves, traditional – an updated expression of state-sangha accommodations that could be traced back to earlier periods of Laṅkan history, going all the way back to the time of the Buddha. Rather than claiming to consolidate and firm up the boundaries of Buddhist monastic law (so as to create an alternative system for governing sangha affairs), monastic lawmakers chose to highlight other legal divisions. They pointed to the importance of sectarian distinctions and the competing claims to orthodoxy advanced by the island's growing number of new fraternities.

[60] Malalgoda, *Buddhism in Sinhalese Society*. [61] Kieffer-Pülz, 'Translocal Debates.'
[62] See also Blackburn, *Locations of Buddhism: Colonialism and Modernity in Sri Lanka*.

Looking outside the imperial archive, therefore, one finds that, rather than being overwritten by colonial law, Buddhist monastic law flourished in the nineteenth century – perhaps even on an unprecedented scale. *Katikāvatas* were created and revised, monastic court decisions were issued and contested, sangha councils and jurists met regularly to decide matters or to challenge the legal pronouncement of colonial officials or other monastic groups. The legal texts and institutions produced by monks during the nineteenth century – and the practices of legal pluralism they communicate – do not reflect an agonistic world of jurispathic legal clashes. Rather, they suggest a jurigenerative atmosphere in which monastic lawmakers adapted and innovated, updating long-standing legal forms and principles 'in accordance with the times'.

This is not to say that the legal changes that came with British colonisation were never seen as disruptive. The jurisdictionalisation of Buddhism described in Chapter 3 was part of what prompted the drafting of new constitutions and rules for monastic life. The nineteenth century was undoubtedly a period of dramatic shifts that could not be ignored. Where pre-colonial polities gave Kandyan rulers ultimate authority over most domains of life, colonisation prised apart sovereign from sangha, the 'order of the Buddha' from the 'orders of the (English) king'. Nineteenth-century monks recognised this. Their work distinguished the normative authority claimed by monastic jurists from that of district court magistrates – and monastic litigants 'forum shopped' accordingly. Monks who felt aggrieved by Ceylonese courts and sanghas even turned to authorities overseas – pleading to monarchs and monks in the Bay of Bengal to intervene in their own local conflicts.[63]

Rather than dampening or displacing Laṅkan monastic law, however, these developments offered new imperatives and incentives for monastic lawmaking. Some constitutions (such as those of Malvatu prelates Galgiriyāvē and Parakum̆burē) affirmed the authority of colonial law and encouraged monks to comply with the new civil court system. Others (such as the Asgiri *Supreme Dhamma Katikāvata*) took a more circumspect approach, advising monks that, when possible, they should avoid colonial courts and follow colonial laws without deviating from the dharma. In other cases, such as the legal decisions (*tīndū*)

[63] Blackburn; Malalgoda, *Buddhism in Sinhalese Society*; Kieffer-Pülz, 'Translocal Debates.'

issued by Parakuṁburē, monastic orders appear to blur the lines between monastic and colonial legal authority. Still others, like the legal decision issued in 1911, offered a two-way approach, producing a style of legal text that spoke both to connoisseurs of monastic law and to state-legal officials charged with upholding colonial laws. Developments in monastic legal practice, in other words, were neither homogenous nor stable over the course of the nineteenth and early twentieth centuries – nor were they feeble.

To look at the monastic legal archive is to observe a combination of new and old techniques used by monastic jurists to address to the situation of colonial governance. The texts of *katikāvata*, *tīndu* and other legal sources recognise and respond to the new multi-legal realities of 'the times'. Yet they also seem to treat this pluri-legal context as something the island had seen before – a feature of life to be acknowledged and managed, but something anticipated by *katikāvata*s, *vinaya* literature and other sources. Rather than emphasising rupture, monastic jurists used their institutional memories to navigate and naturalise a new form of multiplicity. They practised legal pluralism in a manner not unlike the legal entrepreneurs in Nandini Chatterjee's recent account of Mughal legality: Laṅkan monks seem to have blended monastic law together with the other normative forms they encountered, while at the same time '[giving] no indication that they saw themselves as engaging with an eclectic system . . . they saw it all as 'law'.[64]

[64] Chatterjee, *Negotiating Mughal Law*, 40.

PART II

CHAPTER FIVE

LIKE AND UNLIKE 'LAW'

Making a Monastic Judiciary

Studies of legal pluralism suffer from an original sin of analysis, or so some critics argue. Those critics insist that applying the term 'law' to the activities of non-state communities – such as Buddhist monks or garment-factory workers – confuses analogy with equivalence, imposing a model of state governance where it does not belong. They argue that the very concept of law is inseparable from the modern nation-state and its concerns with centralisation, standardisation and the exercise of regulatory power – by universalising the concept, one unwittingly universalises the logic.

These kinds of arguments can be seen across academic disciplines. Legal anthropologist Simon Roberts has admonished scholars to be 'very cautious' in classifying non-state traditions as law for fear of falsely equating the 'negotiated orders' of communities with the top-down regulation of modern governments.[1] Legal theorist Brian Tamanaha sounds a similar alarm when he points to the distinction between conventional approaches to legal pluralism – which imply 'a multiplicity of one basic phenomenon, "law"' – and his 'non-essentialist' legal pluralism, which recognises fundamentally different phenomena that merely share the label of law.[2] Even Sally Engle Merry, an anthropologist and early proponent of legal pluralism, deemed it necessary to treat state law as 'fundamentally different' to other

[1] Roberts, 'After Government?'
[2] Tamanaha, 'A Non-Essentialist Version of Legal Pluralism,' 315.

normative orders, given its uniquely authoritative status and coercive style of enforcement.[3]

Yet, critiques like these, which question the use of 'law' beyond the nation-state, should themselves be treated critically. That is because, in their stronger forms, such critiques imply that modern state law's defining qualities (its formalism or rationalisation, for example) achieve fruition only in the national legal systems of modern countries. Therefore, the argument goes, when one sees those qualities in other domains – for example, in the disciplinary practices of Buddhist monks – it is likely the result of state law's influence.[4] This argument, however, can be deeply misleading when it comes to monastic law.

There is also a second reason that scholars should approach this critique with caution: comparisons to state law are not made by scholars alone. They are also made – and rejected – by legal actors themselves. Melissa Demian, for example, has documented the fluid and context-specific ways that people in Papua New Guinea characterise their 'moral-normative' practices known as *kastom*. In some contexts, she argues, locals construe *kastom* as a species of customary law that exists 'on the scale' of state law and remains comparable to it. In other contexts, they treat *kastom* as an entirely different kind of activity, less akin to legislation and litigation than to other kinds of 'efficacious actions' such as churchgoing or trade.[5]

Similar patterns emerge in discussions of monastic discipline (*vinaya*) in Sri Lanka. Like *kastom*, the presumed commensurability of *vinaya* and state law changes across communities and contexts. In her ethnographies of Buddhist nuns, Nirmala Salgado finds that female renunciants do not speak of *vinaya* as analogous to the juridical practices of the

[3] Merry, 'Legal Pluralism,' 879.

[4] This position, echoed by sociologists of law from Weber to Galanter, portrays modern law (meaning modern state law) as unique precisely to the degree that it 'evolved' these traits. Weber describes modern law as systematic, formal, rational and predictable. Galanter uses the words 'uniform', 'universalistic', and 'regular'. Although both acknowledge modern law's capacity for change over time, they nevertheless stress (as more primary) modern law's demands for uniformity and consistency among social groups, times and spaces. Weber, *Max Weber on Charisma and Institution Building, Selected Papers*, 81–85, 107–111; Galanter, 'The Modernization of Law,' 153–65.

[5] Demian, 'Dislocating Custom.'

Sri Lankan state but as a form of self-cultivation, restraint and moral development.[6]

*

This chapter proceeds in the spirit of Demian and Salgado. Rather than resolving whether monastic law is or is not measurable 'on the scale' of state law, it considers the various practices of legal pluralism that monks use to invite, obscure, affirm, deny – or even avoid asking about – the commensurability of *vinaya* and state law. Drawing on ethnographic and archival research with one of Sri Lanka's three major fraternities, the Rāmañña Nikāya, I introduce readers to the Rāmañña judicial system while also exploring the various ways that monks compare and contrast that system with the judicial architecture of the Sri Lankan state. At times, Rāmañña monks emphasise similarities in institutional structures, legal procedures, or ideas of justice. At other times, they stress fundamental differences, framing monastic and state law either as similar systems with different kinds of content or as regimes that cannot and should not be compared: one oriented toward nirvana, the other toward social regulation (a theme to which I will return in Chapter 6).

DILEMMAS OF COMPLIANCE IN MONASTIC LAW

Rāmañña monks practise legal pluralism in ways that both affirm and reject similarities between state law and monastic law. In so doing, they take part in the longer tradition of collating, characterising and coordinating legal orders – of practising legal pluralism – as described in Part I of the book. This connection is not merely historical. Contemporary monastic law continues to rely on ancient legal sources and to draw on institutions and rules developed during the colonial period.

Today, as in 1900, Buddhist monks reckon with a braided combination of monastic and state-legal authorities. Disputes over monastic property and succession are addressed in monastic courts, using laws and procedures that I will describe below. Those same disputes are also brought before civil courts, where secular judges adjudicate them using the precedents of Buddhist Ecclesiastical Law, a body of case law first

[6] Salgado, 'On the Question of 'Discipline' (Vinaya) and Nuns in Theravāda Buddhism.'

shaped by colonial judges. When monks have concerns about the administration of Buddhist monasteries, they may turn either to their fraternity's courts and executive councils or to the Department of Buddhist Affairs, which takes its mandate from the Buddhist Temporalities Ordinance, a revised version of a law introduced by the British in 1889.[7]

Despite their overlapping authority, monastic and state law do not enjoy equal powers in the eyes of the government. Monastic constitutions (*katikāvatas*) and courts have a status similar to that of other 'voluntary associations', such as sports teams or guilds: unless formally recognised through legislation, contract or by courts, their orders are not enforceable by the police or other government officials. When it comes to enforcing rules, monastic fraternities rely, in the final analysis, on moral suasion, social pressure and the threat of exclusion or ostracism.

Non-coercive techniques like these have precedents in the Vinaya Piṭaka, as discussed in Chapter 2, and can be highly effective in monasteries, just as they are in families, neighbourhoods and professional cohorts. Yet in high-stakes disputes – for example, those concerning property, orthodoxy, membership, disrobing, or high office – many monks worry that these measures alone are not sufficient. As one monastic jurist put it to me:

> We can't do things like putting people in prison; we can't administer fines. ... If [a monk] does not accept the punishment (*danduvama*) we give, there is nothing we can do.[8]

This acknowledgement – that the smooth functioning of monastic law depends ultimately on the voluntary compliance of monks – came up frequently in my interviews. Such concerns date back to the Vinaya Piṭaka itself, which concedes that successful disciplinary actions require that the offenders 'see' their own guilt and voluntarily accept their penalty.[9]

All of this raises a foundational question for monastic fraternities in Sri Lanka: how can groups like the Rāmañña Nikāya foster trust and

7 On the origins of Buddhist Ecclesiastical Law and the Buddhist Temporalities Ordinance, see Chapter 3.

8 Interview with monastic judge (*anuvijjaka*) near Veyangoda, 10 December 2019.

9 Failing to 'see' one's offence (i.e. acknowledge one's guilt) is itself an additional offence, punishable by a suspension action (*ukkhepanīya kamma*), which might be added on to the original offence. Oldenberg, *The Vinaya Piṭakaṃ*, Vin i, 324 and passim.

compliance in a system whose authority, while deeply consequential, cannot be externally enforced?

Although this question arises frequently in Sri Lanka's news media and political debates (a topic that I will return to in Chapter 7),[10] outright acts of defiance are relatively rare occurrences, considering the roughly 42,000 persons living as monks in Sri Lanka. In most cases, committing oneself to a life in robes – particularly after the age of twenty, when candidates can undergo higher ordination[11] – implies a commitment to the institutional and moral legitimacy of the monastic fraternity itself.[12] It is reasonable to assume that most monastics try not to undermine the very system of laws to which they have dedicated their lives. Moreover, the sangha is, at least in theory, a community to which members willingly opt in and from which they may leave at any time. While disrobing carries social consequences, such as family or community disapproval, a significant proportion of monks do so each year.[13]

[10] To give just one example, a senior monk, speaking on a popular Sinhala language television programme in 2016, lamented to the host: 'In the old days, when monks made a decision to expel a bhikkhu from this *sāsana*, or from his monastic council or his fraternity – because it was understood that he had clearly lost his monastic status – the accused who had been charged left on his own, honestly. That was how it worked: whatever the law was, they accepted it; they accepted the disciplinary law (*vinaya nītiya*); they accepted it with extreme deference and left the scene. Now, today, this kind of thing doesn't always happen. There is huge variation among [monks] today as to whether they will accept a disciplinary law decision [even if] that decision would have been accepted in the old days.' *Saṅghādikaraṇaya [The Sangha Court]*.

[11] On the differences between novice monks or novices (*sāmaṇeras*) and full monks (*bhikkhus*), see Chapter 1 of this book.

[12] Individuals ordain as monastics for a variety of reasons and in a variety of ways. In South and Southeast Asia, observers point to two distinct types of ordination. One type of ordination, which is the dominant form in Sri Lanka, is undertaken with the intention of committing to robes for a long period of time, or one's entire life. A second type of ordination, referred to as temporary ordination, is also popular in mainland Southeast Asia. Under temporary ordination, men and women will remain in robes for a discrete period of time – for example, one or three months – with the intention of returning to lay life. This kind of ordination is extremely popular among young men in Thailand, with lifetime ordinations being somewhat less common. In both cases, however, I would suggest that ordination entails a commitment to the institutional legitimacy of the sangha.

[13] In the survey of 1,669 monks conducted for this project (see Chapter 1), respondents indicated that the number one threat facing the *sāsana* was the numbers of monks disrobing. Question 15.

Those who deeply oppose a monastic court's ruling or its prescribed sanctions need not act in open defiance. They may simply leave the order or (in some cases) seek admission in another community.

Just because individuals choose to remain in robes, however, does not mean that they always comply with monastic rulings. Many Sri Lankan temples have extensive landholdings that bring benefits and influence to the chief incumbent monks who oversee those temples.[14] When monastic courts deny these coveted positions to claimants, some resist. Because Sri Lanka's civil courts do not officially recognise the monastic courts' decisions, a monk who is dissatisfied with a sangha court ruling may choose to ignore it and take the matter to civil court, where state-court judges apply Sri Lankan law. One monastic jurist explained the situation this way:

> Currently, when we have some kind of conflict at a temple between monks or between monks and lay persons, we adjudicate it [ourselves]. We hear the case and then give the decision. If they oppose that decision, they appeal it (*äpil ganna*) to the monastic Senior Court [and so on]. . .. However, as it is now, even after [receiving] all those decisions, they can still go to the state court. And then, there will be a different law . . . one that's different from our [monastic] law. In this way, sometimes someone who we have determined to be an offender (*väradikārayā*) is found to be an innocent party in the state court (*niväradikāriyā*).[15]

While it is difficult to determine how often civil courts override monastic rulings, the very potential for them to do so may embolden would-be challengers.[16] This fact unsettles many monks, including

14 Resources like these could, for example, give a chief incumbent monk the ability to create museums, fund schools, upgrade monastic residences, fund charities, or a variety of other things. In some cases, income from temples has been used to purchase luxury items, including cars and other goods. These kinds of property holdings, as well as the office of chief incumbent, are discussed in Chapters 4 and 5 of this book.

15 Interview with monastic judge (*anuvijjaka*) near Colombo, 10 December 2019.

16 While Sri Lanka's state-court judges acknowledge the existence of a monastic judicial system as a factual reality, they do not treat the decisions given by Buddhist monastic judges as authoritative sources of law nor as settled decisions (*res judicata*) that state courts are obliged to follow. One lawyer who regularly litigates cases relating to Buddhist Ecclesiastical Law estimated that roughly one-third of the decisions issued by civil courts go against the decisions made in monastic courts. Interview with senior lawyer, Colombo, 17 December 2014.

72% of survey respondents who agreed that 'when Sri Lankan law and monastic *vinaya* rules and traditions conflict, it is more important to follow monastic law'.[17]

For some, even the act of contesting a monastic court decision undermines the legitimacy and efficacy of the monastic legal system as a whole. As one senior jurist put it:

> We [jurists] try to end [disputes] only within [the monastic courts] themselves because we must protect the public's faith in us [monks] (*janatāvagē pähädīma*). Once you go to the state courts, it will be spread all over the newspapers, radio and television and become an embarrassment to the sangha.[18]

INTER-LEGAL ANALOGIES AND INTRA-LEGAL TRUST

Practices of legal pluralism help address these challenges. Rāmañña lawmakers and jurists carefully compare and contrast their laws with state law in ways that enhance monastic law's legitimacy and authority. As one senior jurist explained, Rāmañña legal experts aim to generate 'trust' (*viśvāsayak*) in the fraternity's legal system – a deep confidence in the fairness and integrity of that system such that 'it will be very rare for a monk not to accept the decisions that are given'.[19] This trust is cultivated through a range of codes, protocols, training programmes, educational syllabi, court records and jurisprudential manuals, all of which communicate in two registers at once. On the one hand, Rāmañña legal practices evoke the form, style and putative impartiality of state-legal authority. On the other hand, these practices remain deeply rooted in monastic legal traditions, drawing heavily on the Vinaya Piṭaka and other *vinaya* literature.

This twofold strategy of cannily comparing and contrasting monastic and state law at different times echoes that of the *katikāvatas* and nineteenth-century legal orders examined in Chapter 4 of this book. By harmonising the styles and idioms of monastic and state law,

[17] Question 10.8.
[18] Interview with justice in monastic Supreme Court 12 December 2019.
[19] Interview with monastic judge (*anuvijjaka*) near Colombo, 10 December 2019.

Rāmañña jurists today – like jurists in the past – underscore the complementarity between the two laws and court systems, using the authority of one to buttress the authority of the other. At the same time, monastic jurists take care not to push the comparison too far. They regularly clarify to fraternity members that Rāmañña legal cases are not simply state-style litigation in saffron garb but another species of adjudication entirely: one that is uniquely Buddhistic (S: *śāsanika*) and based on the Vinaya.

Double-Speak and Double-Law

It is important to note that the parallels between state and monastic law that Rāmañña jurists highlight – or downplay – are not the products of imposition or mimicry. They do not derive from pushing state-legal models onto monastic law under conditions of duress. Arguments like this – that treat religious legal traditions as passive recipients or opportunistic imitators of state law – appear widely in 'law and religion' scholarship.[20] When it comes to monastic law in Sri Lanka, however, such arguments distort the reality. When Rāmañña jurists speak of plaintiffs, evidence, verdicts, litigation and other terms, they do not simply borrow a state-legal vocabulary. Rather, they engage in a sophisticated form of double-speak, drawing on monastic and state-legal registers simultaneously.

This double-speak is possible because monastic and state-legal traditions already share fundamental similarities. The procedures, concepts and categories of adjudication used by Sri Lankan state-legal institutions – such as two-party litigation, the triadic structure of the courts, standards of evidence and other features examined below – bear striking resemblance to those found in the Vinaya Piṭaka and related *vinaya* literature. That is to say, many premodern monastic legal texts already exhibit the kinds of formalism, rationalisation, proceduralism and categorical thinking that scholars associate with the laws of modern nation-states. Indeed, if one were to trace the history of legal borrowing, the chronology would begin not with Sri Lankan state law but with the Vinaya.

These symmetries may simply be serendipitous, reflecting parallel developments across time and legal cultures. Or they may reveal perennial, cross-cultural patterns in the ways humans conceive and resolve

[20] For an excellent overview of this scholarship, see: Oraby and Sullivan, 'Law and Religion.'

disputes. Regardless of their origins, Rāmañña lawmakers and jurists – many of whom also have familiarity with state law – have actively leveraged these similarities to support and defend the integrity of the fraternity's laws.

MONASTIC COURTS IN SRI LANKA

All of Sri Lanka's monastic fraternities rely on a system of monastic courts (S: *saṅghādhikaraṇa*) for managing disputes among members.[21] In Sri Lanka's largest monastic fraternity, the Malvatu Branch of the Siyam Nikāya, the fraternity's executive council appoints a judicial council[22] headed by a judicial chief.[23] That council intervenes when local abbots or regional monastic leaders are unable to resolve a dispute themselves. To involve the judicial council, regional monastic officials must write a formal petition to the executive council, which the judicial chief reviews monthly. If the case is deemed significant, the judicial chief can appoint a subcommittee of the judicial council, consisting of two, three or four members. Those monks review the case at the fraternity's headquarters in Kandy, deciding which of the dozens of petitions received in a year will be given hearings.[24]

The Malvatu method for adjudicating disputes builds upon the fraternity's broader hierarchical structure, which is concentrated in its executive council located at the fraternity's headquarters in the ancient royal capital of Kandy. Rather than a routinised system of lower and higher courts, the Malvatu system relies, in the first instance, on more senior monks settling disputes among their juniors. Only when those interventions fail does the judicial apparatus kick in. The Malvatu court system is, thus, rooted in firm notions of hierarchy, in which power spreads from, but remains centralised in, the leadership in Kandy.[25] This hierarchical and centralised structure parallels the pyramidal structure of contemporary courts; yet it also resembles the

[21] The terms used to describe these bodies sometimes vary. The Kotte Chapter of the Siyam Nikāya, for example, uses the term *viniścaya sabhā* to refer to their courts. Interview with deputy prelate of Kotte Chapter, 19 December 2014.

[22] *Adhikaraṇa saṅgha sabhāva*.

[23] *Adhikaraṇa nāyaka*.

[24] Interview with deputy prelate of the Malvatu fraternity, Kandy, 30 July 2016.

[25] One younger Malvatu bhikkhu stressed to me [in English] the 'full power' that the great leader (*mahānāyaka*) of the Malvatu Chapter has to handle matters of indiscipline, underscoring that, ultimately, difficult judicial matters could be handled directly by him. Interview, Colombo, 21 July 2016.

hierarchical and centralised institutions of justice that were found in the Kandyan kingdom in the eighteenth century, during the fraternity's formative period of growth.[26] In the same way Kandyan legal authority radiated outwards from the king's palace, so too does Malvatu judicial authority radiate from the fraternity's head monastery.[27]

The Malvatu judicial structure is not the only model used in contemporary Sri Lanka. Among the officially recognised monastic groups on the island – with membership ranging from over 6,500 monks (as in the Malvatu) to fewer than 100 in the smallest fraternities[28] – one can find a variety of systems for managing disputes and arriving at authoritative decisions. Of these various monastic legal systems, the most developed and complex is that of the Rāmañña Nikāya, the island's second-largest self-governing monastic group, with approximately 4,000 monks and accounting for nearly 20 per cent of the island's total monastic population.

The Rāmañña Nikāya's legal system not only addresses the challenges of monastic discipline discussed above, but it also plays an important role in the fraternity's history and growth. More than other fraternities, Rāmañña monks have relied on their reputation for discipline to attract lay support and ensure institutional survival. Where older fraternities like the Malvatu received extensive land grants from kings prior to the nineteenth century, the Rāmañña Nikāya – which was formed in 1864 – did not exist during the period of major royal endowments. Few Rāmañña monasteries therefore have ample estates on which they can rely for income. Instead, Rāmañña monks have

[26] See, for example, D'Oyly, 'A Sketch of the Constitution of the Kandyan Kingdom,' 221–48. This link between the Kandyan kingdom and the Siyam Nikāya was a recurring theme among interviews conducted with Siyam monks. As one bhikkhu put it: 'Compared to the other *nikāyas* the traditions within the Siyam Nikāya are unique . . . they come from the royal era (*rajakālē*)'. Interview in Kandy, 20 December 2019.

[27] Thus, rather than the judicial committee hearing its cases in the regions where the dispute occurred, litigants must travel to the fraternity's headquarters in Kandy for a hearing. Similarly, the Malvatu's constitution requires that regional head monks (*pāḷāt nāyakas*) convey all dispute-resolution decisions to a central executive council in Kandy for confirmation (*sthira karanu*). Malvatu Chapter of the Siyam Nikāya, *Malvatu Katikāvata Saha Baṇadaham Pota (1921)*, 10, §9.7.

[28] These numbers come from a document obtained from the Department of Buddhist Affairs in 2013: Government of Sri Lanka, *Vihārasthāna hā Bhikṣūn Vahansē Saṅgaṇaya* [*Census of Bhikkhus and Temples*].

depended, for much of the fraternity's existence, on comparatively smaller donations of money, food and properties from the lay public.[29]

Rāmañña monks also had to cultivate new kinds of donor networks beyond the traditional high-caste aristocrats that sustained the older Kandyan fraternities. Although the founding members of the Rāmañña Nikāya spoke more about piety than caste, the Rāmañña fraternity was among the first groups to ordain men from all castes – defying long-standing restrictions that applied to the Siyam Nikāya and other groups. As such, Rāmañña monks appealed to a different base of lay supporters during their period of formative growth in the nineteenth century. In particular, they attracted support from the island's new middle-class traders and merchants living near the coastal entrepôts of Colombo, Galle and Matara (as described in Chapter 4). Rāmañña monks' popularity among this new donor-class was due, in no small part, to their reputation for the meticulous observance of monastic law secured by a well-functioning legal system.

THE RĀMAÑÑA NIKĀYA JUDICIARY

The procedures, structures and requirements for judging disputes in the Rāmañña Nikāya appear in the constitution (*katikāvata*) promulgated by the fraternity's founders in the 1860s, and amended multiple times since then. The current version (discussed in Chapter 2 of this book) situates the Rāmañña judiciary within a broader system of monastic governance, which includes a set of forty-seven regional sangha councils,[30] an island-wide administrative sangha council[31] with representatives from all the regional councils, and a fourteen-member executive council,[32] headed by the great leader (*mahānāyaka*) in which the 'executive power' of the fraternity is vested.[33]

29 Malalgoda, *Buddhism in Sinhalese Society*, 161–72. To some extent this is true for all fraternities without extensive properties. However, even wealthy institutions rely on lay patrons offerings meals to the monks.

30 *Prādēśika saṅghasabhā*.

31 *Pālaka saṅghasabhāva*.

32 The size of these representative bodies and this executive council (*kāraka sabhāva*) has grown over time.

33 *Vidhāyaka balaya*. Śrī Laṅkā Rāmañña Mahā Nikāya Pālaka Saṅgha Sabhā, *Śrī Laṅkā Rāmañña Mahā Nikāya Katikāvata [The Katikāvata for the Sri Lankan Rāmañña Fraternity]*, 50, §69(i).

The structure of the current Rāmañña judicial system is laid out in Chapter Twelve of the constitution, titled 'The Position of District Judge, Judicial Councils and the Composition of Their Duties'. Here, the *katikāvata* prescribes a multi-tiered system of courts (*adhikaraṇas*) arrayed from the regional to the national level, each with its own jurisdiction and procedures for appeal. Like the Malvatu model mentioned above, the Rāmañña system is overseen by a judicial chief,[34] appointed by the great leader of the fraternity in consultation with the executive council. Assisting him are the posts of chief judicial registrar and deputy judicial registrar,[35] who handle the daily administration of the system.[36] Judicial chiefs are usually very senior monks who serve as long as they are capable, or – as has been the case for three out of the four recent judicial chiefs – until they become the great leader of the fraternity.[37]

At the lowest level is a network of approximately fifty regional judges,[38] who are chosen by the executive council from among the members of the administrative sangha council. The constitution charges these judges with 'taking suitable steps for resolving and settling issues that are causing disagreements and disputes'. If a regional judge cannot settle the issue himself, he will call for the formation of a regional judicial committee[39] – a temporary body consisting of three regional judges appointed by the judicial registrar for the purpose of resolving a particular case.[40]

The constitution presents the duties of regional judicial committees as part-lawyer, part-magistrate. In their lawyerly role, judicial committees assist litigants – both accuser and accused – in preparing

[34] *Adhikaraṇa nāyaka*. The judicial chief must have at least twenty years' experience as a judge in the monastic Supreme Court or Senior Court.

[35] *Pradhāna-* and *nijōjya- adhikaraṇa lekhakādhikāri*.

[36] *Śrī Laṅkā Rāmañña Mahā Nikāya Katikāvata*, 76, §109(i-ii). The judicial chief is also a member of the executive council.

[37] Mātatē Dhammakusala, *Rāmañña Vaṃsaya [The Rāmañña Lineage]*, 32–33.

[38] *prādēśika anuvijjaka*.

[39] *prādēśika anuvijjaka maṇḍalayak*. *Śrī Laṅkā Rāmañña Mahā Nikāya Katikāvata*, 90, §130(ii).

[40] Regional judges are also organised into councils of regional judges (*prādēśika anuvijjaka sabhā*), which do not seem to play a collective role other than to help organise and coordinate the geographically dispersed group of jurists. On this body, see *Śrī Laṅkā Rāmañña Mahā Nikāya Katikāvata*, §132, p. 91.

'accusation papers', filing petitions and submitting responses to the court.[41] In their judge-like role, they either offer solutions to the conflict themselves or reinforce the orders made by higher courts.[42]

This dual function of regional judges conforms with prototypes taken *both* from the *vinaya* and state law. On the one hand, the role of regional judges is modelled on the role of examining judges (*anuvijjakas*) described in the Vinaya Piṭaka.[43] On the other hand, as several monastic judges affirmed to me during interviews, the work of regional judges closely resembles that of 'mediation boards' (*samatha maṇḍala*) operating under Sri Lanka's Ministry of Justice. Like the regional judges in Rāmañña judicial system, these boards consist of local citizens, usually retired professionals, who facilitate discussion and encourage disputants to accept shared principles of justice.[44] The parallel was strongly emphasised at the first judicial training workshop I attended: 'What we're hoping for [in monastic courts] is a settlement (*samathayak*).... Although we call it a court (*adhikaraṇa*), it's a settlement body ... it's similar to a *samatha maṇḍalaya*'.[45] The shared term, *samatha*, used both in the Pali Vinaya and in contemporary state-legal institutions, underscores this connection, referring to the peaceful resolution of a dispute in both contexts.

When regional judicial committees hear a case, the event is referred to as a regional court.[46] The Rāmañña constitution gives these courts the following mandate:

> Examining, formulating a settlement (*samathayak*) (a peace [*sāmadānayak*]) and implementing the required remedy for that settlement as it relates to any accusations (*cōdanā*) other than *uṭṭhāgāminī* and *chēdyagāminī* offenses [the two most serious types of monastic offenses],[47] namely

41 Ibid., 90, §130(iii).

42 Those decisions are called *adikaraṇa tīraṇa*. Ibid., 90, §130(iv).

43 See Chapter 2. See also: Schonthal, 'Buddhist Rules About Rules.'

44 For an ethnographic example of how these bodies work see: de Silva, 'Cultural Practice of Human Rights: An Anthropological Study of Human Rights in Sri Lanka,' 154–57.

45 Training seminar for monastic judges, Colombo, 28 December 2017.

46 *Prādēśikādhikaraṇas*, sometimes also referred to as 'minor adjudications', *khuddakādhikaraṇas*.

47 The earliest use of these terms – *uṭṭhāgāminī* and *chēdyagāminī* (P: *vuṭṭhāgāminī* and *chejjagāminī*) – appears in the commentary on the *Dīghanikāya* attributed to Buddhaghosa, *Sumaṅgalavilāsinī*, in a section discussing different ways in which the Buddha grouped regulations in the Vinaya. They are included as part of a triadic

> disagreements arising among monks or between monks and donors, or between monastic teachers and monastic students, concerning personal property or properties belonging to the triple gem; as well as any other matters that fall within the above-mentioned category as decided by the chief judicial registrar on instruction to the deputy judicial registrar.[48]

The jurisdiction (*bala sīmāva*) of regional courts and regional judges, like that of Sri Lanka's mediation boards, is limited to comparatively minor disputes. According to the legal framework of the Vinaya Piṭaka, these would also be disputes involving small disciplinary offences that do not need to be examined or rehabilitated in front of the entire monastic community.[49] For example, these disputes might involve personality clashes among two or more monks, or accusations that one monk transgressed a minor disciplinary rule (such as misbehaving in public). When a hearing is held, the relevant monks and judges are instructed to gather at an 'adjudication site'[50] that has been agreed upon by all parties and the executive council.[51] Given that minor disagreements are often handled informally by temple prelates, most regional judges do not hear many cases.[52]

contrast between *chejjagāminī*, *vuṭṭhānagāminī* and *desanāgāminī*, which imply, respectively, those offences that lead to being 'cut off' (*chejja*) from the sangha, those requiring rehabilitation (*vuṭṭhāna*) and those requiring simply some form of confession (*desanā*). *Chejjagāminī* corresponds with *pārājika* offences, *vuṭṭhānagāminī* with *saṅghādisesa* and *aniyata* offences, and *desanāgāminī* with the remaining offenses. It is notable that although *vuṭṭhānagāminī* and *desanāgāminī* appear elsewhere as a contrasting binary, for example in the *Samantapāsādikā*, *chejjagāminī* does not. T.W. Rhys Davids and Estlin Carpenter, *The Sumaṅgala-Vilāsini: Buddhaghosa's Commentary on the Dīgha Nikāya*, Vol i, 101.

48 *Śrī Laṅkā Rāmañña Mahā Nikāya Katikāvata*, 92, §134(i). The court is also responsible for recording the decision and sending it to the deputy judicial registrar of the *nikāya*, who then sends copies to the parties as well as other 'relevant regional monastic judges'. Ibid., §134(iii).

49 By 'small offences', I am referring to those offences that, according to the technical reasoning of the Vinaya, do not need to be managed through communal legal actions, or *saṅgha kammas*. For more on these legal actions, see Schonthal, 'Buddhist Rules About Rules.'

50 *Viniścaya sthānayak*.

51 Śrī Laṅkā Rāmañña Mahā Nikāya Pālaka Saṅgha Sabhā, *Śrī Laṅkā Rāmañña Mahā Nikāya Katikāvata [The Katikāvata for the Sri Lankan Rāmañña Fraternity]*, 90, §131(i).

52 Members of the Rāmañña judiciary have recently discussed the possibility of expanding the powers and influence of the regional judges so that they would be able to handle more significant cases that, at present, are heard by higher courts. Not

Above these regional courts sits a Senior Court[53] consisting of three senior judges,[54] selected from a roster of twenty-one. Like the regional judges, the senior judges are selected by the fraternity's executive council based on their experience and learning. The Rāmañña constitution gives the Senior Court the following powers:

> To settle, give decisions (*tīraṇa*) and administer the punishments prescribed in the Vinaya and in this constitution for transgressions relating to complaints involving: the control of movable and immovable property belonging to the *nikāya*, worship sites, the monkhood or individuals as well as a claim to the [position of] chief incumbent of the temple; [the disciplinary offenses of] moral failure, corrupting laypersons and doing evil actions[55]; and also requests and complaints that have been sent to the chief judicial registrar under the provisions laid out in §135 (ii) and (iii) [relating to the appeals process].[56]

According to the Rāmañña constitution, the Senior Court handles relatively serious matters, including property disputes and significant disciplinary infractions – although not matters severe enough to warrant suspension from the fraternity. The Senior Court hears conflicts over temple property or allegations that a monk has been drinking alcohol. The Senior Court also hears cases on appeal.[57] If either party in a regional court dispute – the accuser or the accused – is dissatisfied

only would this relieve some of the caseloads for higher courts, but Rāmañña jurists also expressed that dealing with disputes at lower levels was, generally speaking, preferable. A senior jurist, speaking at one monastic training, put it this way: 'By managing these problems within the regional courts, we can effectively shore up the base (*padanama*) of this fraternity. Doing this, gives us a chance to work on behalf of the fraternity, the executive council and to do everything properly (*hariyaṭa*) . . . the position of regional judge is therefore not secondary to any other role, but is in fact equal even to the Supreme Court'. Training seminar for monastic judges, Colombo, 28 December 2017.

53 *jyeṣṭhādhikaraṇaya.* 54 *jyeṣṭhānuvijjaka.*

55 These three are specific legal categories taken from *vinaya* literature: moral failure (*sīla vipatti*), corrupting laypersons (*kuladūsana*), doing evil actions (*pāpa samācāra*).

56 *Śrī Laṅkā Rāmañña Mahā Nikāya Katikāvata*, 94, §140(i).

57 Although monastic jurists often use the contemporary Sinhala term for appeal (*äpäl karanavā*), the Rāmañña constitution and related legal literature use the phrase *ukkōṭana*, taken from a term in *vinaya* literature that describes the 're-opening' of settled legal cases (*adhikaraṇa*).

with the ruling, they may petition the judicial registrar for an appeal within two weeks of the decision.[58]

At the apex of the Rāmañña judicial system is a Supreme Court[59] consisting of twelve senior monks who are appointed by the executive council along with the judicial chief and the chief judicial registrar. Like the lower courts, the Supreme Court convenes in three-judge benches. However, in exceptional cases, five justices may form a final panel[60] and issue non-appealable decisions.[61] According to the chief judicial registrar at the time of my research, less than 20% of all cases end up in Supreme Court with less than 5% requiring a final panel decision.[62]

The Rāmañña constitution defines the Supreme Court's jurisdiction as follows:

A. [Matters] concerning the membership of regional sangha councils;
B. [Matters] concerning the membership of the administrative sangha council as well as [the process of] selecting [members] for it;
C. [Matters] concerning withdrawing the studentship of monks and novices;
D. [Matters] concerning actions that go against the regulations in the constitution, whether by some activity done in the administration of the fraternity, or by a working committee, or a board or official;
E. [Matters] concerning the rejection of a Senior Court decision [made] without an appeal or the non-implementation of that decision;
F. Accusations that have been advanced concerning the rejection of *katikāvata*-consistent regulations [issued by] officials, executive councils or judicial councils who have been appointed for the administration of the fraternity;
G. Cases relating to decisions made by the Senior Court on appeal (*ukkōṭita*);
H. Cases relating to decisions [issued by] the Supreme Court on appeal that have been advanced with the hope that the decision [will be made by] a final panel of the Supreme Court of five justices;
I. All the questions that have not been addressed by another court in the fraternity which arise from time to time in [the process of those

58 *Śrī Laṅkā Rāmañña Mahā Nikāya Katikāvata*, 92–93, §135(i)–(iii).
59 *Uparimādhikaraṇaya.* 60 *Uttarītara uparimānuvijjaka maṇḍalaya.*
61 *Śrī Laṅkā Rāmañña Mahā Nikāya Katikāvata*, 97, §145(iii).
62 Interview with chief judicial registrar of Rāmañña Nikāya, Anuradhapura, 9 December 2019.

courts] adjudicating, examining or making decisions, including the related punishments that are prescribed in the Vinaya and this constitution.[63]

As can be seen, the Supreme Court is entrusted with the fraternity's most consequential legal matters, including membership disputes, dereliction of official duties and the removal of monks' status as students or novices. Although not stated explicitly, by empowering the Supreme Court to address 'all questions that have not been addressed by another court', the Rāmañña constitution also gives the apical judiciary powers to nullify the memberships of senior monks from the fraternity in cases where they have violated one of the four major *pārājika* offences. Notably, however, the court does not have any power to forcibly expel a monk from the temple. It can only rescind a monk's affiliation and request that the Department of Buddhist Affairs, which keeps records of monastic affiliation, adjust its records accordingly.[64]

Litigants unhappy with decisions given by the Rāmañña Senior Court can appeal to the Supreme Court within three weeks of the decision, in which case the Supreme Court judges may call for a new investigation, summon new witnesses or ask parties to clarify or resubmit their documents. The constitution specifies that the Supreme Court may then 'give its own decision, agree with the original decision, reject [that decision], change it or have that particular case reheard again by the original court'.[65]

In interviews and workshops, Rāmañña jurists pointed out the similarities between the fraternity's higher judiciary – its Senior Court and Supreme Court – and the higher judiciary in Sri Lanka's state-legal system. Both have appellate jurisdiction and multi-judge benches, and both are governed by clearly defined powers exercised by judges promoted from lower courts. Even the technical Sinhala language used to describe these bodies – terms like jurisdiction (*bala sīmāva*) and court (*adhikaraṇa*) – mirrors language found in Sri Lanka's national constitution.[66]

63 *Śrī Laṅkā Rāmañña Mahā Nikāya Katikāvata*, 96–97, §145(i).

64 Interview with former assistant commissioner of the Department of Buddhist Affairs, Colombo, 2 July 2016. See also, Weerasooria, *Buddhist Ecclesiastical Law*, 594–95.

65 *Śrī Laṅkā Rāmañña Mahā Nikāya Katikāvata*, 105, §151(v).

66 Government of Sri Lanka, *Constitution of the Democratic Socialist Republic of Sri Lanka (Amended 2015)*, Chapter XVI. The parallel structure of the state and

At the same time, the Rāmañña constitution blends these state-like elements with categories and content drawn from the Vinaya. The Vinaya, too, refers to hierarchies of authority and multiple opportunities for hearing a dispute.[67] The Rāmañña framework builds on these precedents. In fact, many of the legal terms employed in both Sri Lanka's state and monastic courts – including those for accuser and accused (*codakayā* and *cuditayā*), settlement (*samatha*), evidence (*sākṣyaya*), judge (*viniścakārayā*) and court (*adhikaraṇa*) – can ultimately be traced back to Pali legal terminology found in the Vinaya Piṭaka.

PROTOCOL AND PREDICTABILITY IN THE RĀMAÑÑA JUDICIAL SYSTEM

As elaborated in its constitution, the Rāmañña Nikāya's judicial system solves two organisational problems. First, it clarifies the institutions, officials and protocols for dealing with contentious matters that cannot be resolved informally or within the confines of a given monastery. This clarification is particularly important because the Vinaya Piṭaka, although it contains procedural rules for resolving disputes, does not provide a comprehensive blueprint for how to run a court system.[68] Second, the description of the Rāmañña judicial system also gives monks in the fraternity assurance that disputes will be handled in a fair, systematic and predictable way. As one jurist put it, the system ensures that the courts

> are not unfair and that there's no issue with the qualifications (*sudusukam*) of the adjudicating monks; that [judges] are approaching the facts in a non-partisan way and their giving decisions justly (*sādhāraṇava*).[69]

Rāmañña legal systems was taken for granted among most of the monks that I interviewed. As noted in Chapter 1, the Sinhala term for court, *adhikaraṇa*, traces to an analogous Pali term found in the Vinaya Piṭaka.

67 On notions of 'appeal' in the Vinaya, for example, see Kieffer-Pülz, 'Translocal Debates,' 2016–17. See also: Schonthal, 'Buddhist Rules About Rules', Section VII.

68 von Hinüber, 'Buddhist Law,' 21.

69 Interview with monastic judge (*anuvijjaka*) near Veyangoda 10 December 2019.

Monks I spoke with commented that this sense of impartiality and fairness was reinforced by specific rules embedded in the Rāmañña constitution covering the processes for making allegations and conducting trials. The Rāmañña constitution lays out in lengthy detail – twenty separate clauses – the precise requirements for making an accusation (*cōdanāva*) against another monk. Accusations can be issued against an individual monk or a monastic body (such as a council or committee) and can be issued either by monks or by laypersons. Importantly, both the target of the accusation and the accuser must be affiliated with the Rāmañña Nikāya.[70]

Accusations must take the form of written documents – referred to as charge sheets (*cōdana patrayas*) or petitions (*petsamas*) – which should be sent by registered post to the chief judicial registrar. Those documents outline the nature of the offence and include the names and addresses of the accusers and accused, along with any witnesses.[71] Following submission, the deputy judicial registrar must record the accusations in a logbook and notify the accused party by writing within one week. From there, the chief judicial registrar nominates three judges from the regional, Senior Court or Supreme Court (depending on the matter) to form a court.[72] The constitution lays out additional protocols for cases where a monastic judge is accused of an offence. In such situations, the case cannot be heard by close judicial colleagues and, for matters involving the highest judicial officials (such as the judicial chief), the chief registrar of the fraternity, rather than the chief judicial registrar, acts as presider.

A notable feature of the Rāmañña judicial system are the detailed provisions designed to discourage false accusations and provide remedies for monks whose reputations have been impugned. For example, the constitution explicitly gives authority to monks whose names have been slandered to confront their accusers and obtain a formal legal decision establishing their innocence and purity (*pāriśuddhiya*).[73] It also empowers the chief judicial registrar to review allegations, even in cases where charge sheets have not been

[70] In the case of lay accusers, they should be patrons (*dāyakas*) of a Rāmañña Nikāya temple.
[71] *Śrī Laṅkā Rāmañña Mahā Nikāya Katikāvata*, 97, §147(i); 100, §148(x).
[72] Ibid., pp. 98–99, §148(i)–(vi). [73] Ibid., p. 97, §147(iv).

submitted properly or accompanied by the required information. Doing so, the constitution indicates, helps 'protect the purity of monks and the faith (*śraddhāva*) of lay supporters'.[74] In such cases, the executive council of the fraternity can itself step in to discipline monks who make potentially baseless accusations as a way of protecting reputations and safeguarding the unity (*sāmagriya*, P: *sāmaggi*) of the sangha.[75]

Similar attention to detail and formality can be seen in the protocols judges must follow when conducting hearings. The constitution lays out a list of administrative requirements to which judges are supposed to adhere. These include distributing lists of witnesses, documents and other evidence to all judges and parties involved in the case and sharing any other charge sheets, petitions or 'response sheets' (*uttara patra*).[76] It also gives the chief and deputy judicial registrars powers to issue subpoenas (*kändavīmē ājñā*), with significant penalties if summoned monks do not attend.[77]

For Senior Court and Supreme Court cases, the constitution permits the appointment of 'trial-assisting monks' (*viniścaya sahāyakayan vahansēlā*) who help the litigating parties collect evidence, assess facts and negotiate the process of litigation. Trial-assisting monks also collaborate with judges to help them understand the context and issues being disputed.[78] Given the number of questions that arose during monastic workshops about the nature of this role – such as whether trial-assisting monks should be considered similar to lawyers or court clerks, or whether they should be specially trained in the Vinaya, or if lay lawyers can serve in the role – it seems that they are not used frequently in practice.[79]

GUIDELINES FOR (NON-)CONFRONTATION

In addition to the guidelines laid out in the Rāmañña constitution, monastic judges also receive specific training workshops on how to run

[74] Ibid., p. 97, §147(iii). [75] Ibid., p. 97, §147(v). [76] Ibid., p. 100, §148(xi).
[77] Ibid., p. 102, §149(i); p. 103, §149(v). [78] Ibid., pp. 103–4, §105(i)–(viii).
[79] It is interesting to note that, both in the trainings and one-on-one interviews, monastic judges voiced concern over the potential use of lawyers in the monastic legal context, frequently pointing to the perceived unethical behaviour of lay lawyers, who were seen as more concerned with winning cases than settling disputes or establishing the truth of a matter.

a hearing. At one such training I attended, the instructor led jurists through a booklet that described the process for conducting an adjudication in eleven steps:

1. At the very beginning of the procedure, separate the two parties – accuser/accused – and identify each of them.[80]
2. Obtain a list of names of the relevant persons on both sides who are required for the adjudication.
3. Mark down their birthday, the date of their robing, the date of full ordination, etc.
4. Take down the birthdays of the lay devotees.
5. Get signatures to confirm that [the above people] came.
6. If there are people who are not relevant to the case, remove them from the adjudication hall (*viniścaya śālā*).
7. Administer the five precepts to the lay devotees.
8. For monks, chant in the opening *gāthā*s, namely: [P:] '*sukho buddhānaṃ uppādo*' ('Happy is the arising of the Buddha').
9. Next, the head of the court should offer the moral advice (*dharmānuśāsanāva*).
10. Permission should be sought by the accuser from the accused to present the charge sheet, saying: [P:] '*ahaṃ taṃ vattukāmo, karotu me āyasmā ōkāsanti*' ('Venerable One, please grant me permission to speak'), [S:] [Meaning] 'I am accusing the Venerable One (*āyuṣmatun*) myself. May the Venerable One please give me permission.' Obtaining permission in this way, one should present the charge sheet.
11. With this accusation, [the parties] should be established in the accusation procedure (*cudita pratipattiyehi*).

Over the course of the training, several elements were emphasised, particularly the ideally non-confrontational nature of the proceedings. Unlike the agonistic setting of state courts, I was told, monastic courts aim to avoid conflict. Although the hearing format mirrors that of state courts – with the 'triadic structure'[81] of plaintiff, defendant and judge, along with the binary logic of accuser and accused – monastic judges stress that adjudication should not be a confrontational process. In fact,

[80] Instructions listed verbs in the gerund form, but I give them in the imperative for the sake of clarity. The rest mirrors the grammar of the sheet.
[81] Shapiro, *Courts: A Comparative and Political Analysis*.

except for the opening and closing formalities, where the formal accusation is laid and the trial is concluded, the accuser and the accused do not participate in the trial at the same time. Evidence is presented separately, and witnesses are examined on their own, privately by the judges.

Explaining the protocol, one instructor summarised:

> Judges should call witnesses and interrogate the evidence in such a way that they protect them [the witnesses] while also verifying their assessment [of the facts]. This means that one must bring in [the witnesses] one by one, without face-to-face questioning [by the litigants]. Only by doing it this way can one create an atmosphere that is not conflictual (*gäṭumak äti novena parisarayak*) and suitable for a similarly non-conflictual style of adjudicating.[82]

These themes – of discretion, protection, privacy, and avoidance of conflict – recurred throughout public discussions and individual interviews about monastic legal procedures. In fact, the very choreography and contents of the hearing were often described as ways of de-escalating and pacifying parties, rather than determining fault.

Another booklet distributed at monastic trainings[83] reminded Rāmañña jurists of the moral duties incumbent on the various parties involved in a case, quoting Pali passages from the Enclosing section (*Parivāra*) of the Vinaya (marked with P:) and giving Sinhala glosses (marked with S:):

> [P:] '*Cōdakēna kathaṃ paṭipajjitabbaṃ*' (How should [the procedure] be followed by the accuser?) | [S:] How must an accuser (complainant) comport oneself?
>
> 1. [P:] '*kālēna vakkhāmi no akālena*' (I am speaking at the right time not the wrong time) | [S:] Presenting the complaint having considered whether it is the appropriate (*sudusu*) time to do so.
> 2. [P:] '*bhūtena vakkhāmi no abhūtena*' (I am speaking genuinely, not falsely) | [S:] Presenting the accusation, [thinking] 'I am speaking only the truth about a thing that actually happened; I am not speaking lies about something that did not happen.'

82 Training seminar for monastic senior judges and Supreme Court judges, Colombo, 28 December 2017.

83 Training seminar for monastic judges, Colombo 14 December, 2018. Manual, 'Annual Seminar of Regional Court Judges.'

3. [P:] '*saṇhena vakkhāmi no pharusena*' (I am speaking softly, not harshly) | [S:] The accusation should be presented, [thinking] 'I am speaking in a delicate manner; I am not speaking with bitterness.'
4. [P:] '*atthasaṃhitena vakkhāmi no anatthasaṃhitena*' (I am speaking purposefully, not purposelessly) | [S:] The accusation should be made [thinking] 'I am making this accusation only out of a desire to do something meaningful, not meaningless.'
5. [P:] '*metta citto vakkhāmi no dosantaro*' (I am speaking with a compassionate mind, not out of anger) | [S:] The accusation should be made [thinking] 'I am accusing with a compassionate mind, not out of anger.'

During the training sessions, instructors emphasised both the Vinaya origins of these principles and their differences from state litigation procedures. Monastic judges, they explained, should not operate like civil court judges. They should conduct their inquiries in a discreet, private setting – not a public place – so as to minimise unwanted attention and embarrassment for the parties. Instead of rushing to determine fault, they should remind litigants of their ethical responsibilities to one another and encourage the moral dispositions necessary for resolving disputes harmoniously. They should press accusers not only to adduce facts but also to reflect on their own tact, compassion and intentions in bringing a claim in the first place. Defendants, they insisted, should be reminded to respond patiently and speak only about what happened and nothing else. Supremely important, the instructors made clear, was that a judge should avoid 'bias, hatred, fear or delusion' in writing their judgments and rely closely on dharma, *vinaya* and *sāsana*.[84]

A particularly significant aspect of the monastic adjudication process is the issuing of moral guidance (*anuśāsana*) at the outset of litigation. According to the judicial chief, this step gave judges an opportunity to remind litigants about the relevant *vinaya* principles, procedural steps and moral obligations at play – as well as the potential consequences, both material and karmic, of carrying on with the proceeding. Hearing these

[84] This phrase and these instructions come from a larger set of Pali verses visible in the *Parivāra*: *yena dhammena, yena vinayena, yena satthu sāsanena taṃ adhikaraṇaṃ vūpasammati tathā taṃ adhikaraṇaṃ vūpasametabbaṃ*. Meaning: A court case that is decided in accordance with the dharma, the Vinaya and the *sāsana* of the teacher, that is a case which will be resolved. Oldenberg, *The Vinaya Piṭakaṃ*, Vol. v, 161.

admonitions, he clarified to me in an email, generates a sense of pious despair (*saṃvega*) and fear (*kampana*) in devout monks, which encourages them to settle their disputes.[85] This point was underscored by an instructor at one monastic training who commended the audience:

> sometimes it happens that litigation may end simply by [giving] moral guidance (*anuśāsana*). One doesn't even need to hear the case. [The parties] just leave, saying 'we don't need this anymore.''[86]

CONDUCTING INQUIRIES

One notable parallel between the Vinaya Piṭaka and contemporary state-legal settings is the use of formulaic phrases and rigid syntactic structures to enact the authority of courts.[87] As seen in Chapter 2 of this book, the Vinaya Piṭaka treats the precise repetition of words as one of the three basic requirements for any successful legal action (P: *kamma*, S: *karma*), including the settlement of legal cases. This emphasis on syntactic regularity extends to the judicial examination of litigants and witnesses in Rāmañña Nikāya courts. While questioning may vary in practice, the ideal judicial interrogation – advocated by the fraternity – follows a prescribed script. A booklet from a 2019 training session illustrates this approach:

JUDGE: Are you accusing this monk?
ACCUSER: Yes.

[85] Email with judicial chief of Rāmañña Nikāya, 31 August 2021. It's notable that, although a discrete procedural step of *anuśāsana* cannot be found in the Vinaya's scattered accounts of judicial process, warnings about the existential and karmic dangers of misbehaving in an *adhikaraṇa* can be seen in the verses of the *Parivāra*, as well as other places. 'A person, who impugns [another] out of bias, hatred, fear or delusion, is a fool with damaged faculties who, upon the break-up of the body [at death] will go to hell.' Oldenberg, *The Vinaya Piṭakaṃ*, Vol. v, 161.

[86] Training seminar for monastic senior judges and Supreme Court justices, Colombo, 28 December 2017. It could be argued that a similar moralising (and conflict-diffusing) effect follows from the administering of precepts to laypeople and the chanting of verses that are used to commence the proceedings. In addition to these being conducted collectively (as opposed to the individual oaths given in state courts), the very contents of these chants highlight participants' shared moral universe.

[87] Danet, 'Language in the Legal Process'; Winn, 'Legal Ritual'; Richland, 'Jurisdiction.'

JUDGE: What type of offence do you accuse him of? Is it a failure of morality (P: *sīla vipatti*) etc.?
ACCUSER: It is a failure of morality / viewpoint / behaviour / livelihood? (P: *sīla/diṭṭhi/ācāra/ājīva*)[88] [the accuser chooses one or more].
JUDGE: Do you know what the failure was?
ACCUSER: Yes I know.
JUDGE: What was the failure?
ACCUSER: The offense that arose was ______.
. . .
JUDGE: Do you accuse [this monk] according to something you saw? Or heard? Do you doubt him?
ACCUSER: [chooses one or more][89]

Depending on the accuser's responses to the final question, the booklet recommends a series of follow-up queries. For example, accusers (or witnesses) who claim to have seen a monastic offence being committed ought to be asked the following details to 'confirm their accuracy':

What was seen?
How was it seen?
Who saw it?
Where did they see it?
Did they [actually] see the *pārājika* offense / *saṅghādisesa* offense / etc. committed?
Where were you?
Where was this monk?
What were you doing?
What was this monk doing?

[88] These different types of offences correspond with categories from the Vinaya. The authors of the booklet draw a further correspondence between the type of failure and the type of offence that relates to it: failures of morality (*sīla vipatti*) are linked with *pārājika* and *saṅghādisesa*, the two most serious types of offence in the Vinaya; failures of behaviour (*ācāra*) are associated with any offence other than *pārājika*; failures of viewpoint (*diṭṭhi*) correspond with the offence of holding heretical views (classified by the booklet using the Pali technical terms, *antagāhikādiṭṭhi* or *micchādiṭṭhi*); failures of livelihood (*ājīva*) relate to 'precepts relating to livelihood,' such as those that forbid monks from engaging in commerce and other trades.

[89] Script distributed at training seminar for monastic judges, Colombo, 29 November 2019.

As with other legal procedures examined earlier, the Rāmañña Nikāya rules for trials derive in clear and obvious ways from ancient templates found in the Vinaya Piṭaka and other sources. While the Vinaya does not give step-by-step instructions for judges in quite this way, it does provide lists of questions and criteria for examining cases. For example, one passage in the Enclosing portion of the Vinaya instructs:

> The accuser is to be questioned by the examiner (*anuvijjaka*): 'Sir, this monk who you are accusing, why are you accusing him? Are you accusing him for failing in his moral conduct? Are you accusing him for failing in [his] behaviour? . . . in [his] views?'[90]

The Rāmañña Nikāya legal curriculum draws on Vinaya passages like this, translating and organising them into fixed protocols and scripts that can be followed easily by monastic judges.

The resulting framework looks very much like the protocols of contemporary state courts, incorporating features like meticulously patterned behaviours, clear sequencing of events, standardised formats for inquiry and stereotyped lists of questions and affirmations (e.g., *How do you plead?*). These underlying symmetries allow Rāmañña monks to evoke two idioms of legal authority at once: that of state courts and that of the Vinaya Piṭaka legal settlements. In so doing, Rāmañña jurists reinforce not only the regularity, impartiality and adherence to 'due process' in monastic courts but also their deep grounding in Vinaya legal traditions.

CATEGORICAL THINKING AND ANALYTIC REGULARITY

Judicial procedures are not the only means by which the Rāmañña legal system disciplines and standardises the practices of judges. Through attendance at regular judicial trainings and the study of specialised booklets and handouts, Rāmañña jurists also gain fluency in a specialised legal vocabulary and system of categorical thinking. These categories, most of which come from the Vinaya or its major commentary, the *Samantapāsādikā*, include the following:

- **The four types of cases or disputes that might come before a monastic court**:
  1. disputes over the content of the Buddha's teaching;
  2. accusations of misconduct against a monk;

[90] Oldenberg, *The Vinaya Piṭakaṃ*, Vol. v, 160.

3. disagreements over the nature and severity of an offense that was committed;
4. and conflicts over whether a particular legal action (*karma*) was properly performed.[91]

- **The six facts that should be given special consideration during an adjudication**:
  1. the facts of a case;
  2. the lists of rules contained in the *Pātimokkha*;
  3. the word-analyses that appear in the Explanations section of the Vinaya;
  4. the three-fold casuistic analysis of offenses;
  5. the possibility of secondary offences committed while undergoing penance for another offense;
  6. and the circumstances under which the deed might not be considered an offense.[92]
- **The three types of grounds (*vatthu*) on which an accusation is made**:
  1. grounds that were seen;
  2. grounds that were heard;
  3. grounds that are doubted.
- **The two foundations (*mūla*) for accusations**:
  1. grounded accusations made by persons who directly saw the transgression;
  2. and ungrounded accusations 'made by someone who saw something else associated with the transgression'.
- **The four ways of knowing the Vinaya**:
  1. through the entire text of the Vinaya Piṭaka itself;
  2. through 'the four great standards' (*mahāpadesā*) of juristic interpretation[93];

[91] In Pali: *vivādādhikaraṇam*, *anuvādādhikaraṇa*, *āpattādhikaraṇa*, *kiccādhikaraṇa*.

[92] This list of six – *vatthu*, *mātikā*, *padabhājanīya*, *tikapariccheda*, *antarāpatti* and *anāpatti* – can be found in the *Samantapāsādikā* as part of a list of factors that an expert adjudicator should consider.

[93] These can be found at Oldenberg, *The Vinaya Piṭakaṃ*, Vol. i, 250-251. Kieffer-Pülz translates them as follows:

1. If something is not prohibited as unallowable, but agrees with what is unallowable, then it is unsuitable.
2. If something is not prohibited as unallowable, but agrees with what is allowable, then it is suitable.
3. If something is not allowed as allowable, but agrees with what is unallowable, then it is unsuitable,

3. through the doctrine of the teachers preserved in the commentary;
4. and, if all else fails, through clarifying the matter based on one's own 'reasoned and systematic understanding' of the other three sources.[94]

- **The four duties of a judge**:
  1. knowing the Vinaya (in the fourfold manner above);
  2. having 'exhaustive knowledge of the Vinaya and its commentaries including its vocabulary';
  3. being 'humble but not timid' about one's grounding in the Vinaya;
  4. and knowing about the lineage of eminent teachers that come through the Vinaya and its commentaries.
- **The seven ways of producing a legal settlement** (*samatha*):
  1. through face-to-face litigation;
  2. through a verdict of innocence;
  3. a verdict of insanity;
  4. a confession of guilt;
  5. a majority vote;
  6. a declaration of another's recalcitrant wrongness;
  7. or through 'covering the matter over with grass' and moving on from the dispute.[95]

As presented in training booklets and judicial workshops, these categories serve two primary functions. First, Vinaya categories help jurists

4. If something is not allowed as allowable, but agrees with what is allowable, then it is suitable.

Kieffer-Pülz, 'Translocal Debates,' 112.

94 These sources are *sutta* (referring to the Vinaya as a whole), *suttānulōma* (that which conforms with the Vinaya), *ācaryavāda* (the doctrine of the teachers) and *attanōmati* (one's own opinion), respectively. See Kieffer-Pülz, 'Translocal Debates,' 113–14. The booklet from which I quote also gives a list of authoritative texts one should study. This includes 'accounts of accusations etc.' taken from the twelfth-century summary of the Vinaya, the *Palimuttakavinayavinicchaya* (also known as the *Vinayasaṅgaha*); the seventeenth-century Burmese sub-commentary on that text (the *Vinayālaṅkāraṭīkā*); a collection of essays on *saṅghādhikaraṇa*, some imported from earlier published and unpublished works, published in 2017 under the auspices of the Rāmañña fraternity called *Saṅghādikaraṇa Lekhana Saṅgrahaya*; and the Vinaya commentary, *Samantapāsādikā*.

95 As several jurists pointed out to me during our discussions, the imagery in this last category is of covering over faeces after defecating. These seven methods and their Pali equivalents in the Vinaya Piṭaka are discussed briefly in Chapter 2 of this book.

to identify and dissect key features of a legal dispute, a process Geertz refers to as 'skeletonising' cases.[96] Confronted with the messiness of a real-life conflict, the above categories provide a framework for organising judicial reasoning and prioritising particular features of a case. By classifying a case as one of the four types of disputes, for example, judges know immediately which of the seven settlement options may be used.[97] Similarly, by consulting the four ways of knowing the Vinaya, jurists can hierarchically grade the various sources of monastic law that might apply to a given issue.

Second, the very fact of knowing such categories provides a way for monastic judges to demonstrate their expertise to litigants and peers. Even the ability to explain the six factors that one should consider in a monastic litigation communicates a high level of competency in *vinaya* literature. Thus, by referring to these factors in a hearing or a written judgment, monastic jurists assert their own legal expertise.

Judicial trainings for Rāmañña monks serve as opportunities to build and demonstrate that expertise. Many judicial trainings – including all of those I attended – include a session dedicated to analysing hypothetical cases. These cases offer complex (even extreme) examples of disputes, often touching on several issues at once, such as property, misconduct, conflicts of law and other matters. The following is a summary of one such case:

> The chief incumbent of a monastery dies. His most senior student (student 1), who has been overseas for ten years, returns to Sri Lanka to request incumbency. The local monks and board of trustees (*dāyaka sabhāva*) oppose this and favour the deceased incumbent's second most-senior student (student 2) who has served as his deputy for many years. During the temporary handover of incumbency that occurs at the funeral,[98] student 2 is given control. Student 1 protests this and, asserting his claim to incumbency, begins to cut down and sell off trees that were on the monastery property without any permission. There are also allegations of other misconduct, including the use of alcohol. A formal charge sheet is sent by the monastery's board of trustees to

[96] Geertz, 'Fact and Law in Comparative Perspective.'

[97] For more on this correlation between cases and settlements in the Vinaya, see Chapter 2 of this book.

[98] The technical term here is the *prāpta saṅgha* – meaning the group of monks who gather together at the funeral of a deceased monk. It is an important concept in Rāmañña legal thinking that was regularly invoked in legal cases and judicial trainings.

> the judicial registrar. How should this be solved according to both the dharma and the constitution of the Rāmañña fraternity?

While there are many interesting observations to be made about this hypothetical case – including the role played by lay trustees and the balance between seniority and morality as measures of authority – for our purposes, what is interesting is the way the judicial training booklet advised judges to parse this complex conflict using several categories.

In a series of tables dissecting the example, the matter was classified as an 'accusation case' consisting of four discrete charges, each of which was linked to a particular category of offence. For each offence, the authors specified the type of 'failure' that had occurred. Cutting trees, for example, was linked to the offence of theft, which was associated with a failure of morality, the punishment for which could be removal from the community. The booklet advised jurists that if student 1 accepted his charges, the nature of the case would shift to another kind of case, a 'disagreement over the category of offence', in which case the important action was to decide on which categories of offence matched the facts. (For this, the four ways of knowing the Vinaya would be important.) If the accused party did not admit to the offence, and if the facts proved his culpability, judges were enjoined to settle the matter according to 'a declaration of another's recalcitrant wrongness', one of the seven types of settlement.

This kind of categorical thinking is, of course, not unique to Buddhist legal sources. It can be found throughout Buddhist philosophical and didactic literature as well: from the four noble truths, to the threefold baskets of teachings, to the long lists of qualities and sub-qualities that form the core of the Abhidhamma Piṭaka, the canonical 'basket' most concerned with metaphysics. Similar kinds of categorical thinking can also be found in state-legal regimes, for example, in the various categories of cases and penalties (e.g., civil versus criminal) or types of jurisdictions (e.g., territorial versus personal), and so on.

In the Rāmañña legal order, these two traditions of categorical thinking – one taken from Buddhism and the other from the common law – intersect in a way that amplifies features of both. For instance, Rāmañña legal texts refer to both 'judgments' (*tīraṇa* or *tīndu*) and 'settlements' (*samatha*) using categories from the common law and the Vinaya.[99]

[99] The use of *tīndu* to refer to the decisions of a monastic court has a much longer history, dating back to the 1850s, as seen in Chapter 2.

As deployed in legal manuals, and as used by monastic jurists, the two categories not only interfuse (being used as synonyms in many cases), they also evoke different features of the event that concludes a legal dispute. When monastic jurists spoke about 'decisions', they elicited the idea of official, written documents that announced the outcome of litigation. When they spoke about 'settlements', they cast light on the act of pacifying disputes. A similar pattern can be seen in jurists' twinned use of the state-legal term 'appeal' (S: *äpäl kirīma*) and the Vinaya-derived term for 're-opening' a dispute (P: *ukkoṭana*), each of which calls attention to a different aspect of relitigating an issue in another setting. The former highlights recourse to a higher decision-making body, while the latter stresses the undoing of a prior settlement. Rather than one system imposing on the other, this play of lexemes reflects a felicitous alignment, a productive symmetry between monastic and state law, which enables Rāmañña jurists to practise legal pluralism in an integrative – and institutionally useful – way.

WRITTEN RECORDS AND JUDICIAL DECISIONS

The productive alignment of monastic and state law is particularly visible in the instructions given to Rāmañña judges regarding the writing of judicial decisions. As might be expected, the Vinaya Piṭaka and its major commentaries do not provide instructions for documenting judgments in writing. While nineteenth-century manuscript archives do contain examples of monastic legal decisions – as seen in Chapter 4 of this book – the prototypical structure of contemporary Rāmañña court decisions echoes that of Sri Lanka's state courts.

Rāmañña Nikāya court judgments are official-looking documents, typed in formal Sinhala on fraternity letterhead (complete with a seal), using numbered paragraphs and long case numbers reminiscent of those seen in civil courts (case number '/' year). In the offices of some of the monastic judges I visited, I observed piles of monastic case files stacked in locked glass cabinets, using the same manila-coloured folders commonly seen in the chambers of civil court lawyers and judges. Among the anonymised case files and legal materials that I was able to consult, I noted striking similarities with the format, contents and style of monastic and state-legal briefs.

The written records of law are of tremendous importance to the Rāmañña Nikāya. This can be seen clearly in the Rāmañña constitution, which devotes multiple sections to explaining the proper way to handle documentation relating to all parts of monastic life: from confirming a monk's ordination status, to recognising an official position in the monastic administration, such as chief incumbent. The importance of documentation could also be seen at the judicial trainings that I attended, and the special attention directed to structuring and writing legal judgments. In a pamphlet handed out at one of these trainings, judges were instructed to include all of the following elements in their written decisions:[100]

- Details of the cause (*nimitta*) of action,[101] the place and date of adjudication, and the presiding judges;
- an account of the facts presented by the accuser and the accused;
- a summary of the evidence presented by witnesses for both sides;
- a clarification of the nature and size of the offence based on consideration of the evidence, e.g., whether it is a failure of morality or conduct, etc;
- a summary of the relevant principles within the Vinaya Piṭaka that, in the judges' opinions, relate to the offence – such as whether it be might considered to be a *pārājika* or *saṅghādisesa* offense, etc. – as well as a summary of principles that confirm and/or disconfirm that opinion;
- a summary of the relevant provisions in the fraternity's constitution including their article and clause numbers, relating to the offense;
- a consideration of whether there is a tradition (*sampradāyak*) in the fraternity that might influence the judge's reasoning.

Written judicial decisions, the instructor clarified, should present these elements sequentially. If the case was heard on appeal, he went on, the decisions of lower courts should also be summarised. Although the decision is written up by only one of the judges on a judicial committee (designated as 'secretary' for that particular bench[102]), the judgments are expected to be unanimous. Once written, Rāmañña courts deliver

100 Taken from worksheet distributed at a training seminar for monastic judges, Colombo, 14 December 2018, and discussed.

101 An example of this was given in the discussion. A *nimitta* might be: 'Judgment about the incumbency of monastery ____.' Training seminar for monastic judges, Colombo, 14 December 2018.

102 As mentioned above, with the exception of a full bench of the Supreme Court, all monastic courts meet in three-judge panels called judicial committees (*anuvijjaka maṇḍala*) in which one monk serves as chairman (*sabhāpati*) and one monk as writer (*lekhaka*yā).

their verdicts as formal recommendations to the chief judicial registrar, who, with the authorisation of the fraternity's executive council, communicates the judgment, and any associated judicial orders, to the relevant parties.[103]

For the most part, judicial decisions in the Rāmañña Nikāya are private documents, shared only among litigants and judges before being archived by the fraternity. As such, their imagined audience is relatively small: litigants, monastic judges, senior members of the fraternity and civil court judges who might review the decisions if a civil action is filed. However, from time to time, important verdicts also appear in other places, including national newspapers, the fraternity's periodicals, or books written by important jurist monks. Examples of five very short written decisions appear, for example, in *The Illumination of the* Sangha *Courts* (*Saṅghādhikaraṇa Jotikā*) described in Chapter 2. I have translated one of these judgments – a shorter decision that does not follow all the steps above but gives a sense for the tone and structure of a monastic court decision – in the appendix to this chapter.

INNOVATION, CONSERVATION AND SUPPLEMENTARY SANCTIONS

Legal authority in the Rāmañña court system involves the careful balancing of several sources of law: the Vinaya Piṭaka and related literature, the written *katikāvata* of the fraternity, and the unwritten long-standing traditions (*sampradāyan*) of the Rāmañña Nikāya. As described by members of the fraternity, these sources ideally work in complementary ways, insofar as the fraternity's constitution and its disciplinary traditions are understood to be based on the Vinaya Piṭaka.

Nevertheless, in practice, certain sources take priority for certain matters. For example, when it comes to disputes over leadership roles – such as the hypothetical dispute over chief incumbency in the sample case above – the Vinaya Piṭaka and its commentaries do not provide clear guidance, given the absence of similar offices in those texts. In those cases, the fraternity's constitution and traditions will play a more influential role in determining outcomes. The Rāmañña constitution and traditions also take priority for certain contemporary social issues, such as the explicit prohibition on Rāmañña monks

103 Interview with senior monastic judge (*jyeṣṭhānuvijjaka*) near Panadura, 14 December 2019.

participating in politics – a *katikāvata* rule that itself codifies tradition-based norms. By contrast, the Vinaya Piṭaka and its commentaries take precedence in many other issues, especially matters of monastic comportment or the correct performance of legal actions.

This is not to say that the modern Rāmañña legal system simply fills the gaps left by the Vinaya Piṭaka and its commentaries. In the process of adjudication, judges interpret *vinaya* norms in a modern light. Consider, for instance, a discussion about the appropriate punishment for monks who drink alcohol that occurred at one monastic training. As seen in Chapter 2 of this book, the Vinaya classifies the offence of drinking alcohol as a relatively minor offence, requiring only confession. Despite this fact, one workshop speaker argued to his audience that, in the context of modern Sri Lanka, such a sanction might be reconsidered, given the heavy reputational risks for the fraternity if monks drink alcohol and the associated loss of essential lay support it could provoke. Given these risks, the monk urged, judges should think practically (*prāyōgikava*) about the damages of alcohol consumption and acknowledge that, although it was a minor infraction in the Vinaya, this offence could have more-than-minor implications for the fraternity in the present day.[104]

Another way in which the Rāmañña legal system innovates is in its administration of penalties, which combines the authority of Vinaya Piṭaka and *katikāvata* in striking ways. Given the challenges of enforcing monastic law described above, the fraternity has developed supplementary sanctions that incorporate aspects of the Vinaya's punishments but in a way that acknowledges the authority of the fraternity's constitution and addresses the contemporary challenge posed by monks who refuse to 'see' their transgression. The first such sanction is the 'prohibition on association' (*sambhoga tahanama*), which serves as a kind of general punishment designed to chasten those monks who refuse to comply with the *katikāvata*, the judgment given by a sangha court or the orders given by 'a legally authorised sangha council or official'.[105] As defined in the glossary section of the Rāmañña constitution, the sanction is

> [i]ntended to be a prohibition order[106] that is administered – through an announcement signed by the judicial chief with the permission of the

[104] Training seminar for monastic judges, Colombo, 17 December 2018.
[105] *Śrī Laṅkā Rāmañña Mahā Nikāya Katikāvata*, 6 §3 (xxxxvii).
[106] *Tahanam niyōgaya*.

> great leader – as a way to prohibit a poorly disciplined bhikkhu who is required to undergo monastic legal sanction from participating in the dharma or material resources of the sangha[107] together with his other monastic peers until he has completed the appropriate legal action such as the banishment action.[108]

As explained by senior jurists in the fraternity, *sambhoga tahanama* seems to be a catch-all phrase incorporating many types of probation described in the Vinaya.[109] It is perhaps most similar to the punishment of *brahma daṇḍa*, the total exclusion of an offender from all activities and interactions with other monks – a penalty so serious that it was described by one jurist as like being 'dead to the sangha'.[110] If, after undergoing this penalty, the offending monk remains defiant and fails to 'return to restraint',[111] he may be given 'the punishment of expulsion',[112] which nullifies his membership in the fraternity – an outcome not described in the Vinaya, but seemingly essential in the context of contemporary Sri Lanka, where one's monastic status is not only a sangha matter but a state-legal one as well.[113]

107 *Dharmāmiṣa ṣambhōga no karana.*

108 P: *tajjanīya. Śrī Laṅkā Rāmañña Mahā Nikāya Katikāvata*, 105, §152.

109 In particular, the restrictions covered under *sambhoga tahanama* seem to be associated with the 'fivefold' penalties of *tajjanīya kamma* (blame action), *nissaya kamma* (guidance action), *pabbājanīya kamma* (banishment action), *paṭisāraṇīya kamma* (summons-to-reconcile) and *ukkhepanīya kamma* (suspension action, of three types). Suspension actions, which are considered the most serious, require monks to observe a series of forty-three severe restrictions while also being practically and symbolically excluded from the communion and referred to as those who 'belong to a different communion' *nānā-saṃvāsaka*); so serious are the restrictions that monks who interact, support or live with those undergoing suspension actions will themselves be considered as though they are suspended and belonging to a different communion. On these fivefold penalties, see Nolot, 'Studies in Vinaya Technical Terms IV-X.'

110 Interview with chief judicial registrar and senior jurist, Colombo, 20 December 2017. This punishment was famously imposed on the Buddha's charioteer Channa, who refused to listen to the admonishments of other monks. According to multiple accounts in the Vinaya Piṭaka and Sutta Piṭaka, the Buddha instructed that 'Channa may say what he wants but he is not to be spoken to, instructed, or admonished by the bhikkhus'. The accounts describe that it was the shock caused by this penalty that eventually led Channa to gain enlightenment. Notably, this penalty is not described as a routine sanction used in the sangha, other than in this one instance. Ṭhānissaro Bhikkhu, *The Buddhist Monastic Code*, Vol. ii, 1058.

111 *āyati saṃvaraya.* 112 *nerapīmē dandavama.* 113 See Chapter 2.

Although similar to the prohibition on the association, the Rāmañña constitution prescribes a separate penalty for monks who were proven to have committed defeat-worthy (*pārājika*) offences but failed to accept them. These monks are declared to be 'dubious' (*śaṅkanīya*), a status that the constitution describes as follows:

> *Śaṅkanīya:* Following the judicial investigation of an accusation of *pārājika* made against a bhikkhu, if a judicial committee proves logically that an accused bhikkhu has lost his monastic status (*bhikṣutvaya*) and the accused refuses to accept that [decision], the judicial committee has the power to determine him to be a 'dubious (*śaṅkanīya*) individual.' This does not indicate that his impugned monastic status is in doubt by the judicial committee, [rather] it means that he does not have any monastic status. Any monk who is determined to be *śaṅkanīya*, following the publication of that [determination], they are no longer accepted as an ordained bhikkhu, and all the duties and rights relating to the accused become voided. If [the court] determines that the accused is unfit [for the sangha], after adjudicating an accusation of this type, it is accepted that all the duties and rights possessed by that bhikkhu are nullified.[114]

Here too, the Rāmañña judicial system draws from and augments the various sanctions offered in the Vinaya, in this case creating a constitutional sanction for those who are proven to be *pārājika* but do not consent to that finding. This power to blend Vinaya and fraternity-based sanctions is acknowledged explicitly in the Rāmañña constitution, which grants judges the ability to 'issue punishments taken from the Vinaya for monks who are found guilty of those offences as well as [to issue] punishments taken from the *katikāvata* for monks who violate [the *katikāvata*'s] regulations'.[115]

In addition to aligning (and contrasting) monastic and state-legal elements, therefore, the Rāmañña court system also blends together distinct bodies of monastic law. In their design and implementation of monastic courts, Rāmañña lawmakers bring together elements of the Vinaya Piṭaka (and related literature), *katikāvata* and the customary traditions of the fraternity. These intra-monastic practices of legal pluralism are acknowledged and celebrated by monks in the

114 Śrī Laṅkā Rāmañña Mahā Nikāya Pālaka Saṅgha Sabhā, *Śrī Laṅkā Rāmañña Mahā Nikāya Katikāvata [The Katikāvata for the Sri Lankan Rāmañña Fraternity]*, 6–7 §3(L).

115 105 §152(ii).

fraternity: the Vinaya Piṭaka is considered to be the foundation for Rāmañña law, *katikāvata* clarifies the terms of its application in the present, while *nikāya* traditions encompass important customs that developed over time.

A key motif that recurred throughout the judicial trainings that I attended was the importance of ensuring conformity to these three sources of law when judging legal cases. Speakers insisted that the best judgments – those that would be convincing to litigants and most resistant to contestation by them – were those that precisely documented passages from the Vinaya and *katikāvata* and applied them appropriately to the different elements of a case. In one such training, the speaker advised judges to write their decisions as follows:

> [First] clarify the facts according to the Vinaya Piṭaka . . . Is [the matter] a defeat offence (*pārājika*)? Is it a probationary offence? Next, clarify the facts according to the *katikāvata*. . . This should happen according to this section of the *katikāvata* . . . Then mention the [page] numbers to prove it. Following that, mention any traditions in the fraternity that might apply. . . If we write a report like that, citing the *katikāvata* and the Vinaya [and the traditions], it will be both clear and accepted [by the litigants].[116]

Harmonisation, integration and citation of legal sources is as much a necessity for Rāmañña judges as it is for state-court judges. Commenting on this need for citation, one speaker commented at a workshop for Senior and Supreme Court judges: 'There were no page numbers when the Tipiṭaka was written on palm leaves. Now that they've been printed as books, there are page numbers. When we record evidence or give responses, we should provide [those page numbers] . . . it's necessary'.[117] The same speaker also warned participants that, when copying legal sources, 'Do not write even one extra word!' so that there are no disputes over the accurate use and interpretation of the law.

Although oral evidence is permissible according to the Vinaya, Rāmañña judges were encouraged to prioritise written documentation. One discussant at a workshop in Colombo offered the hypothetical example of an alleged assault in a temple, explaining that, even if

[116] Training seminar for monastic judges, Colombo, 14 December.

[117] Training seminar for monastic senior judges and Supreme Court Justices, Colombo, 17 December 2018.

eyewitnesses could testify that the victim fell accidentally, documentary evidence such as medical reports must be gathered just in case the matter ended up before a civil or criminal court.[118] Another jurist stressed that even the precise meaning of words ought to be clarified in cases where there might be unintentional ambiguity or a shift in meaning over time or in a different context.[119]

The need for monastic courts to maintain a clear written record was a recurring theme in both trainings and interviews. Jurists were reminded that monastic legal records need to match the standards and conventions of state-legal records, given the ever-present possibility that a case might be reviewed by a civil court. This focus on written precision, systematicity, referencing and comprehensiveness – as well as the protocols, procedures and categorical thinking described above – encourages a fastidious style of writing designed to satisfy not only monastic concerns about dharma and *vinaya* but civil concerns with process and procedure.

CONCLUSION

As outlined in the Rāmañña constitution as well as in the worksheets, handbooks and speeches shared at judicial trainings, Rāmañña judges practise legal pluralism in ways that both resist and embrace the parallels between monastic and state law. They resist them in their emphasis on the distinct methods and goals of monastic law, which differ from those of the state courts: rather than guilt, they pursue reconciliation; rather than punishment, they seek concord; rather than upholding legality, they protect unity, morality and dharma. At the same time, monastic lawmakers and jurists also invite comparisons

118 Training seminar for monastic senior judges and Supreme Court Justices, Colombo, 17 December 2018.

119 Interview with monastic Supreme Court justice, near Colombo, 12 December 2019. In making this point, he recounted a story, based on a similar example from a commentary on the Vinaya, of a coconut shell that was stolen in Kandy but then sold in Colombo. The senior judge explained that a proper jurist must consider whether the coconut's value – which is essential for determining the severity of the theft – should be based on the price in Kandy or Colombo. Another senior jurist that I interviewed stressed that a monastic judge must carefully choose the words he uses to describe the qualities or actions of a monk, making sure that the language invoked is simple yet precise. Interview with monastic senior judge, outside of Colombo, 14 December.

between Rāmañña and state law, pointing out their common structures, terminology and concerns for regularity. For its users, this seems to amplify the sense of predictability, systematicity, fairness and impartiality that characterises the fraternity's court system – drawing on the familiarity or prestige of the state-legal structures to communicate the reliability and authority of monastic ones.

Together, these dual practices of legal pluralism – one stressing similarity, the other difference – help to coordinate two modes of legal authority that have salience and status in the eyes of Rāmañña monks: those associated with the state and those associated with the Buddha. Rāmañña jurists place monastic law 'on the scale' of Sri Lankan law while, at the same time, highlighting its superior, more-than-human status.[120] In so doing, they not only broaden the ground of legal legitimacy for Rāmañña jurists but also maintain the doctrinally essential distinction between *vinaya* and other forms of worldly law (a dynamic I examine in Chapter 7 of this book). These two modes of legality merge in the unique form of double-speak employed by Rāmañña jurists, which draws on the shared vocabularies of Vinaya and Sri Lankan law and communicates multiple messages about the relation between the two: a sense of mutuality and overlap, juxtaposition and difference, or some combination of the two.

These practices are powerful, at least when it comes to perceptions about the integrity and legitimacy of Rāmañña law. Although this chapter draws mainly on prescriptive sources, rather than everyday observations of monastic courts, the Rāmañña monks and lay supporters with whom I spoke viewed these sources with pride. They spoke approvingly about the fraternity's 235-page constitution and its judicial trainings, which appear to be unique on the island. For supporters, these artefacts demonstrate the fraternity's commitment to discipline and restraint (S: *hikmīma, saṃvaraya*) while also bringing esteem to the Rāmañña Nikāya. As one senior monk put it, 'if we run [this legal system] in a highly organised manner, I think that all the other monastic fraternities [and lay persons] will have special respect for Sri Lanka's Rāmañña Nikāya... We must therefore take pride in that [system] and protect it well.'[121]

120 This attitude appears to be widely shared among the sangha, given that 83 per cent of the monks I surveyed agreed that 'vinaya rules and traditions provide a better way of resolving common disputes than state law', Question 10.7.

121 Interview with monastic judge (*anuvijjaka*), Colombo, 17 December 2017.

These practices also raise certain questions about the broader methods and aims of Buddhist monastic life. How does one square this complex world of legality with monks' ultimate goal of nirvana? It is to this question that I will return in Chapter 6.

Appendix: Example of a Written Decision Given by a Rāmañña Nikāya Senior Court

Senior Court Decision on the Position of Chief Incumbent for Ven. X*

When making an appointment to chief incumbent, one must consider especially whether the pupils whom the deceased monk mentored (*antevāsikas*) or the residents whom the chief monk ordained (*saddhivihārikas*) are appropriate for the position, as indicated in the 2nd section of the 63rd article [of the *katikāvata*]. Following the order [specified] there, the primary place should be held by the pupils whom the monk mentored. If there is no suitable (*sudusu*) figure among them, the monk should then consider the residents whom the monk ordained, as a second option. If there are no suitable figures even among those residents, the monk should find another suitable person.

The Hambantota Regional Sangha Council does not seem to have given consideration to this constitution [the Rāmañña *katikāvata*] and the sequence [of consideration] and qualifications that must exist for the role of chief incumbent. It is clear in the judgment (*viniścaya*) that Ven. X is not the former pupil of [the deceased incumbent] but one of the residents he ordained.

Moreover, it was revealed in the judgment that Ven. X doesn't even possess the qualifications indicated in the 4th section of the 62nd article. For this reason, the appointment of Ven. X to the chief incumbent position of Monastery Y by the Hambantota Regional Sangha Council is cancelled on the authority of the Sri Lanka Rāmañña Mahānikāya sangha court, under the first section of the 66th article [of the *katikāvata*].

With this, [the complainant] Ven. A is appointed to the chief incumbent position because he was the [deceased monk's] primary

* Note: I have anonymised the names of parties to the litigation contained in this record for purposes of discretion.

antevāsika pupil and had been appointed temporarily to the position of chief incumbent of the above-mentioned monastery under clause 'a' of the revised first section of the 63rd article of the constitution by the committee of monks that met on the day after the cremation of [the deceased incumbent]; he also has all of the qualifications clarified in the 62nd article of the constitution.

With this, before the terms listed in the 3rd section of the 63rd regulation, the position of chief incumbent [we] assign to Ven. A who, as the correct novice student, was correct [for the role.]

In this matter,
1. Veväldeniyē Mēdhālaṃkāra Maha Sthavīra
2. Mirissē Dhammasiri Mahā Sthavira / Jyeśṭha Anuvijjakavaru
Date 1985-08-14

CHAPTER SIX

LAW'S KARMAS

Nirvana, Rebirth and the Cosmological Consequences of Monastic Law

What does law *do*? Common answers are that law ensures justice, discipline, order, control, predictability, coordination, security, and social harmony. Although specifying different kinds of human actions, answers like these nevertheless converge on a single idea: law exists *to regulate* society, to impose a certain structure on it.

For many, regulation is the defining feature of law. According to the theory of law known as legal positivism, what distinguishes law from other human activities is its 'positing' of a command, an order to be heeded. Across most domains of government and scholarship, positivist notions of law remain the dominant, even if unstated, point of view. A certain positivist approach to law can be found, for example, in Chapter 5 of this book. There, I showed how practices of legal pluralism – which aligned monastic and state-legal structures – helped to address problems of compliance in the Rāmañña fraternity, increasing the likelihood that litigants will heed the decisions of monastic judges.

Regulation, however, is only one purpose of law. Viewed holistically and historically, law also contains many other functions and facets. In his well-known article 'Nomos and Narrative', Robert Cover makes the case for viewing law not simply as a tool for 'social control' but as an interpretive framework – a world – in which humans live.

> [Law contains] not only a *corpus juris* but also a language and a mythos ... [which] establish paradigms for behaviour [and] build relations between the normative and the material universe, between the constraints of reality and the demands of an ethic. These myths establish a repertoire of moves,

> a lexicon of normative action – that may be combined into meaningful patterns culled from the meaningful patterns of the past.[1]

For Cover, and the many who have been influenced by him, a narrowly regulatory understanding of law overlooks its many other 'world-creating' powers: its stories, histories, humour and utopianism – its evocation of a broader cosmology through which communities find meaning, purpose and redemption.

These broader features of law – what Caroline Humfress, following Marianne Constable, refers to as law's 'nonpositivist possibilities'[2] – appear clearly in the writing of legal historians and socio-legal scholars. Fernanda Pirie, in particular, cautions scholars not to assume that, where one finds legal texts, those texts necessarily served as tools of regulation.[3] While this may be true in some cases, Pirie identifies a large number of other legal sources – from *fiqh* and *shari'a* in eighteenth-century Yemen, to *dharmaśāstra* in ancient India, to the Tang Code in imperial China, to the various codes produced by German, Frankish and Anglo-Saxon rules in early medieval Europe – which, although filled with specific rules and sanctions, were neither composed nor deployed primarily as instruments of governance. The significance of these laws, Pirie argues, lies less in their practical enforcement than in their symbolic and ideological value. They are expressions of civilisation, erudition, transcendence, cosmic order, piety, collective memory and group identity – not just collections of commands.[4] The same, I suggest, is true of Buddhist monastic law.

Monastic Law beyond Legal Positivism

In this chapter, I explore some of the *nonpositivist* features of monastic law, its purposes beyond maintaining discipline and order. In making this case, I draw primarily on sixty semi-structured interviews with Buddhist monks conducted between 2015 and early 2020. Interviewees came from a range

[1] Cover, 'Foreword: Nomos and Narrative,' 9.

[2] I take this phrase from Caroline Humfress, who is citing the work of Marianne Constable: Humfress, 'Legal Pluralism's Other'; Constable, *Just Silences*.

[3] 'Law before Government: Ideology and Aspiration', *Oxford Journal of Legal Studies* 20: 207–28 (2010). See also Pirie, *The Anthropology of Law*, Chapters Three, Four and Seven.

[4] Pirie, 'Law before Government,' 216–22.

of backgrounds. Most were from the Rāmañña Nikāya and served as monastic judges at the regional, Senior Court or Supreme Court levels. Others were senior monks with administrative roles within the fraternity: heads of monasteries, experts in *vinaya* and high-ranking members of their fraternity's executive councils. A smaller number were non-specialist monks from a variety of fraternities, including younger monks studying at universities around the country, with whom I met in focus groups or during one-to-one sessions. In analysing these interviews, I also draw on findings from other sources used in this book: the island-wide survey of Buddhist monks, ethnographies of monastic judicial trainings and investigation of monastic legal sources.

As I will show, monastic jurists speak about much more than regulation. They present themselves as preserving unity, unanimity and harmony in the sangha. They are said to serve as models of Buddhist virtues – equanimity, compassion and humility – who can inspire piety in those who have lapsed in their discipline. They work to protect the Buddha's legacy in the world (the *sāsana*), enhance the positive karma of those around them and support others' progress towards nirvana.[5]

For all its symmetries with Sri Lankan law, the Rāmañña legal system presumes much broader frames of reference than the country's constitution or civil courts. More than just regulating human society, monastic law also implicates expansive conceptions of space, time and human action: the cosmos as well as the country, countless lifetimes as well as recent events, ultimate salvation as well as human misconduct. What Rebecca French once observed in Tibet, one might also observe in Sri Lanka: monastic law implicates a 'legal cosmology' that extends beyond the here-and-now and connects acts of judging with a broader set of 'myths, relations of power, concepts of time, space and personal identity, legal rituals, history, religious principles, reasoning patterns, procedures, available roles, symbols'.[6]

Practising Pluralism *within* Monastic Law

This chapter considers this larger legal cosmology and its influence on how monks practise legal pluralism – how they bring order and

[5] In his textual study of the Vinaya Piṭaka, Holt makes this point clearly, showing how the rules of the root text form a system that embodies the dharma and prepares one for nirvana. Holt, *Discipline: The Canonical Buddhism of the Vinayapitaka.*

[6] French, 'The Cosmology of Law in Buddhist Tibet,' 97.

meaning to their state of normative complexity. Rather than focusing only on practices that juxtapose or align monastic law with state law, as I have in previous chapters, here I focus on practices that balance the diverse purposes and goals *internal* to monastic laws themselves – practices that relate regulation and salvation, order and morality, procedure and karma, communal harmony and nirvana.

The chapter begins by examining the process of becoming a monastic judge. It then analyses several key principles and themes – many of them soteriological and cosmological in nature – that recurred in discussions about how monastic judges ought to practise their craft. These include ideals of unity, salvation, harmony, karma, defilement, impartiality, rehabilitation, empathy, purifying the mind and lay-monastic reciprocity. By foregrounding these and other nonpositivist dimensions of monastic law, I hope to give readers a fuller view of monastic legal thought and practice and to show that, in Cover's terms, monastic law is much more than a *corpus juris*, a body of rules to be followed. I argue that monastic law's users emphasise not only its regulatory function but to its 'world-making' dimensions: its role in safeguarding the Buddha's dispensation, shaping karmic trajectories across lifetimes, acknowledging human fallibility, defining the proper qualities of a dharmic life and making possible the attainment of nirvana – both now and in the future.

LEARNING THE VINAYA, BECOMING A JUDGE

Knowledge of the monastic legal system is a kind of specialised knowledge that one pursues above and beyond the normal education that monastics receive in *vinaya* literature. In addition to learning about the Vinaya and its related literatures from abbots and teachers in monasteries, the topic of monastic discipline, *vinaya*, is also taught as a mandatory subject in monastic training institutes, or *pirivenas*, around the country. Although the content varies from site to site, training programmes generally follow a syllabus that mixes direct passages from the Vinaya with readings from handbooks, compendia, manuals and secondary sources about the history of the *sāsana* and *vinaya* literature. (On these categories of texts, see Chapter 2 of this book.)

While much more can be said about formative *vinaya* training for monks within and outside of *pirivena* settings,[7] most respondents that

[7] See, for example, Samuels, *Attracting the Heart*.

I interviewed underscored the importance of developing disciplinary knowledge incrementally. Most often, they spoke about the formative importance in their youth of learning the *sekhiya* rules, the seventy-five precepts in the Vinaya Piṭaka relating to everyday conduct, as well as the routines and duties of monastery life (known as *vat piḷivet*). These practical, behavioural dimensions of monastic life feature prominently in many of the preparatory books that a prospective or newly ordained novice monk is encouraged to study – such as the various versions of the *Preaching and Dharma Book for Novices* (*Sāmaṇera Baṇa Daham Pota*), a training manual containing the basic instructions, concepts, principles and chants required of novice monks (discussed in Chapter 2).

For those seeking higher qualifications in *vinaya*, further study is possible through a combination of advanced *pirivenas*, monastic universities, state universities and private education providers. One interviewee described his own academic progression, earning successive qualifications: first being certified as knowledgeable (*vedi*), then as an instructor (*ācāriya*), then as a master (*viśārada*).[8] Monks who demonstrate their mastery of *vinaya* literature through a system of exams and among their peers may be recognised as '*vinaya* experts' (*vinayadharas*).

Although beneficial for monastic judges, ascending to the highest level of formal education is not a requirement for becoming a regional court judge. Rāmañña law has no fixed list of educational qualifications for the role, other than the requirements that the candidate must be a member of the governing council of the fraternity – a position available to all 'disciplined' *bhikkhus* who have maintained good standing with the fraternity for at least ten years.[9] Relevant sections of the Rāmañña

[8] These titles appear to come from certificates given to monks who pass specialised exams. Unlike the state-sponsored monastic exam systems in places like Thailand and Myanmar, this particular exam system is offered through a private education provider, the '*dharmadīpa* institution', as well as through other monastic education centres, including monasteries, with certificates granted by senior monks. Thank you to C.R. de Silva for helping identify this. Interview with chief incumbent monk, Kandy, 27 June 2019. On monastic education in Sri Lanka more broadly, De Silva, 'The Education of Buddhist Monks in Sri Lanka: A Historical Review and Some Suggestions for Reform.' On monastic education in mainland Southeast Asia, see Dhammasami, *Buddhism, Education and Politics in Burma and Thailand*.

[9] *Śrī Laṅkā Rāmañña Mahā Nikāya Katikāvata*, 130, 89, §49(ii).The title *sthavira* (P: *thera*) applies to a bhikkhu who has been in robes for at least ten years following

constitution (*katikāvata*) state simply that a prospective judge must be 'suitable' for the role, a quality that one judge described as follows:

> Unlike becoming a judge or lawyer [in the state system] there are no written exams to determine monastic judges. The primary requirement is a monk's suitability (*sudusukama*): He must be a good person (*honda kenek*) living in accordance with the Vinaya, and free from any obvious flaws. He should be focussed; if he can't speak [confidently], he won't be able to handle a case; he should be someone with the proper personality; he should have the ability, the personality [for it]. This is [what I mean by] suitability.[10]

Similar qualities were stressed by other monks whom I interviewed. What makes a good judge, according to respondents, were attributes such as tolerance, discipline, confidence, impartiality and a general tendency towards honest, frank, direct (*avaṅka*) speech.[11]

Rather than applying for judicial positions, prospective judges are selected by senior monks in the executive council from among active members of the governing council who embody these attributes.[12] New judges serve seven-year renewable terms, with the possibility of promotion within the legal hierarchy. All of the senior jurists that I interviewed started as regional court judges and worked their way up through the system, including the current judicial chief.[13]

In many ways, training for the Rāmañña judiciary happens on the job. Newer judges are encouraged to learn the required skills from more experienced judges who serve on the decision-making panels. One senior judge put it this way:

> It's like this: in the early period, we only learned [about the Vinaya] so that we could pass the exam. But when one's working [in monastic law] practically, we come to understand the use and meaning of it. I studied it around the age of 20 or 25, when I was at university; I was learning it then. But it wasn't until I was 40 or 50 that I became part of the process

ordination, and the title *mahāsthavira* (P: *mahāthera*) applies to a monk who has been in robes for at least twenty years.

10 Interview with monastic judge (*anuvijjaka*) near Veyangoda, 10 December 2019.

11 Interview with monastic judge (*anuvijjaka*) near Moratuva, 17 December 2019.

12 Interview with monastic senior judge (*jyeṣṭhānuvijjaka*) near Colombo, 18 December 2019.

13 Interview with the chief judicial registrar, now judicial chief, of the Rāmañña Nikāya, Anuradhapura, 9 December 2019.

> of monastic litigation (*adhikaraṇa kriyāvaliya*), under the judicial chief, which is to say I engaged with it on a practical level. That's when I engaged with this practically, not just learning about it. That's when I knew I had the desire and the ability to protect the *sāsana* in this way.[14]

In recent decades, this practical learning has been supplemented by judicial training workshops. Since at least 2014, these trainings have been happening two or three times a year, with judges from lower and higher courts meeting to discuss matters of protocol, process, jurisprudence and other topics. As alluded to in Chapter 5, organisers of these trainings have also produced booklets and worksheets to assist judges. By most accounts, the regularity and intensity of judicial trainings have increased over the years.[15] In addition to adding more workshops to the roster and developing a wider range of booklets, the Rāmañña judicial leadership has also invited civil court judges and lawyers to provide instruction on legal reasoning and offer overviews of relevant civil laws, such as the Buddhist Temporalities Ordinance and Buddhist Ecclesiastical Law.[16]

JUDGING JUDGMENTS: THE PLURAL PURPOSES OF LAW

Rāmañña monks characterise the purposes of monastic law in multiple ways, which include and exceed the concerns about regulation discussed in Chapter 5. Although interviewees affirmed monastic courts' role in maintaining order and shaping conduct, they also described the ideal outcomes of adjudication in different terms. Most commonly, they framed adjudication as a process of pacification and calming aimed at resolving conflicts through consensus rather than coercion. The very language of 'settlement' or *samatha*, which is used in the Vinaya and Rāmañña legal institutions, encourages these associations.

During my interviews with monastic jurists and the hours I spent at judicial training workshops, I was repeatedly struck by the strong

[14] Interview with senior monastic judge (*jyeṣṭhānuvijjaka*) near Panadura, 14 December 2019.
[15] This was reported to me in multiple interviews.
[16] Interview with monastic Supreme Court justice, near Colombo, 12 December 2019.

emphasis on mediation and finding common ground. More than half of the jurists I interviewed defined a 'good' settlement or judicial decision as one in which both parties agreed to the outcome. As noted in Chapter 5, some expert jurists might even resolve disputes pre-emptively – before the litigation begins – by simply offering moral admonitions (*anuśāsana*) to the litigants.

Monastic judges thus portrayed their courts as different to the imagined functioning of civil courts. Whereas civil courts create winners and losers, they said, monastic courts create consensus.[17] Whereas civil courts take a 'person-centric' (*pudgala kēndrīya*) approach, monastic courts pursue 'uplift for the *entire* community'.[18] Monastic law, in this framing, is not just an expression of communal harmony but an active instrument in its realisation. As one jurist explained to me, skilful monastic judges bring litigants together and restore their inseparable union, binding them together as though they were mixing water and milk into a single liquid.[19]

Sāmaggi/Unity

Using the technical language of the Vinaya Piṭaka and its commentaries, Rāmañña jurists speak about monastic courts as protecting the unity and unanimity of the monastic community, a quality known in Pali as *sāmaggi* and in Sinhala as *samagrīya*. *Sāmaggi* denotes unity in the strongest possible sense, as a unison both of bodies and minds. It is a condition in which all monks in a given monastery live together harmoniously in a spirit of common purpose. *Sāmaggi* connotes both a social and legal condition. It is not only a quality to which communities ought to aspire but a requirement for the legitimate conducting of legal actions or *karmas* (discussed in Chapter 2).[20] The importance of

17 Interview with *anunāyāka* of Koṭṭē Chapter of Siyam Nikāya, near Colombo, 9 December 2014.

18 Training seminar for monastic judges (*anuvijjakas*), Colombo, 28 December 2017.

19 Training seminar for monastic judges (*anuvijjakas*), Colombo, 28 December 2017. This echoes a famous quote from an important Sri Lankan chronicle, the Cūḷavaṃsa. Kemper, 'J.R. Jayawardene, Righteousness and Realpolitik,' 203.

20 In an interview with the two senior legal officials in the fraternity, I asked the question of what the most important thing was that lay society could learn from monastic law; *sāmaggi* was the answer. Interview with chief judicial registrar and senior jurist, Colombo, 20 December 2017.

sāmaggi as a goal of adjudication was described this way by the head of a monastery in Kandy:

> In the *sangha* [court] the aim is not to have one side lose, but to create a settlement for everyone . . . so that after the mistake (*varada*) is accepted, everyone unites together as a sangha and works together for *sāmaggi*. You can't say 'this person can't come back because of the mistake he made.' Now, this might be the case in civil law . . . but that's not the case here.[21]

Even though litigation might expose a litigant's mistakes, its purpose was not fault-finding (a goal the speaker associated with state courts) but unity-building, restoring a fractured community back to a state of *sāmaggi*. The centrality of *sāmaggi* to the Rāmañña fraternity is even visible in the seal of the fraternity, which appears on all official documents, and bears the motto: *sukhā saṅghassa sāmaggī*, meaning 'happy is the unity of the sangha'.[22]

This focus on *sāmaggi* also implies a broader concern with the welfare of the monastic community, beyond the resolution of individual grievances or the rectification of individual harms. Jurists described their role as one of expressing, protecting, and restoring a unified sangha by illuminating the dharma and *vinaya* and by scrupulously reconstructing events as they occurred.[23] They spoke about exposing the truth – in both the empirical and moral sense – as a consensus-generating act, thought to bring all reasonable and disciplined monks into concord.[24] One jurist explained that, unlike civil courts – which separate law and fact from justice – monastic courts treat them as inseparable.[25] Monastic courts, another explained, were not public spaces for advancing

21 Follow-up interview with head monk (*lokuhāmuduruvo*) of a monastery, Kandy, 28 July 2019.

22 This verse can be found in the Dhammapada, verse 194: *sukho buddhānam uppādo sukhā saddhammadesanā; sukhā saṅghassa sāmaggī samaggānaṃ tapo sukho*. Meaning: 'Happy is the arising of the Buddha, happy is preaching of the true dharma; happy is the unity of the sangha, happy is ascetism of those who are unified.' Carter and Palihawadana, *The Dhammapada*, 250.

23 Training seminar for monastic judges (*anuvijjakas*), Colombo, 14 December 2018.

24 'A fair decision will make both parties happy.' Interview with monastic judge (*anuvijjaka*) near Veyangoda, 10 December 2019.

25 Interview with senior monastic judge (*jyeṣṭhānuvijjaka*) near Kandy, 28 June 2019. Interview with monastic judge (*anuvijjaka*) in Kandy, 19 December 2019.

clever arguments but 'covered spaces' designed to determine the truth and avoid embarrassment.[26]

Echoes of *sāmaggi* also appear in the way monks speak about the interpretive parameters of monastic law. Present in many conversations was the idea that the Vinaya itself guided jurists towards consensus. Properly understood, they argued, the text does not yield an array of competing interpretations but instead leads towards a singular, correct conclusion. The more knowledge one had about the Vinaya, the more likely their conclusion would be correct. According to this logic, the pyramidal structure of courts within the fraternity reflected not so much a cascading set of authorities, each with its discretionary powers, but a system of oversight that deepened *sāmaggi* by ensuring that monastic jurists came to adopt the same high-level understanding of the Vinaya and monastic law. Given that the monastic law might be less transparent to less-experienced readers, it was essential, jurists argued, that the decisions about monastic discipline should be reviewed by more senior authorities – such as *jyeṣṭhānuvijjaka*s or *vinayadhara*s – whose expertise helps sustain and deepen *sāmaggi*.

Compassion, Discretion, Tact

In addition to fostering and securing *sāmaggi*, many monastic jurists identified the cultivation of virtuous behaviours – such as compassion, tact, and discretion – as a central goal of monastic law. These qualities, they emphasised, flow from *sāmaggi*: skilled judges encourage litigants to see each other not as competitors but as temporarily estranged members of a single group, all pursuing nirvana. As one instructor advised attendees of a judicial training:

> [Remember] that the accuser, the accused and all of us who are present share a common goal in the end: that goal is understanding the ultimate dharma and freeing ourselves from the stress (*dukkha*) of *saṃsāra*.[27]

Given these shared goals, he urged judges (as well as litigants) to be considerate and committed to assisting others on their journey towards nirvana. Another senior jurist put it this way:

[26] Interview with senior monastic judge (*jyeṣṭhānuvijjaka*) near Panadura, 14 December 2019.

[27] Training seminar for monastic judges (*anuvijjakas*), Colombo, 28 December 2017.

> When one is a judge and taking the seat of judgment (*viniścaya āsanaya*), he should ... have extreme patience towards whomever [he is judging]. No matter what, it's not good to show any lack of consideration for a person. He should have a pleasant look on his face and work in a way that shows compassion and sympathy, especially to the person who had done the offence, the accused (*cūditayā*). [The judge] should build faith in [the accused's] mind about the court (*adhikaraṇaya*). Then, in every situation, [the judge] should listen attentively to [the accused], showing respect for the Buddha's dharma and *vinaya*, and without showing any disdain for him. He must listen with the utmost attention. It's not good to cut someone off by making some sign with your mouth or your eyes. [A judge] must not do those things. He should not speak while stretching out his legs or arms – he must be in the habit of doing all his duties with extreme discipline and patience.[28]

In this rendering, the ideal jurist cultivates patience, humility and sympathy with both body and mind: he smiles, follows process, listens attentively, shows respect and avoids interruptions and distracting gestures. These displays convey empathy and compassion to the litigants, encouraging them to see the court as a site of concern rather than conflict.

Qualities like these are explicitly mentioned in the instructions that jurists give to monastic accusers at the outset of litigation. Before proceeding with their formal complaint, judges ask accusers to consider the timing, motivations and goals of making an accusation (see Chapter 5). One instructor at a judicial training explained that *how* a litigation is conducted can be as significant as the outcome of adjudication itself:

> If you talk about [a dispute] somewhere [publicly], such as at a bus stand or on a road, you can't solve it. Therefore you should discuss it at a correct and suitable time only.[29]

The principle of 'a correct and suitable time' extends to the mental and emotional state of the accuser:

> Now, sometimes when someone makes a complaint, their mind might be scattered and disorganised, or upset and turbulent. And when I look at it later, I recognise that, because of your stress, the complaint was wrong ... or that it wasn't done in the right way. You understand that

[28] Interview with monastic senior judge, outside of Colombo, 14 December.

[29] Training seminar for monastic judges (*anuvijjakas*), Colombo, 28 December 2017.

> after the fact. Therefore, when you make a complaint, one has to do so in the right mindset, not in a state of mental distortion (*vikṛti manasak nätuva*) or stress; [it must be done] with a serene mind and having given it proper consideration.[30]

Visible in quotes like these are concerns not just with the correct application of judicial protocols but with the recognition and cultivation of 'skilful' (*kusala*) dispositions and intentions, which are essential to progressing towards nirvana. Rather than being portrayed as a contest between antagonistic agents with opposing agendas, the ideal monastic court was described as a venue where temporarily estranged peers were reminded of their mutual obligations and common values.

SKILL IN QUESTIONING

Given the importance of proper mindsets and intention to the litigation process, many interviewees insisted that judges ought to be both sympathetic and discerning in assessing the motives of an accuser, bearing in mind that the goal of accusation was not punishment but 'correction' (*niväradi kara gänīma*).[31] Monastic judges do this by gathering and evaluating information in a certain way. Even more than in civil court cases, monastic judges stand at the centre of hearings: they compile the case files, request evidence and call the witnesses. Litigants may be supported by trial-assisting monks, but it is the monastic judges who ask the questions. This places a significant burden on monastic judges, given that they are responsible both for resolving the case and for ensuring the well-being of participants.

Monastic jurists described the judicial inquiry process as having two major aims: protection (*ārakśāva*) of the parties involved and the pursuit of truth (*satyabhāva*). Perhaps for this reason, they spoke of approaching monastic cases with different assumptions than they would in a state-legal case. Whereas state courts reward craftiness and cunning, they insisted, monastic courts value candour and honesty. Consider, for example, this exchange I had with two very senior jurists in the Rāmañña fraternity, when I asked them about the difference

30 Interview with monastic judge (*anuvijjaka*) near Moratuva, 17 December 2019.

31 Interview with senior monastic judge (*jyeṣṭhānuvijjaka*) in Colombo, 10 December 2019.

between state law and monastic law in the administration of justice (*sādhāraṇatvaya*):

BHIKKHU 1: Yes, in Buddhist law there is justice.
BHIKKHU 2: Justice is given priority. Under state law, it's totally OK to lie as long as you can prove it with evidence.
BHIKKHU 1: With so much technical stuff (*tākṣaṇika dēval*) [in state law], even a lie can be turned into fact. Lies can be made real. But that's not possible here.[32]

This kind of sentiment – that monastic courts encouraged truthfulness more than state courts – carried through many of the conversations I had with jurists. Although monastic courts do not administer oaths, they begin with the chanting of verses and the recitations of moral admonitions. If laypersons are party to the case or asked to give evidence, judges will administer the five precepts, one of which requires the precept-taker to commit to avoiding lies. These rituals reinforce a shared moral commitment to honesty and warn, directly or indirectly, of the karmic consequences of lying. As one monk put it, 'if you lie, even about a small thing, it is something that affects your whole life, your entire [journey in] *saṃsāra*'.[33]

This is not to suggest that jurists are naive to the possibility of distorting facts. Several monks told me that, although most monks were truthful in the days of the Buddha, deception had become more common in the modern world. As described in workshops and by interviewees, the ideal monastic judge should cut through such dishonesty through, for example, limiting the time given to assertive, voluble monks to present their cases, while extending the time given to more timid and shy litigants. One young *vinaya* expert at a training session framed the judge's role in this way:

> Judges (*anuvijjakas*) should be able to recognise aggressiveness and acrimony on the side of the accusers and skilfully take steps to control that. If not [those accusers] might use their abilities in rhetorical force and wordplay to pervert the workings of the case and confuse the matter such that an effective solution cannot be given to deal with the issue. Therefore, you should carefully scrutinise and recognise the reality of the

[32] Interview with chief judicial registrar and senior jurist, Colombo, 20 December 2017.

[33] Interview with senior monastic judge (*jyēṣṭhānuvijjaka*) near Panadura, 31 June 2019.

> persons that are involved in the issue. If one party is weak (*durvala*), encourage them and assuage their fear. Conduct your inquiry with them thoroughly, respectfully, asking about the injustice (*asādhāraṇaya*), as it relates to them. If there are parties that are speaking harshly or bitterly or playing with words or trying to create a conflict, you should be able to control those people.[34]

During interviews and workshops, jurists mentioned a variety of strategies they used to determine the truth. The head monk of a monastery in Kandy analogised the matter to a parent judging a child: just as a mother distinguishes truth from fiction in the stories of her children, so too should judges compassionately but scrupulously distinguish fact from fiction among litigants.[35] One participant at a judicial training for higher court judges suggested that his peers ask the same questions multiple times over consecutive days, paying special attention to any inconsistencies in the details given.[36] Several jurists emphasised the importance of verifying claims against other forms of documentation, such as police reports or medical certificates, if they are available.[37] Other jurists advocated a more meticulous scrutiny of the actual statements made by witnesses using a set of probing follow-up questions – including those advised by the Enclosing section of the Vinaya discussed in Chapter 5.[38]

At a training for higher court judges, one well-known monastic jurist cautioned the attending judges that when words are presented to them in a case, orally or in written form, they 'put aside how we [judges] would understand that word' and instead treat the language in a highly contextual way.[39] He admonished that a careful judge always

[34] Training seminar for monastic judges, Colombo, 28 December 2017.

[35] Follow-up interview with head monk (*lokuhamuduru*) of a monastery, Kandy, 28 July 2019.

[36] Training seminar for senior monastic judges (*jyeṣṭhānuvijjaka*) and Supreme Court Justices in Colombo, 28 December 2017.

[37] Training seminar for senior monastic judges (*jyeṣṭhānuvijjaka*) and Supreme Court justices in Colombo, 17 December 2018. This imperative was confirmed to me by the chief judicial registrar who agreed in an interview: 'we do not accept [evidence] that cannot be proved'. Interview with two senior monastics, both members of the Rāmaññā Nikāya in Colombo, 20 December 2017.

[38] Interview with monastic judge of the Rāmañña Nikāya Supreme Court (*uparimādhikaraṇaya)* near Kandy, 20 December 2019.

[39] Training seminar for senior monastic judges (*jyeṣṭhānuvijjaka*) and Supreme Court justices in Colombo, 17 December 2018.

scrutinises the intended meaning behind a term, especially when that term can have multiple denotations. Even the word bhikkhu can have many meanings, he warned.[40]

Another senior jurist praised the value of experience, referring to a well-known story in which the Buddha, in one of his past lives, served as a judge. In that story, two women claimed to be the mother of an infant, and the judge was tasked with determining the rightful parent. To determine the correct one, the judge asked the claimants to take hold of the child's legs and arms and engage in a tug-of-war. When one claimant refused and started to cry, the judge recognised her as the true mother. Reflecting on the story, the monastic jurist explained that this kind of wisdom epitomised the accumulated knowledge of experienced judges who learn to see the truth beneath appearances in the same way that a doctor, following years of practice, can diagnose patients simply by observing them.[41]

JUDGMENTS

Metaphors of depth abound in descriptions of adjudication given by monks. The act of resolving disputes is analogised to digging beneath the exterior of things and penetrating appearances. Warnings were forthcoming, both in judicial trainings and interviews, that looks can be deceiving and that what appears one way 'on the surface' can be very different 'on the inside'. Practices of adjudication drew, in this way, on a kind of epistemology that moves beyond the superficial facts to reveal the more fundamental, karmic causes of misconduct.

This imperative to look for underlying causes can be seen in the Rāmañña Nikāya's judicial training materials, which draw on imagery and techniques taken from *vinaya* literature. Training handbooks direct jurists' attention to the roots (*mūla*) of misconduct, which may come from several kinds of failures: a failure to uphold moral principles (*sīla*), a failure to observe behavioural standards (*ācāra*), a failure to hold correct viewpoints (*diṭṭhi*) or a failure to engage in moral ways of subsisting (*ājīva*). As seen in Chapter 5, the process of analysing a case requires monks to work from an 'exterior' observable action to its

[40] Training seminar for senior monastic judges (*jyeṣṭhānuvijjaka*) and Supreme Court justices in Colombo, 17 December 2018.
[41] Interview with senior monastic judge (*jyeṣṭhānuvijjaka*) in Kandy, 28 June 2019.

constituting category of misconduct, and, from there, to the misguided dispositions or urges that gave rise to it.

Judicial training materials extend this kind of causal induction by encouraging jurists to understand the various factors that give rise to conflicts in the first place. A booklet distributed at one judicial training identified the six root causes of 'dispute cases' (*vivāvādhikaraṇa*), one of the most common of the four types of cases that might come before a monastic judge. Drawing on passages in the Vinaya and *Sāmagāma Sutta*, it identified six pairs of roots (*mūla*) that underlie such disputes: hatred and anger, vindictiveness and spite, jealousy and self-absorption, treachery and deceitfulness, evilness and wrong views, obstinance and attachment to one's own views.

Such analyses promote an understanding of wrongdoing that surpasses the negligence or corrupt character of the individual wrongdoer, pointing instead to the underlying mental 'defilements' (*kilesa*) that afflict all non-enlightened beings. Jurists often referred to the fact that, according to the Vinaya, the Buddha created disciplinary rules because most of his later followers were not-yet-awakened monks who, by virtue of their fallible, non-awakened minds, could not help but misbehave. One instructor put it this way during a workshop:

> Those who come to work within this Buddha *sāsana* are people with defilements – they are persons who have *kilesas*. They come to this Buddha *sāsana* to become undefiled, to become free from the *dukkha* of *saṃsāra*. Hardly anyone comes to the Buddha *sāsana* without defilements. Most of the people who came to join the Buddha had minds that were afflicted by passion, hatred and delusion (*rāga*, *dosa*, *mōha*). They were all people who were burning with those *kilesas*; and it was through listening to the sweet dharma of the Buddha, that [those *kilesas*] were extinguished (*nivā gatte*). Today, when problems arise among us [monastics] concerning the robes, or donated alms, or monastic residences, or medicines, or whatever – whether in the environment we're living in, or in our social system, whether it impacts us mentally or physically – all of these problems come into being because of the *kilesas*, because we go about our business with a defiled mind. This is certainly a truth that all of us [should] accept. Given that's the case, we need to find a solution to this problem, all of us monks should study, teach and discipline ourselves in such a way as to remove these defilements.[42]

[42] Training seminar for monastic judges, Colombo, 28 December 2017 (Pos. 23).

According to this speaker, and many other monks I spoke with, adjudication was a process of accounting for and addressing *kilesas* within the sangha. It was a way of confronting the fact that even those who dedicated their lives to dharma could not help but struggle with 'lust, anger, delusion and other *kilesas*'.[43]

This focus on penetrating appearances to discover their internal, motivating causes places an added burden on judges to make sure that they investigate cases with a 'calm, free, soft mind' that does not add additional *kilesas* into the dispute. A composed and disciplined judge not only ensures a just outcome but also serves as a model of virtuous behaviour that might inspire and guide the litigants. Several monks described the ideal judge not simply as a 'decider' or 'arbitrator' of cases (as the Pali word *anuvijjaka* is sometimes translated) but as a guide or exemplar to whom the offending monk can look for inspiration. As one instructor put it, if judges can conduct themselves in a disciplined, restrained, humble manner, 'it is worth a thousand dharma stories'.[44]

Avoiding Bias (and Its Karmic Consequences)

Given the weight placed on the demeanour and mind-state of judges – so as to avoid bringing additional *kilesas* to bear on the dispute – it is unsurprising that jurists, both in workshops and interviews, spoke extensively about the importance of avoiding bias in judging disputes. The methodical avoidance of bias serves both a practical and soteriological function when it comes to the Rāmañña monastic court. From a practical standpoint, impartiality is essential for maintaining trust in the monastic court system. Judges must not only avoid bias but also the appearance of bias, as even a perception of unfairness can undermine confidence in the system as a whole. From a soteriological perspective, judicial neutrality helps limit the impacts of hatred, greed and delusion on judges, thereby reducing the risk of improper decisions and the negative karma such decisions accrue.

In a relatively small and close-knit community like the Rāmañña fraternity, avoiding bias can be difficult. Despite institutional measures designed to avoid conflicts of interest – such as the *katikāvata* rule prohibiting regional court judges from hearing cases in their own region – jurists cannot always avoid familiarity with litigants. Rāmañña monks see each other regularly at collective rituals, and they

[43] Training seminar for monastic judges, Colombo, 28 December 2017. [44] Ibid.

often share ordination or educational experiences. An instructor at one monastic training commented:

> We know [litigants]. We have relationships with them. However, when we go to the adjudication place ... we have to conduct ourselves in the manner prescribed [in our judicial training]. ... If we go there and talk to [the litigants] and chat with them and go and have a cup of tea with them, the others there will think that our comments are based on past experience with them. We should never drink tea like that; if the plaintiff and defendant are there, we should not make conversation with them because it might sow a seed of doubt: 'these people are drinking tea with him while undertaking judicial work.' Be very careful. We [judges] must have a pure and chastened (*saṃvega*) mindset, which means there should be no predetermined decisions. ... You should go in there like a blank piece of paper ... with no underlying ideas about a person, only an understanding of dharma and *vinaya*.[45]

Procedural and soteriological admonitions come through the instructor's words. He presents lapses in legal procedure (such as drinking tea with a litigant) as, on the one hand, a practical problem for judges and litigants, something that will cause disputants to lose confidence in the neutrality of the court. On the other hand, he also describes such lapses in soteriological terms: to behave too casually is to be without *saṃvega*, a complex Pali term that refers to a wise person's appropriate shock and despondency at the miseries of *saṃsāra*. *Saṃvega* constitutes the appropriately chastened attitude one should bring to serious matters like legal disputes. Lapses in protocol, the speaker suggests, are avoided by cultivating *saṃvega* and the associated desire for nirvana.

The Vinaya Piṭaka acknowledges the possibility of partiality and favouritism in monastic courts, particularly in the Enclosing section, passages of which were discussed by instructors at several monastic workshops. Referring to a chapter on 'minor conflicts' (*cūḷasaṃgāma*), an experienced jurist presented the following to an audience of Senior Court and Supreme Court jurists:

> The monk who is doing the judgment should never under any circumstances ask the following questions of either the accuser or the accused monks: What is their monastic lineage (*paramparāva*)? Who is their primary teacher? Where are they from? How long have they studied?...

[45] Training seminar for monastic judges, Colombo, 14 December 2018.

> How many [texts] have they learned? How many temples do they have? That is, you can't inquire into anything like this at all because when one looks into these things and learns about them, one's bias (*agatiya*) grows with each detail. This is explained in the *Parivāra*[46]. . . . It means that one should be a person who always respects the sangha, not someone who respects the individual. That is to say that when a case arises involving a monk that you know and like, when you are conducting the case, when you are judging the case, you should not be thinking: 'Oh, I like this monk; I know this monk well; this monk has helped me out a lot with the fraternity; he has done so much for the fraternity, etc.' To do that is to respect the person, rather than the dharma.[47]

Both speakers quoted above, and many others, described the conundrum posed by monastic judges' familiarity with litigants and the mixture of personal and communal concerns this dilemma entails. Personally, the fact of familiarity poses a threat to the cultivated mindset that an ideal judge ought to have: one that is wholly free from preconceptions about the case or the litigants and therefore untainted by any associated forms of harmful bias, specifically the four 'bad ways' (*agati*) of fear, desire, hatred and ignorance.[48] (A just decision is, by definition, a decision that is free from these influences.[49]) Communally, the appearance of familiarity can generate negative impressions (and associated *kilesas*) in monks who may be observing the case, including litigants and others.

This sensitivity to the relationship between appearances and internal states is foundational to the functioning of the sangha as a whole. Among the major reasons given by the Buddha for promulgating rules of monastic conduct was to create a renunciant community so disciplined and well-behaved that they would 'bring faith in the *sāsana* to those who have none and to increase the faith of those who have it' (*appasannānaṃ vā pasādaya, pasannānaṃ vā bhiyyobhāvāya*).[50] I heard

[46] This was interrupted for a short clarification specifying where in the *Parivāra* these matters were discussed. One can find this discussion in the following citations, where a fuller list of taboo questions appears, including questions about the status or standing of one's family. The Oldenberg, *The Vinaya Piṭakaṃ*, Vol. v, 164; Horner, *The Book of Discipline (Vinaya Piṭaka)*, Vol. vi, 264.

[47] Training seminar for senior monastic judges (*jyeṣṭhānuvijjaka*) and Supreme Court justices in Colombo, 28 December 2017.

[48] These are *bhaya-, chanda-, dosa-, moha- agati.*

[49] Interview with monastic judge (*anuvijjaka*) near Veyangoda, 10 December 2019.

[50] Oldenberg, *The Vinaya Piṭakaṃ*, Vin. iii, 20.

this Pali phrase intoned regularly over the course of my fieldwork whenever the topic of proper judicial behaviour was discussed. This phrase also appears in the Explanations section of the Vinaya, repeated anew with the introduction of each *Pātimokkha* rule.[51]

The implication is that avoiding the *appearance* of bias or favouritism in judging was equally important as avoiding the internal state of bias. The imperative to appear as unbiased, even if one was already unbiased, was put vividly by one instructor at a judicial training:

> Whenever you go to a judgment hall to judge a case . . . one should enter the hall with extreme humility, without looking at the surroundings; one should enter without looking around to see who the monks are on both sides of the case because if one sees that a familiar monk has come it might lead to partisanship (*pakṣagrāhī*). Therefore, keep your eyes on the ground when entering. When it comes time to do the judgment, don't blink your eyes or nod your head. This means that it is the dharma, the *vinaya* and the *sāsana* of the teacher that are speaking.[52]

As presented by this speaker, the ideal monastic judge does not exercise authority as an individual, an opinionated specialist in legal analysis. (These qualities were associated with state-legal professionals during the discussion that preceded the quote.) The monastic judge is rather a conduit for the law, an expert in its true meaning who lets the Buddha's teachings speak through him. He does not expatiate on the teaching or give original interpretations. A monastic judge's virtues, in this view, come not from his cleverness but from his accuracy, impartiality and consistency. Rather than an exponent of the law, the idealised monastic judge temporarily abandons his ego in order to adopt a 'personality made by dharma and *vinaya*'.[53]

LAW'S KARMA

Rāmañña jurists practise legal pluralism in ways that align monastic law's practical and soteriological aims. Indeed, a striking feature of their legal discourse is the fluid movement between earthly and cosmological

[51] This does not appear in the standard transliteration of the Vinaya from the Pali Text Society because it is often omitted or replaced by '. . .'

[52] Training seminar for senior monastic judges (*jyeṣṭhānuvijjaka*) and Supreme Court justices in Colombo, 28 December 2017.

[53] Training seminar for senior monastic judges (*jyeṣṭhānuvijjaka*) and Supreme Court justices in Colombo, 28 December 2017.

frames of reference. Even the most technical discussions – such as the proper procedures for contacting witnesses or converting the ancient currencies and measures from the Vinaya into modern Sri Lankan Rupees and kilometres – frequently give way to broader discussions of rebirth and salvation, *saṃsāra* and nirvana. When senior jurists instruct monks to approach legal procedures with an attitude of *saṃvega*, they call into view this larger frame of reference.

This soteriological frame of reference was also evident in the responses of monks that I surveyed. Much to my surprise, 81 per cent of respondents agreed (51% strongly) that 'a/the foundational objective' (*mūlika aramuna*) of monastic laws and traditions was to 'help monks in obtaining nirvana'.[54] Among respondents from the Rāmañña Nikāya, agreement was even stronger, with 84 per cent concurring (60% strongly) that the pursuit of nirvana was a core function of monastic law.

An example of this frame-shifting occurred during a judicial training for higher court jurists that I attended in 2018. During a conversation about the various administrative units within the fraternity that might become involved in a judicial matter, one of the senior jurists leading the conversation paused to offer the following reflection before returning to the procedural details:

> The Buddha once said something about there being no beginning and no end to the cycle of rebirths (*saṃsāra*). He gave the example that the Ganges was approximately 2500 kilometres long and several kilometres wide. How much sand is on both sides of the river? Even if we were to count the grains of sand, our number of future rebirths would exceed that. Our journey in *saṃsāra* goes even beyond that, and it's the same with the journey we've travelled already. How much further will you go on that long journey? We should think about that when we're working [as judges]. We should also be mindful that our destination could be hell. We should think about that, too . . . we should think about whether we are stretching out our *saṃsāra* or bringing a stop to it.[55]

The speaker's comments, which were received approvingly by other monks, demonstrate what Lina Verchery has referred to as 'perspectival dexterity', a bifocality of viewpoint in which the immediate is juxtaposed

[54] Question 5.3.
[55] Training seminar for monastic judges, Colombo, 28 December 2017.

with the ultimate such that the former seems more significant and the latter more imminent.[56] While it is impossible to know whether Rāmañña judges think more about future rebirths than legal protocols when crafting their decisions, it is nevertheless clear that Rāmañña legal elites speak regularly about the work of judging in ways that draw together procedural imperatives (send subpoenas by registered post!) with soteriological ones (do not prolong *saṃsāra*!).

Nowhere was this conjunction of proximate and ultimate concerns more visible than in the various warnings issued by monastic jurists regarding the consequences of biased or shoddy acts of judging. The warnings draw on cautionary words in *vinaya* literature. The Enclosing section of the Vinaya, for example, includes verses that warn unscrupulous litigants and judges of the frightening consequences that follow from abusing the legal process. Early modern Buddhist legal texts from Burma include similar admonitions, cautioning that even well-intentioned judges who make errors in their verdicts risk unfortunate karmic repercussions.[57]

Read through these texts, the vocation of a monastic judge has much higher stakes than his civil court counterparts. Monastic judges who give unjust (*ayukti*) decisions or who conduct a faulty investigation don't just face dismissal but a variety of other penalties in this world and the next. The dynamics of double-bind were expressed to me in an interview with a former monastic Supreme Court jurist:

> Do you know why we give [*pārājika* decisions relating to expulsion from the fraternity] only through the Supreme Court or the Final Panel of the Supreme Court? Because if you have a case and you give an incorrect decision that harms someone who is not guilty, the person who gave the decision will also have a *pārājika*. Now, let's say there is some accusation of stealing, of taking what is not given (*adinnādāna*), and we give a decision following the evidence [that it is] a *pārājika* offense but, in fact, it's actually not that bad. . .. If [judges] give that decision, they are denying the rights of those monks. Or if you decide that the rightful incumbent of a temple is not the rightful incumbent based on an accusation, you are stealing that monk's privileges and thereby committing your own *pārājika*.[58]

[56] Verchery, 'Seeing with the Imagination Relational Ontologies and Perspectival Dexterity in the Chinese Buddhist Insect Imaginaire'

[57] Lammerts, *Buddhist Law in Burma*.

[58] Interview with monastic judge of the Rāmañña Nikāya Supreme Court (*uparimādhikaraṇaya*) near Kandy, 20 December 2019.

Unlike state courts, where judges' positions of authority largely insulate them from the negative consequences of an errant judgment or insufficient investigation, monastic judges remain 'on the hook' even for mistakes committed in good faith. One instructor at a judicial training put the matter starkly:

> Judges need to put in their utmost effort because if they do not and, for some reason, a dispute comes up between two parties and it is handled incorrectly (*väradi lesa*) perhaps on account of some prejudice such as desire, there is a possibility that, through judging that case, one or both parties might be destined for negative rebirths, or incur bad [karmic] effects, or go to hell. That's why the Buddha said that [judging] is a serious responsibility.[59]

This means that, to quote the then-chief judicial registrar of the Rāmañña Nikāya, '*vinaya* judging is a very dangerous thing', risking unfortunate consequences for all parties involved, including the judges.[60] 'Litigation (*naḍukīma*)', in his words, 'is unlucky for everyone'.[61] Or, as another jurist put it, given the consequences, 'it's better not to be a judge, if you can avoid it'.[62]

In spite of these dangers, a skilful judge is thought to have a profoundly positive impact on the sangha and the wider cosmos. One instructor offered the following encouragement at a judicial training in 2017:

> There are multiple types of court decisions that one can give in this world. But the decisions given by us as monastic judges are decisions that influence the entire world, together with the world of the gods. Therefore, this opportunity is like the opportunity given to the founders of the sangha: it is a chance to do good and ground the sangha in skilfulness (*kusala*), in dharma, in *vinaya*, in morality (*guṇa*), in the *sāsana* of the teacher. And if we solve problems that way, if we offer solutions like this, if we think about issues in this way, . . . you, my great monastics, will absolutely be healing the minds of the entire world and that of the gods.[63]

[59] Training seminar for monastic judges, Colombo, 28 December 2017.

[60] Interview with chief judicial registrar of Rāmañña Nikāya, Anuradhapura, 9 December 2019.

[61] Ibid.

[62] Interview with senior monastic judge (*jyeṣṭhānuvijjaka*) in Colombo, 14 December 2019.

[63] Training seminar for monastic judges, Colombo, 28 December 2017.

This speaker, like other jurists I spoke to, characterised monastic judging – for all its hazards – as one of the most profound and consequential vocations a bhikkhu can undertake. Preserving *sāmaggi*, preventing schism and redeeming discipline and virtue in the face of threats are said to be essential for the survival and vitality of the *sāsana* and the continuity of the fraternity. This idea is encapsulated in another Pali phrase repeated frequently by monastic jurists: '*Vinayo nama sāsanassa ayu*', meaning that the *vinaya*, and by extension its jurists, is the very life of the *sāsana* itself.

As one can see, in spite of the deeply regulatory features of the Rāmañña court system – its emphasis on order, procedure, regularity, categorisation, protocol and other qualities – Rāmañña jurists do not speak about monastic legality in narrowly regulatory terms. Instead, they frame judging as an act of immense soteriological and karmic importance. The procedures that govern adjudication are not merely administrative directives designed to ensure consistency. They are also guardrails designed to minimise the possibility of karmic catastrophes and to mitigate this-worldly and other-worldly risk. These guardrails include giving the most soteriologically 'dangerous' cases to those jurists who have the most experience and wisdom, namely the monastic judges of the Supreme Court, who are least likely to endanger the karmic futures of all parties involved. In this way, the logics of monastic judging are not unlike the historical rationales behind the 'reasonable doubt' standard in criminal trials. In both cases, procedural rules not only ensure due process for litigants but also mitigate the chances of hell in the world to come.[64]

THE IMPORTANCE OF REHABILITATION

I noticed a similar plurality of purposes when speaking with monastic judges about the administration of penalties and penance. Here, too, judges spoke concurrently about this-worldly regulatory concerns, such as the fairness of the sanction and the feasibility of enforcement, as well as about other-worldly soteriological concerns, such as limiting *saṃsāra* and expediting nirvana.

The nature and aim of 'punishment' have long been a topic of discussion among Buddhists and Buddhologists. As Steven Collins

[64] Whitman, *The Origins of Reasonable Doubt*.

and Michael Zimmerman have documented, Buddhist texts frequently caution readers about the karmic consequences of bodily punishments meted out by kings and their ministers. These sources describe a double-bind similar to that faced by Rāmañña judges: monarchs and ministers are expected to punish in order to preserve justice, yet those punishments also carry karmic consequences for the punishers themselves, affecting their own rebirths.[65] A similar aversion to violence also appears in accounts of monastic punishments, which, while not entailing acts of bodily harm, are nevertheless said to have a powerful emotional and psychobiological impact.[66]

The question of whether *vinaya* sanctions can be called punishments in the Western legal sense is itself a matter of some debate. Although *vinaya* literature uses the same term to describe the sanctions issued by monks and kings (P: *danduvam*), some scholars, such as Malcolm Voyce, have warned against treating *vinaya* sanctions as punishments in the conventional sense of the term. For Voyce, sanctions in the Vinaya Piṭaka differ from contemporary notions of punishment because they are not acts of punitive force intended to repay transgression with some form of physical or emotional pain. Rather, they are understood to be medicine-like 'treatments' designed to encourage spiritual development.[67] Ṭhānissara Bhikkhu makes a similar case, clarifying that transgression in the Vinaya is not corrected with practices of retribution or the payments of damages but with procedures that seek to 'stand [the offender] back up' (P: *vuṭṭhāna-vidhī*), which repair his morality and moral status in the community.

Similar sentiments to those of Ṭhānissaro and Voyce were expressed to me by monastic judges in the Rāmañña Nikāya, who were also keen on stressing the differences between *vinaya* sanctions and the punishments of civil law. One jurist argued that, where state law used physical

[65] Collins, *Nirvana and Other Buddhist Felicities: Utopias of the Pali Imaginaire*, Chapter Six; Zimmerman, 'Only a Fool Becomes a King: Buddhist Stances on Punishment.'

[66] One can point to several accounts in the Vinaya where monks who are convicted of offences are observed to become depressed or ill. In one famous case that was recounted multiple times during my research, the Buddha's charioteer Channa is reduced to fainting from the force of the Buddha's announcement that he will be given the *brahma danda* punishment of excommunication.

[67] Voyce, 'The Communal Discipline of the Buddhist Order of Monks,' 149; Voyce, 'Ideas of Transgression and Buddhist Monks.' See also the recent work of Salgado ('On the Question of 'Discipline" (Vinaya) and Nuns in Theravāda Buddhism, 2019) as it relates to punishment among contemporary Sri Lankan nuns.

coercion to enforce rules, sangha courts used sanctions compassionately as a way to 'help the offender understand [his offence], to rehabilitate him as though he were a drug addict'. He clarified that, in correcting those who failed to uphold the Buddha's instructions, monastic sanctions did not aim to maintain sangha hierarchies or penalise transgressions for their own sake; rather, they served as a kind of therapeutic technique, which worked positively on the psyches of monks and helped them to restore a healthy frame of mind.[68] Notable in this particular judge's comments was his use of the Sinhala term for rehabilitation (*punarutthāpanaya*), which echoes etymologically the Vinaya-based idea of 'standing someone up' (P: *uṭṭhāpanaṃ*) after an offense.[69]

In this and other conversations, monastic jurists spoke about sanctions as edifying in nature, designed to redirect and retrain the mind of the offender so that he does not damage his own karmic journey:

> In Buddhist law most things are for educating persons. This means there are no serious physical punishments (*däḍi danduvam*).... Sometimes giving a [physical] punishment will itself corrupt the person's mind.... In civil [and criminal] law, one punishes mistakes, but here [in the *sangha*], we avoid any physical punishments and implement various psychological processes to correct the person. When one uses Buddhist law the goal is nirvana; it is to direct a person who has been on the wrong path back towards the path to nirvana; it is for the nirvana of all four groups [of Buddhist followers] – monks, nuns, lay men and lay women. There is no such [concern for] liberation (*vimukti*) in civil law.[70]

Striking in these discussions was the relative absence of stigmatising terms. There is no discussion of a corrupted category of person that differs fundamentally from others. Misconduct was frequently described as a 'mistake', using the same Sinhala term (*väradi*) that one might use to denote a spelling mistake. Rather than *committing* offences, monks were often described as *arriving at* them, reinforcing the idea that wrongdoing stemmed not from malice but temporary lapses in self-control or clarity of mind.

The chief judicial registrar at the time summed up the matter with reference to the Buddhist notion of thirst (*tṛṣṇā*), the idea that non-

68 Interview with monastic judge (*anuvijjaka*) near Moratuva, 17 December 2019.
69 On this idea, see Ṭhānissaro Bhikkhu, *The Buddhist Monastic Code*, Vol. ii, 358.
70 Interview with monastic judge (*anuvijjaka*) near Moratuva, 17 December 2019.

enlightened beings tend to be controlled by constant, nagging desires. He reflected that, in most cases, 'thirst is the problem, [because] it can't be satiated'.[71] Another jurist commented that, ultimately, the causes of an offender's misconduct cannot be inveigled from them through interrogation; it was a question that 'must be answered by oneself'.[72]

In the world of monastic punishment, as described by Rāmañña jurists, the aim is not retribution but restoration. Despite observers' common fixation on the expulsion-worthy *pārājika* offences, the jurists I spoke with seemed more concerned with preserving a community of fallible-but-fixable members than with expelling bad seeds from their midst. One senior judge explained that the same person who commits an offence and is called a bad (*naraka*) person will, after some time, again be seen as a good person. Therefore, we can't just call him an evil person and eliminate him (*ayin karana*), and kick him out'.[73] Care is needed to address the underlying issues and repair the individual.

Another monastic judge put it this way:

> When we [administer sanctions] we do our best to give the offender advice, to assist him. For us, this is a method of rehabilitation. We're trying to help them. You could say that monks are a rare treasure. Hardly anyone is ordaining these days; there's no one . . . therefore we need to make sure that there's no injustice (*asādhāraṇayak*) within the group of monks that have been ordained. We try to make decisions in such a way that we do not damage their minds or discourage them so as to help them stay [within the sangha]. As much as possible, we try to keep them here. We look to correct (*harigassaganna*) them, to correct their errors, to help them become a more productive person. That is to say, when we hear a legal case, we do so as people hoping to hold on to people, not to send them away.[74]

This focus on rehabilitation has multiple implications. On the one hand, rehabilitation aligns with the *telos* of discipline in the Vinaya: rules and sanctions serve to instruct, guide and improve a person rather than deter and punish them. On the other hand, the imperative to

71 Interview with chief judicial registrar of Rāmañña Nikāya, Anuradhapura, 9 December 2019.
72 Interview with monastic judge (*anuvijjaka*) near Moratuva, 17 December 2019.
73 Interview with senior monastic judge (*jyeṣṭhānuvijjaka*) near Panadura, 14 December 2019.
74 Interview with monastic judge (*anuvijjaka*) near Veyangoda, 10 December 2019.

restore and retain misbehaving *bhikkhus* rather than remove them also recognises the existential challenges faced by the monkhood itself, now and in the past. Monastic life is difficult, and fully committed monks are both imperfect and increasingly rare. Indeed, the precarity of the monastic vocation and concerns about future recruitment were key findings in the survey. When asked about the most difficult challenges facing Buddhism, respondents ranked the decline in new monastic recruits and the large numbers of monks leaving the sangha as the two most pressing challenges.[75]

The idea that monastic legal sanctions serve as didactic devices for not-yet-awakened monks has found its way into the very institutional fabric of the Rāmañña Nikāya. One can see this, among other places, in the way that the Rāmañña fraternity handles the week-long penance called *mānatta*, which the Vinaya Piṭaka describes as a sanction that must be imposed on monks who commit the second-most serious category of offences called penance offences (P: *saṅghādhisesa*). While the Vinaya treats *mānatta* as a penalty for misdeeds, members of the Rāmañña fraternity have transformed the *mānatta* penance into an annual practice conducted before the start of important legal actions (*kammas*), especially higher ordination rites. Prior to these events, bhikkhus will undertake the full six-day and six-night *mānatta* practice (very similar to that prescribed in the Vinaya) as a way of making sure they are fully pure even from offences they committed knowingly or unknowingly.[76]

[75] In a section of the survey that permitted respondents to indicate which problems were 'one of the biggest' facing the sangha, 61 per cent indicated 'the lack of people entering the monkhood'. Fifty-one per cent indicated that 'too many bhikkhus leaving the monkhood' was one of the biggest challenges. Questions 15.4 and 15.5. The other seven (of nine) challenges named in the survey include (along with the percentage of respondents who marked these as 'one of the biggest problems'): insufficient lay support (35%), insufficient government support (48%), too much unwanted government interference (40%), lack of discipline among bhikkhus (33%), too much influence by foreign governments and NGOs (39%), conversion to other religions (32%), and other problems coming from other religious groups (36%). Respondents evaluated each of these 'challenges' along a five-point scale ranging from 'one of the biggest problems', to 'a significant problem', to 'a medium-sized problem', ' to 'a minor problem', to 'not a problem'.

[76] As with the descriptions given in the Vinaya, these *mānatta* practices will be preceded by a preliminary probation (*parivāsa*) period and will conclude with reinstatement actions (*abbhāna*). In many cases, the probation period is only observed at night for practical reasons. This allows bhikkhus to participate fully in religious duties during the day. A group of pure monks who are not undergoing

As with the discussion of judging above, here too, the emphasis extends beyond the immediate regulation of sangha members. Jurists also identify a larger soteriological frame in which the 'correction' of mistakes is not simply a matter of paying off a debt to the community or 'doing one's time' before being restored to full status. Practices like *mānatta* also facilitate monks' journey through *saṃsāra* for the benefit of themselves, the community of monks and the lay devotees who support them. In this perspective, the coercive logic of state punishments makes little sense, given that, in ultimate terms, the punishment does not advance the salvation of the offender or the sangha. Considered cosmologically, and karmically, a sangha sanction is even more consequential than its civil or criminal equivalents. One head monk put it this way:

> Let's say one were to break some article in the civil law, there'd be a punishment [and that's it]. But if someone offends in Buddhist law, the punishment follows from dharma. If I do something serious as a bhikkhu, I can't be freed (*nidahas venavā*) from a dharma punishment in the same way.[77]

When it comes to administering sanctions, then, monastic jurists practise legal pluralism in two ways. They practise an *intra-legal* pluralism in their acknowledgement of the proximate and ultimate goals of correcting actions: order and justice in this life and a better rebirth in the life to come. They also practise legal pluralism in an *inter-legal* sense, recognising that while monastic courts may share certain regulatory concerns with state courts, their goals and methods diverge significantly.

Where state courts focus primarily on punishment as a tool of regulation, monastics operate with a broader set of objectives: rehabilitation, correction, restoration of the individual and guiding both offenders and affected parties back to the path towards nirvana. Rather than imposing punitive measures on individuals, monastic courts offer opportunities

penance or probation must oversee the actions of confession and reinstatement that are essential to this process. For this purpose, a group of senior monks, at minimum the twenty who are required for *abbhāna*, will act as leaders of the action. Interview with senior monastic judge (*jyeṣṭhānuvijjaka*) in Colombo, 17 December 2019. Further clarified by Ven. Raluvē Padmasiri in email communication, 5 February 2025.

77 Follow-up interview with head monk (*lokuhamuduru*) of a monastery, Kandy, 28 July 2019.

for offenders to reaffirm their normative commitments. One senior monastic judge explained this to me by referring to the rhetorical form of the Vinaya's precepts:

> All our precepts[78] say [in English] '*I take refuge in the Buddha.*' We say [in Pali] '*Buddhaṃ sāraṇaṃ gacchāmi.*' I won't kill living beings ... you could say [in English] '*do not kill, do not steal.*' However, I take these [precepts] because I *understand* them. I don't just do them. These aren't at all like state laws, where you're punished if you don't follow them. Vinaya laws, which is to say the Buddha's dharma, are totally different.[79]

Notable in this conversation was the word used to discuss these Buddhist imperatives. Rather than calling them 'rules' or 'regulations', the speaker referred to them as acts of 'I undertake' (*samādiyāmi*) – using the verbal form of the precepts as a way to highlight their personal, voluntary character. He argued that, unlike the state-legal model of rule and punishment, in which the punishment guarantees adherence to the rule, in the Buddhist legal model, people willingly undertake precepts as individual expressions of their commitment to the Buddha's teaching and aspiration for nirvana.

LAITY AS A GOAL AND INSTRUMENT OF LEGALITY

While monastic courts and sanctions are primarily matters for the sangha, the issue of monastic misconduct sometimes involves laypersons as well. The Vinaya acknowledges this fact in its multiple passages dealing with the proper ways that monks and laity should interact. The Vinaya prohibits monastics from having too much contact with the laity and exhorts monks, when they do see laity, to behave in ways that inspire faith and respect.

Lay devotees influence monastic courts in formal and informal ways. Formally, the Rāmañña constitution permits laity to act as parties in sangha court cases, either as witnesses or as litigants. Informally, lay communities have their own ways of applying pressure. In a focus group

[78] The speaker referred to 'all the *samādhiyāmis*,' literally all the 'I undertakes', which is the verb that concludes the recitation of the five and ten precepts as chanted by Buddhists on special occasions.

[79] Interview with senior monastic judge (*jyeṣṭhānuvijjaka*) in Colombo, 17 December 2019.

with several young monks at the University of Colombo, one of the respondents explained:

> In some cases, a monastic court settlement (*adhikaraṇa samatha*) is not implemented. If court settlements are not done, the villagers will get together and deal with the matter themselves. That's why, in serious matters, monks choose to do a settlement. If not, a group of villagers might throw out the accused monk; they might even beat him and chase him away. They might also write letters to the senior monks . . .they will do things like write petitions explaining that such and such an offence has been done, etc. That is to say, people generally take action. People take action when the monks fail to take action. . .. Sometimes the monks can expel the offender after a monastic court settlement. Sometimes they might transfer him to a remote temple. Or perhaps the senior monks will bring the monk close and try to place him under the precepts (*śikṣaṇaya karanna*). If not, people will come together and kick him out. A lot of the time in Sri Lanka, if a monk who has committed an offence does not go to a court,[80] the people will get together and expel him from the temple themselves.[81]

Accounts like this illustrate how monastic jurists, in fact, navigate three legal traditions in their practices of legal pluralism: that of monastic law, that of state law, and that of popular moral expectations.[82] Across several interviews, monastic jurists recounted cases in which monks engaged in misconduct – selling temple property, flouting disciplinary rules – but refused to comply with monastic court rulings and could not be prosecuted under state law. In many of these instances, local lay donors (*dāyakas*) stepped in to assert their own notions of right and wrong. For example, in one case, about which I have written elsewhere, local laypersons staged a protest in the village streets to show their displeasure at a monk who had tried to obtain a driving license.[83]

Stories like this confirm the important role that the laity plays in shaping and upholding monastic discipline. These narratives also seem

80 Unclear whether the speaker intended a sangha court or state court.

81 Focus group interview with three monks, Colombo, 26 July 2019.

82 For analogous arrangements in Thailand, see: Borchert and Darlington, 'Political Disrobing in Thailand'; Chladek, 'Imagined Laity and the Performance of Monasticism in Northern Thailand'; Schedneck, 'The Lay Buddhist Gaze and Femininity in Thai Male Monasticism.'.

83 Schonthal, 'The Impossibility of a Buddhist State.'

to support the Vinaya's admonition that monks must act in ways that 'increase the confidence' of lay Buddhists and enhance their faith in the *sāsana*. Such confidence not only ensures the sangha's popular legitimacy; it is also essential for fraternities' survival. As one interviewee put it, 'a wise monastic jurist understands the importance of working well with donors'.[84]

CONCLUSION

Conversations with monastic jurists suggest a portrait of monastic law that goes well beyond the concerns with regulation described in Chapter 5. While compliance and procedural regularity are clearly important to monastic judges, they are not ends in themselves. Rather, according to the monastic jurists in this chapter, these features also serve higher-order goals: preserving unity and unanimity (*sāmaggi*) among monks; maintaining discretion and protecting reputations; avoiding further conflict and identifying strife's root causes; minimising judicial prejudice by eliminating the mental defilements (*kilesa*) that give rise to them; restoring offenders to the community – 'standing them back up' – by applying therapeutic sanctions; and, most importantly, shortening one's time in *saṃsāra* and hastening nirvana. Monks also recognise the importance of monastic law for aligning the conduct of monks with the concerns and norms of local laity and temple donors. This not only brings the two normative traditions closer, it also serves as a means of attracting laity to the *sāsana* and deepening their faith in it.

Speaking with Buddhist monks about monastic law – or 'listening in' as they speak to each other in workshops and in written works – highlights the limits of the dominant categories we use to conceptualise

[84] 'If the incumbent monk can't work well with donors, then he can't maintain the temple... Therefore, we take care to ensure that they can work well with donors. Interview with senior monastic judge (*jyeṣṭhānuvijjaka*) near Panadura, 14 December 2019.
In settings where the monastic-lay relations are particularly strong, monastic jurists may also deal with matters beyond just monastic misconduct. In several interviews, monks relayed examples of senior sangha members, many of them jurists, helping to resolve disputes in the local area. In one case, a senior jurist helped resolve a property dispute between parties as a way to prevent the matter from being escalated to the local police or courts. Interview with senior monastic judge (*jyeṣṭhānuvijjaka*) in Kandy, 28 June 2019.

law. As discussed by specialist and non-specialist monks, Buddhist monastic law is both positive law and natural law: it is authorised by this-worldly actors and aligned with a more-than-worldly order. Monastic law's technologies, material forms, institutions, logics, processes and officials resemble those of state law. Yet, they also claim fidelity to the teachings of the Buddha and the universal laws of dharma – a cosmic legal order that, according to some traditions of Theravāda Buddhism in Southeast Asia, is literally inscribed on the boundary-wall of the universe in letters the size of cows.[85]

The Buddha, himself, offers ten reasons for the creation of monastic law in the Vinaya Piṭaka, which blend together these regulatory and cosmological dimensions. Monastic law, he explains, ensures the excellence and comfort of the sangha; it reproaches difficult persons and comforts good monks; it restrains the mental cankers in this world and repels them in the next life; it supports the faith of those who do not believe and to increases the belief of those who already believe; and it establishes the true dharma while also elevating monastic discipline (*vinaya*).[86] Even in the Vinaya, therefore, the purposes of monastic law are themselves plural, implicating social order as well as comfort, discipline, karma, lay-monastic relations, *sāmaggi* and faith. Monks express this plurality – that is, they practise legal pluralism – by framing these multiple aims of monastic law as complementary goals, commensurable practices dedicated to the shared goals of preserving *the sāsana* and progressing towards nirvana.

Attending Rāmañña judicial trainings and speaking with monks revealed the many 'nonpositivist possibilities' embedded in monastic law. Monks framed their law's positivist and nonpositivist elements not as distinct features but as intertwined ones: a legal order that regulates conduct while also impacting karma, *saṃsāra* and the path to nirvana. Interviewees suggested a deep connection between monastic law's material forms (its codes, courts, judicial offices) and its soteriological significance (as embodying a salvific dharma). To understand monastic law *solely* as a tool of social control *or* as a system of spiritual guidance is to miss half of the picture.

85 Lammerts, *Buddhist Law in Burma*, 63–64.

86 These reasons are given initially as a justification for the first *pārājika* rule against sex. Elsewhere in the Vinaya, the rationales are applied to all of the rules. Oldenberg, *The Vinaya Piṭakaṃ*, Vol. iii, 21, 15–16.

The monastic opinions above display a similar ambivalence about monastic law's similarities with state law as those discussed in Chapter 5. In speaking about the regulative and soteriological goals of law, interviewees made it clear that comparisons with state-legal structures were adequate in some ways but not others. In certain cases, a jurist who spoke casually about Rāmañña laws and regulations (*nīti rīti*) as naturally aligned with those of the Sri Lankan state would – when asked about such comparisons explicitly – suddenly appeal to the nonpositivist features of monastic law and reject any similarities between *anuvijjaka*'s work and the techniques of state governance. Some even argued that the word 'law' (*nītiya*) did not accurately capture the nature of monastic discipline, preferring terms such as precepts (*śikṣā*) or guidelines (*paññattī*).

These rhetorical shifts suggest not so much a denial of the state-like features of monastic law so much as an unwillingness to reduce monastic legality to one framework or the other – to treat monastic laws as entirely analogous to state law or entirely incompatible with it.[87] In this way, monastic jurists practise legal pluralism in ways that both invite and resist comparisons with Sri Lanka's national legal system. They construe the Rāmañña system as both an embodiment of state-like legal rationalism and an expression of Buddhist soteriological activism. The first invites recognition by Sri Lankan state law; the second resists it, positioning monastic law as a regime whose authority, aims, and connection to ultimate truth render its translation into state legal language or its absorption into state-legal institutions as a kind of boundary violation – an act of government overreach that compromises monastic law's legitimacy and taints its 'purity'.

The tensions between these framings of monastic law and their political and legal implications will be examined in Part III of this book.

[87] A similar kind of bifocality has been observed by scholars of Sri Lankan religions, who point out the juxtaposition of 'worldly' (P: *lokika*, S: *laukika*) and 'more-than-worldly' (P: *lokuttara*, S: *lokottara*) intentions that devotees bring to rituals: a simultaneous desire for the benefits of wealth, success and health in this life and a concern with the loftier, and seemingly incompatible, goal of extinguishing their cycles rebirth altogether.

PART III

CHAPTER SEVEN

'LEGALISING' MONASTIC LAW

The Politics of Legal Recognition in Post-Colonial Sri Lanka

A surprising reference to monastic law lies hidden in plain sight in Sri Lanka's constitution. Although largely ignored by lawmakers and judges, the provision comprises the entire fourth paragraph of the constitution's chapter on the judiciary (XV). It reads:

> Parliament may by law provide *for the creation and establishment of courts, tribunals or institutions for the adjudication and settlement of matters relating to the discipline* (S: *vinaya*) of *bhikk[h]us* or any dispute between *bhikk[h]us* or any other dispute relating to the performance of services, in, or in relation to, temples.
>
> Such law may... make provision –
>
> (a) for the appointment, transfer, dismissal and disciplinary control (S: *vinaya pālanaya*) of the member or members of such courts, tribunals or institutions by the President or by such other person or body of persons as may be provided for in such law;
> (b) for the exclusion of the jurisdiction of any other institution referred to in paragraph (1) of this Article [on the structure of state courts] in relation to such matters and disputes.
>
> In this paragraph the expressions '*bhikk[h]u*' and 'temple' shall have the same meanings as in the Buddhist Temporalities Ordinance, as at the commencement of the Constitution.[1]

This provision – which invites parliamentarians to draft a new law establishing monastic courts – is unique in Sri Lanka's constitution.

[1] Chapter XV 105(4). Italics mine.

Nowhere else in the country's fundamental law does one find a similar statute-in-waiting. The provision also stands out among global constitutions as an oddly specific encouragement for the government to produce a particular kind of legislation – even suggesting its own list of topics and definitions.

This section of the constitution, its monastic courts clause, serves as a conspicuous symbol of – or perhaps a monument to – Sri Lankans' ongoing attempts to harmonise monastic law and state law. These attempts are by no means new. For more than 200 years, colonial and postcolonial governments have attempted to legislate the proper relationships between monastic and state laws. In the nineteenth century, British officials addressed this issue by 'jurisdictionalising' Buddhist law in ways that distinguished temple lands from taxable lands and 'purely spiritual' matters from civil ones. By the 1940s, monastic law was acknowledged in two forms of state law: a body of case law, known as Buddhist Ecclesiastical Law, which purported to recognise key rules of monastic behaviour and succession; and a Buddhist Temporalities Ordinance, which granted trustee-like powers to the 'chief incumbent' monk of temples. I explore these developments in Part I of this book.

Rather than settling the relationship between monastic law and state law, however, these legal innovations have often been criticised on account of the overlapping structures of authority that they seem to establish. When it comes to monastic succession, membership, property and other matters, Sri Lanka's laws require the island's monks to navigate two sources of normativity: that of monastic courts and executive councils, and that of civil courts and government officials – each of which claims their own powers to interpret and enact the instructions of the Buddha (as described in Part II of this book). This doubled authority has been an ongoing cause for concern for both monastics and lawmakers. Indeed, disputes about how (and whether) to recognise monastic law in courts and legislation have been some of the most enduring features of public policy on the island – a national debate that has continued virtually without stop for more than two centuries.

'Legalising' Monastic Law

In recent decades, the terms of this debate have acquired a distinctive framing in Sinhala, Sri Lanka's most-spoken language and the vernacular used by most of the country's Buddhists. Expressed in Sinhala, the debate is said to concern the question of 'legalising' (*nītigata kirīma*) monastic law, an ambiguous phrase that means different things to different people. For some, this phrase implies the absorption of monastic law into state law, such that monastic codes and courts would be integrated in the country's larger juridical apparatus. For others, it means the granting of 'state-legal power' (*nītiyānukula balayak*) to monastic legal institutions, a one-way transfer of authority from the state to monastic fraternities. Visible in Sinhala-language debates, therefore, is a basic uncertainty about the relationship between the two legal traditions: does *legalising* imply a merger of monastic law with state law? Or does it imply some kind of devolution of legal powers away from the government and towards the monastic groups themselves?

Alongside this uncertainty about what it means to legalise monastic law sits another uncertainty about how that legalising should occur. Those who seek to legalise monastic law generally have in mind one of two types of reform. The first reform entails the creation of new statutes that would grant formal, legal recognition to the monastic constitutions (*katikāvatas*) used by fraternities to govern their members. This reform would permit Sri Lankan judges to use *katikāvatas* as they would any other state law when addressing disputes among Buddhist monks. Under this scheme, monastic constitutions would acquire a status similar to *Thesavalamai*, a body of personal law that, since its codification by the Dutch in the early eighteenth century, has been used by civil courts to govern matters of marriage, inheritance and divorce for Jaffna Tamils.[2]

The second type of reform seeks to expand the authority of monastic courts rather than codifying monastic rules. Proponents of this reform argue that the state should not incorporate monastic laws directly, but devolve decision-making authority to monastic tribunals themselves, either in their existing form or as part of a national, government-backed Buddhist judicial system. This reform would grant monastic courts a legal status similar to that of the island's state-appointed Quazi Courts, which have civil jurisdiction over marriage, divorce, succession and inheritance under Sri Lanka's regime of Muslim personal law.[3]

[2] Guruparan, 'Customary Law of Stateless Nations.' This code-like quality was not intrinsic to the laws themselves, but the product of Dutch attempts to stabilise Thesavalami for the purposes of colonial governance. By contrast, proposals to codify monastic constitutions made clear that, in the first instance, they were to be drafted by monastic fraternities themselves.

[3] On this, see Schonthal, 'Environments of Law.'

At the time of writing, neither reform has succeeded. As a result, Sri Lanka remains the only Buddhist-majority country in the world without a state-backed monastic legal system. Myanmar has its official monastic bureaucracy, called the State-Sangha Mahanayaka Committee, which oversees an official hierarchy of monastic Vinicchaya Courts. Thailand has a similar monastic bureaucracy and judicial system, guided by an apical 'Council of Elders' (*mahatherasamakhom*) which in principle oversees a nationwide network of sangha officials. Similar bureaucracies, if less stable ones, can also be found in the histories of Bhutan, Laos and, to a lesser degree, Cambodia.

Sri Lanka, by contrast, continues to rely on institutional arrangements established during British colonial rule: civil courts hear disputes over monastic property, while monastic tribunals adjudicate their own disputes over the conduct of fraternity members.[4] Sangha court rulings and monastic constitutions influence state law only in an indirect way – as evidence of 'customary practices' that may inform judicial decisions or government reports – but they carry no official legal status or mechanism of enforcement.[5]

And yet, the issue of legalising monastic law has consistently been portrayed as urgent. Not a single decade has passed since independence without some high-profile attempt to better integrate monastic law and state law. This sense of urgency endures today. Seventy-four per cent of the monks surveyed for this research agreed that the government should be involved in helping 'improve the situation of the bhikkhu vinaya and its traditions'.[6] Eighty-eight per cent responded that 'it would be good to establish a monastic court for all monks in Sri Lanka'.[7] Although lawmakers frequently propose these very changes, no new solutions have been implemented.

What is going on?

Pursuing Purity with Failed Laws

Understanding this dilemma requires one to look beyond legal pluralism as an empirical condition, a state of legal multiplicity that one simply encounters. Sri Lanka's difficulties in 'legalising' monastic law

[4] That is, unless they involve other violations of state law, such as criminal law or constitutional protections for human rights. For more on cases like these, see Chapter 8. On the colonial roots of the current system, see Chapter 3.

[5] Weerasooria, *Buddhist Ecclesiastical Law*, 161 and ff. [6] Question 12.1.

[7] Question 12.3.

do not stem from monastic law's rigidity or its in-born resistance to secular lawmaking. There is no intrinsic disharmony to the 'stuff' of monastic and state law that makes the two incompatible. In fact, the legal systems of sanghas and states have intertwined and coevolved for centuries, each acknowledging the authority of the other.[8] Of the 1,669 Buddhist monks surveyed for this project, more than 75 per cent responded that they perceived no foundational clash (S: *gäṭumak*) between monastic and state law.[9]

To explain the persistence of disputes over legalising monastic law, one must look, instead, to the ways that monks, politicians, jurists and others have given order and meaning to that legal 'stuff' in the first place – the ways they have *practised* legal pluralism. Legalising monastic law has failed because Sri Lanka's monks and lawmakers have repeatedly practised legal pluralism in an agonistic way, which fetishises the *purity* of law. Their ways of expressing and enacting legal multiplicity have not sought to reconcile legal authorities but to defend the autonomy and integrity of one law or another.

This chapter follows a seemingly non-stop series of debates and legislative proposals concerning whether and how to legalise monastic law that took place between the 1940s and the 2000s – a period of profound economic, political and social change, only some of which can be considered in the pages that follow.[10] I show how, in each of

8 The Vinaya Piṭaka itself contains passages requiring that monastics observe 'the orders of the king' unless they are manifestly unjust. von Hinüber, 'Buddhist Law,' 29. The important Vinaya commentary *Samanatapāsādikā* distinguishes between conduct that 'is condemned by the world' (P: *lokavajja*) and conduct that 'is condemned by [monastic] rules' (P: *paṇṇattivajja*) while recommending that the two should be harmonised (see Chapter 2). However, older attempts to distinguish between monastic law and worldly law can also be found the youngest part of the Vinaya, the *Parivāra*. For an investigation of these earlier terms and their application, see Kieffer-Pülz, *Verlorene Gaṇṭhipadas zum buddhistischen Ordensrecht*, I, 322f., fn 1.

9 S: *bhikkhu vinaya nīti saha sampradaya*. Question 10.6.

10 I consider even more recent proposals and debates in Chapter 8. Major transformations during the period examined here include the spread of Sinhala nationalism and Tamil separatism, the onset of civil war (from 1983 to 2009), two leftist insurgencies (in 1971 and 1987–1989), economic nationalisation (during the SLFP-led Sirima Bandaranaike government of 1970–1976) followed by widespread and ongoing economic liberalisation (starting in 1977, with the UNP government led by JR Jayawardene), constitutional transformations, and many other things. For a more comprehensive treatment of these decades, see, among others: De Silva, *A History of Sri Lanka*; DeVotta, *Blowback: Linguistic Nationalism, Institutional Decay*

these debates, advocates for legal change *as well as* critics of those changes practised legal pluralism in ways that fixated on laws' purity. While some portrayed schemes for legalising monastic law as ways to protect the independence and orthodoxy of law (both state and monastic law), others portrayed the proposed reforms as dangerous interventions that would contaminate otherwise pristine sources of authority.

These practices of legal pluralism often followed lines of political affiliation. Monks and laymen who had strong links to the United National Party (UNP) supported that party's proposals for reform; those aligned with the country's other major political party, the Sri Lankan Freedom Party (SLFP), supported its proposals. As these two dominant parties grew more polarised in the years following Sri Lanka's independence in 1948, so too did their associated practices of legal pluralism.

For all sides, the language of legal purity proved useful and resonant. Some used the language of purity to invoke Euro-American ideals of state laws as neutral, secular and self-contained.[11] Others drew on notions of purity and purification taken from Laṅkan Buddhist history, especially the idea that monastic discipline and the *sāsana* were susceptible to corruption and in periodic need of purification (P: *sodhana*) to ensure that the island remained a place of pure (*qua* untainted, S: *nirmala*) dharma. In this way, ideals of legal purity taken from accounts of positivist law aligned with concepts of doctrinal purity taken from Buddhist religious texts, further fortifying arguments that one kind of law ought not to be mingled with the other.[12]

and Ethnic Conflict in Sri Lanka; De Silva, *Sri Lanka: A History*; Wickramasinghe, *Sri Lanka in the Modern Age: A History*; Rambukwella, *The Politics and Poetics of Authenticity*.

11 These ideals are most fully expressed, perhaps, in Kelsen's 'pure theory of law', which relied on 'preclud[ing] from the cognition of positive law all elements foreign thereto'. Kelsen, 'The Pure Theory of Law and Analytical Jurisprudence,' 44. See also, Fish, 'The Law Wishes to Have a Formal Existence.'

12 Notions of purity and reform are also closely related linguistically in Sinhala and other Indic languages. In Sinhala, the word for reform or amendment *saṃśōdhana* derives from the Pali word for purification, *sodhanaya*. On 'purifying' the *sāsana* and monastic law, see Aung-Thwin, 'The Role of Sasana Reform in Burmese History'; Bechert, 'Theravada Buddhist Sangha: Some General Observations on Historical and Political Factors in Its Development.'

Ultimately, this chapter offers a history of failed law. It presents a story of draft bills, committee reports, policy proposals and white papers that never found their way into legislation. Yet, as I hope to show, this history of legal failure – of failures to legalise monastic law – offers powerful insights into the dilemmas of monastic law in contemporary Sri Lanka. In particular, it explains the longevity and persistence of confounding questions that continue to shape the practices of legal pluralism in Sri Lanka today: questions about the relative authority and independence of state and sangha, the separation or integration of 'monastic society' (*bhikṣu samājaya*) with 'normal society' (*sāmānya/podu samājaya*), and the ideal unity or multiplicity of Sri Lanka's monastic community.

PURIFYING THE SANGHA IN THE 1940S

Although visible throughout the nineteenth century, practices of legal pluralism gained renewed relevance in the years surrounding Sri Lanka's independence as part of a broader effort to reverse colonial policies thought to have been harmful to Buddhism.[13] When it came to monastic law, critics pointed to two policies as being particularly damaging: the creation of Buddhist Ecclesiastical Law, that body of case law which granted civil court judges authority over certain kinds of monastic disputes; and the introduction of the Buddhist Temporalities Ordinance, a controversial law that, among other things, gave chief incumbent monks and government officials (initially the Public Trustee, later the Commissioner of Buddhist Affairs) control over Buddhist monasteries.

Initially, it was not Buddhist monks who led the push for legal reform but Buddhist lay groups, educators and politicians. One of the most influential was G.P. Malalasekera, Professor of Pali at the newly formed University of Ceylon, president of the island's leading Buddhist lay organisation (the All-Ceylon Buddhist Congress, or ACBC) and editor of the popular monthly magazine *The Buddhist*. Although Malalasekera led multiple initiatives relating to Buddhism, he treated the legal recognition of monastic law as particularly important. He argued that

[13] Schonthal, *Buddhism, Politics and Limits of Law: The Pyrrhic Constitutionalism of Sri* Lanka, Chapter Two. See also Part I of this book.

legal change was needed to 'reform the sangha', which, in the lead-up to independence, had become increasingly involved in national politics.

Of particular concern to Malalasekera (and other elites) was a cohort of young monks from the island's second-largest monastic college, the Vidyalaṅkāra Pirivena. Influenced by more radical anti-colonial nationalisms in India, monks at the college had been campaigning for leftist politicians, appearing at their rallies and canvassing votes for them. This monastic-political alliance posed a threat to the dominant UNP, which represented elite interests and advocated a more gradual path to independence.

By the late 1940s, tensions between the UNP and the Vidyalaṅkāra monks had escalated, and questions of law – both monastic and state law – quickly rose to the surface. In January 1946, the leader of the UNP and soon-to-be Prime Minister, D.S. Senanayake, gave an address attacking the Vidyalaṅkāra monks for ignoring their obligations to the Vinaya. He helped form a '*sāsana* cleansing committee' (*sāsana sōdhana sabhāva*), which proposed to recognise the Vinaya Piṭaka in state law, making its disciplinary rules enforceable by national courts.[14] In response, the Vidyalaṅkāra monks published a 'declaration' arguing that the Vinaya not only permitted monks to engage in political activities, it *obligated* them to do so.[15]

[14] The *sāsana* cleansing committee (*sāsana sōdhana sabhāva*) was a group of prominent Buddhist professionals. During a conference organised at one of Colombo's most important Buddhist sites, the group endorsed a set of six proposals which, they asserted, would preserve both the purity of the sangha and the secularity of the state. The ACBC, unsurprisingly, also supported the efforts of this committee. Abeysekara, *Colors of the Robe: Religion, Identity, and Difference*, 86.

[15] Authors of the declaration insisted that *vinaya* (the Sinhala term being ambiguous as to its connotation of the Vinaya Piṭaka or the wider corpus of monastic discipline) did not contain a set of fixed and unchangeable guidelines that restricted monks' activities. It was instead an evolving corpus that accommodated the changing conditions of monastic life and the needs of the laity. They argued that *vinaya* required monks to support the 'development of the religion (*āgama*) and . . . those citizens who adhere to it'; and, to the extent that 'any program for [improving] human welfare in the world today is part of politics', *vinaya* actually *required* monks to participate in politics. They also argued that the perceived chasm between political activity and monastic affairs, or between national laws and *vinaya*, came not from Buddhism itself but from colonial and Christian schemes to 'separate monks and laity'. Walpola Rāhula, *Bhikṣuvagē Urumaya [Heritage of the Bhikkhu]*, 120–21.

For Malalasekera, using law to restrain this cohort of politically active monks was, in his words, 'the burning question of the hour'.[16] He blamed colonial laws for eroding the standards of monastic discipline. Laws such as the Buddhist Temporalities Ordinance, he argued, undermined *vinaya* by shifting disciplinary authority away from the leaders of monastic fraternities and into the hands of local chief incumbents. This meant that monastic fraternities (whose hierarchies were national, not local) could not enforce their laws in a top-down way. It also meant that defiant younger monks, like those from Vidyalaṅkāra, could disregard the orders of hierarchs: '[i]t is positively harmful,' Malalsekera decried in his presidential address to the ACBC given in September 1946, 'to have Nayakas or [monastic] Leaders who are so only in name, whose leadership is not only not recognised but often openly repudiated'. To restore monastic discipline, he called for 'a through-going reform in the present system of administration of Bhikkhus'.[17] He stressed that '[t]he future of the Sāsana is inextricably bound up with the *purity* of the Sangha'[18] – and the purity of the sangha depended on the promulgation of appropriate state laws.

THE BUDDHIST JUDICIAL COUNCIL

Between 1946 and 1959, Malalasekera and the ACBC led multiple attempts at law reform, each of which sought to 'purify' or 'reform' the sangha by creating a system of state-supervised monastic courts. The earliest blueprints for this system appear in Malalasekera's collected papers, housed in the Sri Lankan National Archives. There, sandwiched among the newspaper clippings and letters, one finds handwritten drafts as well as (presumably) final printed copies of a 'Proposed Bill

[16] Malalasekera, 'Bhikkhus and Politics.' Although Malalasekera, who was the editor of the journal, had supported monks from Vidyalaṅkāra in their studies, he sided with Senanayake, pleading with monks not to 'throw themselves into the maelstrom of party politics and electioneering' and, by so doing, 'prostitute their calling'.

[17] In addition to the agenda for the July 1946 meeting, the creation of a judicial council (*adhikaraṇa maṇḍalayak*) was also one of three proposals agreed to. That council would consist of monks and lawyers who were empowered to address disputes concerning monastic appointments and temple property. Pamphlet titled '*samasta laṅkā bauddha mahā sammelanaya, 27 veni sāṃvatsarikotsavya*' [27th Anniversary Conference of the ACBC]. 25–26 August. The subtitle specifies that it is 'led by Chairman Guṇapāla Malalasēkerara'. SLNA box 25.34/124.

[18] Printed leaflet from 'All Ceylon Buddhist Congress 28th Annual Sessions,' Amabalangoda, 8 September 1946. SLNA box 25.34/124.

for the Creation an Order that will Establish and Empower a Buddhist Judicial Council (*bauddha adhikaraṇa maṇḍalaya*)'.[19]

The bill offers the blueprint for a national body of monastic and lay experts who, convening as a Buddhist Judicial Council, would oversee the practice of monastic law. The head, or chairman (*sabhāpati*), of the body, was to be a Buddhist layman, specifically a lawyer who had practised in the Supreme Court for more than ten years. The Council's general members would be made up of ten to thirty bhikkhus representing each of the major fraternities (*nikāyas*), with formal appointments made by the governor on the recommendation of the fraternity's great leader (*mahānāyaka*).[20]

When disputes between bhikkhus arose, the Buddhist Judicial Council members would convene in seven-person courts (called *adhikaraṇa*) consisting of a chairman, four bhikkhus and two laymen, chosen by lottery among all members.[21] Lay lawyers or other delegated representatives were permitted to represent litigating parties. Verdicts were to be reached by majority vote among the judges, with appeals to the Supreme Court possible on questions of law and procedure but not Buddhist doctrine. Under this scheme, no disputes between monks could be heard in state courts without the permission of the Buddhist Judicial Council.[22]

The authors of the bill practised legal pluralism in a way that fit Malalasekera and the ACBC's elite-led visions of monastic reform.

[19] Handwritten draft titled '*bauddha sāsaṇika adhikaraṇa maṇḍala pihiṭuvīma hā patkirīma piṇisa panavanu labana āṇā panatayi*' [Proposed Order for Establishing and Empowering a Buddha Sāsana Judicial Council]. SLNA box 25.34/340. Mimeographed copy titled '*bauddha adhikaraṇa maṇḍala pihiṭuvīma hā patkirīma piṇisa āñā panatak äti kirīma saňdahā idiripat karanu labana keṭumpatayi*' [Proposed Draft Bill for the Creation of an Order that will Establish and Empower a Buddhist Judicial Council] SLNA box 25.34/279. All quotes below come from the mimeographed version, which is largely identical to the handwritten text.

[20] This reference to the governor, rather than the governor general, suggests that the bill was drafted and designed for implementation before independence. §2–3 of Proposed Bill.

[21] The courts would have discretion as to whether the proceedings were private or public and which language was used (§9–12). The draft bill also gave considerable leeway to the Council over courtroom protocol and procedure. The Buddhist Judicial Council could decide, for example, where the court would meet and the rules of evidence that would apply. The chairman was given powers similar to those of a district court judge: he could issue subpoenas and orders, and even prescribe punishments.

[22] §14 of Proposed Bill.

Purifying monastic law, in this model, depended on bringing *vinaya* under the control of both monastic and state elites, with the latter having oversight and the former providing the manpower. In personal letters from 1946, Malalasekera wrote that the survival of the sangha, and therefore the *sāsana*, depended on the efforts of determined laypersons to 'stop the rot that has obviously set in [to the sangha]'.[23] In another letter, he opined that 'the brilliance of the *sāsana* depends mainly on the bhikkhus', making it 'essential to raise up the situation (*tatvaya*) of monks and protect their honour . . . so that they may fortify the *sāsana* against its destruction and decline, of which several signs can already been seen'.[24]

For Malalasekera and the authors of the bill, 'raising up' the sangha meant reinforcing the authority of monastic hierarchies using state-legal mechanisms. The proposed Buddhist Judicial Council did not displace sangha courts so much as establish a hybrid institution (part sangha court, part state tribunal) that could strengthen the authority of the fraternities themselves.[25] To prevent outright conflict between the monastic and state court systems, and to ensure the relative autonomy of each, the draft bill mandated that would-be litigants could not apply to the Buddhist Judicial Council directly. Rather, they would first need formal approval to do so from the executive council of their own fraternity.[26] Even then, the Buddhist Judicial Council would only grant leave to the most difficult kinds of disputes, such as those involving monks from different fraternities. Rather than nationalising monastic law, therefore, the bill reaffirmed the legal boundaries of individual fraternities,[27] while also giving new powers to high-ranking monks.[28]

[23] Letter dated 30 March 1946 addressee's name unclear. SLNA box 25.34/340.

[24] Letter dated 10 June 1946 addressed to 'sir' (*mahatāṇeni)* SLNA box 25.34/340.

[25] The court could use its hybrid legal authority to compel monks to comply with the monastic court system by issuing enforceable subpoenas to no-show litigants (§14–15).

[26] *Svakīya nikāyika kāraka saṅgha sabhāva* (§15).

[27] The bill even made provision that litigants appealing to the Buddhist Judicial Council could request judges from their own *nikāyas* (§5).

[28] Were the bill to have passed, senior monks would have been able to issue expulsion orders to misbehaving members who, under penalty of criminal sanctions, would be 'prohibited from wearing the saffron robe and behaving like a monk (*cīvaraya daramin bhiṣuvak sē häsuruṇe*)' (§22). The bill inhibited monks who were expelled from one fraternity to join another, by mandating that such monks present to the new hierarchs permission from the *mahānāyaka* of their previous fraternity. Only those fraternities that were officially recognised by the government – and scheduled

USING LAW TO SAVE LAW: SANGHA COUNCILS AND SANGHA COURTS

In the 1950s, Malalasekera's draft bill served as the prototype for two other major attempts at legislative reform. Both initiatives grew out of public inquiries designed to recommend new policy frameworks for protecting Buddhism. The first inquiry, which ran from 1954 to 1956, was led by an ACBC-sponsored 'Buddhist Committee of Inquiry' consisting of seven monks and five laypersons. The second inquiry, which was modelled on the first,[29] was set up in 1957 by Prime Minister S.W.R.D. Bandaranaike, after his SLFP defeated the UNP in the 1956 general elections. Bandaranaike named his government-sponsored investigative body the 'Buddha Sāsana Commission'.

The two inquiries – led by the *Committee* and the *Commission* respectively – took place at a time of heightened enthusiasm and activity around Buddhism. Sri Lankan Buddhists had designated 1956 as the 2,500-year anniversary of the Buddha's birth. It was an especially significant event, given predictions that the Buddha's dispensation would only last for a total 5,000 years. To mark this moment, Bandaranaike's government supported a range of educational, religious and legal projects. They sponsored projects to translate the Tipiṭaka into Sinhala[30] and create an Encyclopaedia of Buddhism; they supported a Professorship in Buddhist Studies and convened numerous public rituals and celebrations.[31]

In this context of Buddhist activism, both the Committee and the Commission produced long reports recommending new laws and institutions that would help 'rehabilitate' Buddhism from its depredations

in the bill – would count as valid, thereby preventing a proliferation of self-made sangha groups (§16, 23). Under one section (§16), the bill even promised that 'all constitutions (*vyavasthāvan*) that had been enacted by the executive councils of fraternities and which had been published in the official government gazette would have the same legal force as if they were published in the bill itself' – a line that essentially gave *katikāvatas* the force of a government regulation.

29 In fact the composition of the two bodies overlapped considerably: of the ten monks and six laymen that comprised the government commission, three monks and two laymen had served on the ACBC Committee.

30 Deegalle, 'The First Sinhala Tripiṭakaya Translation.'

31 For a helpful account of these celebrations, referred to as the *Buddha Jayanthi*, see Bond, *The Buddhist Revival in Sri Lanka.*

under colonialism.[32] Their recommendations reflected similar concerns about the purity of monastic law and the necessity of protecting the sangha's autonomy. Ultimately, each of them recommended an institutional solution that looked similar to Malalasekera's Buddhist Judicial Committee: a hybrid judicial body that would ensure, in the words of the government report, that 'ecclesiastical courts [had] exclusive jurisdiction in matters relating to the Sangha'.[33]

A clear vision of this system can be seen in the recommendations of the government-appointed Buddha Sāsana Commission. The Commission proposed that sangha courts should be established as part of a national system of Buddhist governance, inspired partially by legal innovations in Burma.[34] The system would be overseen by a Sāsana Council (*sāsana maṇḍalaya*) administered collaboratively by two bodies: one consisting of laity and monks together, the other consisting of monks alone.[35] The first body, called the Sāsana Union

[32] So similar were the two projects, in fact, that Malalasekera even wrote to the Minister of Cultural Affairs expressing concerns that those who had contributed to the ACBC *Committee* might see the new government *Commission* as simply replicating and undermining the work they had done. Consider, for example, a letter written from Malalasekera to the Minister of Cultural Affairs on 8 January 1957 expressing 'misunderstanding and misgiving in certain quarters regarding the powers and functions of the Buddhist Commission' and a concern for the 'unity and solidarity of the Buddhists'. Letter archived in SLNA box 25.341/124.

[33] Government of Ceylon, *Interim Report of the Buddha Sāsana Commission (Sessional Paper XXV of 1957)*.

[34] In 1949, Burma successfully enacted its own sāsana-purifying legislation in the form of the Vinicchaya-thāna and Vinicchaya Tribunal Act, which established an official system of 'Ecclesiastical Courts' to manage the disputes over the Vinaya, including a hierarchy of tribunals from the local to national levels. This was modified in the subsequent Provisional Vinicchaya-Htana Act of 1951. In 1950, Burma's lawmakers introduced the Buddha Sāsana Act, which established a 'Buddha Sāsana Council' consisting of lay and monastic members who, together, served as a national body that could oversee the practice of Buddhism and represent the country's Buddhists. Although not modelled precisely on these statutes, the ACBC recommendations were certainly inspired by them. Events in Burma were followed closely in Buddhist publications, and ACBC writers even appended excerpts from Burma's Buddha Sāsana Act to the end of their petition. On developments in Burma during this period of legal change, see: Ashin, 'Die-Human, Born Human. The Life and Posthumous Trial of Shin Ukkaṭṭha, a Pioneering Burmese Monk during a Tumultuous Period in a Nation's History,' 92.

[35] Government of Ceylon, *Buddha Śāsana Komiṣan Vārtāva (Buddha Sāsana Commission Report)*, 242 (§820). The idea behind creating two distinctive organisations was that the commissioners felt that it was inappropriate (*nusudusu*) for laity to make decisions about monastic issues.

(*sāsana saṅgamaya*), would represent a variety of Buddhist societies and organisations.[36] Its responsibilities would include overseeing Buddhist finances and education, organising rituals and cultural events, administering and developing Buddhist sacred sites, registering monks and overseeing a nationwide system of 'temple societies' (*vihārasamiti*).[37]

The second (monastic) body was to be called the Supreme Sangha Council (*uttara saṅgha sabhāva*). It would consist of fifty members, both appointed and elected, representing all fraternities and regions of the country.[38] The body would have authority over the 'same duties that were assigned to Sinhalese kings previously',[39] including overseeing the discipline, education and unity of the island's monks and administering the newly proposed sangha court system. The Supreme Sangha Council would also be charged with developing 'religious constitutions' governing the practice of Buddhism of monks

[36] As presented in the bill, this body was to have fewer than 101 members, consisting of five groups: laypersons elected from Buddhist societies, an equal number of laity and monks representing regional associations, a variable number of laity and monks appointed by a 'nomination committee' consisting of laity and monks appointed by various other Buddhist societies, and three ex-officio members: two bhikkhus from the Supreme Sangha Council, including the chairman and the chief lay official for the Temple of the Tooth. Government of Ceylon, 258 (§879 and ff.).

[37] Government of Ceylon, 251 (§842 and ff.). A key element of the administrative scheme imagined in the draft bill is the creation of temple societies (*vihāra samiti*) consisting of monks and laity living near a particular Buddhist temple. These groups would be registered with the Department of Cultural Affairs and would help oversee the routine administration of the temples, including maintaining a register of devotees. These groups would also help to ensure that the appointment of monastic incumbents followed a set of defined rules, which the draft bill spelt out in detail.

[38] The proposed representation seems to be based on the Burmese law. It consisted of appointed and elected members. Among the twenty-one members were fifteen senior monks representing the Siyam, Amarapura and Rāmañña Nikāyas (roughly in proportion to the size of those groups) as well as six ex-officio members: the *mahānāyakas* of the Malvatu and Asgiri Chapters of the Siyam Nikāya; one *mahānāyaka* from the Amarapura Nikāya (the confederation of sects not having elected a supreme *mahānāyaka* at that point); the *mahānāyaka* of the Rāmañña Nikāya; and the principals of Vidyodāya and Vidyalaṅkāra Pirivenas, the two major higher institutions of monastic learning at the time. The thirty elected members were to be chosen from a pool of candidates representing the entire country. Aside from the appointed and elected members, the body was to be run by an executive council consisting of a chairman, three vice-chairman and six executive council members. Government of Ceylon, 255–256 (§866 and ff.).

[39] Government of Ceylon, 234 (§ 787).

in a manner similar to the Supreme Patriarch (*sangharāja*) in Thailand.[40]

A national system of sangha courts (*saṅghādhikaraṇa*) was a centrepiece of the new organisational strategy, earning its own major chapter in the Commission's final report. As imagined by the drafters, the system looked similar to Malalasekera's Buddhist Judicial Councils. As with Malalasekera's scheme, sangha courts would operate at two levels. At the first level was the fraternity sangha court, which would acquire 'all the powers that a district court currently has'. However, given that it would be 'unfitting' (*yōgya novana*) for monastic judges to issue subpoenas and warrants, press charges or deliver punishments and enforcement orders, such actions would be delegated to local courts.[41]

At the second level would be the 'great monastic court', a *mahāsaṅghādhikaraṇa*, consisting of eleven persons, appointed by the Minister of Cultural Affairs in consultation with the *nikāya* leadership: ten bhikkhus representing the three major *nikāyas* and a single Buddhist layperson, such as a retired judge or senior lawyer. A lawyer (also a Buddhist layperson) would be appointed as judicial registrar. The court would meet in three-judge benches to hear:

1. Minor (*suḷu*) criminal cases in which a Buddhist monk is either plaintiff or defendant and for which both parties agree to hear the matter in sangha court rather than normal court.
2. Normal (*sāmānya*) civil law cases involving a Buddhist monk as plaintiff or defendant and for which both parties agree to adjudication in a sangha court.
3. Civil cases in which both parties are monks (to be heard initially by the sangha courts of the three fraternities).

40 On the reasons for this, see: Government of Ceylon, *Buddha Śāsana Komiṣan Vārtāva (Buddha Sāsana Commission Report)*, 242 (§821). The Supreme Sangha Council could also advise the government on sangha affairs and – importantly for the authors – provide a network of scholars who could ensure that Buddhism remained effective in the modern world by adapting and interpreting its teachings 'according to the needs of the present world'. The example given is preaching sermons, which, the report speculated, had lost popularity because it has not been adapted to the times (*kālanurūpa no vana*). Government of Ceylon, 236.

41 Although the details were somewhat hazy, the imagined protocol seems to be that fraternity-based sangha courts would undertake the entire adjudication and rely on local judges only to issue orders in circumstances where the parties refused to appear or the sangha courts' judgments were ignored.

4. Court cases relating to the appointment of chief incumbents (*vihārādhipatis*).
5. Cases pertaining to the removal of [monks] from [such] appointments.
6. Cases declaring one to be stripped of his monastic status (*bhikṣutvaya*) (first heard by the sangha courts of the three fraternities).[42]

Under this proposal, the monastic court would have broad powers to rule on virtually any case involving Buddhist monks, with the exception of serious criminal offences.[43]

Compared with Malalasekera's draft law, the government-sponsored Commission proposed to hand over even more authority to monks and individual fraternities. Malalasekera's 2:1 ratio of monks to laity was replaced by a 10:1 ratio of monks to laity in the new apical judicial body. Moreover, the devolution of judicial authority to the fraternities created the impression that the government was ceding jurisdictional autonomy rather than asserting control. The commissioners framed their proposals not as mechanisms for state-led reform of the sangha but as instruments for the fraternities to regulate themselves – a means for them to enforce discipline internally and to have the ability to expel rule-breakers from their ranks. By preserving fraternities' own sangha courts as the tribunals of first instance and carefully uncoupling the acts of making and enforcing sangha court decisions, the commissioners offered up a purist vision of legal pluralism – one that promised to bolster monastic law without tampering with it.

[42] Summary of §687. Government of Ceylon, *Buddha Śāsana Komiṣan Vārtāva (Buddha Sāsana Commission Report)*, 205.

[43] Some sections deal with the issue of serious criminal cases. The authors essentially recommend that, after such matters are decided by a monastic court, local monks or members of the temple societies can bring those published judicial decisions to a local district court, which will then issue an order removing the monk from any position of authority he might have, such as chief incumbent. Government of Ceylon, 204–5.

Also under this proposal, the monastic court would be responsible for disputes over appointing and dismissing temple incumbents – which had long been the responsibility of civil courts. As imagined by the authors, cases like this could be filed only by members of temple societies or registered Buddhist monks. The *nikāya*'s own courts would continue to operate. But, under the new regime, civil disputes between monks or cases involving disrobing could be appealed to a national sangha court.

JUDGING SANGHA COURTS

From today's vantage point, the sangha court systems proposed by the Committee and the Commission seem to resolve many of the frustrations expressed by monks in Chapter 5. Several monks that I interviewed mentioned these 1950s proposals by name and lamented that none of the recommendations had ever been implemented. Indeed, as reported above, 88 per cent of the monks surveyed in 2017 agreed that it would be 'good to establish a sangha court for all monks in Sri Lanka'.[44]

In the 1950s, however, the legal proposals suggested by the ACBC and the Bandaranaike government faced fierce opposition in the island's major newspapers and parliament. The proposed schemes for 'legalising' monastic law drew particularly strong reproval from two groups of critics, each of whom accused the proposal writers of threatening the essential character and autonomy of law – both state law and monastic law.

One set of criticisms came from political elites, such as the Prime Minister and leader of the UNP, D.S. Senanayake, who portrayed the suggested reforms as endangering the pristine secularity of state law. Although sympathetic to the project of limiting monks' involvement in politics, Senanayake vehemently rejected the idea that the government should establish new institutions to oversee Buddhism. During a parliamentary debate on the ACBC proposals, he rebuked his political rival, SWRD Bandaranaike (who had introduced the proposals), quipping in front of the entire House of Representatives, 'we have come to Parliament to do public service, not to send you to nirvana'.[45]

In taking this strongly separationist position, Senanayake echoed the stance of the island's civil courts. In the decades leading up to the 1950s, Sri Lankan judges were also stressing the importance of keeping 'ecclesiastical courts' separate from state law – albeit for different reasons to Senanayake. In a series of judgments from the 1910s to the 1940s, judges argued that monastic courts, not civil courts, should make decisions about the conduct of monks because only they had the

[44] Question 12.3.

[45] Debate on 24 July 1951 as reported in: Government of Ceylon, *Hansard Debates in the House of Representatives*, 1550.

appropriate powers and expertise.[46] For both the civil courts and Senanayake, then, government intervention in monastic courts was not only unwarranted but harmful, as it risked perturbing the nature and integrity of both legal regimes.[47]

Monastic Opposition

More significant in derailing the proposals, however, were the negative reactions of monastic groups themselves, some of whom characterised the creation of a state-supervised monastic court system as attempts by an immoral government to control – and therefore corrupt – monastic authority. One powerful group that advocated this position consisted of the high-ranking monks from the Siyam Nikāya who, as in the 1890s (see Chapter 3), were suspicious of any state intervention in monastic affairs. Not only did the Siyam Nikāya monks boycott the government Commission and refuse to send delegations to its meetings, they even wrote a letter to the Governor General, imploring him, as the Crown's representative, to restrain the Commission from encroaching on the sangha's autonomy. In their appeal, they warned that, without such restraint, Buddhism might become 'the playground of the country's politicians'.[48] As a further rebuke, the Malvatu and Asgiri *mahānāyaka*s appointed their own '*sāsana* reform committee', which would 'set up a code for the administration and control of any arbitration on all

[46] Important decisions include the 1908 case of *Sumangala v Dhammarakkita* as reported in 11NLR360; the 1928 case of *Atadasi v Ratwata* as reported in 29NLR361; and the 1913 case of *Dharmarama v Wimalaratna* as reported in Balasingham, *Notes of Cases*, 57 and ff.

[47] One of the clearest statements of this position can be seen in the case of *Kirikitta Saranankara Thero v Medegama Dhammananda Thero* as reported in 55NLR313. In this case, rival monks from the Malvatu Chapter of the Siyam Nikāya ended up in the Supreme Court on appeal, with one litigant asking the judges to quash a decision given by the Malvatu sangha courts and the other litigant asking that it be enforced. Although the court stopped short of formally recognising the decisions given by the monastic courts as binding, the decision did (citing the case of *Dharmarama v Wimalaratna*) stress that it was 'a well-established rule of law whereby persons who voluntarily submit a dispute to a non-judicial or domestic forum must abide by its decision unless it be vitiated by misconduct or substantial irregularity of procedure or by a violation of the principles of natural justice'.

[48] *Times of Ceylon*, 21 January 1957 as quoted in Phadnis, *Religion and Politics in Sri Lanka*, 214.

matters in the Buddhist religion *and not look to the secular State* for such control'.[49]

A second group of monks opposing the government-supervised sangha courts came from the Vidyalaṅkāra Pirivena. Like the Siyam Nikāya, these activist monks drew on similar images of a pure, self-governing system of monastic law to condemn the work of the legal reform committees. In a long editorial in Vidyalaṅkāra's regular journal, *Nava Lokaya* or 'The New World', one influential monk conceded that although some change was needed,

> the change should not come from looking at the other countries of the world [e.g., Burma] nor from some [government-established] *sāsana* council. But from looking towards the original (*ādikalpika*) monastic society. It is from monks that the necessary changes must come[,] and not from a government or from pleasure-seeking laity. Therefore, if some desire-filled householders want to make some code (*saṅgrahayak*) for the *sāsana*, they should do so only if they don't place even a toe in the affairs of bhikkhus.[50]

This editorial, and others like it, cast both the ACBC and government reforms in the same light: as the unwelcome meddling of corrupted lay elites and a few, uninformed collaborationist members of the sangha. 'The time has arrived', the author wrote, 'to rescue the Buddha *sāsana* from the English-educated black-whites (*kaḷu suddangen*) and the politicians ... [who are] trying to make a mess out of the Buddha's dharma'.[51]

At the core of the impasse in the 1940s and 1950s then were not just politics and self-interest, but conflicting practices of legal pluralism that justified or rejected the act of 'legalising' monastic courts. Like the colonial commissions before them, Malalasekera, the ACBC and the Bandaranaike government argued that state involvement in sangha affairs was nothing new. Lawmakers were just carrying on the traditions of Laṅkan kings who, as the 'secular head[s] of Buddhism', also created

[49] Quotation from the *Ceylon Daily News* as reported in *World Buddhism* March 1953, p. 6. *Italics added.* Note: the intentions of the ACBC Committee had already been announced in 1951. All-Ceylon Buddhist Congress, *Buddhism and the State: Resolutions and Memorandum of the All Ceylon Buddhist Congress.*

[50] Nārāvimala Dhammaratana, '*Śāsana Komisama* [Sāsana Commission],' 140. The journal, *Nava Lokaya*, or *The New World*, was started by another Buddhist monk, Ven. Udakendawala Siri Saranankara in the 1940s.

[51] Ibid. 133.

laws and bureaucracies governing monks.[52] In the logic of the reports' authors (both monastic and lay), the government was not usurping monastic authority so much as empowering fraternities to enforce the rules of the Vinaya Piṭaka themselves.

For critics of these proposals, however, the mere possibility of government involvement in monastic discipline would sully the very thing reformers aimed to protect. Monastic groups accused lay officials of tainting the autonomy and discipline of the sangha and tampering with monastic legal traditions. Politicians like Senanayake pointed to the fact that establishing hybrid institutions to administer monastic law would undercut both the independence of the government and the purity of monastic law. In a notable parliamentary exchange, Senanayake condemned the ACBC's proposals as

> [reminiscent] of the old saying, *pīlle hakuru sangavenvā vāgeyi*, which means 'like hiding jaggery in the gutter'. In this case it is not in the gutter, it is in a worse place because in that place they will not find protection for Buddhism or any other religion; there they will meet with the destruction of all religion. It will be a case of '*Stalin saranam gachchami*' ['I take refuge in Stalin].[53]

SANGHA COURTS IN THE 1960S AND 1970S

Despite the public impasse over sangha courts in the 1950s, monks and politicians continued to create and debate proposals in the years that followed, all the while drawing on purist notions of law and agonistic practices of legal pluralism. Monastic courts remained at the forefront of politics in part due to the assassination of SWRD Bandaranaike by a Buddhist monk in September 1959, which provoked renewed public outcry over the perceived decline of *vinaya* among the island's monks. In the months following the murder, even monastic groups that had opposed the idea of government-backed sangha courts appeared to

52 All-Ceylon Buddhist Congress, *Buddhism and the State*, iv.

53 Debate on 24 July 1951 as reported in: Government of Ceylon, *Hansard Debates in the House of Representatives*, 1538–39. The Sinhala quotation appears in the original. In this quip, Senanayake is inserting Stalin's name in place of the Buddha's name in a set of vows that all Buddhists repeat regularly. The typical sequence for reciters is: 'I take refuge in the Buddha; I take refuge in the dharma; I take refuge in the sangha.'

reconsider.[54] Proposals for sangha courts resurfaced in parliament, along with other Buddhism-focussed policies.[55]

Partisanship followed as well and, by this time, the roles were familiar. When, during the first half of the 1960s, the SLFP-led government tried to implement elements of the Buddha Sāsana Commission report, the UNP opposition accused them of overstepping their legal powers and trying to control the sangha – tainting both state law and sangha law. Following the UNP's election victory in 1965 the roles were reversed, with the SLFP-led opposition levelling similar accusations against the new government. Monastic groups aligned themselves on both sides of the divide.[56]

Despite these political tensions, the push for legalising sangha courts endured, even as government officials and monastic leaders disagreed over precisely how it should happen. Sangha courts legislation was emphatically endorsed by the Chief Justice of the country in 1963 and declared a priority of the incoming UNP government in 1965.[57] The creation of 'ecclesiastical courts' garnered the support of

[54] For example, leaders of the largest monastic activist organisation on the island – the United Monastic Front (or EBP, *eksat bhikkhu peramuna*) – pledged to refrain from political action, with similar statements from other monastic organisations following suit.

[55] *World Buddhism* April 1960, p. 139. These included policies relating to the creation of a *sāsana* council (*sāsana maṇḍalaya*), the teaching of Buddhism in schools, the creation of monastic universities, the prohibition of monks engaging in politics or salaried employment, the state registration of monastics, interdictions on gambling and blasphemous films (about the Buddha), the reform of the Buddhist Temporalities Ordinance and the recognition of Buddhist public holidays (including recommendations to replace the existing Saturday-and-Sunday weekends with weekends reckoned according to the lunar calendar).

[56] Wilson, 'Buddhism in Ceylon Politics,' 527. Debates over regulating Buddhism took a slightly different hue in the 1960s on account of events in Asia. Writers in national newspapers and Buddhist journals warned readers about the state repression and control of Buddhism by autocratic regimes in China, Vietnam, Burma and Thailand. Aided by politicised suspicions of the country's Marxist parties (who were in coalition with the SLFP for most of the 1960s), UNP politicians cautioned against legislative reforms that might covertly seek to control Buddhism and co-opt its monks. This climate of politicised panic over state control of Buddhism immediately disqualified a number of recommendations made by the Bandaranaike-led government commission, including the formation of a national Buddhist council as well as state oversight over the ordination, economic activity or employment of monks.

[57] *World Buddhism*, September 1963, p. 11. Reporters recalled how the Chief Justice had, in front of a large crowd of Siyam Nikāya monks, repudiated the 'slur on a

major Buddhist lay organisations, with the ACBC making the issue one of its three foundational resolutions for 1966.[58] According to the Minister of Justice, all three *nikāyas* also supported sangha court legislation, which, he announced, would be drafted in 1966 with the help of a special 'advisory council for Buddhist Affairs' consisting of monks and laity.[59]

As the government moved forward, the fraternities prepared for the anticipated reforms by reviewing their monastic constitutions (*katikāvatas*). By 1963, the Malvatu and Asgiriya chapters of the Siyam Nikāya had reconstituted their joint committee (reviving their initiative from 1953) to draft a new joint constitution, with the other fraternities following suit.[60] Siyam Nikāya leaders weighed in on the legislative process underway with the government, expressing their concerns about the idea of a national monastic court that would preside over all fraternities and insisting that only monks from the same fraternity should judge the conduct of their peers.[61]

By 1970, the Siyam Nikāya leaders left no doubt as to where they stood on the proposed monastic court system. In a set of proposals submitted to the committee charged with drafting the island's new constitution, they urged lawmakers to include a clause guaranteeing that the government,

> *[S]hall not impose legislation, orders and regulations pertaining to the disciplinary activities of the sangha (Vinayakamma)*, its ancient and traditional customs and manners, the administrative institutions or the sect or the Board of Administration and its internal affairs.[62]

This proposal – which claimed to represent nearly half of the country's monks – made clear that while monastic leaders were happy for the

predominately Buddhist country like Ceylon for bhikkhus to resort to the law courts [which were] primarily intended for laymen' and called for 'immediate steps' to be taken to establish monastic courts.

58 *World Buddhism*, January 1966, p. 20–22.

59 *World Buddhism*, October 1967, pp. 74–75; *World Buddhism*, July 1968, p. 323. Representatives would come from all the *nikāyas*, along with lay representatives from the major Buddhist lay groups, including the ACBC.

60 *World Buddhism*, August 1963, p. 24. Mātalē Dhammakusala, *Rāmañña Vaṃsaya [The Rāmañña Lineage]*, 6.

61 Phadnis, *Religion and Politics in Sri Lanka*, 228.

62 Submission to Constituent Assembly from the *mahānāyakas* of the Malvatu and Asgiri branches of the Siyam Nikāya, submitted 10 September 1970. SLNA MCA 73/2/1. Italics are my own.

government to grant legal authority to monastic courts and constitutions, legalising monastic law should *not* entail government interference in fraternities' internal affairs.

Legal Reform as an Inside Job

The Siyam Nikāya proposals reflected a shift in public debates about monastic law during the early 1970s. Whereas earlier proposals for monastic courts from the 1940s and 1950s had tilted the centre of authority towards the state, the emerging consensus in the 1970s sought to devolve legal authority entirely to monastic fraternities. Legalising monastic law – according to this model – meant granting state-legal power (*nītiyānukula balayak*) to the *nikāyas* themselves rather than to some new conjoint judicial body composed of both monks and state officials. 'Purifying the *sāsana*' would be an inside job, undertaken within the monastery by 'pure' monastic authorities.

In anticipation of taking on these new powers, all three of the major fraternities undertook their own law-reform activities. In 1973, both the Rāmañña and Amarapura Nikāyas amended their constitutions (*katikāvatas*) to give greater coherence and unity to their administrative and judicial structures. Rāmañña lawmakers formally established their current three-tier system of Regional, High and Supreme Courts, discussed in Chapter 5.[63] The Amarapura Nikāya, a federation of more than twenty largely independent sub-fraternities, created an overarching administrative charter which, among other things, outlined a 'federal' court system that would sit above its many separate sangha councils.[64] In February 1972, the heads of the Malvatu and Asgiri chapters of the Siyam Nikāya convened a meeting of 'the four chapters of the Siyam Nikāya' – the Malvatu, Asgiri, Koṭṭe and Kelaniya *sabhāvas* – and appointed a nine-member subcommittee to draft a new Nikāya-wide constitution establishing a collective Siyam Nikāya sangha court overseen by a trans-chapter advisory committee of fifteen members.[65]

63 Śrī Laṅkā Rāmañña Mahā Nikāya Pālaka Saṅgha Sabhā, *Śrī Laṅkā Rāmañña Nikāya Vyavasthā Saṅgrahaya [The Constitutional Code of the Rāmañña Fraternity of Sri Lanka]*. Also see: *World Buddhism*, February 1972, p. 191.

64 *Amarapura Mahānikāyē Saṅghādhikaraṇaya Hā Śrī Laṅkā Amarapura Mahāsaṅgha Sabhāvē Vyavasthā Saṅgrahaya [Collection of the Constitution of the Amarapura Fraternity, the Monastic Court of the Amarapura Fraternity and the Constitution for the Sangha Council of the Amarapura Great-Fraternity]*.

65 *World Buddhism*, February 1972, p. 188.

As an important symbolic and political gesture, all three major fraternities had submitted copies of their monastic constitutions to the government at the start of 1974. In so doing they followed long-standing traditions: historically, Sri Lankan monks had presented important decisions, such as the appointment of a new *mahānāyaka*, to island's rulers. In the context of ongoing debates about legalising monastic law in the early 1970s, the presentations of these monastic constitutions carried additional weight. When a fifteen-member delegation from the Siyam Nikāya formally presented its new constitution and monastic court (*saṅghādhikarana*) 'acts' to the President and Prime Minister in May 1973, it was clear that they expected some imminent grant of new legal powers.[66]

Similarly, when the leader of the Amarapura Nikāya, Ven. Balangoda Ananda Maitreya, wrote the preface to his fraternity's 1973 constitution, he pointed out explicitly that the new charter would enhance the viability of an intra-sangha legal system:

> We now put into your hands the Amarapura fraternity *katikāvata*, together with the charters [of the different sub-fraternities] and the legal scheme for the fraternity's monastic court system. We do this with the hope that this will be a tremendous support and ensure the continuation and unity of the fraternity by providing the necessary systematic arrangements for unifying all the branches (*śākhaval*) of the sanghas that exist within our great Amarapura confraternity.

Maitreya's words reflected a broad expectation likely shared among leaders from all three *nikāyas*: the sangha was ready and waiting for the devolution of state-legal power in the near future.

For a time, such devolution seemed likely indeed. In 1976 the government prepared three draft bills 'to frame a new system of ecclesiastical laws for each of the three Buddhist *nikāyas* in Sri Lanka' for presentation to the state assembly by the Minister for Cultural Affairs.[67] When general

[66] *World Buddhism*, June 1973, p. 285

[67] *World Buddhism*, June 1976, p. 301. It is interesting to note that not all monks were happy with the three separate systems being recognised. For example, one assistant secretary monk from the Sri Kalyāṇavaṃsa Nikāya expressed simultaneous frustration that the government was giving up on the possibility of a singular code for all monks (given that they follow 'one and the same code discipline') and the fact that his own fraternity, which was 'a unique and distinct *nikāya* and not on offshoot of another', was not granted its own judicial system. *Ceylon Daily News*, 14 June 1976, p. 8.

elections rolled around the following year, the SLFP even included the creation of a monastic courts law as part of its election manifesto – a commitment echoed by the soon-to-be Minister of Cultural Affairs from the UNP.[68]

Lawyers, Monks and Lawyer-Monks

Efforts in the 1970s to legalise monastic courts and constitutions drew on particular practices of legal pluralism and assumptions about monastic and state law. Monastic law, the assumptions went, entailed the rules of conduct and behaviour particular to Buddhist monks, such as the imperatives to avoid contact with women or to follow the orders issued by sangha councils. It was thought to derive primarily from the Vinaya Piṭaka, as interpreted over time in commentarial literature and in the constitutions and courts of monastic fraternities. This way of thinking about monastic law gave the impression that 'legalising' monastic courts was easy because it simply involved recognising an already-existing jurisdictional split: monastic courts would handle *vinaya* while state courts would handle everything else. On its face, the arrangement promised to eliminate the need for monks to go to secular courts for anything but the most serious matters, such as criminal offences.

A single court case in the 1970s would fundamentally rattle this way of looking at things. The case involved Ven. Nakulugamuvē Sumana, a bhikkhu ordained in the Kalyāṇavaṃsa sub-fraternity of the Amarapura Nikāya and a graduate of the national university, where he earned a Bachelor of Laws degree. On graduation, Sumana applied for admission to the Sri Lankan bar as a lawyer. However, when his name was published in the newspaper alongside other candidates, it provoked widespread controversy among Buddhists. Within days, virtually every major Buddhist lay organisation on the island had filed petitions with the Supreme Court seeking to stop Sumana from taking his oaths as a lawyer.

In making their petitions, the Buddhist organisations appealed to the newly established chapter on 'Buddhism' that had been included in the

68 Sangha court legislation would be 'the piece of legislation concerning the welfare of the Sāsana moved in the National State Assembly'. *Ceylon Daily News*, 12 January 1978, n.p.: 'Sanghadhikarana will benefit 20,000 Bhikkhus.' It is interesting to note that a similar momentum was generated for reforming other religious legal structures at the time, as well.

new 1972 Sri Lankan Constitution. That chapter (Chapter II) gave Buddhism 'the foremost place' and obligated the government to 'protect and foster' it. Permitting a Buddhist monk to practise as a lawyer, the petitioners argued, would violate these obligations.

Sumana's case quickly became a cause célèbre in the country, reaching the front page of newspapers around the island. Noting the public outcry and legal significance of the case, the Chief Justice of the Supreme Court appointed a full five-judge bench to hear the matter. At its core, the case challenged popular assumptions about the nature of monastic law. For years, the issue of sangha courts had come up regularly in political debate. Yet this was the most high-profile court case to consider the content, sources and jurisdictions of monastic law – and to pit one set of Buddhist legal authorities against another.

Legal submissions in the Sumana case seemed to pit the authority of the Vinaya Piṭaka against the authority of monastic fraternities. A large coalition of Buddhist lay organisations and monastic supporters who opposed Sumana argued that the idea of a lawyer-monk was 'in contravention of the Vinaya Pitaka' and therefore 'contrary to the larger interests of Buddhism'. Supporters of Sumana, both laity and monks, rejected this position, arguing that monastic legal authority came not just from the Vinaya Piṭaka but from the organisational hierarchy of the fraternities themselves, and *their interpretations* of the Vinaya. These supporters included the highest-ranking monks in Sumana's own fraternity: the great leader (*mahānāyaka*) of Sumana's chapter, as well as the supreme leader (*uttarītara mahānāyaka*) of the entire Amarapura confraternity, who represented nearly one-third of the island's monastics.

The Amarapura approach was ultimately affirmed in a majority decision of the Supreme Court. When it came to monastic law, the court argued, institutions trumped texts. It was the fraternity's leaders 'whose opinion matters, and who have the power to examine the conduct of the Bhikkhu concerned'. Although others may read the Vinaya Piṭaka in a different light, the majority opinion concluded, only senior monks within a fraternity had the power to determine and enforce its rules.[69]

Sumana's case unsettled several key assumptions that had guided discussions about 'legalising' monastic law up until that point. Where

[69] *In the Matter of an Application by Rev. Sumana Thero to Be Admitted and Enrolled as an Attorney-at-Law* (Enrolment Application No. A 6851) as reported in 3SLR365 (2005), p. 372.

the architects of sangha court legislation had assumed that senior monks across the fraternities shared a more-or-less common model of monastic behaviour, the Sumana case exposed differences. Events in the Supreme Court cast a vexing light on the multiple conflicting authorities and texts that claimed to speak for monastic law: laity versus monks, legal texts versus legal experts, monks in one fraternity versus monks in another.

Not only did the litigants clash in Sumana's case, but the judges did as well. Chief Justice Samarakoon's eight-page majority opinion was followed by an extensive thirty-five-page dissent from Justice Wanasundara, who took an entirely different approach to monastic law. Wanasundara argued that questions of conformity with the Vinaya did not need to be deferred to monastic hierarchs. If judges wanted to know the correct standards of monastic law, they could simply examine the Vinaya oneself to see 'what the Buddha has actually said on these topics'.[70] When it came to monks' serving as lawyers, he argued, that answer was obvious:

> The Vinaya rules themselves are most exhaustive in nature and contain the training rules, prohibitions, allowances, and regulations, governing the life of a bhikk[h]u. They ... are intended to [commit] a monk to a life of seclusion and purity which will facilitate his mental development. They deal *inter alia*, with such minute matters as of dress deportment and propriety of conduct of eating, wearing the robe and even against causing harm to seeds and plants. It is not necessary here to refer to them in any detail as even a cursory perusal of the 227 rules will reveal this. These rules will give fair idea of the great degree of restraint and control over the faculties demanded from a monk and how incompatible such conduct is with the life of a layman. By no stretch of imagination could it be said that the profession of the law with [its] pre occupation with criminal and civil matters and its atmosphere of debate and contention heat and tension can be reconciled with the calm and detached life expected of a monk as indicated by the Vinaya.[71]

For Wanasundara, the inappropriateness of monks practicing law was obvious to anyone who read the Vinaya Piṭaka.To deny this conclusion was, therefore, not only to transgress the Buddha's sacred instructions, but to abandon the state's constitutional obligations to 'protect and foster' Buddhism – obligations which, according to Wanasundara,

[70] 3SLR365 (2005), p. 387. [71] 3SLR365 (2005), pp. 391–2.

included the government's duty to protect Buddhism's 'purity' against 'laxity and degeneracy'.[72]

Similarly polarised responses emerged in newspapers and journals, many of which made a direct link between the proposals for sangha courts and the issues raised by the Sumana case. Polarisation even appeared within the Amarapura confraternity itself. On one side stood the prominent scholar monk Ven. Walpola Rahula, who had filed affidavits of support for Sumana. Rahula envisioned a beneficial nexus between monk-lawyers and sangha courts, remarking to a journalist that 'society needed 20 to 30 bhikkhus like Ven. Sumana who were conversant with law' because they could bring that knowledge to the sangha courts.[73] Rahula's views were echoed by the registrar of the Amarapura Nikāya Ven. Pimburē Sōrata, who also welcomed the idea, suggesting that the legal training of lawyers would undoubtedly benefit the fraternity's own monastic courts.[74]

On the other side of the issue was Ven. Madihē Paññasīha, a popular and influential leader of the Sri Dharmarakkhita sub-fraternity of the Amarapura Nikāya and a member of Bandaranaike's Buddha Sāsana Commission. He insisted that the Sumana case was a perfect example of why the country needed an official sangha court system. The Sumana case, he commented, was 'the most opportune time for the Government to step in and take appropriate and immediate steps to prevent the recurrence of this kind of activity which was injurious to the Sasana'.[75]

Despite their opposing conclusions, both sides framed their arguments in terms of the purity and autonomy of monastic law. Only they

[72] The question was simply whether its mandates were both retrospective and prospective in nature: 'When it is said that Buddhism should be protected, does this envisage a restoration of the religion to its original purity or merely its preservation from further degeneracy and depredation? The issue becomes further complicated by the fact that, as stated earlier, it is still possible to see in this country the Dhamma Vinaya in its *pure form*, not only preserved as theory or text but also in practice as a living example. Side by side with this, we also see in certain quarters the spectacle of a departure from those high ideals where laxity and degeneracy prevail. . . . One may pose the question whether the provisions of [the Buddhism Chapter] should be regarded as a sword or as a shield. That is to say, should [they] be applied in a positive sense so as to undo even earlier transgressions and transactions, or only negatively in a defensive way, to prevent and ward off threatened dangers.' 3SLR365 (2005), p. 403.

[73] *Ceylon Daily News*, 28 January 1978, p. 4.

[74] *Ceylon Daily News (City Edition)*, 29 December 1977, p. 1.

[75] Ibid., p. 1.

fundamentally disagreed on where monastic authority was most rightfully located: in the interpretations of senior monks, or in the textual directives of the Vinaya Piṭaka itself.

THE ANSWER IS SANGHA COURTS, WHAT'S THE QUESTION?

It is difficult to overstate the significance of the Sumana case for practices of legal pluralism in Sri Lanka. With this case, questions about how to 'legalise' monastic law that had been submerged or overlooked were suddenly propelled to centre stage in public discussions: What might happen if legal authorities from one monastic group disagreed with those of another? What would happen if the norms endorsed by sangha courts conflicted with lay readings of the Vinaya or popular expectations about monastic discipline?

The contentiousness of these questions became starkly visible when, having won his case, Sumana returned to the Supreme Court to take his oaths as a lawyer. Under the weight of public pressure, the same court that had granted Sumana the right to apply to the bar now denied him entrance to the event. The reason was procedural: to take his oaths as an attorney, the monk would have to give up his saffron robes and put on the black and white suit required of lawyers – something Sumana was not prepared to do.[76]

While the Sumana case failed to resolve these tensions, it did manage to ignite an even broader public commitment to establishing monastic courts as a tool for addressing the conundrums that Sumana himself seemed to embody. The prominence of this commitment can be seen in the drafting of the sangha courts clause in country's second independent constitution in 1978, described in the introduction to this chapter. Also visible in the sangha court clause and the parliamentary debates surrounding it are the ongoing disagreements about the nature and reconcilability of monastic and state-legal authority.

At one stage during the parliamentary debates about the sangha courts clause, a prominent minister recommended that drafters add precision by inserting the phrase 'according to the Vinaya law' (*vinaya nītiyaṭa anuva*). That phrase, he argued, would clarify 'that the control of monks did not happen through worldly law (*laukika nītiyaṭa*)' because the Vinaya was

[76] Ceylon Daily News, 8 April 1978, n.p.: 'Monk in Robes not Permitted to Enrol.'

'already constitutionalised (*vyavasthāgata kalāma*) ... and valid even without [the support of] state law'.[77] To this suggestion, a senior minister quickly spoke out, rejecting any such attempt at disambiguation:

> This [provision] merely authorises the creation of *some kind of court* (*yamkisi adhikaraṇayak*) through the constitution. The ideas that the Honorable Minister advanced very much relate to the question of '*What is Buddhist law in Sri Lanka?*' And this is an issue that we don't need to pursue in this [1978 draft] constitution.[78]

Palpable in the Minister's comments is the same unease that had shaped public discourse during the Sumana case: a discomfort with confronting the deeper questions about the nature, scope and sources of monastic law. That discomfort was evidently shared by the Prime Minister, who, soon thereafter, called an end to the discussion, insisting that the provision was *not* designed to clarify the matter of sangha courts but was merely

> a way of making space in the constitution for accepting those acts ... relating to the creation of sangha courts (*saṅghādhikaraṇa*) which had been agreed upon by the esteemed Laṅkan sangha.[79]

As with the deliberately ambiguous phrase 'foremost place' that drafters used to describe the special status of Buddhism in Chapter II of the constitution, the ambiguous language concerning sangha courts served to paper over and temporarily evade larger and more divisive questions – questions about the precise scope and authority (*balaya*) that would be given to such courts and the legitimate sources of monastic law itself.

MONASTIC COURTS AND *KATIKĀVATAS* IN THE 1980S, AND BEYOND

By 1980, debates over legalising monastic law had moved, if not towards resolution, at least towards certain points of agreement.

[77] Speech by W.J.M Lokubandara (then a non-cabinet minister for Indigenous Medicine) on 16 August 1978 as reported in Government of Sri Lanka, *Hansard Parliamentary Debates*, 2028.

[78] Speech by Minister of Trade, Lalith Athulathmudali on 16 August 1978 Government of Ceylon, *Hansard Debates in the House of Representatives*, 2028–29. *Emphasis added.*

[79] Speech given on 16 August 1978 Government of Ceylon, 2029.

Firstly, the primary vehicle for legal recognition would be the monastic courts (*saṅghādhikaraṇas*), with monastic constitutions (*katikāvatas*) playing a secondary role. Secondly, the government would give up on creating its own national council of monks and officials that could resolve monastic disputes; it would instead delegate state-legal power (*nītiyānukula balaya*) to the sangha courts already operating within the fraternities. Using this approach, lawmakers could avoid accusations of undermining sangha autonomy while also sidestepping foundational questions about the nature and sources of Buddhist law.

Over the next twenty years, successive governments and monastic fraternities took steps to pave the way for such a system. A major White Paper was issued in 1981, followed by a presidential commission on the matter in 2001. Discussions were held in the newly formed Department of Buddhist Affairs (established in 1981), and monastic groups continued preparations for a formal handover. Even the judges of Sri Lanka's higher judiciary seemed to be preparing for such a delegation of legal authority. Yet, no legislation would be enacted, owing, in large part, to the persistence of purist models of law and agonistic practices of legal pluralism that dominated public discussions and parliamentary debates.

Legalising monastic law was initially championed by J.R. Jayawardene's UNP government (1978–1988), which was followed by six more years of UNP-led parliaments. It was under Jayawardene's leadership that the sangha courts clause was incorporated into the revised constitution. Jayawardene presented himself as a pious Buddhist but one who favoured clear boundaries between sangha and state. He had been one of the UNP's chief critics of the politically engaged Vidyalaṅkāra monks in the 1940s and remained an advocate of strong leadership in the monkhood, seeing clerical hierarchy as a means of controlling the political activism of younger monks. Shortly after taking office, he created a Department of Buddhist Affairs, convened a national committee to standardise Pirivena education and founded a 'Buddhist and Pali University' – all with the ostensible aim of making sure that monastic life remained disciplined and separate from mainstream politics and secular education.[80] As Steven Kemper has written, Jayawardene supported 'a certain kind of Buddhist monk – senior,

[80] On these issues and Jayawardene more generally see: Abeysekara, *Colors of the Robe*, 97–104; Kemper, 'J.R. Jayawardene, Righteousness and Realpolitik'; Schonthal, *Buddhism, Politics and Limits of Law*, 159–61.

high-ranking officials of the various fraternities and scholarly monks – and a certain kind of Buddhism – the kind that is lived out in monasteries, not on political platforms or behind police barricades'.[81]

The White Paper on sangha courts

In January 1981, Jayawardene's Ministry of Cultural Affairs published a 'White Paper on the Proposed Establishment of Saṅghādhikaraṇa (sangha court) Committees', which it released to the public. The introduction framed the initiative in grand historical terms. According to the authors, Sri Lanka's ancient kingdoms had once enjoyed a seamless integration of society, king, religion, tradition and laws (*sampradāyan sirit virit, nīti rīti*) such that 'the most important aspect of the Sinhala state was the connection between the foundations of society and its body of laws that entrenched, supported and protected the Buddha *sāsana*'.[82] This integration, they argued, had been severed by colonisation, harming monastic groups and their laws. By undermining Buddhist legal institutions – the Vinaya, *katikāvatas* and sangha courts – the British had eroded the sangha's legal authority and allowed foreign ideas to corrupt monastic life.

The White Paper promised to remedy this historical damage by proposing new laws that would

> giv[e] the necessary legal recognition to the decisions of sangha courts which had been the foremost element [upholding] the autonomy of (*svāyatna bhāvaya*) of our bhikkhu *sāsana*. And by doing so, to give an opportunity for monks to govern their own affairs according to things like *vinaya* rules and regulations and *katikāvatas*. This goal can be achieved through establishing monastic adjudication bodies (*bhikkhu viniścaya sabhās*) like those in the past.[83]

A notable shift in tone distinguished this proposal from previous proposals drafted in the 1940s and 1950s. Whereas those initiatives had framed legislation as a means of reforming the sangha or consolidating monastic authority under state oversight, the 1981 White Paper framed its recommendations as a means of devolving authority to the monastic fraternities (*nikāyas*) themselves – leaving it up to them to

[81] Kemper, 'J.R. Jayawardene, Righteousness and Realpolitik,' 201.

[82] Government of Sri Lanka Ministry of Cultural Affairs, *Yōjita Saṃghādhikaraṇa Sabhā Pihiṭuvīma Piḷibanda Dhavala Patrikāva [White Paper on the Proposed Establishment of Sanghadhikarana Sabhas]*, 1.

[83] Ibid., 2.

undertake their own acts of internal purification. Just as Jayewardene's economic policies emphasised privatisation and decentralisation in contrast to the state-centralising policies of the previous SLFP-led government, his government's vision for monastic courts similarly promoted a devolved form of self-governance rather than a centralised state-led project.[84]

Although claiming to move beyond previous efforts, the White Paper clearly built upon earlier legal proposals. The jurisdiction of the proposed monastic courts was similar to that envisaged in the 1950s and 1960s. Monastic judges would hear cases relating to the incumbency of temples, the conduct and punishment of monks, disputes between bhikkhus, and complaints made by lay donors about the activities of monks or use of temple property. A hierarchy of judicial bodies was also imagined. However, this time, the drafters proposed a three-tier, rather than a two-tier system, in which *all* of the courts – not just the lower ones – would come under the direct authority of the three major *nikāyas*. The proposed structure was as follows:

> Regional Judicial Councils (*prādēśīya anuvijjaka sabhā*) would act as a court of first instance for disputes among monks who were affiliated to the same sub-fraternity or chapter.
>
> High Court Judicial Councils (*mahā saṅghādhikaraṇa anuvijjaka sabhā*) would have powers to hear appeals from the regional courts, issue court orders enforcing regional court decisions, resolve disputes within executive councils and adjudicate disputes among different chapters (*pārśvayan*).
>
> Supreme Court Councils (*utttarītara saṅghādhikaraṇa sabhā*) would hear High Court cases on appeal and have original jurisdiction over 'petitions' (*petsam*) submitted by *mahānāyakas* as well as petitions made by monks or laity relating to major questions affecting the *nikāya* and the *sāsana*. These councils would also have powers to 'adjudicate on any issues that arise relating to *dharma-vinaya*'.[85]

Unlike previous proposals, which had envisioned hybrid institutions guided by a degree of state oversight, the White Paper underscored the legal autonomy (*svāyatna bhāvaya*) of the fraternities themselves. Yet it was an autonomy imagined in hierarchical, state-like terms. Legal

[84] Schonthal, *Buddhism, Politics and Limits of Law*, 159–67.

[85] Government of Sri Lanka Ministry of Cultural Affairs, *Yōjita Saṃghādhikaraṇa Sabhā Pihiṭuvīma Piḷibanda Dhavala Patrikāva*, 3 and ff.

powers would be granted, but on the assumption that fraternities maintained a pyramidal court structure analogous to that of the Sri Lankan judiciary.

Jayawardene's government presented the White Paper proposals to parliament as the product of extended consultation with Buddhists throughout the country. In a long and meandering speech, Jayawardene's Minister of Cultural Affairs, E.L.B. Hurulle, recounted the many conversations with 'the revered *mahānāyakas*, *anunāyakas* and *nāyakas*', 'leaders from among the collection of Buddhist organizations', and a dizzying number of ministers, 'Buddhist lawyers', jurists from the law commission and attorney general's office, working groups and other government bodies.[86] The grand description of this tripartite group – including the administrative 'triple gem' of Buddhist monks, lay organisations and government officials – sought to reassure the audience that the project was not an act of government intrusion on monastic autonomy. Rather, it reflected the admonishments (*anuśāsanā*) and instructions (*upades*) given by monastic leaders themselves. Its ultimate goal, he insisted, was to protect the integrity of monastic law by granting 'whatever power was necessary through the law so that monks could implement Vinaya, *katikāvata* and other things necessary for the respect of the sangha'. The White Paper proposals, in this way, helped guarantee that Sri Lanka would remain a bastion of 'pure Theravāda Buddhism'.[87]

The proposals were welcomed enthusiastically by major sections of the monkhood. At an ordination ceremony in August 1981, for instance, Rāmañña Nikāya leaders implored the president and other senior members of government in attendance to implement the proposed sangha court system as soon as possible. The fraternity's great leader proclaimed that such legislation would not only grant legal powers to the sangha courts, but it would also shield the sangha from monks who use civil court actions to challenge fraternities' rulings. Actioning the proposals in the White Paper, he suggested, would

[86] Speech given on 20 February 1981, as recorded in Government of Sri Lanka, *Hansard Parliamentary Debates*, 579.

[87] Ibid., 582, 581. The recommendations in the White Paper were not perfect solutions, he admitted, on account of the fact that, although the *sāsana* is singular, 'there are unfortunately today three *nikāyas* that, by tradition, are in existence' and 'a single law cannot change that fact'. Nevertheless, he predicted, the provisions in the White Paper were a step in that direction; and he submitted the document with the 'hope as Buddhists that one day the monks will be united into a single *nikāya*'.

safeguard both state law and monastic law, restoring to monastic fraternities 'the same ancient authority (*balaya*) that we [once] had to undertake monastic affairs without the interference of government'.[88]

The Fate of the White Paper

The plans laid out in the 1981 White Paper never eventuated, perhaps on account of the cascade of crises and tragedies that gripped the country during Jayawardene's government. This included a series of vicious, island-wide pogroms against the country's Tamil communities in 1983, followed by the onset of full-scale civil war between the government and the Liberation Tigers of Tamil Eelam (LTTE), resulting in the deaths of many thousands and the displacement of many more.[89] Unable to defeat the LTTE, Jayawardene accepted a controversial plan to deploy peacekeeping soldiers from India in the island's north while also devolving greater political authority to the island's provinces. These actions triggered a massive political backlash, motivating widespread protests and helping to fuel a violent Marxist insurgency led by the Janatha Vimukti Peramuna (People's Liberation Front, or JVP). Between 1987 and 1989, the JVP engaged in targeted assassinations and other violence, prompting a brutal counter-insurgency campaign by the government, during which thousands of suspected JVP members and sympathisers were detained or killed.

Despite these and other major events, the government did not abandon its plans to legalise monastic law. As Ananda Abeysekara and others have shown, scenes of Buddhist monks protesting the Indian Peacekeeping Force or supporting the JVP only further confirmed for Jayawardene and his deputies the urgent need for sangha reform.[90] During the same period, at least one monastic leader broke away from the powerful Asgiri Chapter of the Siyam Nikāya to form his own independent sub-fraternity in open defiance of sangha and political

[88] *Sasuna* [journal of the Rāmañña Nikāya], September 1981, p. 4.

[89] Estimates are that, between 1983 and 2009, around 100,000 people were killed in Sri Lanka's civil war, with nearly a million more people displaced.

[90] Schalk, 'Unity and Sovereignty: Key Concepts of a Militant Buddhist Organization in Sri Lanka MSV, Movement for the Protection of the Motherland'; Amunugama, 'Buddhaputra and Bhumiputra?'; Abeysekara, 'The Saffron Army, Violence, Terror (ism): Buddhism, Identity and Difference in Sri Lanka.'

leaders.[91] In the early 1990s, when Jayewardene's successor, Ranasinghe Premadasa, assumed office, the push to legalise monastic law was refreshed as a stated objective of government policy.

UPGRADING *KATIKĀVATAS* IN 1990S AND 2000S

In many ways, attempts to legalise monastic law in the 1990s and 2000s looked the same as in previous decades. Successive governments led the change, only to face resistance by opposition parties, who – invoking their own purist models of law and legal pluralism – stalled any new initiatives. Meanwhile, the institutional conditions of monastic life largely continued as they were. Monks continued to attend *pirivenas* and universities. They engaged in development work and charitable activities. Some worked as social workers and teachers. They joined activist groups and political movements – some of them inclusive, others fiercely nationalistic and anti-Muslim, anti-Christian or anti-Tamil in their rhetoric.[92]

One shift in governmental practices of legal pluralism, however, was the increasing emphasis on monastic constitutions (*katikāvatas*) rather than monastic courts (*saṅghādhikaraṇas*) as the key instruments for legal change. This is visible in a 1990 memorandum on 'legislative activities' produced by the Department of Buddhist Affairs.[93] In it, the authors lay out several measures that must be taken to prepare for the devolution of legal authority to monastic fraternities:

1. The fraternities should update their *katikāvatas* and basic rules for conducting monastic-court cases (*saṅghādhikaraṇas*) in accordance with the Vinaya Piṭaka;
2. The Minister of Buddhist Affairs should register the updated *katikāvatas* and take steps to ensure that they are given legal authority (*naitika balaya*);

[91] Abeysekara, 'Politics of Higher Ordination, Buddhist Monastic Identitiy, and Leadership at the Dambulla Temple in Sri Lanka.'

[92] On some of the diverse roles and activities of Buddhist monastics during this period see, Abeysekara, *Colors of the Robe*; De Silva, 'Vigilant Steps'; Fedricks, 'Accessibility of Nirvāṇa: The Language and Media of Sri Lankan Buddhist Televangelists and Their Followers'; Kahandagama, 'New Buddhist Trends in Post-War Sri Lanka'; Seneviratne, *The Work of Kings*.

[93] Thank you to Steven Kemper for sharing a copy of this memorandum with me.

3. Steps should be taken to adjudicate disputes among bhikkhus belonging to particular *nikāyas* according to the *katikāvatas* that have been accepted by those *nikāyas*;
4. Steps should be taken to establish an inter-*nikāya* working committee (*bala maṇḍalayak*) which can expand on these measures and also settle inter-*nikāya* problems as they arise, drawing on their experiences with resolving conflicts within their *nikāya*. ('*Nikāya*' should be interpreted as including all chapters (*pārśva*) that have fulfilled the obligations according to Section 41 of the Buddhist Temporalities Ordinance.)

According to field notes taken by Steven Kemper – who met with officers in the Department of Buddhist Affairs in October 1990 and obtained a copy of the memorandum – these updated proposals emerged out of discussions with government officials earlier that year. Comments made by one of the officers help explain the rationale behind turning legislative attention from the sangha courts to *katikāvatas*. The court system proposed by the 1981 White Paper, the officer reported, had been opposed by monks in the Siyam Nikāya because it appeared to apply the Rāmañña model of sangha courts to all fraternities on the island.[94] If the government was truly committed to sangha autonomy, the officer suggested, it should instead recognise the distinct legal institutions used by each of the fraternities – institutions that were differently laid out in each of the fraternities *katikāvatas*.

Following this line of thinking, government reforms since the 1990s have focussed almost entirely on the narrower issue of how and whether to recognise *katikāvatas* in law. A key moment came in 2001, when President Chandrika Bandaranaike – the daughter of the Prime Minister who had convened the 1957 Buddha Sāsana Commission –

[94] This certainly seems plausible. Although unstated in the White Paper itself, the proposed court hierarchy bears striking resemblance in its structure and terminology to the three-tier court structure employed by the Rāmañña Nikāya at that time. Similarly to the Rāmañña system, monks would collectively form a regional judicial committee (*anuvijjaka maṇḍalaya*) and would convene for adjudication in three-judge panels. Rāmañña-like judicial registrars (*lekhakādhikārīn*) were also proposed as officers who could administrate the judicial system as a whole, including issuing summons, keeping records, and publicising decisions. Also similar was the process of selecting senior court judges from the pool of existing *anuvijjakas* by the *mahānāyakas* and executive councils.

formed a *new* Buddha Sāsana Commission.[95] Members of the new Commission recommended working with *katikāvatas*, rather than sangha courts, as a way to ensure the fraternities' legal independence: 'Instead of a *saṅghādhikaraṇa* act', the commissioners proposed, 'we should give legal power (*nītimaya balaya*) to the *katikāvatas* of the various *nikāyas*'.[96]

Two years later, the government introduced to parliament a new *Katikāvata* Registration Bill permitting all recognised monastic fraternities to register their *katikāvatas* with the Commissioner of Buddhist Affairs.[97] The bill also stipulated a list of four topics that each *katikāvata* should cover in order to receive approval (§6(1)):

(a) The rules governing the discipline and conduct of a bhikkhu;
(b) All matters relating to bhikkhuhood and bhikkhu life;
(c) The procedure to be adopted in resolving disputes arising between and among bhikkhus pertaining to the observance of bhikkhu

[95] By then, the format for this work was well established: a committee was formed consisting of five Buddhist laypersons and six high-ranking monks, chaired by the *mahānāyaka* of the Kotte Chapter of the Siyam Nikāya after the Malvatu *mahānāyaka* declined. The group then received a mandate from the president to survey the condition (*tattvaya*, the same word used by previous commissions) of Buddhism in Sri Lanka and to identify the key issues facing the *sāsana*. The commission began its work in September of 2001 with the publication of newspaper notices in English, Sinhala and Tamil inviting Buddhist monks and the general public, along with Buddhist organisations, to make submissions responding to the mandate. A programme was broadcast on one of Sri Lanka's public television stations on 30 November, further advertising the event. By January 2002, the commission had received 443 letters. Between December 2001 and 2002, the commission held eighty-two working meetings, reviewed previous legislation and reports (including those mentioned above), met with key government officials and oversaw a series of public hearings in different parts of the country where there were large Buddhist populations. Government of Sri Lanka, *Report of the Buddha Sāsana Presidential Commission: Summary of Conclusions and Recommendations*, 1–3, Schedule IV.

[96] Government of Sri Lanka, 54.

[97] *The Katikāvata Registration Bill* was presented to parliament on 12 July 2004 and gazetted on 9 July 2004. According to the bill, a single *katikāvata* could be made to govern multiple *nikāyas*. This provision was included ostensibly to accommodate fraternities like the Amarapura Nikāya, which had established a shared overarching *katikāvata* endorsed by all its varying chapters. The list of recognised fraternities draws from lists kept with the Department of Buddhist Affairs and includes nine branches of the Siyam Nikāya, twenty-one branches of the Amarapura Nikāya and two branches of the Rāmañña Nikāya (see Appendix X). All quotations are from the English version of the bill.

vinaya rules, misconduct and misdemeanours of the bhikkhus, and the incumbency of [monastic] property; and
(d) The establishment and the functions of a Karaka Sangha Sabha for each Nikaya.

Rather than directly incorporating sangha courts, the bill sought to recognise the *katikāvatas' rules* concerning sangha courts and the standards of monastic conduct. This meant that, if a dispute were to arise among bhikkhus, state courts would have the authority to enforce sangha court decisions because the authority of the decision-makers and the regulations they applied would have been recognised in state statute. If a disgruntled monk 'resist[ed]' the sangha court's decisions, fraternity leaders could, by prevailing on the Commissioner of Buddhist Affairs, seek a district court order compelling the monk's compliance using police assistance if needed.

The 2004 *Katikāvata* Registration Bill was built on the principles and procedures laid out in the 2001 Report, which in turn drew on ideas and debates dating back to the 1940s. Nevertheless, as with previous proposals, the new bill also aroused fierce opposition from those who took a purist view of monastic and state law. Claiming it was a violation of monastic autonomy, critics condemned the bill for giving a list of topics that fraternities must include in their *katikāvatas*. Critics also decried the idea that civil courts (rather than sangha courts) retained ultimate powers to enforce the orders. As in previous decades, opponents cast the bill as a device for intervening in monastic affairs, permitting lay bureaucrats to taint what should be a pure legal order rooted in the Vinaya Piṭaka.

These agonistic practices of legal pluralism won the day: the *Katikāvata* Registration Bill never received a second reading in parliament, and the matter largely faded from view for the next ten years as other forms of 'Buddhist interest litigation' took centre stage.[98] Yet, as history had repeatedly shown, the issue would not remain dormant. In 2016, the question of *katikāvata* legislation resurfaced again in a highly public and acrimonious way – one that will be examined in Chapter 8.

CONCLUSION

In 2018, a Sri Lankan television programme hosted a live debate on the topic of monastic courts, in which one of the two monastic

[98] Schonthal, 'Securing the Sasana through Law.'

interviewees summarised the history of events described in this chapter as follows:

> [The debates today] are part of the same history, the idea of having a sangha courts [bill] was first introduced [during the time of] D.S. Senanayake [in the 1940 and 50s]. From that day – and I'm not making a criticism here – there's been opposition to that. This opposition starts and stops with that. In this way, all of [these current debates] have been part of that history. Now, maybe sometimes this is done falsely for political reasons. Sometimes, there may be radicals (*rädikalvādī*) saying that if they [pass a bill] we monks will lose our freedom. Regardless, there are always some who are dead set against it, no matter what.[99]

A similar sense of frustration, and history, was evident among many of the monks I interviewed. One exasperated Rāmañña jurist put it this way:

> We've been asking since 1956 [to legalise monastic law]. . .. In the past, as far back as the reign of King Aśoka, there has been a purification of the sangha (*saṅgha śōdanayak*). It's happened several times. . .. Now, *katikāvatas* have been promulgated, such as the *Dambadeni Katikāvata*, the *Poḷonnaruva Katikāvata* and others. . .. Over time, these [laws] had to be reformed (*śaṅśōdanaya karanna*). . .. [In the past] there were strong figures who could do that. They stood behind the idea that the *sāsana* must be protected. Today, [Sri Lankan politicians] are not like that. They are only focused on their [own political] survival.[100]

In both quotes, and the larger conversations from which they were taken, one finds even further concerns with establishing or defending legal purity. These monks blame political opportunism combined with ineffectual governments for the ongoing failures to legalise monastic law, and this failure has, in turn, interfered with the purity of the sangha and its legal system. From their perspectives, state recognition and reform of monastic law – whether in the 1950s, or in Aśoka's time – are not new tools used to limit monastic independence. They are part of a much older tradition of using state power to purify monastic laws in ways that ensure the flourishing of the sangha and *sāsana* together. Their voices are part of a decades-long chorus of demands

[99] 'Television Broadcast: *Theravādī Bauddha Saṅghādhikaraṇaya* [*The Monastic Court in Theravāda Buddhism*].'

[100] Interview with chief judicial registrar and senior jurist (*jyeṣṭhānuvijjaka*) in Colombo 20 December 2017.

made by politicians and monks calling on the Sri Lankan state to 'legalise' monastic law.

To understand why, despite this chorus, Sri Lanka has never managed to enact substantive reforms, one must acknowledge the twofold character of legal pluralism as presented in this book. Legal pluralism is not just an empirical condition, an assemblage of normative artefacts (codes, customs, tribunals, procedures and norms) emanating from monastic and state-legal authorities. It also entails a set of *practices* that collate, connect and characterise those artefacts – giving order and meaning to the diverse 'stuff' of law.

Understood this way, the failure to legalise monastic law is not due to any inherent incompatibility between the 'stuff' of monastic law and state law. It is due to the agonistic practices of legal pluralism advanced by the island's influential elites, both lay and monastic, who – for a variety of reasons – have consistently framed attempts to legalise monastic law as a mixing of pure, autonomous systems that should be kept apart. Drawing on these purist conceptions of law, critics have repeatedly mobilised the public against legal change by accusing would-be reformers of tainting laws that were otherwise pristine and should be free from normative mixing.

For nearly a century, these purist frameworks have helped ensure that monastic-state legal pluralism continues to be presented as problematic and unstable. That is because the same purist notions of law used to legitimate legal reforms *have also* been used to sabotage those same reforms in parliaments, courtrooms and monasteries. The government politicians who support *katikāvata* bills as a way to protect the purity and autonomy of monastic law, when in opposition, criticise those same reforms as corrupting the Vinaya and violating the sangha's autonomy.

At the same time, public protests over laws' threatened purity ignore entirely the many everyday practices that place monastic and state law in a more flexible and accommodationist relationship. Practices like these appear throughout Parts I and II of this book: civil lawyers and judges help draft some *katikāvatas*, monastic jurists identify symmetries between *vinaya* and state law, and monastic lawmakers and civil judges look to the other legal tradition to remake and reform their own laws. The Vinaya Piṭaka itself enjoins monastics to reconcile monastic rules with 'the orders of the king', unless they are manifestly unjust.[101]

[101] von Hinüber, 'Buddhist Law,' 29.

Of course, purist arguments do not explain everything. The governments of Bhutan, Myanmar, Vietnam and Thailand have all established official sangha courts and hierarchies, despite periodic protests made by monastic groups and politicians. To do so, they relied on modes of authority other than parliamentary debates, drawing on the charisma of kings and the coercive power of militaries. Viewed in this way, it is not simply factionalism, political polarisation and agonistic practices of legal pluralism that are to blame in Sri Lanka. One must also credit the robustness of Sri Lanka's democracy and the decentralised nature of its monastic groups for the persistence of the debate and the lasting inability to create a singular top-down solution. In issues of monastic law, as in all things, democracy and decentralisation both invite and prolong difficult conversations – a good thing, provided those conversations take place in good faith.

The history of legislative failure and purist visions of legal pluralism can be seen in other contexts as well. Wherever governments are asked to 'legalise' the laws of non-state groups, one finds similar debates over tainting, corrupting or coopting those laws. The politics of recognising monastic law in Sri Lanka may be compared with the politics of recognising forms of Indigenous law in Australia, Canada and New Zealand. In India, Pakistan, Malaysia, Egypt and elsewhere, political and religious elites have also faced similar kinds of double binds when it comes to the status of Islamic law.[102] To assent to acts of state legalisation is always, in some ways, to confront the idea of a pure and fully autonomous system of law.

What is ironic about this process in Sri Lanka is that agonistic, purist practices of legal pluralism – which are mobilised in the name of protecting monastic law – have served to hold in place the very colonial-era institutions that all parties claim to be inadequate. Monastic law continues to remain in thrall to colonial legal structures in Sri Lanka in large part because would-be reformers and, more importantly, their critics have insisted on a purist vision of multilegality that has likely never existed. The impacts and legacies of this history will be explored in Chapter 8.

[102] Kamal, 'A Theory of Religious Sovereignty Private Law Disputes and State-Religion Relations in Bangladesh and Pakistan.'

CHAPTER EIGHT

CONSTITUTIONALISING VINAYA

In July 2021, amid growing frustration over the government's pandemic response, surging commodity prices and political corruption, then Prime Minister Mahinda Rajapaksa issued a memorandum to his cabinet announcing his intention to introduce a new bill purporting to safeguard the core texts of Theravāda Buddhism.[1] Entitled the 'Tipiṭaka Conversation Act', the bill sought to criminalise actions that would 'alter, distort, destroy or have destroyed, disrespect or use illicitly' the three 'baskets' of texts – or Tipiṭaka – thought to contain the Buddha's original words.[2] Commentaries and sub-commentaries on the Tipiṭaka were also protected by the bill, including a large number of works relating to the 'basket' of monastic law, the Vinaya Piṭaka.

In his cabinet memorandum, the Prime Minister claimed the law would protect Buddhist texts from 'active vicious forces which distort the pure dharma and ... thereby damage the values system of Buddhism'. Such protection, he clarified, was not simply important for Buddhists. Rather, it was required by the Constitution of Sri

[1] *Vikṛti kirīma*. '2021 *aṅka ... darana tripitaka saṁrakṣaṇa panata*' [the Tripiṭaka Conservation Act of 2021, number...'] Unpublished copy of the bill in possession of the author.

[2] §(2)(i) of draft bill. The bill thus extended protections also to the 'official' Sinhalese language translation of the Tipiṭaka, which had been commissioned by the government in 1956. On the status of the Tipiṭaka, see Chapter 2.

Lanka, which placed a responsibility on the government to preserve 'pure Buddhism for the future generation[s]'.[3]

Visible in this episode is a particular practice of legal pluralism that has defined Sri Lankan politics for decades, one that construes monastic and state law in certain ways and places them into a particular kind of relationship. Since independence, lawmakers in Sri Lanka have characterised the laws of the state not simply as distinct from the laws of the Buddha but as the guarantor and protector of them. Starting in 1972, this approach to legal pluralism has been embodied in the second chapter of Sri Lanka's constitution, entitled 'Buddhism':

> The Republic of Sri Lanka shall give to Buddhism the foremost place and accordingly it shall be the duty of the State to protect and foster the Buddha Sāsana, while assuring to all religions the rights granted by Articles 10 and 14(1)(e) [namely, 'freedom of thought, conscience and religion' and freedom 'to manifest one's religion or belief in worship, observance, practise and teaching'].[4]

As presented in the Buddhism Chapter, the laws of the republic and the laws of the Buddha stand as separable entities, with the former having a responsibility to secure the latter. It is a binary approach to legal pluralism that – not unlike the colonial frameworks discussed in Chapter 3 – presumes that the Buddha's dispensation can be straightforwardly identified and 'fostered' through the instruments of state law.

For decades, the Buddhism Chapter of Sri Lanka's constitution has loomed in the background of virtually all public discussions concerning the relationship between monastic and state law. Among other things, politicians, jurists and monks have interpreted constitutional obligations to protect the Buddha *sāsana* as requiring the state to protect monastic law – especially the Vinaya Piṭaka, which is said to constitute the very life of the *sāsana* itself.[5] Readers have already encountered one instance of this in Chapter 7, with the legal controversies surrounding Ven. Sumana's application to become a

3 Cabinet Memorandum No: MBRCA/01/07/2021/CP/07 on 'Enacting an Act for the Preservation of Thripitaka' February 2, 2021.

4 The Chapter was first ratified in 1972 and then modified very slightly in 1978, to replace '. . .protect and foster Buddhism' with the current '. . .protect and foster the Buddha Sāsana'. On that change, and its broader implications, see Schonthal, 'Buddhist Perspectives on Freedom of Religion or Belief.'

5 On this quote and this idea, see Chapter 2.

lawyer. In that case, the Buddhism Chapter, and its presumed mandate to protect the Vinaya, featured centrally in the petitions made for and against the lawyer-monk. The Buddhism Chapter also featured prominently in the majority and minority decisions of the Supreme Court, which offered their own conflicting interpretations of the Vinaya Piṭaka's contents, alongside a broader discussion about the nature of monastic legal authority.

Neither the Tipiṭaka Protection Bill nor Ven. Sumana's case is unique in Sri Lankan history. Ever since the Buddhism Chapter's introduction, the constitutional obligation to 'protect and foster the Buddha Sāsana' has repeatedly been used to justify legislative initiatives and judicial rulings concerning monastic law. Yet, as I will demonstrate in this chapter, these interventions have consistently failed to stabilise monastic law in the ways imagined by lawmakers and litigants. Rather than shielding the contents and status of the Vinaya Piṭaka from disturbance (as imagined in the Tipiṭaka Conservation Bill above), legal appeals to the Buddhism Chapter have done opposite: they have invited and amplified disputes about the nature, structure and state-legal status of the Vinaya and monastic law – stimulating rather than reconciling competing practices of legal pluralism.

Invoking the Buddhism Chapter in lawmaking and litigation has cast a spotlight on difficult questions about the sources and status of monastic law. It has sparked debates about how to rank and assess the relative authority of monastic legal sources, including the Vinaya Piṭaka, monastic constitutions (*katikāvatas*), monastery traditions and institutional hierarchies. It has prompted arguments about the compatibility of monastic law with bureaucratic decisions, parliamentary statutes, court orders and constitutional law. At the same time, appeals to the Buddhism Chapter in courts and parliament have also attracted national media attention, helping to turn even minor administrative disputes into national controversies.

These dynamics can be seen clearly in three higher court cases linking constitutional obligations to Buddhism with questions of monastic law. In the first case, a Buddhist monk petitioned the Court of Appeals to compel a government officer to issue him a driving licence. In the second case, two Buddhist monastics lodged a fundamental rights petition with the Supreme Court seeking an identity card with the title 'bhikkhunī' or nun. In a third case, a coalition of Buddhist monks and laypersons mounted a successful political and legal challenge to a new bill proposing to recognise monastic constitutions (*katikāvatas*).[6]

Drawing on legal submissions, petitions, draft bills and newspaper coverage as well as interviews with litigants, lawyers and observers, this chapter examines the competing practices of legal pluralism elicited by the three cases. It considers how and why claims to protect the *sāsana* and Vinaya in law ended up mobilising – and publicising – differing expressions of monastic law and its ideal relationship to state law. What becomes clear through this examination is that, despite what the Buddhism Chapter would suggest, the coincidence of monastic law and state law in Sri Lanka is neither simple nor stable. Even those who agree on the goal of protecting monastic law using state law differ in their presumptions about what those laws contain as well as where and how they should coexist. Rather than a single multi-legal environment that individuals negotiate differently, one finds a landscape of divergent, overlapping and contested legal pluralisms – a diversity of ways that actors express and enact the 'fact' of legal multiplicity.

THE CASE OF THE DRIVING MONK

This plurality of legal pluralisms can be seen clearly in a court case questioning whether state officials ought to grant driving licences to Buddhist monastics. While there is no explicit legal ban on monks driving in Sri Lanka, there are strong societal norms against it. Few Buddhist monks attempt to drive, and those who do often face public censure. Against this backdrop, it was perhaps unsurprising that when Ven. Paragoḍa Vimalavaṃsa approached his local Commissioner of Motor Traffic (CMT) to apply for a licence, his request was denied. What was unexpected, however, was his decision to challenge the decision in court. Filing a petition with the Court of Appeal, Vimalavaṃsa accused the CMT of violating not only his constitutional right to equal treatment under the law but also the state's obligation, under the Buddhism Chapter of the constitution, to 'protect and foster the Buddha Sāsana'. By prohibiting him from driving, Vimalavaṃsa argued, the government was impeding his ability to teach and spread

[6] The long history leading up to and motivating this bill is explored in Chapter 7 of this book.

the dharma – and therefore violating constitutional obligations to 'foster' the Buddha *sāsana*.[7]

What makes this case particularly revealing is the way in which Sri Lanka's legal system became a forum for competing practices of legal pluralism. Over the course of more than a decade, the Appellate and Supreme Courts became public spaces for debating questions of monastic and state law, drawing attention to fundamental disagreements about their contents and how they should interact. At stake was not simply whether monks could drive but how state institutions should engage with monastic discipline, and which authorities – both lay and monastic – should have the power to interpret the Vinaya Piṭaka. From the courtroom, these debates spilt over into public life through Sinhala and English language media, where they were framed as part of a broader clash between monastic norms and contemporary life.

Taking Sides and Drawing Lines

In keeping with the adversarial format of litigation, the court received a large number of intervening petitions filed either for or against Vimalavaṃsa's claims. Many of these petitions came from Buddhist monks. Chief-incumbent monks from around the country wrote in support of Vimalavaṃsa, agreeing that denying licences to Buddhist monks violated monks' rights to equality under the law and undermined their important work in supporting the *sāsana*.

Opposing petitions came from a raft of important monastic leaders, including some of the most influential monks in the country. This group included the four great leaders (*mahānāyakas*) of the island's major fraternities (*nikāyas*) as well as a body of respected scholar monks representing the Tipiṭaka Compilation Board, a prestigious committee charged with compiling a new edition of the Buddhist teachings. These opponents argued that Vimalavaṃsa had the facts all wrong: denying a driving licence did not damage the *sāsana*; it protected Buddhism because it upheld the key principles of monastic discipline contained in the Vinaya Piṭaka.

The opponents of Vimalavaṃsa had a more difficult job, legally speaking. Not only did they need to demonstrate that the Vinaya prohibited monks from driving, they also had to make the case that monks' behavioural obligations under monastic law should override a

[7] For a different analysis of this case, focusing on different texts and facts, see: Schonthal, 'The Impossibility of a Buddhist State.'

monk's rights as a citizen to obtain a driving licence. Aware of this tension, Vimalavaṃsa repeatedly stressed that, when it came to Sri Lanka's courts, monks should be viewed *only* as citizens with rights and duties under Sri Lankan law, rather than as subjects of monastic law. As such, he insisted, judges should focus on monks' constitutional rights – not their obligations under the Vinaya Piṭaka. In any case, he warned, government officials have no jurisdiction to pronounce on monastic discipline because '[m]atters pertaining to the Vinaya are outside the domain of the Court'.[8]

Avoiding this jurisdictional trap required nimble thinking on the part of those who opposed Vimalavaṃsa. Their solution, a rather ingenious one, was to analogise the Vinaya to the professional codes of conduct observed by doctors and lawyers. Just as doctors and lawyers must abide by ethical guidelines that limit their freedoms, they argued, monks too were bound by Vinaya rules that limited their conduct. From this perspective, denying a monk a driving licence was no different than upholding the ethical standards of lawyers or doctors. Moreover, Vimalavaṃsa's opponents argued, the Vinaya represented 'the supramundane (*lōkōttara*) law' of the Buddha, which stood above – not outside – the 'temporal (*laukika*) law' of the state[9]:

> [T]he rights of a lawyer can be considered [only] upon taking into consideration the fact that he is bound by the regulations of the legal profession. This situation applies to other professions as well. When the rights of Buddhist clergy are analysed, these rights must be analysed *as below* (*yaṭat*) the law of the Vinaya Piṭaka.[10]

As framed by Vimalavaṃsa's opponents, then, Buddhist monks did not operate within two separate legal spheres, one dominated by the Vinaya the other by state law. Rather, they lived within both simultaneously, with monastic law, not state law, being primary.

This analogy to lawyers and doctors, however, had limits. Unlike professional codes of conduct in law and medicine, the Vinaya Piṭaka was not a document over which civil court judges were meant to exercise interpretive authority. If the Vinaya had the qualities of

[8] Written Submissions from Petitioner-Respondent Ven. Dr. Paragoda Wimalawansa Thero *in SC 84/2007 (SC/Sp.LA/240/2007*, CA *Writ. App. 1978/2004)*. Submitted Feb 24, 2014, p. 24. (Submission in English.)

[9] Letter Submitted as Evidence (R11) Letter to Commissioner of Buddhist Affairs in CA Writ. App. 1978/2004, dated November 11, 2006. (Submission in Sinhala.)

[10] Letter Submitted as Evidence (R11). (Submission in Sinhala).

prescriptive law, it was a law that was meant to be read and interpreted by Buddhist monks only. Yet, if monks were proper interpreters of Vinaya, what happened when they disagreed?

Interpreting Authority

For those who opposed Vimalavaṃsa, the answer seemed obvious. The most trustworthy interpretations of the Vinaya Piṭaka came from the highest-ranking monks – namely the *mahānāyaka*s and other senior clergy. Keeping with the analogy to the legal profession, Vimalavaṃsa's opponents argued that what higher court judges were to state law, higher-ranking monks were to monastic law.

This position was echoed in the submissions made by lay trustees from Vimalavaṃsa's own temple, who also opposed his driving. Referring to the lawyer-monk case discussed in Chapter 7 of this book, the trustees insisted that

> the opinions provided by Mahanayake Theros ... are the final interpretations on Vinaya Rules and that even the Supreme Court of this country cannot venture to interpret such religious rules.[11]

According to the trustees, as well as others, the Vinaya provided not only a code of conduct but an institutional blueprint for interpreting and enforcing that code: the Vinaya should be interpreted by the sangha's most senior monks, and national monastic bodies should set the terms for local monasteries.

Vimalavaṃsa disagreed vociferously. In his view, interpretive authority for the Vinaya Piṭaka did not rest in the hands of a narrow elite. Any educated, senior monk could apply the Vinaya themselves. In fact, the very notion of a single monastic hierarchy was, for him, a misinterpretation of Buddhist history and doctrine. He explained to me in a letter:

> There are no Mahanayakas or Nayakas in Buddhism. But, nominal Buddhists don't know that ... The 'Mahanayaka titles' were created by [Kirti] Sri Wickrama Rajasinha, the ruling king of the Kandy about 200 years ago.... Owing to his inadequate knowledge of Buddhism, he appointed [a] Mahanayaka for the Bhikkhu society... Even most powerful and favourable Emperor in the Buddhist History[,] the great Asoka[,] did not appointed (sic) a superior monk for the Bhikkhu Society [because] he had some sort of knowledge [about] Buddhism.

[11] Written Submissions on behalf of the Second to Fifth Added Respondents in CA *Writ. App. 1978/2004*, dated 5 February 2014. (Submission in English.)

> Unfortunately, Sri Lankan Buddhists do not know this . . . [T]hey think that the Mahanayakas are [in charge] of Buddhism.[12]

For Vimalavaṃsa, reading and interpreting the Vinaya was the prerogative of all qualified monks. Therefore, letters written by *mahānāyakas* and the Tipiṭaka Board should not be seen as binding legal opinions but simply 'expressions of . . . personal opinion'.[13]

Living Law or Fixed Code?

Having characterised monastic legal authority in this way, Vimalavaṃsa offered his own defence of the fact that the Vinaya Piṭaka did not prohibit driving. Drawing on passages of the Pali Vinaya along with other sources,[14] Vimalavaṃsa advanced two main arguments. First, he pointed out that the Vinaya Piṭaka contained no explicit prohibitions against operating automobiles. Second, he argued that, in the absence of a clear prohibition, one should look to more the general interpretive principles of monastic law, which gave guidance about how monks should handle issues that did not come up during the Buddha's time, such as the issue of driving cars.

According to Vimalavaṃsa, the Vinaya's rules of interpretation permitted monks to alter their behaviour slightly in order to accommodate changes in technology and lifestyle. He argued that a close reading of the Vinaya reveals that the Buddha had relaxed minor rules of monastic comportment over time, adapting them to his surroundings. Except for the four major offences that warranted removal from the monastery (*pārājikas*),[15] the Vinaya did not contain rigid and inflexible rules. Instead, he argued, the Vinaya was a living law designed to evolve over generations and allow for the 'broadening of the activities of the Bhikkhus' in society.[16]

12 Personal communication from Ven. Vimalavaṃsa.

13 Written Submissions from Petitioner-Respondent Ven. Dr. Paragoda Wimalawansa Thero *in SC 84/2007 (SC/Sp.LA/240/2007, CA Writ. App. 1978/2004)*. Submitted Feb 24, 2014, p. 20. (Submission in English.)

14 For example, quotes from the scholar monk Walpola Rahula as well as other passages from the Tipiṭaka, such as the *Kālāma Sutta* of the *Aṅguttara Nikāya*.

15 The four are killing, stealing, having sex or falsely claiming to have supernatural powers.

16 Written Submissions from Petitioner-Respondent Ven. Dr. Paragoda Wimalawansa Thero *in SC 84/2007 (SC/Sp.LA/240/2007, CA Writ. App. 1978/2004)*. Submitted 24 February 2014, p. 31. (Submission in English.)

Vimalavaṃsa's living-law portrait of the Vinaya may have seemed unorthodox for some, but it could not be ignored. The rhythms and requirements of litigation – which oscillated between argument and counterargument, petition and response, claim and objection – required that Vimalavaṃsa's opponents respond to the provocative (and, strictly speaking, accurate) claim that the Vinaya contained no prohibition against driving automobiles.[17] One practice of legal pluralism demanded another.

The opponents of Vimalavaṃsa argued that, when it came to the issue of monks' driving, he was simply looking in the wrong place in the Vinaya. Rather than looking topically for the subject of cars (e.g., in the list of rules contained in the Explanations section of Vinaya[18]), Vimalavaṃsa should have been looking at the Vinaya's collections of meta-rules for determining whether new kinds of practices, unknown during the Buddha's time, were permissible under the strictures of monastic discipline. This argument is underscored stridently in the letter from the Tipiṭaka Board.

> The basic argument of several of the monks who are demanding permission to drive is that, because there is not an [explicit] disciplinary prohibition relating to driving, it must, in time, be allowed.... [However] it is clear from looking at the history of Vinaya precepts that [those] precepts were enacted by the Buddha because monastic behaviour was occurring which was inappropriate within the social climate of

[17] In the Pali Vinaya there is a reference to monks 'going by' or 'driving' vehicles (*yāna*) as being an offence, but only a minor one requiring confession: [P:] *na bhikkhave yānena yāyitabbaṃ. yo yāyeyya, āpatti dukkaṭassa* [Monks, one should not drive with (or go by) a vehicle. He who drives (or goes by) a vehicle commits an offence of wrongdoing (Vin i, 191,21f.).] Interestingly, the rule for monks is not part of the standard list of 227 rules contained in the *Pātimokkha* and the Explanations section of the Vinaya for monks. It appears instead in the Chapters section, as a subsidiary rule. In the case of the Vinaya for nuns, however, the prohibition figures in the Explanations section and *Pātimokkha* as one of the confession offenses (*pācittiya* number 85). This section glosses the word *yāna* as: a litter (*vayha*) chariot (*ratha* or *sandamānikā*), cart (*sakaṭa*), palanquin (*sivikā*) or sedan chair (*pāṭankī*) (Vin iv, 339,8 ff). Applying these rules to modern Sri Lanka is tricky not only because it raises questions about whether the rules are amendable, but because the meaning of *yāyitabbaṃ* and *yāyeyya* can encompass *both* driving *and* riding in cars, depending on how one chooses to translate them. And, while it is unusual to see monks driving cars, it is very common to see monks *riding* in them. Thank you to Petra Kieffer-Pülz for directing me towards these passages. All Vinaya citations are from Oldenberg, *The Vinaya Piṭakaṃ*.

[18] On the structure of the Vinaya Piṭaka, see Chapter 2 of this book.

> that time and which aroused the displeasure of the populace.... [For this reason] the Buddha considered several social criteria when enacting precepts. For this, the Vinaya Piṭaka illuminates ten reasons. Two of these disciplinary reasons include [the admonition to] give confidence (*pähäduṇu*) to those who do not have confidence [in the *sāsana*] and to increase the confidence of those who [already] have confidence ([as in the Pali phrase] *appasannānaṃ vā pasādāya, pasannānaṃ vā bhiyyobhāvāya)*. The aforementioned criteria are applicable even today for determining whether a monastic action is appropriate or inappropriate.

The letter then goes on:

> One can see how Lord Buddha made appropriate decisions concerning situations not mentioned in the Vinaya in the four 'Mahāpadēsa' Vinaya laws in the *Mahāvaggapāḷi* in the *Bhēsajjakkhandhaka*. They are:[19]
>
> 01. *Even if* a thing was not forbidden [by the Buddha] as being unsuitable (*akäpa*), *it is unsuitable* if it comports with (coheres with) an unsuitable nature.[20]
> 02. *Even if* a thing was not forbidden [by the Buddha] as being unsuitable, *it is suitable* if it comports with a suitable nature.
> 03. *Even if* a thing was not permitted [by the Buddha] as being suitable, *it is unsuitable* if it comports with an unsuitable nature.
> 04. *Even if* a thing was not permitted [by the Buddha] as being suitable, *it is suitable* if it comports with a suitable nature.
>
> Through these Mahāpadēsa standards, the 1st through the 3rd, [which are] cited here, it is possible to decide whether monks' driving is suitable or unsuitable.[21]

[19] This is my translation of the Tipiṭaka Board's Sinhala description of these rules. The original list of rules can be found in Pali at Oldenberg, *The Vinaya Piṭakaṃ*, Vin i, 250, 31–251, 6. To make it easier for the reader to follow, I included some italics in my translation.

[20] The word I translate here as 'comports with' is, in the original Sinhala, *anulom [vē]*. *Anulom* derives from the Pali/Sanskrit term *anuloma*, meaning 'with the direction' of the hair or the grain of the wood. *Anuloma* is a technical term found widely in *dharmaśastra* and Buddhist texts, where it refers adjectively to something that is acceptable within a normative regime. *Anulom venavā* is not a common phrase in colloquial Sinhala, which is probably why the authors included the parenthetical explanation as *sudusu [vē]* (which I translate above as 'coheres with' but can also mean 'to become acceptable').

[21] Letter Submitted as Evidence (R12) Letter to Commissioner of Buddhist Affairs in *CA Writ. App. 1978/2004*, dated 16 November 2006. (Submission in Sinhala.) Italics my own.

The monks of the Tipiṭaka Board argued that the issue of driving was, indeed, addressed in the Vinaya Piṭaka. Only it was covered by a set of specific criteria for evaluating the propriety of monastic behaviour. These criteria appeared not in the list of prescriptive rules contained in the first part of the Vinaya, the Explanations section, but in the principles and procedures contained in the second part, the Chapters section.[22] Rather than gradually accommodating Vinaya rules to society, Vimalavaṃsa's opponents argued, monks should continually reapply these higher-order principles in the face of new dilemmas. Vinaya rules did not change over time; rather, they were more fully realised and more completely elaborated. The Vinaya Piṭaka was not a living law, in other words, but an invariant and consistently applied code of conduct.

In the end, the Court of Appeal rejected Vimalavaṃsa's petition, ruling that monks could not obtain driving licences.[23] Rather than settling the issue, however, the ruling deepened the controversy. This was because both sides – the 'winners' and 'losers' of the litigation – had doubts about civil judges' own practices of legal pluralism. Although they disagreed with each other, Vimalavaṃsa and his opponents *both* rejected the expression legal pluralism embodied in the court's decision: one that placed state law above the Vinaya, and gave state-legal authorities, such as judges, the authority to pronounce on complex matters of monastic law.

THE CASE OF THE BHIKKHUNĪ ID CARDS

A second high-profile court case from the 2010s was unfolding in the judiciary while the Vimalavaṃsa case was still being litigated. This case, too, offers a striking example of public, agonistic and dialectical practices of legal pluralism catalysed by legal appeals to the Buddhism Chapter. Unlike the case of the driving monk, this dispute – concerning the legal status of Buddhist nuns (bhikkhunīs) – had not concluded at the time of writing this book.[24] Yet, even before it concluded, the

[22] This is the Bhesajjakkhandhaka section mentioned above.

[23] For more on the decision, see Schonthal, *Buddhism, Politics and Limits of Law*, Chapter Six.

[24] For an update on the case which, which was eventually decided in June 2025, see footnote 47. In total, the judgment came twelve years after the initial petition, and after I submitted a complete manuscript of this book.

process of litigation served to spotlight and further sharpen existing practices of legal pluralism that had been visible on the island for some time.

The case began with a fundamental rights petition filed in the Supreme Court by two monastics: Ven. Inamāḷuvē Śrī Sumaṅgala Thero, the chief incumbent of Rangiri Dambulla Temple, and Ven. Välimaḍa Dhammadinnā Bhikkhunī, a Buddhist nun affiliated with the same temple. Sumaṅgala was a powerful and (for some) controversial figure in the sangha. He began his monastic career as a member of the Asgiri Chapter of the Siyam Nikāya, but he broke away in 1985 with the bold act of conducting a separate higher ordination ceremony (*upasampadā*) at his own temple in Dambulla.[25] Sumaṅgala's ordination ceremony, and those that would follow, not only flouted the long-standing Asgiri tradition of ordaining monks at the Asgiri head-temple in Kandy, they also defied the Asgiri chapter's caste-based norms concerning who could join the fraternity. Rather than restricting ordination to persons from the traditional rice-farmer caste (*goyigama kula*), Sumaṅgala admitted monks from a variety of backgrounds.[26]

Like Sumaṅgala, Dhammadinnā had also been involved in contested ordination traditions. She received higher ordination at Sumaṅgala's temple as part of a series of bhikkhunī ordination ceremonies that he conducted starting in 1998. With these ordinations, Sumaṅgala broke even further with Asgiri conventions, as well as conventions shared by the island's other monastic bodies: before 1998, there had been no bhikkhunī ordinations conducted in Sri Lanka since the ancient period.[27] By participating in this newly confirmed lineage, Dhammadinnā became part of a revival movement that challenged deeply entrenched norms regarding the legitimacy of female ordination in Sri Lanka's monastic community.

[25] Abeysekara, 'Politics of Higher Ordination, Buddhist Monastic Identity, and Leadership at the Dambulla Temple in Sri Lanka.' By 'his own' I mean that Sumaṅgala was the chief incumbent monk of that site. Interestingly, the official monastic register with the Department of Buddhist Affairs refers to the monastic body in Dambulla as a temple council (*vihāra saṅgha sabhāva*) rather than a chapter (*pārśvaya*) or great monastic council (*mahāsaṅgha sabhāva*), as it does with other sub-groups within the Siyam Nikāya.

[26] Some consideration of caste dynamics in Sri Lankan monasticism appears in Chapter 4 of this book.

[27] Salgado, *Buddhist Nuns and Gendered Practice*, Chapter Six.

Similarly to the case of the driving monk, the issue at the core of Sumaṅgala and Dhammadinnā's petitions was a seemingly minor administrative matter. In 2013, Dhammadinnā applied to the Department for the Registration of Persons (DRP) to renew her national identity card using her ordination name, including the title, 'nun' or bhikkhunī. Although some bhikkhunīs had used this title on identity documents in the past, the DRP officer would only issue Dhammadinnā with an identity card showing the title *sil mātāva* or 'precept mother' on it. *Sil mātāva* (pl. *mātā*) is the name given to non-ordained female renunciants in Sri Lanka, who live like fully ordained monastics but formally follow only ten precepts, instead of the 311 rules traditionally designated for fully ordained Buddhist nuns.[28]

Citing her higher ordination in the Dambulla lineage, Dhammadinnā and Sumaṅgala filed a fundamental rights petition in the Supreme Court insisting that the DRP's refusal to write bhikkhunī on the ID card amounted to a violation of Dhammadinnā's rights to equality under the law, as protected by Article 12(1) of Sri Lanka's constitution.[29] Over the course of the case, their petition expanded into a broader constitutional challenge, implicating the Buddhism Chapter of the constitution and the government's associated obligations to protect the *sāsana*.

Dhammadinnā's case drew attention to the inconsistencies within Sri Lankans' approach to Buddhist nuns and their laws.[30] Although Sumaṅgala estimated 1,600 bhikkhunīs in Sri Lanka,[31] the Sri Lankan government – like the governments of Thailand, Myanmar and Cambodia – does not formally recognise their existence in law. Nor is the legitimacy of bhikkhunī ordinations accepted by many of the

[28] Informally, they often follow many more precepts. On *sil mātā* see, De Silva, 'Vigilant Steps'; Mrozik, 'Sri Lankan Buddhist Nuns'; Salgado, *Buddhist Nuns and Gendered Practice*.

[29] The Supreme Court of Sri Lanka has original jurisdiction over all fundamental rights claims. Article 12(1) reads: 'All persons are equal before the law and are entitled to the equal protection of the law.'

[30] This ought not to be confused with popular attitudes towards bhikkhunī. There are many people in Sri Lanka who, de facto, accept the legitimacy of bhikkhunī ordination even if it is not recognised de jure. Salgado, 'Tradition Power and Community among Buddhist Nuns in Sri Lanka.' On the analogous situation in Thailand, see Ito, 'Questions of Ordination Legitimacy for Newly Ordained Theravāda Bhikkhunī in Thailand.'

[31] Interview with Ven. Sumaṅgala, in Dambulla, 31 July 2016.

island's senior monks and lay Buddhist leaders. Only *sil mātā* have official legal status.

As in other parts of Southern Asia, objections to bhikkhunī ordination in Sri Lanka centre on two doctrinal points. First, critics argue that a valid ordination lineage must trace an unbroken chain of higher ordinations back to the time of the Buddha. Second, they insist that a legitimate Theravāda monastic order must have a continuous history of using the Pali Vinaya as its legal foundation. According to opponents, Sri Lanka's modern bhikkhunī lineage, which was revived with assistance from East Asian nuns in the late twentieth century, fails on both counts: it emerged with the support of Mahāyāna nuns, and it draws on a chain of transmission linked to the Dharmaguptaka (rather than the Pali) variant of the Vinaya.[32]

Resistance to bhikkhunī ordination is not limited to government officials and monks, however. Even some *sil mātā* express scepticism about the validity of bhikkhunīs.[33] As one *dasa sil mātāva* explained to me in an interview:

> Some *sil mäṇiyo* [*mātā*] have become bhikkhunī in Dambulla. Our teacher did not like it. Our mäṇiyo said, 'we have the ten-precept [mothers]; we have Mahāyāna bhikkhunīs; . . . but, in the world, there are no Theravāda bhikkhunīs.' There should be a continuous stream of bhikkhunīs in order to have a [bhikkhunī] ordination. Mahāyāna bhikkhunīs cannot give higher ordination to Theravāda bhikkhunīs. For this reason, the teacher went to many countries such as China, Myanmar, Vietnam etc. [She discovered that] the discipline (*sīla*) of the ten-precept mothers is a valuable thing. Mahāyāna nuns are doing jobs.

32 For much more on some of the doctrinal questions, see, for example: Anālayo, 'The Revival of the Bhikkhunī Order and the Decline of the Sāsana'; Anālayo, 'The Cullavagga on Bhikkhuni Ordination'; Heirman, 'Buddhist Nuns: Between Past and Present'; Hüsken, 'The Legend of the Establishment of the Buddhist Order of Nuns in the Theravada Vinaya-Pitaka'; Kieffer-Pülz, 'Re-Ordination of Former Buddhist Nuns in the Theravāda Tradition'; Mrozik, 'We Love Our Nuns'; Seeger, 'The Bhikkhunī-Ordination Controversy in Thailand.'

33 On ten-precept mothers and the formations of female renunciation in the contemporary Theravāda world, see: Bartholomeusz, *Women under the Bo Tree: Buddhist Nuns in Sri Lanka*; De Silva, 'Vigilant Steps'; Falk, *Making Fields of Merit: Buddhist Female Ascetics and Gendered Orders in Thailand*; Jordt, *Burma's Mass Lay Meditation Movement: Buddhism and the Cultural Construction of Power*; Kawanami, *Renunciation and Empowerment of Buddhist Nuns in Myanmar-Burma: Building a Community of Female Faithful*; Salgado, 'Religious Identities of Buddhist Nuns.'

> Their attitudes (*ākalpa*) are very much different from us. In this way, one can say that the pure [observance] of the ten precepts is much better.[34]

This perspective – which emphasises the non-local, non-traditional, non-orthodox nature of bhikkhunī ordination in Sri Lanka – circulates widely among Sri Lankan laity and monastics alike. Yet it makes the legal status of bhikkhunīs somewhat fraught: although state officials and senior monks reject bhikkhunī ordinations, there are many on the island who accept them.

Practices and Counter-Practices of Legal Pluralism

In this context of conflicting views, the Sri Lankan state has taken an official position about the status of bhikkhunīs and their laws. The Department of Buddhist Affairs refuses to register bhikkhunī ordinations. The Buddhist Temporalities Ordinance excludes bhikkhunīs from its definition of Buddhist monks.[35] Legal mechanisms like these imply to Sri Lankans that the Theravāda bhikkhunī Vinaya has no official status in Sri Lanka. Through litigation, Sumaṅgala and Dhammadinnā contested this position, challenging the government's paradigm of legal pluralism and offering their own competing account of monastic law, its sources and its relationship to state-legal authority.

At the core of their petitions is an argument that Dhammadinnā's bhikkhunī ordination should be officially validated because it had followed the proper Vinaya procedures. The ordination (*upasampadā*), they asserted, was conducted

> with strict adherence to Vinaya Rules and the Buddhist Teachings, in the presence and with the participation of over 200 Vinaya Dhara Bhikkhus [monks who are expert in Vinaya] from all the chapters of the Siyam, Siyamopali,[36] Amarapura and Ramannya.[37]

As used in their petitions, the term 'Vinaya' referred both to the basic rules of conduct outlined in the first part of the Vinaya Piṭaka, the

[34] Interview near Colombo, 18 July 2016.

[35] *Buddhist Temporalities Ordinance* No. 19 of 1931 (amended most recently in 1992).

[36] Even though Sumaṅgala separates them here, Siyam and Siyamopali (Sinhala: *syāmōpāli*) are usually used interchangeably to refer to the lineages descended from the monk, Ven. Upāli of Siam.

[37] Written Affidavit from Ven. Welimada Dhammadinnā Bhikkhuni, dated 19 June 2013, in *Ven. Welimada Dhammadinnā Bhikkhuni and others v RMS Sarath Kumara and Others SC(FR) 28/2013*, Paragraph 8. (Submission in English.)

Explanations section, and to the ritual instructions outlined in the second part, the Chapters section – which, among other things, clarifies the protocols for admitting new monks into the sangha. It was these procedural protocols, they argued, that determined whether ordinations were licit or not. All of these protocols had been followed in Dambulla: bhikkhunī ordinations took place through unanimous decision by the Dambulla temple's sangha council; they were conducted within the perimeter of the temple's formal ritual boundary, or *sīmā*; they included the correct number of higher ordained monks and nuns. Most importantly, the ordinations were approved unanimously, without any objections being made during the course of the ceremony.

Reflecting on these matters in a book published in 2015, Sumaṅgala took the argument even further. Not only had the ordination ritual conformed to the requirements of the Vinaya Piṭaka, he argued, but anyone who questioned that conformity was, themself, transgressing the Vinaya Piṭaka:

> According to the Vinaya Piṭaka, when there is a higher ordination ceremony at the ceremonial hall, with the participation of sangha, if there is a transgression (*virōdhayak*) of dharma or the Vinaya it must be reported at that very higher ordination event. [Those conducting the ceremony] ask three times, in fact, to see if there is a transgression of this type to announce. If no noise is made, [those people] will declare the fact that the higher ordination is finalised, and that no one has objected to it. It is itself a violation of the Vinaya law to proclaim in the media or [in other] publications, after a higher ordination (*upasampadā*) like this, that there was the violation [of the Vinaya] or that the act can be reversed after the *upasampadā* has been agreed upon.[38]

Sumaṅgala's reasoning relies on a particular framing of the Vinaya Piṭaka, one that stresses the central importance of the text's procedural rules for legal actions (*vinaya karmas*). This approach can be seen in Sumaṅgala's meticulous use of the phrase *upasampadā vinaya karmaya* to refer to the bhikkhunī ordinations. That phrase, although common in specialist commentaries and *vinaya* literature,[39] makes a striking impression in the context of books and legal petitions written for non-specialists.[40] It calls

[38] Ināmaḷuvē Sumaṅgala, *Śrī Laṅkāvē Bhikṣunī Parṣadaya Piḷibaňda Vimarśanayak [A Review of the Assembly of Bhikkhunis in Sri Lanka]*, 25. Italics mine.

[39] For example, Rērukānē Candavimala, *Vinaya Karma Pota [Book of Vinaya Acts]*.

[40] Dhammadinnā and Sumaṅgala's English-language petitions further reinforce this procedural, technical approach to the Vinaya by rendering the phrase 'Vinaya Karma' in capitals, untranslated.

readers' attention, again and again, to the technical, procedural aspects of bhikkhunī ordination – reminding them that this is a specialised type of legal action the legitimacy of which comes from its conformity with the minute ritual requirements of the Vinaya rather than the opinions of government bureaucrats or other monks.

Originalism against Traditionalism

Sumaṅgala's legal arguments reflect a broader rendering of the Vinaya, which carries through his writings. Rather than a specialist code interpretable only by monastic elites, the Vinaya should be treated as a primary and self-sufficient source of law itself. In this view, the Vinaya serves as a foundational charter for monastic action that stands apart from and above later commentaries and traditions. Sumaṅgala's practices of legal pluralism draw a strong line between the root text of the Vinaya and the larger body of monastic rules, customs and institutional frameworks that come after it (see Chapter 2).

During an interview I conducted with him in 2016, Sumaṅgala made this distinction explicit, differentiating between the ancient Vinaya and those legal texts and traditions (*sampradāyan*) that came later. The Vinaya, he pointed out, contained the Buddha's *original* teachings, while the later sources were less reliable, even corrupted:

> Now, when one thinks about tradition (*sampradāya*) one thinks about Mahāyāna, Theravāda or Vajrayāna. There are mainly these three vehicles (*yāna*). However, Lord Buddha did not belong to any one of these [vehicles]. These were created by monks. They were created by monks after the Buddha's enlightenment. Do you know what Theravāda is? In saying 'the Theravāda [tradition]' [one speaks about] the first dharma conference (*saṅghāyana*), which took place three months after the Buddha's enlightenment, [under the direction of the monk] Ven. Mahākāśyapa. The collection of dharma and *vinaya* was compiled there. They pieced together the teachings that the Buddha gave. The dharma and the *vinaya* that were pieced together [at that first conference] is the Pali Tipiṭaka that we use today. . . . From its beginnings at that time, until today things are being added to it. During the Tipiṭaka's codifying, mistakes (*aḍupāḍu*) were made. One of these mistakes is this narrative about the bhikkhunīs.[41]

According to the Sumaṅgala, the text of the Vinaya Piṭaka that sits on the shelves of monasteries and libraries should not be read as the

[41] Interview with Ven. Sumaṅgala, in Dambulla, 31 July 2016.

true instructions of the Buddha, faithfully transmitted over time. Rather, modern variants of the Vinaya ought to be seen as imperfect transcriptions of those instructions – core teachings filtered through the corrupting frame of tradition. To interpret the Vinaya correctly, one must separate these core teachings from their later corruptions – particularly in the case of bhikkhunī ordinations, which, he argues, were accepted by the Buddha, but disparaged by later redactors.[42]

Sumaṅgala's tradition-free interpretation of monastic law bears striking similarities to Vimalavaṃsa's *nikāya*-free interpretation in the driving licence case. Both monks practised legal pluralism in ways that elevated the Vinaya Piṭaka above institutional hierarchies, rejecting the authority of monastic fraternities and their regulatory codes in favour of an unmediated reading of the Buddha's original instructions. In both cases, the imperatives of litigation sharpened these viewpoints further, encouraging more strident and uncompromising assertions about law.

Continuity as Legitimacy

Opponents of Sumaṅgala and Dhammadinnā practiced of legal pluralism in an entirely different way, one which grounded monastic law in the idea of institutional and historical continuity. Central to opponents' submissions was a claim about the proper locations of monastic legal authority. Dambulla's *vinaya karmas* lacked legitimacy, opponents argued, because they had not been sanctioned by Sri Lanka's national monastic leadership. This objection can be seen clearly in a letter drafted by the chief monks of the island's major fraternities and submitted as evidence to the court:

> It has come to our attention that recently, in the last two or three years, a group (*koṭasak*) has come into existence calling themselves 'nuns' (*meheṇin*) [.] [They] follow the bhikkhunī higher ordination tradition coming from a Mahāyāna source that does not fulfil any of the fundamental elements required for completing a higher ordination Vinaya act (*upasampadā vinaya karmayak*) under the Theravāda Vinaya and is outside the agreed upon Vinaya procedures.[43] This '*vinaya karma*' is

[42] Ven. Sumaṅgala has in mind, in particular, a portion of the Pali Vinaya that describes the Buddha's reluctance to consent to bhikkhunī ordination because it might hasten the decline of *sāsana*. On this topic in particular, see: Anālayo, 'The Revival of the Bhikkhunī Order and the Decline of the Sāsana.'

[43] *Sammata vinaya paripāṭiyen paribāhirava.*

> being carried out, having made no inquiries from us, nor with our approval or sanction[;] nor were we even informed. It came to our attention that having been influenced by a certain bhikkhu chapter (*pārśvayak*), [the group] was striving to restore anew something like a nuns' *sāsana* [*meheṇi sāsana*]. This order, which is not recognised by the entire Buddhist population nor by the ancient Theravāda tradition [*sampradāya*], should never be allowed. It must be emphasised that no campaign should be tolerated for the legal recognition of this order, which is based on Mahāyāna principles by a [Sri Lankan] government (or one of its departments), which aspire to preserve the pure Theravāda *sāsana* and which strive to establish firmly within the island of Sri Lanka the pure Theravāda Buddhist teaching.[44]

In the letter, the *mahānāyaka*s draw a clear line between the Vinaya-based legal action (*vinaya karma*) of higher ordination and the Theravāda Vinaya itself. What made a legal action of higher ordination legitimate, they argued, was not simply its fulfilment of the Vinaya's procedural requirements. Ordinations also had to be conducted with the permission of the island's major monastic lineages.

According to Sumaṅgala and Dhammadinnā's opponents, fraternity hierarchies and lines of succession were not corrupting forces on the Vinaya but the very structures that guaranteed monastic law's integrity and validity.[45] Tradition (*sampradāya*) underwrote and ensured the accuracy of monastic law. The Vinaya was not an independent source of authority that could be understood in isolation. Institutional continuity and accrued wisdom also mattered, as did other written sources such as the chronicles (*vaṃsas*) and commentaries composed on the island since the ancient period.[46] Monastic law was more than fidelity

44 Letter to the Commissioner General of the Department of Buddhist Affairs, dated Oct. 7, 2010, submitted as evidence in *Ven. Welimada Dhammadinnā Bhikkhuni and others v RMS Sarath Kumara and Others SC(FR) 28/2013*. (Submission in Sinhala.)

45 This is not a minor issue since Mahāyāna monastics observe different versions of the Vinaya; and, in certain places in those Vinayas, the rules and procedures prescribed for ordination differ from the Theravāda version.

46 They also cited a portion of the Pali Vinaya that Sumaṅgala claimed had been corrupted over time, the 'Nuns Chapter' (*bhikkhunī khandhaka*). That portion recounts the Buddha's initial reluctance to ordain bhikkhunīs and his prophecy that doing so would hasten the decline of the *sāsana*. This, the *mahānāyakas* argued, justified further their stance against reviving bhikkhunī ordination. The historical interruption of the lineage was not just a procedural lapse, in their logic, it was part of the mandated trajectory of the monastic order, one that should not be overturned by a unilateral decision from a single temple.

to procedures contained in the Vinaya, they argued. It required institutional validation, historical continuity and alignment with the broader structures of the sangha – all three of which were absent from the Dambulla ordinations.

The dispute over bhikkhunī ordination, like the driving monk case, elicited and publicised competing understandings of monastic law circulating in Sri Lanka. Both sides invoked constitutional obligations to protect the *sāsana* and the Vinaya, yet they arrived at entirely different conclusions about what such protection entailed. For Sumaṅgala and Dhammadinnā, protection meant upholding the procedural rules of the Vinaya gathered through a direct, originalist reading of the Vinaya. For their opponents, protection meant safeguarding the larger network of monastic institutions and traditions that clustered around the Vinaya and mediated its application in the world.

Faced with these opposing views, the Supreme Court delayed deciding the case for more than a decade. Although it initially gave the case leave to proceed, following preliminary hearings and written submissions, the country's most powerful judges and government lawyers effectively brought the matter to halt. Rather than moving to clarify the issue, they chose instead to avoid the controversy by delaying and cancelling hearings. Eventually the court did issue a judgment (as this book was going to press) affirming nuns' rights to have 'bhikkhunī' written on their identity cards. Nevertheless, it remains to be seen how (or whether) this decision will alter the landscape of competing legal pluralisms that has impacted the issue of bhikkhunī ordination for decades.[47]

THE CASE OF THE *KATIKĀVATA* BILL

In both the bhikkhunī case and the driving licence case, legal petitions submitted to Sri Lanka's higher judiciary by Buddhist monastics

[47] In the very final stages of publishing this book, Sri Lanka's Supreme Court issued a sudden and very surprising landmark judgment regarding this case. In a 2–1 majority opinion the court affirmed Dhammadinnā and Sumaṅgala's claims that, by denying the title 'bhikkhunī' on Dhammadinnā's ID card, the officer did indeed breach her constitutional rights. While it is too late in the publication process to write about this decision here, readers are directed to the following: Schonthal, Benjamin. 'Judging Bhikkhunis'. *Tricycle: The Buddhist Review*, 6 September 2025. https://tricycle.org/article/bhikkhuni-ordination-sri-lanka/?utm_campaign=02655378&utm_source=p3s4h3r3s

stimulated and amplified competing practices of legal pluralism. Courts served not only as arenas for adjudicating disputes but also as consequential platforms where monks, lay supporters and legal experts could pronounce publicly on the boundaries, composition and status of law.

These cases attracted the attention of more than just litigants and judges. They also attracted widespread public interest, thanks to the reporting of journalists and online bloggers. Vimalavaṃsa's case became a *cause célèbre*, appearing regularly in the headlines of national newspapers. Although Sumaṅgala and Dhammadinnā's petitions garnered somewhat less attention, they nevertheless helped to hold national debates over bhikkhunī ordinations in the public eye.

In recent years, Sri Lankan governments have sought to address some of the questions concerning the relationship between monastic and state law that were raised in these (and other) cases. For the most part, they have done so through proposing new legislation. One important example of this occurred in January of 2016 when the government of Maithripala Sirisena introduced to parliament a bill designed to resolve some of the legal dilemmas that had become visible in the cases examined above.[48] The bill, called The Theravāda Bhikkhu *Katikāvatas* (Registration) Bill,[49] enabled fraternities to register their constitutions, or *katikāvatas*, with the government, making them an enforceable source of rights and interests in the island's civil courts. The bill was based on the similarly named Katikāvata Registration Bill, withdrawn in 2004, discussed in Chapter 8 of this book.

As with earlier attempts to 'legalise' monastic law, supporters argued that the new bill would help monastic fraternities discipline monks who refused to follow their *katikāvatas*. One senior monk, speaking on national television, articulated the concern as follows:

> The biggest problem at the moment is that, even if we have *katikāvatas*, not one of them has any legal authority (*naitika balayak*). This makes it impossible to enforce any law or order that's been promulgated by their

[48] For other relevant cases, see Schonthal, *Buddhism, Politics and Limits of Law*, Chapter Five.

[49] In Sinhala: *theravādī bhikṣu katikāvat (liyāpadiṅci kirīmē) panata*. The English-language version of the bill was published: Government of Sri Lanka, Theravadi Bhikkhu Kathikawath (Registration) Bill (published in Gazette on 14 December 2015, presented to parliament on 12 January 2016). An excellent article-length treatment of the politics surrounding this bill can be found in Herath, 'Reforms via Katikāvat.'

> great leaders or executive councils against a monk from any tradition, or chapter or fraternity. . . . There needs to be something put in place legally for [dealing with] a *vinaya*-flouting monk who is behaving in ways that are indecent and undisciplined. Because as it is now, there's no way to enforce [rules] even if they are already in the *katikāvatas*, and this is why there has been this increase in misbehaviour in modern sangha society. It's because of this that [monks] have been petitioning [the government] saying that we need to give legal powers and legal status (*naitika tatvayak*) to *katikāvatas* now.[50]

Although unstated, the types of misbehaviour that were most concerning to the bill's supporters were activities that might be permissible in the state-legal system but which were offensive according to the rules of monastic discipline. This included things like cavorting with women, attending films or, as seen in the Vimalavaṃsa case, driving cars. Under the existing legal regime, monasteries could only enforce compliance through persuasion, exclusion or communal pressure.[51] Yet, for many monks, including the speaker, even one monk's misbehaviour could damage the reputation of the entire sangha.[52]

A New Bill to Solve Old Problems

The 2016 *Katikāvata* bill[53] proposed to legalise monastic constitutions using two administrative steps. The first step was to standardise the content of the *katikāvatas* by requiring that all registered *katikāvatas* would, at a minimum, address the following four topics[54]:

(1) the composition and functions of the sangha's executive council (*kāraka saṅgha sabhāva*);

[50] 'Television Broadcast: *Theravādī Bauddha Saṅghādhikaraṇaya* [The Monastic Court in Theravāda Buddhism].'

[51] See Chapter 5 of this book for a more complete discussion of these dilemmas.

[52] Citing the Buddha's injunction in Pali to 'give faith to those who have no faith and to increase the faith of those who have faith [P: *appasannānam vā pasādāya, pasannānam vā bhiyyobhāvāya]*', he underscored that monks have an obligation to 'further increase the confidence of Buddhist people' such that 'if they are behaving in a way that actually damages the minds of Buddhists or diminishes their faith or devotion (*śraddhāvak, bhaktiyak*), the *saṅgha sabhāvas* must take steps to deal with that'.

[53] I rely primarily on the Sinhala copy of the bill, which has legal priority over the English and Tamil copies that are produced by the government.

[54] These are similar to those laid out in the 2004 bill, described in Chapter 7.

(2) a code (*saṅgrahayak*) covering disciplinary matters (*vinaya karuṇu*) and behaviours that a monk must follow;
(3) information about how the executive council will investigate those monks who violate the disciplinary code; and
(4) information about punishments.

Beyond these minimum requirements, the bill recommended a list of possible punishments that might also be spelt out in laws, ranging from temporary expulsion from the monastery at which the monk resided to the nullification of the bhikkhu's formal registration (with the Department of Buddhist Affairs).

As with the previous legal proposals (see Chapter 7), the 2016 bill required that fraternities register their *katikāvatas* with the commissioner of Buddhist Affairs, who would then vet those documents in order to make sure they complied with dharma, *vinaya* and other monastic customs (*cāritra*). Rather than leaving it up to the commissioner, the vetting would be done by an 'expert council' consisting of three monks and two lawyers 'with a knowledge of Vinaya rules (*vinaya rīti*)'. Once registered, the *katikāvatas* would be recognised as valid law, meaning that, if fraternities requested it, civil courts could be enlisted to enforce their rules.[55]

The bill responded directly to the history of litigation involving Buddhist monks in Sri Lanka. In fact, drafters listed in the bill a range of controversial behaviours that had previously come before the island's judges, recommending that these behaviours be prohibited in *katikāvatas*. These included:

(a) engaging in practices of esoteric knowledge or similar activities and publicising it;

[55] §10–11, 12. To enforce those orders, fraternities' executive councils could simply write to the local magistrate and request a summary order against the offender. The court could then impose a range of penalties, starting with six months in prison and/ or a fine of SLR 50,000 (approximately 200 US dollars). In addition, the offending bhikkhu would be forbidden from re-ordaining in another monastic chapter (a significant problem according to several monks that I interviewed).
Beyond these quasi-judicial powers given to executive councils (*saṅgha sabhā*) and great leaders (*mahānāyakas*), the Katikāvata Bill also gave special recognition and authority to the great leaders of the three major fraternities. In a final section, §13, relating to the implementation of the law, the Katikāvata Bill specified that the minister of Buddhist Affairs would implement the bill in consultation with the 'most revered monks of the three *nikāyas*', thereby singling them out in law as the supreme authorities for monastic affairs on the island.

(b) participating in business or commercial activities;
(c) obtaining driving licenses and driving vehicles;
(d) having some kind of public or private employment apart from [employment] in the fields of education, social service or religious affairs; and
(e) engaging in activities that are inappropriate (*akäpa*) for monks or contrary to the bhikkhu Vinaya in public places.[56]

The list of potential prohibitions contains virtually every contentious issue that had come before the courts in the last half-century. In the third example, one can see direct echoes of the Vimalavaṃsa case. In the last example, concerning inappropriate behaviour, one sees a reaction to the matter of bhikkhunī ordinations insofar as the text only mentions the bhikkhu Vinaya (the monks' law) and not the bhikkhunī Vinaya (the nuns' law).

The government and its allies justified the bill as a means of safeguarding monastic law while also preserving monastic autonomy. Unlike earlier proposals that sought to regulate monks directly, the 2016 *Katikāvata* Bill positioned the government as a facilitator rather than an enforcer of monastic legal authority. As drafters explained, the bill did not seek to legislate the Vinaya itself but rather to give force to the decisions made by monastic leaders within the framework of their *katikāvatas*.

Many monastics supported the bill, and its vision of legal pluralism. The *mahānāyaka* of the Amarapura Nikāya, for example, issued a strong message to the Sinhala-language press arguing that the bill was essential for creating 'a monastic society that accords with the Vinaya (*vinayānukūla*)' because it would give 'legal power (*nītyā[nu]kūla [sic] balayak*) to agreements and decisions made by the monks in accordance with the Vinaya'.[57] Moreover, he suggested, the bill devolved authority in a way that confirmed monks' sole prerogative to make rulings about monastic law. Because monastic constitutions were one step removed from the Vinaya Piṭaka, they were safe instruments for transmitting legal authority, allowing for the state-legal recognition of Vinaya-derived norms without giving the government a say over the Vinaya itself.

56 §3(2).

57 Pamunuva, '*Theravādī Bhikṣu Katikāvat Panata Saṅgha Samājayaṭat Behevin Hitakara Vēvi* [The Theravada Bhikshu Katikavata Bill Will Be Very Beneficial for Saṅgha Society].'

The Backlash: Opposing Visions of Monastic Law

Despite widespread support among government ministers and elite monks, the bill ultimately became a lightning rod for disagreement.[58] Opposition came not only from those who had long resisted state involvement in monastic affairs, but also from monastic groups that had initially supported legal recognition for *katikāvatas* and now feared that the specific mechanisms proposed in the bill threatened monastic autonomy. Protests against the bill appeared in newspapers and in street protests. Opponents also went to the Supreme Court, where they successfully challenged certain sections by claiming that they violated several articles of Sri Lanka's constitution – including the Buddhism Chapter.[59]

Those who challenged the bill in public and in court practised legal pluralism in very different ways from the bill's defenders. For the bill's opponents, *katikāvata*s did not stand apart from the Vinaya; they were embodiments of it. The bill, therefore, did not insulate the Vinaya from state law – using *katikāvata*s as a kind of buffer law – but intruded on it directly. The head of the National Patriotic Monks Front, for example, declared to the country's media that 'Parliament cannot change the Vinaya rules of the Theravāda monks. ... If this Bill goes through, the Buddhist law will be overridden by the government law'.[60]

Another senior monk put the matter differently:

> In Sri Lanka, the sangha has social power (*samājya balayak*). [This is] not true in Thailand, nor in any other country. These people [the government introducing the bill] want to break down the power held by the sangha [here]. That would make things easier for them. But we cannot let that happen. ... We're saying [we want] something else, but not this. Give legal powers to our own *katikāvatas*. That way if we reform something and make some mistakes, we [monks] can talk it over and correct them. That will not happen with government-made *katikāvatas*. Give us the legal authority to do it.[61]

58 An excellent analysis of 'social debates' provoked by the bill can be found in Herath, 'Reforms via Katikāvat.'

59 The Supreme Court determinations on the petitions were delivered collectively, on 10 February 2016: SC(SD) 1/2016, 2/2016, 7/2016 '*In the matter of Petitions under Article 121(1) of the Constitution against a Bill titled 'Therawada [sic] Bhikkhu Kathikawath (Registration) Act*.' The Sri Lankan Constitution provides for a process of pre-enactment constitutional review of legislation. This is explained in Schonthal, 'Securing the Sasana through Law.'

60 Seneviratne, 'Sri Lanka Buddhists Divided over Bill to Control Monks.'

61 Interview with monastic judge (*anuvijjaka*) in Diwulpitiya 29 July 2016.

According to this quote, and others like it,[62] the bill threatened monastic law not only by giving the government powers over the Vinaya, but by attempting to standardise Vinaya rules for all fraternities, thereby ignoring key differences in the ways that *nikāyas* applied and interpreted those rules. Not only would the government proposals overstep the boundary between the Vinaya and state law, they would also confuse the important institutional boundaries between *nikāyas* as well as their different legal traditions.

In its coverage of the *Katikāvata* Bill, Sri Lanka's Sinhala-language media amplified the different visions of monastic law expressed by supporters and critics. When speaking to the media, many of those who criticised the bill referred to it not by its official title but as the 'Vinaya Bill' (*vinaya panata*), giving the impression that parliamentarians sought to register the entire Vinaya Piṭaka, rather than just *katikāvatas*.

Some critics went even further, warning that the bill not only misinterpreted Vinaya, but it ignored the island's older, more traditional norms around monastic conduct and monks' relationships with the laity. This argument, which gained considerable traction in the media, was picked up by a group of four student monks at a Sri Lankan university with whom I spoke as a focus group. Reacting to the bill's suggested list of proscribed behaviours, one member of the group worried that legally enforced *katikāvatas* would strain the long-standing bonds between monks and local communities:

> There are certain things that people expect [from monks]: the name-giving after a child is born, determining the auspicious time for a house-opening [ritual], etc. That is to say, people expect various things from monks. People expect this in addition to [following] the Vinaya precepts and preaching [the dharma]. Monks cannot develop relationships with people without doing things like looking after auspicious times and

62 For example, the chief monk for the Southern Province for Rāmañña Nikāya voiced frustration that, although his fraternity had been asking 'for three decades' for laws that would 'give legal powers to the *katikāvatas* of the *nikāyas*', many of the provisions in the new bill seemed unnecessary and an intrusion on monastic autonomy: 'The government does not have any authority to impose laws on Buddhist monks.... Individual fraternities, through their *katikāvatas*, should be authorised to expel from the *sāsana* those individuals that they [themselves] have put into robes, if those persons conduct themselves in immoral and unethical ways that are inappropriate for monks.' Pamunuva, '*Saṅgaruvanaṭa Nīti Dānna Rajayaṭa Balayak Næ* [Government Has No Power to Impose Laws on the Sanghas].'

> horoscopes. However, according to this new bill, monks are not able to do this kind of astrological work. No one agreed to this [because] it's through those things that people and monks maintain a relationship. Looking at horoscopes, advising people what to do in hard times, doing blessings (*set kavi*), giving auspicious times for house-openings, giving three letters (*akuru tunak*) [for babies' names] – these are the things that people trust in (*viśvāsa karanavā*) and that monks ought to attend to. If we can't do those things, what will happen? People will blame us and a chasm will grow between monks and people. For that reason no one likes this [bill].[63]

These comments generated nods of agreement with the rest of the focus group. They also resonated with media statements made by prominent politicians. In one major Sinhala-language daily, then opposition leader Mahinda Rajapaksa called the bill a 'totally direct blow to the cultural identity of Sri Lanka' which would 'create problems for the continuation of the Buddha *sāsana* in the future'.[64] Monastic law, these critics agreed, was not the kind of law that could be standardised and mechanically enforced for all places and times. It was something that must be considered in the context of local Buddhist practices.

While many opponents of the bill feared that it would impose excessive uniformity on monks, another group of critics rejected it for the opposite reason – arguing that it would further entrench existing divisions within the sangha. In particular, they objected to the fact that the bill appeared to endorse the separate authorities, hierarchies and laws of individual *nikāyas* which, they argued, did not always align with Vinaya principles. As one monastic critic put it:

[63] Focus group interview, 21 July 2016.

[64] He stressed, predictably, that 'bhikkhus alone should govern bhikkhus' and that 'law cannot remove the robes of a monk and nullify his monasticism (*bhikṣutvaya*)'. Responding to the prohibitions against things like astrology and medicine, Rajapaksa stated:

> From time immemorial our villagers went to the temple to get cured by monastic doctors (*veda hāmuduruvan*). They would determine the date of the Sinhala New Year by consulting the horoscope. These were monks in the temple. This did not make them business people. They only accepted something if the villager gave it voluntarily. Throughout history, when the country faced challenges, the jewel of the great sangha was the first to raise its voice.

Gamagē, '*Himivarunṭa Nīti Dāna Panata Saṁskṛtiyaṭa Gäsu Paharak* [The Bill that Imposes Laws on Monks is a Blow against [Our] Culture].'

> The proposed *katikāvata*[s] will follow the *nikāyas*. That's what the government says. Now, the divisions that have occurred among most of the *nikāyas* in our country were not there in the time of the Buddha. In the Buddha's time, divisions arose when there were questions over the dharma. But here it was questions about caste (*kula praśna*) that arose and led to the creation of [the current] fraternities. Therefore, in saying that we are creating a *katikāvata* for the *nikāyas*, they're really saying that they are legalising caste divisions.[65]

For monastic critics like such as this, the problem was less one of government intrusion into monastic affairs than the bill's deepening of divisions within the sangha. Such critics saw the bill as giving *too much* weight to *nikāya* identities and, by so doing, further embedding sectarianism, and its associated inequalities, in law.[66]

Opposing the Opposition

The divisive nature of the debates over the *Katikāvata* Bill reflects a familiar pattern in Sri Lankan legal history, one that goes back to the nineteenth-century struggles over monastic and colonial law described in Part I of this book: laws that structured legal pluralism in one way give rise to opposition movements advocating opposing practices of legal pluralism, which, in turn, lead to new legal actions – and so on.[67]

[65] *Kula bhedaya nītigata karanava kiyana eka*. Interview with head monk (*lokuhamadur-uvo*) in Southern Province, 20 July 2016.

[66] Interview with monastic judge (*anuvijjaka*) near Colombo, 10 December 2019.

[67] The examples here only offer some of the myriad comments about the bill in the public media. Multiple others followed suit. For example, a group of deputy leaders (*anunāyakas*) from the Malvatu and Asgiri Chapters of the Siyam Nikāya spoke out soon after the publication of the law, opposing it as an attempt to 'control members of the sangha' and demanding more consultation. A week later, the chief leaders (*mahānāyakas*) of the Malvatu and the Asgiri publicly underscored the importance of supporting the bill. A conference of 'independent monks' (*svādhīna bhikṣus*) expressed concerns that the act would discourage young men from joining the monkhood, reinforce differences among monastic groups and distract from the other more pressing issues facing monks, such as better education, the protection of sacred sites and the creation of island-wide sangha organisations. Other activist monks, familiar with media exposure, also weighed in. Galagodaṭṭhē Gñānasāra decried the bill for controlling Buddhist monks in ways that Muslim and Christian clergy were not. Wimalasurendre, 'Malwatte, Asgiriya Oppose Laws to Control Monks'; Alwis, '*Theravādī Bhikṣu Katikāvat Panataṭa Ekañga Næ* [No Agreement on the Theravādī Bhikṣu Katikāvat Act]'; n.a., 'Bhikku Bill a Timely Need – Asgiriya Mahanayake Thera'; n.a., '*Panat Keṭumpata Desa Paṭu Paramārthayen Nobalanna* [When Looking at the Bill, Don't Look [Only] at the Narrow Purpose].'

In keeping with this pattern, the Supreme Court's ruling against parts of the *Katikāvata* Bill did not end the matter. It only gave rise to a new chorus of counter-arguments demanding that the bill be quickly revised and reintroduced.

Nearly a year after the Supreme Court's decision, for example, a senior monk appeared on national television urging the government to revive the bill, arguing that it was essential to ensuring the purity and independence of the sangha. He insisted that monastic hierarchies must be given the legal means to expel monks who had been declared *pārājika* ('defeated'), as this authority constituted the very essence of monastic sovereignty (*bhikṣu-paramādhipatyaya*):

> It is a *katikāvata* that brings this [power and independence] into effect; that is what is being confirmed legally and what is being implemented.... We must address this need, to create within the sangha a *sāsana* that is completely pure and clear by giving legal authority, legal confirmation, to this *katikāvata*.... There are today various bodies (*saṃsthā*) and collections (*khaṇḍa*) of monks that have been working to destroy the *sāsana*. It's a crime to do this to the *sāsana*, is it not?...
>
> It is clear that each and every government has a responsibility for this. In the constitution there is a clause saying that the Buddha *sāsana* is to be protected and safeguarded; the government is sworn to follow that.... Therefore ... the government must support this *Katikāvata* Bill as a way to protect the image of monks, to protect monks' sovereignty (*svairitvaya*), so that they can fulfil their mission. They [the government] must legalise it ... or we ought to consider them opponents of Buddhism.[68]

This appeal to the government was just one among many. Shortly following the bill's defeat in court and its disappearance from the order paper of parliament, a resurgent wave of support started to rise again in Sri Lanka's public sphere, urging forward long-standing dynamics of legal creation and opposition, one practice of legal pluralism followed by another.

Within a short span of time, a new dialectic of competing practices took shape, which, as in the past, drew on old stereotypes and alliances. Supporters of reform blamed the bill's failure on wealthy and powerful monks who, they speculated, had blocked bill's progress so as not to

68 'Television Broadcast: *Theravādī Bauddha Saṅghādhikaraṇaya* [The Monastic Court in Theravāda Buddhism].'

'decentralise' their powers (*vimadhyagata kirīma*).[69] Others, including many high-ranking monks, blamed schismatic and heterodox monastic groups, arguing that they opposed the bill because weak monastic hierarchies permitted them to behave in unorthodox ways. Through all of it, public debates about the bill – amplified, as they were, by the island's news media – showcased a plurality of legal pluralisms.[70]

PRACTICES AND PLURALITIES OF LEGAL PLURALISM

Legal pluralism is often imagined as an empirical condition, a multiplicity of free-standing legal orders to be navigated by individuals. What matters most, in this view of things, are the strategies used by legal actors to reconcile one system with another or to manage perceived points of conflict. The case studies above, however, offer a different starting point for analysis, one that treats this ostensibly obvious condition of legal pluralism as itself contested and unstable, a construct differentially (even agonistically) produced by persons who claim to be simply observing or protecting 'their' laws. This chapter demonstrates how litigants, lawmakers and judges draw on the same set of normative artefacts – the same texts, obligations, institutions and authorities – to assemble very different accounts of laws' nature, locations and defining qualities. Viewed in this second way, the cases discussed above reveal less about the challenges of balancing two otherwise independent 'systems' than about how human communities engage normative complexity in the first place. Rather than encountering a single

69 Interview with monastic judge (*anuvijjaka*) in Diwulpitiya 29 July 2016.

70 Many high-ranking monks from all three major *nikāyas* conceded that, while the bill may not be perfect in its current version, the project of granting legal powers to *katikāvatas* was itself a long-standing and important one; therefore, the bill should be supported in principle. This included the *mahānāyakas* of the Malvatu and Asgiri chapters of the Siyam Nikāya, as noted above. It also included the supreme *mahānāyaka* of the Amarapura Nikāya, who, after consultation with the executive council of the broader Amarapura confraternity, issued a long statement outlining the roots of the bill in the reform activities of the 1950s (see Chapter 7). He also underscored that the bill is not 'the forceful imposition of laws on monks', but 'the conferring of legal authority (*nītyā[nu]kūla balayak*) on agreements and decisions made by monks in accordance with the Vinaya.' Pamunuva, '*Theravādī Bhikṣu Katikāvat Panata Saṅgha Samājayaṭat Behevit Hitakara Vevi* [The Theravādī Bhikṣu Katikāvat Bill Will Be Very Beneficial to Monastic Society].'

phenomenon, a settled state of multi-legality, laws' users confront a collection of (often competing) constructs – a plurality of legal pluralisms.

This observation has significant implications for how scholars and policymakers ought to think about legal multiplicity. It urges observers to acknowledge the disconcerting possibility that even the very 'facts' of legal pluralism cannot be taken for granted. There is no uncontested normative map, no single superstructural reality, to which we can retreat for analysis. In Sri Lanka, as well as parts of the world, people disagree not only about how to manage overlapping legal orders, but how to construe them in the first place – how to determine their constituents, their sources of normativity and the authorities who can speak on their behalf. Nearly all the actors described in this chapter claimed to use state law to safeguard the *sāsana*, the Vinaya and monastic law. Yet, in so doing, they called into being very different facts about the composition, complementarity, unity, multiplicity and adequacy of those supposedly stable categories.

The legal disputes discussed in this chapter also share dynamics with the longer history of debates about legalising monastic law described in Chapter 7 of this book. In both cases, practices of legal pluralism operated in a dialectical manner, with one expression of legal pluralism giving rise to another: assertions of monastic law's unity (in constitutions or legislation), elicited demonstrations of its multiplicity (by litigants or critics), which called forth attempts to ensure its unity (by court determinations or new legislation). Practices of legal pluralism predicated on the idea that state law could protect the Buddha's law while remaining separate from it gave rise to further practices of legal pluralism that exposed the internal multiplicities of both: the multiple fora for state-legal action; and the multiple norms, texts, interpretations and practices governing the *sāsana*.

Using the Buddhism Chapter to foster *the sāsana* (and, with it, *the* Vinaya) elicited legal actions and events that called into question the singularity of those objects. The Buddhism Chapter was construed as guaranteeing *nikāyas*' autonomy as well as some kind of sangha-wide orthodoxy. It was thought to secure monks' dependence on the Sri Lankan state as well as its independence from it. Monastic law was also characterised in manifold ways: as adaptive and invariant; as hierarchical and egalitarian; as tradition-based and tradition-free; as within the scope of government authority and as entirely outside of it. So too was the term *vinaya* multiply construed. To speak of *vinaya* in these cases was to refer to disciplinary rules and procedural norms, root-text provisions and commentaries, Pali manuscripts and customary practices, *katikāvatas* and the decisions of monastic prelates.

Rather than differing responses to the same legal pluralism, we have a more confounding situation: differing solutions proposed for differing problems. What is at stake is, then, not simply how monastic and state law interact, but how their boundaries and identities are drawn and redrawn, construed and contested. Legal pluralism, in Sri Lanka as elsewhere, is never just one thing. It is a shifting, recursive process – one in which the very nature of 'law' and its diversities remain persistently unsettled.

CONCLUSION

PLURALISING LEGAL PLURALISM

In August 2018, a group of more than 200 Buddhist monks, many of them monastic judges, gathered at a meditation centre in central Colombo. Assembling two by two, they set off barefoot through the streets of the capital city carrying a banner that read: 'A March Demanding State-legal Powers (*rājya balaya*) for the Sangha Courts'. Having walked for five kilometres in the afternoon sun, they arrived at the residence of Sri Lanka's president. There, they delivered a formal letter requesting that his government take immediate action to make monastic court decisions enforceable in state law.

Leaving the residence, the monks held a press conference, where the march organiser addressed a crowd of waiting reporters. He explained to the media that the protestors were not asking for anything unreasonable. Their demand was simple: to be given legal powers to enforce monastic discipline, or *vinaya*. Such powers would not only protect monastic law on the island, he insisted, they would also take a burden off the country's civil courts, which would be freed from having to adjudicate disputes between monks. Moreover, none of this was novel. Other forms of religious law were already recognised in state law, he pointed out, and state-supported monastic courts were part of the island's 'ancient heritage'.[1]

[1] Pieris, '*Mahā Saṅgharatnayaṭa Erehi Naḍu Vibhāgayaṭa Venama Adhikaraṇayak Pihiṭuvanna* [Set up a Separate Court for Litigation against Monks].'

Several weeks later, in December 2018, I attended a judicial training in Colombo, in which the march organiser updated attendees on progress in this area:

> We have come together for today's seminar at an extremely important landmark. What is the reason? This is the era (*yugaya*) in which we are seeking state power (*rājya balaya*) for [our] sangha courts. . ..
>
> My fellow monks may remember that some time ago, bhikkhus went on foot to make [that] request from the president. In a context in which some people were saying, 'We don't want a court, or rules and regulations to control us,' the Rāmañña Nikāya has already requested these things. We ask that [the government] empower our constitution (*vyavasthāva*), which we already use to administer our fraternity. This alone is the request that we made.
>
> Now, in the past [others] had asked for those powers, and a bill was drafted with the relevant provisions and directed to the relevant minister. However, in the end, it came to light that there were some problems relating to how that would be administered. . .. [Now] we're saying give us constitutional power (*vyavasthāmaya balaya*) for our courts. Give us state power (*rājya balaya*). Why, you might ask? Simply because we want to implement our verdicts and decisions in a way that accords with the discipline of the Vinaya Piṭaka.[2]

*

These events, and the rhetoric surrounding them, encapsulate centuries of debates about legal pluralism in Sri Lanka. In his equation of the Vinaya Piṭaka and disciplinary practice (*vinaya kriyāmārga*) with the constitutions and courts of his fraternity, the speaker pointed simultaneously to the unity and multiplicity of monastic law – its ideal unification around a single code (the Vinaya Piṭaka) and its practical application in the various texts and institutions of law examined in Chapter 2. In his references to the country's civil courts and their caseload of litigation among monks, the speaker gestured towards the enduring effects of Buddhist Ecclesiastical Law, a body of case law created by the British (and examined in Chapter 3) that continues to govern monastic succession and property today. In highlighting the special capacities of the Rāmañña court system, the speaker evoked a long history of characterising the laws of monastic fraternities in ways

[2] Speech given by senior monastic judge (*jyeṣṭhānuvijjaka*) at training workshop for monastic judges, 14 December 2018.

that accentuate both their similarities and differences with state legality – themes that I explored in Chapters 4, 5 and 6.

In total, the speaker's comments reflected an institutional reality that is, in many ways, the same today as it was in 1900. Sri Lanka's monastic courts still overlap in jurisdiction with civil courts. Monastic leaders still share authority over ordination and property with bureaucrats whose powers flow from legislation such as the Buddhist Temporalities Ordinance. The norms of monastic life continue to be shaped by the complex interplay of monastic law, state law – themselves differently construed – and the normative expectations of laity. Although case law has evolved, ordinances have been amended, and monastic constitutions have been updated, Buddhist monks today continue to operate within a complex world of overlapping obligations and liabilities, to which they respond by both inviting and resisting state intervention, as seen in Chapters 7 and 8.

Yet continuity does not mean stagnation. Over the past two centuries, Sri Lankans have not simply lived *with* legal pluralism, they have actively created and recreated it – calling forth multiple versions of multi-legality, often concurrently, each with their own calls to action and their own implications for collective life. What counts as Vinaya or monastic law or common law or constitutional law – or, at least, legitimate expressions of them – have been subject to ongoing disagreement, such that the 'facts' of legal pluralism have themselves remained contested. Looking closely at this history over the last two centuries, especially from the perspectives of laws' users, points to the unsettling, if unavoidable, conclusion that legal pluralism is itself plural – a state of normative complexity that is expressed and enacted in multiple ways.

PRACTICES OF LEGAL PLURALISM

This book asks readers to acknowledge the pluralism of legal pluralism and to take it seriously. It argues that our encounters with normative complexity depend not just on the 'stuff' of laws – the courts, constitutions and codes that stand as artefacts of laws' existence – but the ways we bring order and meaning to that stuff: the ways we align or oppose those artefacts, compare or contrast them, reconcile or rank them, and position them as (or against) the category of law; that is to say, it depends on *practices of legal pluralism*.

Recognising the plurality of legal pluralism, however, is not the end of the analysis. Practices of legal pluralism, as I have hoped to show, tend to take finite, patterned forms, drawing on assumptions and assertions that recur across times and places. In Part I of this book, I highlighted practices that stress laws' *separation or integration*, the drawing and dissolving of boundaries within and between monastic and state law in the nineteenth century. Part II examined questions of laws' *commensurability or incommensurability* and the ways in which Rāmañña monks express monastic law's symmetry or dissonance with state-legal forms. Part III highlighted ideals of *purity and adulteration* as guiding motivations for, and definitive critiques of, attempts to 'legalise' monastic law or protect it in court. Running through all parts of this book were practices of legal pluralism fixated on concerns about *continuity or rupture*, the preservation or erosion of law's links with the past.

In all of this, practices of legal pluralism oscillate between two powerful tendencies: the search for unity and the acknowledgement of diversity. On the one hand, humans construe laws as closed systems: integrated bodies of norms, self-contained and free from outside influence. On the other hand, they treat laws as clusters of polycentric authority whose injunctions must be reconciled: Vinaya must be aligned with *katikāvata*s, customs, traditions and so on. What this means is that laws are never entirely unified or fragmented. Like a mosaic, they are both segmented and held together by human practices; and also like a mosaic, the image may change depending on the artist or viewer.

Over the past two centuries, Sri Lankans have assembled this mosaic in differing ways. At some points, Sri Lanka's multi-legal mosaic has offered up a vision of two monoliths – monastic law and state law – set in a relationship of tension or reciprocity. At other points, the mosaic has brought attention to other legal unities: the laws of monastic fraternities, the competition between civil courts and monastic courts, the contradictory imperatives coming from the Department of Buddhist Affairs and the Buddhism Chapter of Sri Lanka's constitution. At yet other times, the mosaic accents more fundamental contrasts within monastic law between mundane concerns with social order and ultimate concerns with karma, self-restraint (*sīlā, hikmīma*) and the pursuit of nirvana.

To practise legal pluralism in these differing ways is to activate multiple stakes and incentives for action. Where laws are rendered as separate, incompatible and pristine embodiments of authority – as in Part III of this book – the stakes of inter-legal negotiations are high, with only a small set of institutional solutions being acceptable:

jurisdictional carve-outs, walls of separation, and rigid forms of 'bridging norms' that limit the ways and circumstances in which laws come into contact. By contrast, where practices of legal pluralism stress the integration, commensurability, hybridity or transformations of laws, the stakes of legal change are lowered and a greater number of solutions may be proposed, such as those documented in Parts I and II of this book.

Across Sri Lankan history, monastics and state officials have practiced legal pluralism in agonistic and purist modes as well as in complementary and hybrid ones. They have scaled 'up' to monolithic visions and 'down' to more polycentric ones. They have framed their concerns as questions of institutional integrity as well as questions about the future of the *sāsana* and the possibility of nirvana. No single practice captures the full compass of multi-legality on the island, although some permit more possibilities for change than others.

PRACTISING LEGAL PLURALISM, EVERYWHERE

We all practise legal pluralism, even if we don't notice it. We take as self-evident the boundaries between religious obligations and secular ones, customary traditions and common law, failing to notice the historicity and particularity of the lines we draw and the relationships we assume. Often, we fail to notice that other distinctions are also possible, other frames of encounter and analysis. Like the Buddhist monastics discussed in this book, our milieu of multi-legality may be fixed, or relatively so, but it permits different expressions and enactments of order.

To recognise this is to recognise something fundamental about legal and communal coexistence. If legal clashes imply contrasting practices more than colliding norms, then conflicts of law are not so much discovered in the world as they are projected onto it. There can be no intrinsic incompatibility between monastic and state law, only incompatible ways of bringing them into proximity.

These observations apply well beyond the shores of Sri Lanka and the walls of Buddhist monasteries. Consider, for example, the legal history of India and its contentious debates over the recognition of religious laws. To focus on the practices of legal pluralism, rather than the empirical field of normative artefacts, is to acknowledge that India's legal frictions emerge not from some foundational tension between, for example, *shari'a* and state law, but from discrete acts of collating, characterising and coordinating laws in such a way as to render them monolithic, agonistic and 'purist' in nature.[3] It is these *practices* within a legally plural country – and not the 'fact' of legal pluralism itself – that explain popular frustrations about the use and misuse of Islamic legal principles in state courts or calls for a Uniform Civil Code.

Similar dynamics apply to debates over the recognition of Māori customary laws, *tikanga Māori*, in my own home country of Aotearoa New Zealand. Here, too, a focus on the contents of normative artefacts emanating from Indigenous and state law has obscured important differences in the ways that people express and frame the parameters of multi-legality in the first place. I would suggest that the question of whether Māori legal concepts align with common-law principles depends less on some objective definitional criteria applied by jurists (e.g., is there a common-law equivalent to *kaitiakitanga* or *mana*?) than on the practices through which legal pluralism is expressed and enacted. It depends on whether one accepts *tikanga* as law; and, if so, whether that law is considered unchanging or evolving, a single body or a collection of diverse traditions, commensurable or incommensurable with state law.

One could go even further. Given their antiquity, sophistication and near-constant history of interactions with other laws, I would suggest that none of the world's major normative traditions can be considered innately resistant to integration with the laws of others.[4] Studies of Islamic law, imperial law and, now, Buddhist monastic law have demonstrated that even those legal traditions that are imagined to be most aloof from or impervious to other forms of law, in fact contain rules, resources and traditions used to accommodate the laws of others. In the same way that all religion is inter-religion, so too might one say that *all law is inter-law*.[5]

LAWS IN CONFLICT, AND COMPROMISE

To understand how and why humans experience laws in conflict, scholars should move beyond the question of whether laws are or are

[3] See, for example: Redding, *A Secular Need*; Lemons, *Divorcing Traditions*.

[4] In most places, for most of history, humans have lived with multiple centres and sources of law. Among others, see: Benton and Clulow, 'Interpolity Law and Jurisdictional Politics'; Davis, 'Centres of Law'; Herzog, 'The Uses and Abuses of Legal Pluralism.'

[5] GhaneaBassiri and Robertson, *All Religion Is Inter-Religion*.

not compatible, as though one could predict social harmony on the basis of some normative algebra that weighed up the various obligations emanating from the laws that we purport to follow. Instead, they should look at the practices of legal pluralism that make such compatibility seem natural or permissible, exceptional or impossible. They should probe the various frames and enactments of multi-legality expressed by laws' drafters and users and the aesthetics, politics and techniques of persuasion that they use. Inter-legal harmony is not a technical feat; it is a social, political and emotional achievement – one that is often precarious.

This is not to say that conditions of legal pluralism, absent of politics, would be tension-free. A key argument of this book is that everyday encounters with legal pluralism, as both an empirical condition and a set of practices, are not acts of traction-like balance. One does not 'hold' multiple laws like one holds a yoga pose, as a kind of equipoise between competing forces. Judging from the chapters of this book, experiences of legal pluralism look more like tennis matches than *āsanas*: humans express and engage with multi-legality through dynamics of push and pull, framings and counter-framings, chains of cause and effect. Moreover, these chains are themselves dialectically related, karmically connected, with one practice of legal pluralism eliciting another: assertions of unity evoking assertions of multiplicity; claims of compatibility giving rise to claims of tension, which, in turn, give rise to new forms of double-speak expressing two normative orders at once. The default state is dynamism, not stability. Legal pluralism is not a problem to solve, but a process to engage.

It is this process that I have tried to document in this book: the shifting and concurrent practices used by Buddhist monks and others to engage laws – some integrative, some confrontational, some influential, some idiosyncratic – all of them 'true' in their own ways. This process and these practices constitute the human experience of legal pluralism, its expression on the ground. They reveal legal pluralism to be more than just the 'stuff' of law, but the changing and recursive *actions* that help people do what we all do: reckon with diverse obligations, assemble normative worlds and forge meaningful pathways forward in our collective and ever-changing lives.

GLOSSARY

Adhikaraṇa	In Sinhala, *adhikaraṇa* refers to courts and adjudication. In Pali it refers to monastic adjudication and legal cases, of which there are four types: dispute cases, accusation cases, offence cases, and action cases. All of these are described in Chapter 2.
Adhikaraṇa samatha	Settlements for legal cases.
All-Ceylon Buddhist Congress (ACBC)	One of Sri Lanka's largest lay-Buddhist organisations which engages in political and legal advocacy. A key actor in Chapter 7.
Amarapura Nikāya	One of the three major monastic fraternities in Sri Lanka. It functions as a federation of more than twenty largely independent sub-fraternities.
Anunāyaka	Deputy leader of a monastic fraternity.
Anuśāsana	Moral instructions or admonishments given by monastic judges at the outset of litigation.
Anuvijjaka	Monastic jurist, judge.
Bhikkhu	Fully ordained male monastic, enjoined to follow 227 precepts in the Pali Vinaya tradition (including 7 rules for adjudicating disputes).
Bhikkhunī	Fully ordained female monastic, enjoined to follow 331 rules in the Pali Vinaya tradition (including 7 rules for adjudicating disputes).
Buddhism Chapter	Chapter Two of the Sri Lankan Constitution that gives to Buddhism 'the foremost place' and obligates the state to 'protect and foster the Buddha Sāsana'. First appeared in 1972 and was slightly revised in 1978.
Buddhist Ecclesiastical Law	A body of civil court doctrine, first developed under British colonial rule in the nineteenth century, relating to topics such as monastic

	succession and the use of temple property. See Chapter 3.
Buddhist Temporalities Ordinance	Legislation governing the use and administration of 'temple' property, defined as including 'any place of Buddhist worship' such as monasteries and pilgrimage sites. The law was first introduced by the British in 1889, with amended versions continuing to be in force today. See Chapter 3.
Chapters section (of the Vinaya)	See *khandhaka*.
Chief incumbent	See *vihārādhipati*.
Constitution	Where unspecified, refers to monastic constitutions, or *katikāvatas*. See *katikāvata*.
Defeat (offence)	See *pārājika*.
Deputy leader	See *anunāyaka*.
Dēvāla	Deity shrines established during the Kandyan period that came under the legal category of 'temples' during the colonial period. See Chapter 3.
Dharma/dhamma	Important and multivalent word that refers, among other things, to the teachings of the Buddha and the laws of the cosmos. See Chapters 1 and 2.
Enclosing section (of the Vinaya)	See *Parivāra*.
Executive Council	See *kāraka sabhāva*.
Explanations section (of the Vinaya)	See Suttavibhaṅga.
Great leader	See *mahānāyaka*.
Hybrid laws	Laws and institutions that purposefully blend monastic and state-legal authority. See Chapter 2.
Jyeṣṭhānuvijjaka (also: *jeṭṭhānuvijjaka*)	Senior monastic judge in the Rāmañña Nikāya judicial system.
Karma/kamma	A multivalent word, which literally means 'action'. Karma/kamma can refer to the cosmic laws of cause and effect that influence all things in *saṃsāra* and which reward skilful (*kusala*) actions with positive results in the future.

	Karma/kamma can also refer to the various legal 'actions' undertaken by sanghas, including ordination, litigation and other matters. See Chapter 2.
Kammavācā	Literally 'words for [legal] actions'. Standard formulas, generally taken from the Vinaya Piṭaka that must be repeated precisely for a legal action to be considered valid.
Katikāvata	Monastic constitution. Important genre of monastic legal texts in Sri Lanka that contains collections of administrative rules and guidelines clarifying the core rules, offices and procedures of monastic life. Roots of genre go back more than a millennium.
Kāraka sabhā	Executive councils for monastic fraternities and sub-fraternities, generally consisting of senior monastics who make important decisions and issue orders regarding the fraternity.
Khandhaka	Part of the Vinaya Piṭaka that provides information about the history, rituals and institutional protocols of the Buddhist monkhood. Referred to in this book as the Chapter section of the Vinaya.
Kusala	'Skilful' ways of acting in the world that align with the Buddha's teaching and bring positive karmic results, moving one towards the ultimate goal of nirvana.
Mahānāyaka	'Great leader' and highest office in a monastic fraternity. In Sri Lanka today it is common that, when people refer to 'the *mahānāyakas*' or the 'four *mahānāyakas*', they have in mind the great leaders of the Asgiri and Malvatu Chapters of the Siyam Nikāya, the great leader of the Rāmañña Nikāya and the 'supreme great leader' (*uttarītara mahānāyaka*) of the Amarapura Nikāya, who functions as the head of the Amarapura confederation. However, the term is also used to refer to the paramount leaders within the chapters and sub-fraternities of the Siyam, Amarapura and Rāmañña Nikāyas.

Mānatta	A period of penance prescribed by the Vinaya, which runs for a period of six days and six nights. During that time, monastics must observe ninety-four restrictions that limit their ability to participate in monastic life.
Monastic judge	See *anuvijjaka*.
Nikāya/*nikāya*	A polysemous term that refers to monastic groupings, generally translated as fraternity. In Sri Lanka, the term is mainly used to refer to the three major monastic groupings, which I refer to in this book as fraternities: the Siyam Nikāya, the Amarapura Nikāya and the Rāmañña Nikāya. Yet, within these large groupings, there are other monastic groups that also refer to themselves as *nikāya*, especially within the Amarapura confederation – a usage that I signal in this book by using the lower-case, italicised version of the term (*nikāya*, rather than Nikāya). I also default to the generic term, *nikāya*, whenever the intended meaning appears to be monastic fraternities in general, rather than the three major Nikāyas specifically.
Nirvana	The ultimate goal of Theravāda Buddhism. One's release from painful cycles of rebirth.
Novice	See *sāmaṇera*.
Ordination (or Higher Ordination)	See *upasampadā*.
Pārājika	Defeat offence. For bhikkhus, these are the first four prohibitions listed in the Explanations section of the Vinaya Piṭaka, which prohibit sex, murder, theft and claiming supernatural powers. (Bhikkhunīs are enjoined to observe eight *pārājikas*.) Committing *pārājika* offences results in one's disrobing and/or expulsion from a monastic community.
Parivāra	The third section of the Pali version of the Vinaya, composed after the other two, which features prominently in the practice of law among Sri Lankan monks. This section contains nineteen chapters, many of which summarise

	and analyse the other two parts of the Vinaya. Referred to as Enclosing section in this book.
Parivāsa	A period of additional probation added on to *mānatta*. In cases where monks conceal their offences deliberately for a period of time, the Vinaya advises that, prior to commencing *mānatta*, monks should observe a period of probation for the number of days equal to the length of time the offence was concealed.
Pārśva	Divisions or chapters of a fraternity, used to describe sections within the Siyam Nikāya in particular.
Pātimokkha(s)	Bare collections of rules that correspond with those in the Explanations section of the Vinaya. Such collections have circulated independently from the Vinaya. The list of rules is intended to be chanted fortnightly by monastics during the *uposatha* rite. See Chapter 2.
Penance offence(s)	See *saṅghādisesa*.
Pirivena	Monastic training institutions in Sri Lanka.
Rāmañña Nikāya	Third largest monastic fraternity in Sri Lanka, most of which functions as a single body, alongside a smaller group of highly ascetical, forest-dwelling monks. Examined closely in Part II.
Regional court	The lowest level of tribunal in the Rāmañña Nikāya judicial system. In Sinhala: *prādēśikādhikaraṇaya*.
Sāmaṇera	Novice monks generally under twenty years old who are not considered full monastics for the purpose of legal actions and who are only enjoined to follow ten basic rules, compared to the 227 for bhikkhus.
Sāmaṇera Baṇa Daham Pota	*Preaching and Dharma Book for Novices*. A training manual for novices who are joining the monkhood. See Chapter 2.
Samantapāsādikā	Extremely important Pali-language commentary on the Vinaya Piṭaka attributed to the monk Buddhaghosa around the fifth century CE. See Chapter 2.

Samatha	Settlement. Can refer to the modes of settlement used to address legal disputes (*adhikaraṇa*) in the Vinaya or to the act of settling disputes more generally. Important term in monastic law.
Saṃsāra	The unpleasant cycle of rebirths in which all sentient beings are trapped until they achieve nirvana.
Saṃvega	Strong feelings of fear and despair caused by thinking about the miseries of *saṃsāra*.
Sangha	The community of monastics. Although the term can refer to individual groups of monastics, it is often used more expansively to refer to all monastics in a given area.
Saṅgha sabhā	Sangha councils that often function as executive committees for monastic groups. Also used to describe sub-branches of the three major Nikāyas.
Saṅghādhikaraṇa	Monastic court.
Saṅghādisesa	The second most serious category of offences in the Vinaya. For bhikkhus, violating these thirteen rules (e.g., making sexual innuendos, touching women, creating schisms in the sangha) requires special periods of penance and probation as well as formal meetings of the monastic order.
Saṅghakarma/ saṅghakamma	'Legal action'. A collective legal procedure undertaken by a community of monks. Also referred to in Sri Lanka as a *vinayakarma*.
Sāsana	Important term, especially in Southern Asian Buddhisms. Refers to the total institutional, social, material and doctrinal legacy of the Buddha. In its inclusion of things like property, artefacts, relics, manuscripts and institutions, *sāsana* is generally thought to have a broader semantic range than the term 'religion'.
Sekhiya	A category of 75 precepts in the Pali Vinaya referred to as 'training rules'. It encompasses a long list of detailed instructions concerning how

	monastics are supposed to conduct themselves while eating, walking, preaching and performing other everyday activities. Transgression of these norms, which is acknowledged to be unavoidable for most monastics, requires no formal confession.
Senior monastic judge	See *jyeṣṭhānuvijjaka*.
Silmātā	'Precept mothers'. Renunciant women in Sri Lanka who live monastic lives but are not bhikkhunīs. Formally, they observe ten precepts, the same as novice monastics. But in practice, they often observe many more. Discussed in more detail in Chapter 8.
Sīmā	Ritual-*cum*-legal boundaries, the proper establishment of which is essential for monastic legal actions.
Siyam Nikāya	The largest of the three major fraternities in Sri Lanka, with eight recognised subgroups, including the important Malvatu and Asgiri Chapters, which are the oldest and largest monastic bodies on the island.
Suttavibhaṅga	The 'Explanations section' of the Vinaya. That part of the Pali Vinaya which offers a detailed account of the origins and meanings of the bhikkhus' 227 precepts and (in the Bhikkhunī Vinaya) the bhikkhunīs' 331 precepts. 'Sutta' is the shorthand for the *Pātimokkha-sutta*, the bare list of rules that also circulates independently. See *Pātimokkha(s)* above.
Tīndū/tīṇḍū	Legal determinations or decisions issued by monastic courts.
Tipiṭaka	The 'three baskets' of texts thought to contain the original words of the Buddha. Includes the basket of discipline (Vinaya Piṭaka), the basket of discourses (Sutta Piṭaka) and the basket of further teachings (Abhidhamma Piṭaka). Sometimes referred to, albeit problematically, as the 'canon' of Theravāda Buddhism.

Theravāda	Also Theriya. The school of Buddhism that predominates in Southern Asia, including in Sri Lanka, and draws on Pali textual sources.
Uposatha	A fortnightly practice prescribed in the Vinaya during which members of a monastic community gather to recite the *Pātimokkha* and confess their offences.
Upasampadā	'Higher ordination' ceremony in which persons over twenty years of age are formally 'accepted' into the monastic community.
V*ihārādhipati*	Chief incumbent monk of a monastery. An office that, since the British colonial period, has come to be recognised in both monastic and state-legal systems as having trustee-like control over the assets and property associated with a monastery. One monk can be Chief incumbent of multiple sites.
vinaya (lower-case, italicised)	A multivalent term in Sinhala and Pali that refers to discipline, especially monastic discipline.
Vinaya (upper-case, unitalicised)	See Vinaya Piṭaka.
Vinayakarma	See *saṅghakarma*.
vinaya literature	Phrase referring to the broader body of texts that discuss monastic law and discipline, including commentaries, digests, handbooks, and other sources described in Chapter 2.
Vinaya Piṭaka	'Basket of Discipline'. The text said to contain the original instructions of the Buddha concerning monastic discipline. Handed down in multiple languages and versions. In Sri Lanka, the Pali version dominates.
Viniścaya/vinicchaya	Adjudication.

REFERENCES

A note on references: The following list refers only to the published sources, including published pamphlets, used for this research. References to other archival sources – including monastic and state legal sources, bills, petitions, submissions, interview transcripts, reports and other unpublished materials – appear in the footnotes of the individual chapters of this book.

Abeyawardhana, H. A. P. *Boundary Divisions of Mediaeval Sri Lanka*. Polgasovita, Sri Lanka: Academy of Sri Lankan Culture, 1999.

Abeysekara, Ananda. *Colors of the Robe: Religion, Identity, and Difference*. Columbia, SC: University of South Carolina Press, 2002.

'Politics of Higher Ordination, Buddhist Monastic Identitiy, and Leadership at the Dambulla Temple in Sri Lanka.' *Journal of the International Association of Buddhist Studies* 22 (1999): 255–80.

'The Saffron Army, Violence, Terror (ism): Buddhism, Identity and Difference in Sri Lanka.' *Numen* 48 (2001): 1–46.

Acevedo, Deepa Das. 'Divine Sovereignty, Indian Property Law, and the Dispute over the Padmanabhaswamy Temple.' *Modern Asian Studies* 50, no. 3 (2016): 841–65.

Adcock, C.S. *The Limits of Tolerance: Indian Secularism and the Politics of Religious Freedom*. New York: Oxford University Press, 2013.

Agostini, Guilio. *The Ornament of Lay Followers: A Translation of Ananda's Upasakajanalankara*. Bristol, UK: Pali Text Society, 2016.

Agrama, Hussein Ali. *Questioning Secularism: Islam, Sovereignty, and the Rule of Law in Modern Egypt*. Chicago: University of Chicago Press, 2012.

All-Ceylon Buddhist Congress. *Buddhism and the State: Resolutions and Memorandum of the All Ceylon Buddhist Congress*. Maradana: Oriental Press, 1951.

Alwis, Kamini. '*Theravādī Bhikṣu Katikāvat Panataṭa Ekan̆ga Næ* [No Agreement on the Theravādī Bhikṣu Katikāvat Act].' *Dinamina*, 22 January 2016. http://dinamina.lk/?q=2016/01/22/පුවත්/ථෙරවාදී-භික්ෂු-කතිකාවත්-පනතට-එකඟ-නෑ.

Amarapura Mahānikāyē. *Amarapura Mahānikāyē Katikāvata, Amarapura Mahānikāyē Saṅghādhikaraṇaya Hā Śrī Laṅkā Amarapura Mahāsaṅgha Sabhāvē Vyavasthā Saṅgrahaya [Collection of the Constitution of the Amarapura Fraternity, the Monastic Court of the Amarapura Fraternity and the Constitution for the Great Sangha Council of the Amarapura Fraternity]*. n.p., 1973.

Amarapura Sirisaddhammavaṃsika Nikāya. *Mahāvihāra Paramparānugata Amarapura Sirisaddhammavaṃsika Nikāyē Katikāvata [The Katikāvata of the Amarapura Sirisaddhammavaṃsika Nikāya Following the Tradition of the Great Vihāra']*. Colombo: Subodha Printers, 1904.

Ambalaṅgoḍa Dhammakusala. *Athakathācārya Buddhaghoṣa Sthavirapādayan Visin Viracita Samantapāsādikā Vinayaṭṭhakathā: Pārājikakāṇḍaya: Siṃhala Parivartanaya [The Eminent Samantapāsādikā Vinaya Commentary by the Commentator Ven. Buddhaghośa: A Sinhala Translation of the Pārājika Section]*. 3 vols. Colombo: Bauddha Saṅskṛtika Madhyasthāna [Buddhist Cultural Centre], 2003.

Amunugama, Sarath. 'Buddhaputra and Bhumiputra?' *Religion* 21 (1991): 115–39.

Anālayo, Bhikkhu. 'The Cullavagga on Bhikkhuni Ordination.' *Journal of Buddhist Ethics* 22 (2015): 401–49.

'The Revival of the Bhikkhunī Order and the Decline of the Sāsana.' *Journal of Buddhist Ethics* 20 (2013): 147–94.

Anderson, Carol S. "'For Those Who Are Ignorant': A Study of the Bauddha Ädahilla.' In *Constituting Communities: Theravada Traditions and Religious Cultures in South and Southeast Asia, Essays in Honor of Frank Reynolds*, edited by John Holt and Jake Kinnard, 171–88. Buffalo: SUNY Press, 2003.

Anderson, M. R. 'Islamic Law and the Colonial Encounter in British India.' In *Institutions and Ideologies: A SOAS South Asia Reader*, 165–85. London: Curzon Press Ltd., 1993.

Appadurai, Arjun. *Worship and Conflict under Colonial Rule: A South Indian Case*. Cambridge South Asian Studies. London: Cambridge University Press, 1981.

Arvind, T. T. 'Religious Endowments and Trusts Law in Colonial India.' In *Asia-Pacific Trusts Law, Volume 2: Adaptation in Context*, edited by Ying Khai Liew and Ying-Chieh Wu. Oxford: Hart Publishing, 2022.

Aung-Thwin, Michael. 'The Role of Sasana Reform in Burmese History: Economic Dimensions of a Religious Purification.' *Journal of Asian Studies* 38, no. 4 (1979): 671–88.

Balasingham, K. *Notes of Cases: Decided by the Supreme Court of Ceylon, Volume 5*. Colombo: Ceylonese Union, 1916.

Barrow, Ian Jeffrey. 'Surveying in Ceylon during the Nineteenth Century.' *Imago Mundi* 55 (2003): 81–96.

Bartholomeusz, Tessa J. *Women under the Bo Tree: Buddhist Nuns in Sri Lanka*. New York: Cambridge University Press, 1994.

Baynes, Herbert. 'A Collection of Kammavācās.' *The Journal of the Royal Asiatic Society of Great Britain and Ireland*, 1892: 53–75.

Bechert, Heinz. 'Theravada Buddhist Sangha: Some General Observations on Historical and Political Factors in Its Development.' *The Journal of Asian Studies* 29 (1970): 761–78.

Benton, Lauren. 'Colonial Law and Cultural Difference: Jurisdictional Politics and the Formation of the Colonial State.' *Comparative Studies in Society and History* 41, no. 3 (1999): 563–88.

Benton, Lauren, and Adam Clulow. 'Interpolity Law and Jurisdictional Politics.' *Law and History Review* 42, no. 2 (2023): 1–13.

Benton, Lauren, and Lisa Ford. *Rage for Order: The British Empire and the Origins of International Law, 1800–1850*. Cambridge, MA: Harvard University Press, 2016.

Benton, Lauren, and Richard J. Ross. *Legal Pluralism and Empires, 1500–1850*. New York: NYU Press, 2013.

Berman, Paul Schiff. 'Towards a Jurisprudence of Hybridity Symposium: Non-State Governance.' *Utah Law Review* 1 (2010): 11–30.

n.a. 'Bhikku Bill a Timely Need-Asgiriya Mahanayake Thera.' *Daily Mirror*, 26 January 2016.

Bianchi, Ester, and Daniela Campo, eds. *'Take the Vinaya as Your Master': Monastic Discipline and Practices in Modern Chinese Buddhism*. Leiden: Brill, 2023.

Blackburn, Anne M. *Locations of Buddhism: Colonialism and Modernity in Sri Lanka*. Chicago: University of Chicago Press, 2010.

Buddhist Learning and Textual Practice in Eighteenth-Century Lankan Monastic Culture. Princeton: Princeton University Press, 2001.

'Looking for the Vinaya: Monastic Discipline in the Practical Canons of the Theravāda.' *Journal of the International Association of Buddhist Studies* 22, no. 2 (1999): 281–309.

Bond, George. *The Buddhist Revival in Sri Lanka*. Columbia, SC: University of South Carolina, 1988.

Borchert, Thomas, and Susan M. Darlington. 'Political Disrobing in Thailand.' *Buddhism, Law & Society* 3 (2017/2018): 113–56.

Borgland, Jens W. 'A Study of the Adhikaraṇavastu: Legal Settlement Procedures of the Mūlasarvāstivāda Vinaya.' Ph.D. Dissertation, University of Oslo, 2014.

'Some Reflections on Thích Nhất Hạnh's Monastic Code for the Twenty-First Century.' In *Buddhist Modernities: Re-Inventing Tradition in the Globalizing Modern World*, edited by Hanna Havnevik, Ute Hüsken, Mark Teeuwen, Vladimir Tikhonov, and Koen Wellens, 259–81. London: Routledge, 2017.

'Undetermined Matters: On the Use of Lay Witnesses in Buddhist Monastic Procedural Law.' *Buddhism, Law & Society* 2 (2017/2016): 1–57.

Bujjampola Dhammaparāyanatissa. *Prātimokṣa Vivaraṇaya*. Bataramula: Ratna Pot Prakāśayō, 2016.

Burset, Christian R. *An Empire of Laws: Legal Pluralism in British Colonial Policy*. New Haven: Yale University Press, 2023.
Buskens, Léon. 'Sharia and the Colonial State.' In *The Ashgate Research Companion to Islamic Law*. New York: Routledge, 2014.
Campo, Daniela. 'A Different Buddhist Revival: The Promotion of Vinaya (Jielü 戒律) in Republican China.' *Journal of Global Buddhism* 18, no. 1 (2017): 129–54.
Carbine, Jason A. 'How King Ramadhipati Handled His Boundary Case: Sima, Sasana, and Buddhist Law.' *Buddhism, Law & Society* 1 (2016/2015): 105–64.
Carbine, Jason A., and Erik W. Davis. 'Introduction.' In *Sīmās: Foundations of Buddhist Religion*, edited by Jason A. Carbine and Erik W. Davis, 1–22. Honolulu: University of Hawai'i Press, 2022.
Carter, John Ross. 'The Origin and Development of 'Buddhism' and 'Religion' in the Study of Theravada Buddhism.' In *On Understanding Buddhists: Essays on the Theravāda Tradition in Sri Lanka*, 9–26. Albany, NY: SUNY Press, 1993.
Carter, John Ross, and Mahinda Palihawadana. *The Dhammapada*. New York: Oxford University Press, 1998.
Chatterjee, Nandini. *The Making of Indian Secularism: Empire, Law and Christianity, 1830–1960*. London: Palgrave Macmillan, 2011.
Negotiating Mughal Law: A Family of Landlords across Three Indian Empires. Cambridge: Cambridge University Press, 2020.
Chiu, Tzu-Lung. 'An Overview of Buddhist Precepts in Taiwan and Mainland China.' *Journal of the Oxford Centre for Buddhist Studies* 13 (2017): 150–96.
'Bodhisattva Precepts and Their Compatibility with Vinaya in Contemporary Chinese Buddhism: A Cross-Straits Comparative Study.' *Journal of the Oxford Centre for Buddhist Studies* 17 (2019): 193–224.
Chladek, Michael R. 'Imagined Laity and the Performance of Monasticism in Northern Thailand.' *Buddhism, Law & Society* 3 (2018/2017): 157–90.
Clarke, Shayne. 'Monks Who Have Sex: Pārājika Penance in Indian Buddhist Monasticisms.' *Journal of Indian Philosophy* 37 (2009): 1–43.
'Vinayas.' In *Brill's Encyclopedia of Buddhism*, edited by Jonathan A. Silk, I: Literature and Languages: 60–87. Leiden: Brill, 2015.
Clauson, G.L.M. 'A New Kammavācā.' *Journal of the Pali Text Society* 5 (1907/1906): 1–7.
Cohen, Bernard. 'Law and the Colonial State in India.' In *History and Power in the Study of Law: New Directions in Legal Anthropology*, edited by June Starr, 132–51. Ithaca, NY: Cornell University Press, 2018.
Collins, Steven. *Nirvana and Other Buddhist Felicities: Utopias of the Pali Imaginaire*. Cambridge: Cambridge University Press, 1998.

Collins, Steven, and Andrew Huxely. 'The Post-Canonical Adventures of Mahasammata.' *Journal of Indian Philosophy* 24 (1996): 623–48.

Constable, Marianne. *Just Silences: The Limits and Possibilities of Modern Law*. Princeton: Princeton University Press, 2008.

Cover, Robert M. 'Foreword: Nomos and Narrative.' *Harvard Law Review* 97 (1984/1983): 4–68.

Crosby, Kate. 'A Theravāda Code of Conduct for Good Buddhists: The 'Upāsakamanussavinaya." *Journal of the American Oriental Society* 126, no. 2 (2006): 177–87.

'Sāriputta's Three Works on the Samantapāsādikā.' *Journal of the Pali Text Society* 28 (2006): 49–59.

Crouch, Melissa. 'Islamic Law and Society in Southeast Asia.' In *The Oxford Handbook of Islamic Law*, edited by Anver M. Emon and Rumee Ahmed, 589–608. Oxford: Oxford University Press, 2018.

'Promiscuity, Polygyny, and the Power of Revenge: The Past and Future of Burmese Buddhist Law in Myanmar.' *Asian Journal of Law and Society* 3 (2016): 85–104.

Danet, Brenda. 'Language in the Legal Process.' *Law & Society Review* 14, no. 3 (1980): 445–564.

Davis, Donald R. 'Centres of Law: Duties, Rights, and Jurisdictional Pluralism in Medieval India.' In *Legalism: Anthropology and History*, edited by Paul Dresch and Hannah Skoda, 85–114. Oxford: Oxford University Press, 2012.

Davis, Donald R., and Timothy Lubin. 'Hinduism and Colonial Law.' In *Hinduism in the Modern World*, edited by Brian A. Hatcher, 96–108. New York: Routledge, 2015.

De Kretser, O. L. *Matara Cases, Being a Collection of Hitherto Unpublished Decisions by the Supreme Court of Ceylon, on Appeal from the District Court of Matara*. 2 vols. Matara: Ceylon Examiner Press, 1911.

De Silva, C. R. *Sri Lanka: A History*. New Delhi: Vikas, 1997.

'The Education of Buddhist Monks in Sri Lanka: A Historical Review and Some Suggestions for Reform.' *The Sri Lanka Journal of the Humanities* 42, no. 1–2 (2018): 1–28.

De Silva, Gihani. 'Vigilant Steps: A Study of Buddhist Female Renunciant Groups in Contemporary Sri Lanka.' Ph.D., University of Otago, 2022.

De Silva, K. M. *A History of Sri Lanka*. Colombo: Vijitha Yapa Publications, 2005.

Social Policy and Missionary Organizations in Ceylon: 1840–1855. London: Longmans, 1965.

De Silva, Premakumara. 'Colonial Governmentality: Legal and Administrative Technologies of the Governance of Sri Pada Temple in Sri Lanka.' In *Theravada Buddhism in Colonial Contexts*, edited by Thomas Borchert, 121–37. New York: Routledge, 2018.

De Soysā, Ahungallē Dē Sū. '*Vasara 167-k Pärani Amarapura Samāgamē Katikāvata* [A 167-Year-Old *Katikāvata* from the Amarapura Samāgama].' In *Amarapura Udāva*, n.d.

Deegalle, Mahinda. 'Politics of the Jathika Hela Urumaya Monks: Buddhism and Ethnicity in Contemporary Sri Lanka.' *Contemporary Buddhism* 5 (2004): 83–103.

'The First Sinhala Tripiṭakaya Translation: De Zoysa's 'Protestant' Buddhist Project for Mass Literacy in Twentieth Century Sri Lanka.' *Vidyodaya Journal of Humanities and Social Sciences* 7, no. 2 (6 July 2022): 28–45.

Demian, Melissa. 'Dislocating Custom.' *PoLAR: Political and Legal Anthropology Review* 38, no. 1 (2015): 91–107.

Department of Buddhist Affairs. *Śrī Laṅkāvē Nikāyayan Pilibaňda Toraturu [Report on the Nikayas in Sri Lanka]*. Colombo: Bauddha Kaṭayutu Piḷibaňda Depārtmēntuva, 1984.

DeVotta, Neil, and Jason Stone. 'Jathika Hela Urumaya and Ethno-Religious Politics in Sri Lanka.' *Pacific Affairs* 81 (2008): 31–51.

DeVotta, Neil. *Blowback: Linguistic Nationalism, Institutional Decay and Ethnic Conflict in Sri Lanka*. Palo Alto, CA: Stanford University Press, 2004.

Dewaraja, Lorna S. *A Study of the Political, Administrative, and Social Structure of the Kandyan Kingdom of Ceylon, 1707–1760*. Colombo: Lake House, 1972.

Dhammasami, Khammai. *Buddhism, Education and Politics in Burma and Thailand: From the Seventeenth Century to the Present*. London: Bloomsbury Publishing, 2018.

Dharmapala, Anagarika. *Return to Righteousness: A Collection of Speeches, Essays, and Letters of the Anagarika Dharmapala*, edited by Ananda Guruge. 1 vol. Ceylon: Anagarika Dharmapala Birth Centenary Committee, Ministry of Education and Cultural Affairs, 1965.

Dickson, J. F. 'The Upasampadā-Kammavācā: Being the Buddhist Manual of the Form and Manner of Ordering of Priests and Deacons. The Pāli Text, with a Translation and Notes.' *Journal of the Royal Asiatic Society of Sri Lanka (n.s.)* 48 (2003): 149–59.

Disānāyaka, Jayaratna Baṇḍā. *Encyclopaedia of Sinhala Language and Culture*. Colombo: Sumitha Publications, 2012.

D'Oyly, John. 'A Sketch of the Constitution of the Kandyan Kingdom.' *Transactions of the Royal Asiatic Society of Great Britain and Ireland* 3, no. 2 (1833): 191–252.

Dreyfus, Georges B. J. *The Sound of Two Hands Clapping: The Education of a Tibetan Buddhist Monk*. Berkeley: University of California Press, 2008.

Dutt, Sukumar. *Early Buddhist Monachism*. London: Kegan Paul, Trench and Trubner, 1924.

Evers, H. D. 'Buddhism and British Colonial Policy.' *Asian Studies* 2 (1964): 323–33.
'Monastic Landlordism' in Ceylon.' *Journal of Asian Studies* 28 (1969): 685–92.
Monks, Priests and Peasants: A Study of Buddhism and Social Structure in Central Ceylon. Leiden: Brill, 1973.
Falk, Monica Lindberg. *Making Fields of Merit: Buddhist Female Ascetics and Gendered Orders in Thailand*. Copenhagen: NIAS Press, 2007.
Fedricks, Krishantha. 'Accessibility of Nirvāṇa: The Language and Media of Sri Lankan Buddhist Televangelists and Their Followers.' Ph.D. Dissertation, University of Texas at Austin, 2023.
Finnegan, Damchö Diana. "'For the Sake of Women, Too': Ethics and Gender in the Narratives of the Mūlasarvāstivāda Vinaya.' Ph.D. Dissertation, The University of Wisconsin at Madison, 2009.
Fish, Stanley. 'The Law Wishes to Have a Formal Existence.' In *There's No Such Thing as Free Speech and It's A Good Thing, Too*, edited by Stanley Fish, 141–79. New York: Oxford University Press, 1993.
Fleming, Christopher T. *Ownership and Inheritance in Sanskrit Jurisprudence*. New York: Oxford University Press, 2021.
French, Rebecca Redwood. 'The Cosmology of Law in Buddhist Tibet.' *Journal of the International Association of Buddhist Studies* 18 (1995): 97–116.
Friedrich, Philip. 'Merchants, Ministers, and Monks: Making Buddhist Power and Place in Medieval Sri Lanka.' Ph.D. Dissertation, Univesity of Pennsylvania, 2020.
Galanter, Marc. 'The Modernization of Law.' In *Modernization: The Dynamics of Growth*, edited by M. Weiner, 153–65. New York: Basic Books Press, 1966.
Gamage, Karuṇāratna. '*Amarapura Hā Rāmañña Nikāyan Deka Ek Nikāyak Bavaṭa Pat Karanavā* [the Two Fraternities of Amarapura and Rāmañña Are Becoming One Nikāya].' *Divaina*, 23 June 2019.
Gamagē, Saman. '*Himivaruntạ Nīti Dāna Panata Saṁskṛtiyaṭa Gäsu Paharak* The Bill That Imposes Laws on Monks Is a Blow against [Our] Culture].' *Divayina*, 14 January 2016.
Geertz, Clifford. 'Local Knowledge: Fact and Law in Comparative Perspective.' In *Local Knowledge: Further Essays in Interpretive Anthropology*, edited by Clifford Geertz, 167–234. New York: Basic Books, 1983.
GhaneaBassiri, Kambiz, and Paul Robertson. *All Religion Is Inter-Religion: Engaging the Work of Steven M. Wasserstrom*. London: Bloomsbury, 2019.
Ginsburg, T., Z. Chernykh, and Z. Elkins. 'Commitment and Diffusion: How and Why National Constitutions Incorporate International Law.' *University of Illinois Law Review* 1 (2008): 201–37.
'*Gnānasāra Himigē Upasampadāva Naeti Karanna Kaṭavat Baeae – Tripiṭakācārya Talaṅgama Sudhīrānanda Himi* [Ven. Gnanasara Cannot

Be Nullified by Anyone – Ven. Talagama Sudhiranandа].' YouTube video, 2018.
Godakumbura, C. E. *Sinhalese Literature*. Colombo: Godage, 2013.
Gogerly, D. J. 'On Buddhism.' *The Journal of the Ceylon Branch of the Royal Asiatic Society of Great Britain & Ireland* 1, no. 1 (1845): 7–29.
'On Buddhism, No. 2.' *The Journal of the Ceylon Branch of the Royal Asiatic Society of Great Britain & Ireland* 1, no. 1 (1845): 93–117.
Gombrich, Richard F., and Gananath Obeyesekere. *Buddhism Transformed: Religious Change in Sri Lanka*. Princeton, Princeton University Press, 1989.
Gornall, Alistair. *Rewriting Buddhism: Pali Literature and Monastic Reform in Sri Lanka, 1157–1270*. London: UCL Press, 2020.
Government of Ceylon. *Buddha Śāsana Komiṣan Vārtāva [Buddha Sāsana Commission Report]*. Colombo: Government Press, 1959.
Government of Ceylon. *Correspondences Relating to the Buddhist Temporalities Ordinance (Sessional Paper IV of 1907)*. Colombo: Government Printers, 1907.
Government of Ceylon. *Hansard Debates in the House of Representatives*. Colombo: Government Press, n.d.
Government of Ceylon. *Interim Report of the Buddha Sāsana Commission (Sessional Paper XXV of 1957)*. Colombo: Government Press, 1957.
Government of Ceylon. *Memorial of the Buddhists of the Kandyan Provinces (Sessional Paper XIII of 1888)*. Colombo: Government Printers, 1888.
Government of Ceylon. *Papers Relating to the Proposed Amendment of the Buddhist Temporalities Ordinance, No. 3 of 1899 (Sessional Paper XXXIII of 1904)*. Colombo: Government Printers, 1904.
Government of Ceylon. *Record of Legislative Acts of the Ceylon Government from 1796: Distinguishing Those Now in Force, Vol II, Containing Ordinances, Orders in Council and Letters Patent from 1833 to 1852*. Colombo: Government Printers, 1854.
Government of Ceylon. *Record of Legislative Acts of the Ceylon Government from 1798 to 1833*. Vol. 1. Colombo: Government Printers, 1853.
Government of Ceylon. *Report of the Commissioners Appointed to Inquire into the Administration of the Buddhist Temporalities (Sessional Paper of the Legislative Council, Paper XVII)*. Colombo: Government Printers, 1876.
Government of Ceylon. *Report of the Temple Land Commissioners on the Progress and Results of the Commission from Its Constitution, in February 1857, to the End of 1858*. Colombo: Government Press, 1859.
Government of Ceylon. *The Buddhist Temporalities Bill, Petitions (Sessional Paper No. IX of 1889)*. Colombo: Government Printers, 1889.
Government of Ceylon. *Legislative Acts 1796–1833*. Colombo: William Skeen, Government Printer Ceylon, 1833.

Government of Sri Lanka. *Constitution of the Democratic Socialist Republic of Sri Lanka*. Colombo: Government Publications Office, 1978.

Government of Sri Lanka. *Hansard Parliamentary Debates*. Colombo: Government Printers, n.d.

Government of Sri Lanka. *Report of the Buddha Sāsana Presidential Commission: Summary of Conclusions and Recommendations*. Colombo: Ministry of Buddha Sasana, 2002.

Government of Sri Lanka. Theravadi Bhikkhu Kathikawath (Registration) Bill 2016.

Government of Sri Lanka. '*Vihārasthāna hā Bhikṣūn Vahansē Saṅgaṇanaya [The Census of Bhikkhus and Temples]*. Colombo: Department of Buddhist Affairs, 2012.

Government of Sri Lanka Ministry of Cultural Affairs. *Yōjita Saṃghādhikaraṇa Sabhā Pihiṭuvīma Piḷibanda Dhavala Patrikāva [White Paper on the Proposed Establishment of Sanghadhikarana Sabhas]*. Colombo: Government Printers, 1981.

Gunawardana, R. A. L. H. *Robe and Plough: Monasticism and Economic Interest in Early Medieval Sri Lanka*. The Association for Asian Studies: Monographs and Papers, No. XXXV. Tucson: University of Arizona Press, 1979.

Guruparan, Kumaravadivel. 'Customary Law of Stateless Nations: Some Observations on the Question of Who Can Reform the Thesawalamai, the Customary Laws of the Tamils in Sri Lanka.' *Jindal Global Law Review* 7, no. 1 (2016): 49–59.

Hallisey, Charles. 'Apropos the Pāli Vinaya as a Historical Document.' *Journal of the Pali Text Society* XV (1990): 197–208.

Haniffa, Farzana. 'Who Gave These Fellows This Strength? Muslims and the Bodu Bala Sena in Post-War Sri Lanka.' In *The Struggle for Peace in the Aftermath of War*, edited by Amarnath Amarasingham and Daniel Bass, 109–27. London: Hurst & Co, 2016.

Hardy, R. Spence. *British Government and the Idolatry of Ceylon*. London: Crofts and Blenkarn, 1841.

Harris, Troy L. 'Secularizing a Religious Legal System: Ecclesiastical Jurisdiction in Early Eighteenth Century England.' *British Journal of American Legal Studies* 8, no. 1 (2019): 1–36.

Hayley, Frederic Austin. *Laws and Customs of the Sinhalese; Or, Kandyan Law*. Colombo: H.W. Cave and Co., 1923.

Heim, Maria. *The Forerunner of All Things: Buddhaghosa on Mind, Intention, and Agency*. New York: Oxford University Press, 2013.

Heirman, Ann. 'Buddhist Nuns: Between Past and Present.' *Numen* 58 (2011): 603–31.

'Vinaya: From India to China.' In *The Spread of Buddhism*, edited by Ann Heirman and Stephan Peter Bumbacher, 167–202. Leiden: Brill, 2007.

Herath, Nuwan. 'Reforms via Katikāvat: Dissension among Buddhist Monks in Sri Lanka over the Code of Conduct Bill.' *South Asia: Journal of South Asian Studies* 44, no. 1 (2021): 52–70.

Herzog, Tamar. 'The Uses and Abuses of Legal Pluralism: A View from the Sideline.' *Law and History Review* 42, no. 2 (2023): 211–222.

Hinüber, Oskar von. *A Handbook of Pāli Literature*. Indian Philology and South Asian Studies, Vol. 2. New York: Walter de Gruyter, 1996.

'Buddhist Law According to the Theravāda-Vinaya: A Survey of Theory and Practice.' *Journal of the International Association of Buddhist Studies* 18, no. 1 (1995): 7–46.

(ed.) 'Buddhist Law and the Phonetics of Pāli (Das Buddhistische Recht Und Die Phonetik Des Pāli).' In *Selected Papers on Pāli Studies*, Oskar von Hinüber, 198–232. Bristol, UK: Pali Text Society, 1994.

'Everyday Life in an Ancient Indian Buddhist Monastery.' *Annual Report of the International Research Institute for Advanced Buddhology at Soka University* 9 (2006): 3–31.

Holt, John. *Buddha in the Crown: Avalokitesvara in the Buddhist Traditions of Sri Lanka*. New York: Oxford University Press, 1991.

Discipline: The Canonical Buddhism of the Vinayapitaka. Delhi: Motilal Banarsidass, 1995.

The Buddhist Visnu. New York: Columbia University Press, 2004.

Horanē Vajirajñāna Himi. *Lakdiva Vinaya Sāhityaya [Sri Lankan Vinaya Literature]*. Colombo: S. Goḍagē saha Sahōdarayō, 2000.

Horner, I. B. *The Book of Discipline (Vinaya Piṭaka)*. 6 vols. London: Pali Text Society, 1938–1966.

House of Commons (UK). 'Hansard Reports for the House of Commons Vol. 123,' 29 November 1852.

Houtman, Gustaaf. 'How a Foreigner Invented Buddhendom in Burmese: From Tha-Tha-Na-to to Bok-Da Ba-Tha.' *Journal of the Royal Anthropological Society of Oxford* 21, no. 2 (1990): 113–28.

Humfress, Caroline. 'Legal Pluralism's Other: Mythologizing Modern Law.' *Law and History Review* 42, no. 2 (9 2023): 155–168.

Hüsken, Ute. 'The Legend of the Establishment of the Buddhist Order of Nuns in the Theravada Vinaya-Pitaka.' *Journal of the Pali Text Society* 26 (2000): 43–69.

Hussin, Iza R. *The Politics of Islamic Law: Local Elites, Colonial Authority, and the Making of the Muslim State*. Chicago: University of Chicago Press, 2016.

Huxley, Andrew. 'Buddhist Case Law on Theft: The Vinītavatthu on the Second Pārājika.' *Journal of Buddhist Ethics* 6 (1999): 313–30.

'Lord Kyaw Thu's Precedent: A Sixteenth-Century Burmese Law Report.' In *Legalism: Anthropology and History*, edited by Paul Dresch and Hannah Skoda, 229–60. Oxford: Oxford University Press, 2012. https://doi.org/10.1093/acprof:oso/9780199664269.003.0009.

'Positivists and Buddhists: The Rise and Fall of Anglo-Burmese Ecclesiastical Law.' *Law and Social Inquiry* 26 (2001): 113–42.

'Studying Theravada Legal Literature.' *Journal of the International Association of Buddhist Studies* 20 (1997): 63–92.

Ikeya, Chie. *Refiguring Women, Colonialism, and Modernity in Burma*. Honolulu: University of Hawai'i Press, 2011.

Ilangasinha, H. B. M. *Buddhism in Medieval Sri Lanka*. Sri Satguru Publications, 1992.

Ināmaḷuvē Sumaṅgala. *Śrī Laṅkāvē Bhikṣunī Parṣadaya Piḷibaňda Vimarśanayak [A Review of the Assembly of Bhikkhunis in Sri Lanka]*. Dambulla: Rangiri Dambulu Vihāraya, 2015.

Ito, Tomomi. 'Questions of Ordination Legitimacy for Newly Ordained Theravāda Bhikkhunī in Thailand.' *Journal of Southeast Asian Studies* 43, no. 1 (2012): 55–76. https://doi.org/10.1017/S002246341100066X.

Jackson, Sherman A. *Islamic Law and the State: The Constitutional Jurisprudence of Shihāb Al-Dīn Al-Qarāfī*. Leiden: Brill, 1996.

Janaka, Ashin. 'Die-Human, Born Human. The Life and Posthumous Trial of Shin Ukkaṭṭha, a Pioneering Burmese Monk during a Tumultuous Period in a Nation's History.' Ph.D. Dissertation, King's College London, 2016.

Jansen, Berthe. *The Monastery Rules: Buddhist Monastic Organization in Pre-Modern Tibet*. Berkeley: University of California Press, 2018.

Jayavardhanapura Kōṭṭē Śrī Kalyāṇī Sāmagrīdharma Mahāsaṅghasabhāva. *Jayavardhanapura Kōṭṭē Śrī Kalyāṇī Sāmagrīdharma Mahāsaṅghasabhāva: Sampādaka Labugama Laṅkānanada Sthavira [The Great Sangha Council of the Jayavardhanapura Kōṭṭē Śrī Kalyāṇī Sāmagrīdharma Chapter: Compiled by Labugama Laṅkānanada Sthavira]*. Maradana, Sri Lanka: Samayawardhana Press, 1964.

Jayawardena, Kumari. *Nobodies to Somebodies: The Rise of the Colonial Bourgeoisie in Sri Lanka*. Delhi: Zed Books, 2002.

Jordt, Ingrid. *Burma's Mass Lay Meditation Movement: Buddhism and the Cultural Construction of Power*. Athens, OH: Ohio, 2007.

Kahandagama, Anushka. 'New Buddhist Trends in Post-War Sri Lanka.' Ph.D. Dissertation, University of Otago, 2025.

Kamal, Faisal. 'A Theory of Religious Sovereignty, Private Law Disputes and State-Religion Relations in Bangladesh and Pakistan.' Ph.D. Dissertation, University of Toronto, 2025.

Kaplan, Uri. 'Updating the Vinaya: Formulating Buddhist Monastic Laws and Pure Rules in Contemporary Korea.' *Contemporary Buddhism* 17, no. 2 (2016): 252–74.

Kariyawasam, Tissa. *Religious Activities and the Development of a New Poetical Tradition in Sinhalese 1852–1906*. Colombo: Godage, 2009.

Kawanami, Hiroko. *Renunciation and Empowerment of Buddhist Nuns in Myanmar-Burma: Building a Community of Female Faithful*. Social Sciences in Asia, 33. Leiden: Brill, 2013.

Kē Ñāṇavimala. *Bauddha Vihāra Devālaya Gam Ājñāpaṇata Hā ē Sambandha Guṇadrōṣa Sat Darśanaya [Buddhist Temporalities: The New Ordinance with a Critical Study of the Same]*. Henaratagoḍa Lankātilaka: M. S. Perērā, 1921.

Kelsen, Hans. 'The Pure Theory of Law and Analytical Jurisprudence.' *Harvard Law Review* 55, no. 1 (1941): 44–70.

Kemper, Steven. 'J.R. Jayawardene, Righteousness and Realpolitik.' In *Sri Lanka: History and the Roots of Conflict*, edited by Jonathan Spencer, 187–205. New York: Routledge, 2002.

The Presence of the Past: Chronicles, Politics, and Culture in Sinhala Life. Ithaca: Cornell University Press, 1991.

Kieffer-Pülz, Petra. *A Manual of the Adornment of the Monastic Boundary: Vācissara's Sīmālaṅkārasaṅgaha*. Studien Zur Indologie. Wiesbaden: Harrassowitz Verlag, 2021.

'Brief Summary of the Development of Buddhist Monastic Law Codes and Institutions.' *Buddhism, Law & Society* 6 (2022/2021): 147–84.

Die Sīmā. Vorschriften Zur Regelung Der Buddhistischen Gemeindegrenze in Älteren Buddhistischen Texten. Berlin: Monographien zur indischen Archäologie, Kunst und Philologie, 1992.

'*Kammavācā* Manuscripts: Written Artefacts for Ordination (*upasampadā*) as a Buddhist Monk or Nun?.' In *Written Artefacts in Rites of Passage: On the Material Culture of Initiation*, edited by Jochen Hermann Vennebusch in collaboration with Karin Becker, 63–86. Stuttgart: Franz Steiner Verlag, 2025.

'Officials: Buddhist.' In *Encyclopedia of Monasicism*, edited by William M. Johnston and Christopher Kleinhenz, 953–56. London, 2000.

'Re-Ordination of Former Buddhist Nuns in the Theravāda Tradition.' *Buddhism, Law & Society* 1 (2015/2016) : 1–32.

'Reuse of Text in Pāli Legal Commentaries.' *Buddhist Studies Review* 33, no. 1–2 (2016): 9–45.

'Review of Silk, Jonathan A., Managing Monks. Administrators and Administrative Roles in Indian Buddhist Monasticism (Oxford University Press, 2008).' *Indo-Iranian Journal* 53 (2010): 71–88.

'Stretching the Vinaya Rules and Getting Away with It.' *Journal of the Pali Text Society* 29 (2007): 1–49.

'The Law of Theft: Regulations in the Theravāda Vinaya and the Law Commentaries.' *Journal of the Pali Text Society* 31 (2011): 1–54.

'Translocal Debates and Legal Hermeneutics: Early Pali Vinaya Texts in the Adjudication of Sīmā Procedures, c. 1200–1900 CE.' *Buddhism, Law & Society* 2 (2016/2017): 103–58.

Verlorene Gaṇṭhipadas zum buddhistischen Ordensrecht: Untersuchungen zu den in der Vajirabuddhiṭīkā zitierten Kommentaren Dhammasiris und Vajirabuddhis. 3 vols. Akademie der Wissenschaften und der Literatur, Mainz, Veröffentlichungen der Indologischen Kommission, Bd.1. Wiesbaden: Harrassowitz Verlag, 2013.

'Vinaya Commentarial Literature in Pali.' In *Brill's Encyclopedia of Buddhism*, edited by Jonathan A. Silk, I: Literature and Languages: 430–41. Leiden: Brill, 2015.

'What the Vinayas Can Tell Us about Law.' In *Buddhism and Law: An Introduction*, edited by Rebecca French and Mark Nathan, 46–62. New York: Cambridge University Press, 2014.

Kirichenko, Alexey. 'The Thathanabaing Project: Monastic Hierarchies and Colonialism in Burma.' In *Theravada Buddhism in Colonial Contexts*, edited by Thomas Borchert. London: Routledge, 2018. https://doi.org/10.4324/9781315111889.

Kitsudō, Masahiro. *Pāli Texts Printed in Sri Lanka in Sinhalese Characters with Supplementary Information on Related Texts*. London: Pali Text Society, 2015.

Kitulgoda Araṇya Sēnāsanaya. *Bhikṣu Prātimōkṣaya Saha Vinaya Karuṇu (Siṁhala Anuvāda Sahitayi)*. Horaṇa, Sri Lanka: C.S. Karuṇaratna saha Putrayō, 2017.

Klabbers, Jan, and Gianluigi Palombella, eds. *The Challenge of Inter-Legality*. ASIL Studies in International Legal Theory. Cambridge: Cambridge University Press, 2019.

Kleinhans, Martha-Marie, and Roderick A. Macdonald. 'What Is a Critical Legal Pluralism?' *Canadian Journal of Law and Society / La Revue Canadienne Droit et Société* 12, no. 2 (1997): 25–46.

Kozlowski, Gregory C. *Muslim Endowments and Society in British India*. Cambridge: Cambridge University Press, 1985.

Krisch, Nico. 'Entangled Legalities in the Postnational Space.' *International Journal of Constitutional Law* 20, no. 1 (2022): 476–506.

'Framing Entangled Legalities beyond the State.' In *Entangled Legalities Beyond the State*, edited by Nico Krisch, 1–32. Cambridge: Cambridge University Press, 2021.

Krishnaswamy, Sudhir. *Democracy and Constitutionalism in India: A Study of the Basic Structure Doctrine*. New York: Oxford University Press, 2010.

Kugle, Scott A. 'Framed, Blamed and Renamed: The Recasting of Islamic Jurisprudence in Colonial South Asia.' *Modern Asian Studies* 35, no. 2 (2001): 257–313.

Kumāra, Bulita Pradīp. '*Allas Katā Jampara Katā Saṅśodhana Yaṭapat Kaḷa Gothā Hitlar Bhitakāva* [The Gota Hitler Scare that's being Supressed by the Bribery Stories and Jumper Stories].' *Divayina Irida Saṅgrahaya*, 24 June 2018.

Lammerts, D. Christian. *Buddhist Law in Burma: A History of Dhammasattha Texts and Jurisprudence, 1250–1850*. Honolulu: University of Hawai'i Press, 2018.

'Genres and Jurisdictions: Laws Governing Monastic Inheritance in Seventeenth-Century Burma.' In *Buddhism and Law: An Introduction*, edited by Rebecca French and Mark Nathan, 183–99. Cambridge: Cambridge University Press, 2014.

Laṅkādīpa. '*Gnānasāra Himiṭa Set Patā Nuvaraeḷiyē Pāgamanak* [Procession in Nuwara Eliya to Bless Ven. Gnanasara].' 17 June 2018.

Lariviere, Richard W. 'Justices and Paṇḍitas: Some Ironies in Contemporary Readings of the Hindu Legal Past.' *The Journal of Asian Studies* 48, no. 4 (1989): 757–69.

Lawrie, Archibald Campbell. *A Gazetteer of the Central Province of Ceylon (Excluding Walapane)*. 2 vols. Colombo: G.J.A. Skeen, Govt. Printer, Ceylon, 1896.

Lemons, Katherine. *Divorcing Traditions: Islamic Marriage Law and the Making of Indian Secularism*. Ithaca: Cornell University Press, 2019.

Lhost, Elizabeth. *Everyday Islamic Law and the Making of Modern South Asia*. Durham: University of North Carolina Press, 2022.

Lin, Pei-Ying. 'Bodhisattva Precepts in East Asian Perspectives and Beyond: Introduction.' *The Eastern Buddhism* 49, no. 1–2 (2018): 1–12.

Liu, Cuilan. *Buddhism in Court: Religion, Law and Jurisdiciton in China*. New York: Oxford University Press, 2024.

'Hybrid Courts and Hybrid Laws: The Legal Governance of Buddhism in Imperial China.' *Journal of Chinese Religions* 47, no. 2 (2019): 153–93.

Luce, G.H., and Tin Htway. 'A Fifteenth Century Inscription and Library at Pagan.' In *Malalasekera Commemoration Volume*, 203–56. Colombo: n.p., 1976.

Malalasekera, G.P. 'Bhikkhus and Politics.' *The Buddhist* 16, no. 11 (March 1946): 87–88.

Malalgoda, Kitsiri. *Buddhism in Sinhalese Society, 1750–1900: A Study of Religious Revival and Change*. Berkeley: University of California Press, 1976.

'Concepts and Confrontations: A Case Study of Agama.' In *Sri Lanka Collective Identities Revisited*, edited by Michael Roberts, 55–77. Colombo: Marga Institute Press, 1997.

'New Manuals for New Times: A Comparative History of Buddha Ädahilla and A Buddhist Catechism.' In *Buddhism in Asia: Revival and Reinvention*, edited by Nayanjot Lahiri and Upinder Singh, 193–240. Delhi: Manohar, 2016.

Malvatu Chapter of the Siyam Nikāya. *Abhinava Katikāvata Saha Baṇadaham Pota [The Modern Katikāvata and Preaching Book]*. 1921. Reprint, Maradana, Sri Lanka: Samayawardhana Press, 1984.

Marglin, Jessica, and Mark Letteney. 'Legal Pluralism as a Category of Analysis.' *Law and History Review* 42, no. 2 (May 2024): 143–53.

Marshall, Charles, ed. *Judgments and Other Decisions and Directions of the Supreme Court of the Island of Ceylon, from the Promulgation of the New Charter, 1st Oct. 1833 to March 1836*. Paris: Printed by Boule and Co., 1839.

Mātatē Dhammakusala. *Rāmañña Vaṃsaya [The Rāmañña Lineage]*. Colombo: V.S. Līlā Printers, 2001.

McKinley, Alexander. 'Mountain at a Center of the World.' Ph.D. Dissertation, Duke University, 2018.

Meegama, Sujatha Arundathi. 'From Kôvils to Devâles: Patronage and 'Influence' at Buddhist and Hindu Temples in Sri Lanka.' Ph.D. Dissertation, University of California, Berkeley, 2011.

Merry, Sally Engle. 'An Anthropological Perspective on Legal Pluralism.' In *The Oxford Handbook of Global Legal Pluralism*, edited by Paul Schiff Berman, 169–86. New York: Oxford University Press, 2020.

'Legal Pluralism.' *Law & Society Review* 22, no. 5 (1988): 869–96.

Meyer, Éric P. 'Lekam Miti: Les Registres Du Royaume De Kandy (Sri Lanka).' In *Encyclopédie des historiographies: Afriques, Amériques, Asies*, edited by Nathalie Kouamé and Anne Viguier, 1: 999–1001. Paris: Presses de l'Inalco, 2020.

Michaels, Ralf. 'Tertiary Rules.' In *Entangled Legalities Beyond the State*, edited by Nico Krisch, 424–48. Cambridge: Cambridge University Press, 2021. https://doi.org/10.1017/9781108914642.021.

Milligan, Matthew D. 'Monastic Buddhist Asset Capitalization in Ancient Sri Lanka.' *Journal of Cultural Economy* 16, no. 5 (2023): 1–16. https://doi.org/10.1080/17530350.2022.2135576.

Mirissē Dhammasiri. *Saṅghādhikaraṇa Jotikā [Elucidations of the Monastic Court]*. Mirissa: Mirissē Guṇasiri Mahāthera Bhāraya, 1993.

Modder, Earle. 'The Principles of Buddhist Ecclesiastical Law: Being a Manual of the Customary Law, Decided Cases, and the Statute Law of the Buddhist Church of Ceylon [Unpublished Manuscript in Mimeograph] (SLNA 25.98/19-20),' 1933/1926.

Moore, Sally Falk. 'Law and Social Change: The Semi-Autonomous Social Field as an Appropriate Subject of Study.' *Law & Society Review* 7, no. 4 (1973): 719–46. https://doi.org/10.2307/3052967.

Morgan, W. C., ed. A *Digest of the Decisions of the Supreme Court Sitting at Colombo, Since the Promulgation of the Charter of 1833: Pt. 1. Oct. 1833 to May 1837, Ed. by Owen W.C. Morgan. 1857*. Colombo: n.p., 1857.

Moustafa, Tamir. *Constituting Religion: Islam, Liberal Rights, and the Malaysian State*. New York: Cambridge University Press, 2018.

Moustafa, Tamir, and Jeffrey Adam Sachs. 'Islamic Law, Society, and the State.' *Law & Society Review* 52, no. 3 (September 2018): 560–73.

Mrozik, Susanne. 'Sri Lankan Buddhist Nuns: Complicating the Debate over Ordination.' *Journal of Feminist Studies in Religion* 36, no. 1 (2020): 33–49.

'We Love Our Nuns: Affective Dimensions of the Sri Lankan Bhikkhuni Revival.' *Journal of Buddhist Ethics* 21 (2014): 57–95.

Muller, A. Charles, ed. *The Collected Works of Korean Buddhism. 11: Exposition of the Sutra of Brahma's Net*. Translated by A. Charles Muller. Seoul: Jogye Order of Korean Buddhism, 2012.
Müller, Edward. 'Khuddasikkhā and Mūlasikkhā.' *Journal of the Pali Text Society* 1 (1883): 86–132.
Nārāvimala Dhammaratana. '*Śāsana Komisama* [Sāsana Commission].' *Nava Lōkaya*, July 1958, 133–34, 139–40.
Nelken, David, and Johannes Feest. *Adapting Legal Cultures*. London: Bloomsbury Publishing, 2001.
Nietupski, Paul. 'Guṇaprabha on Monastic Authority and Authoritative Doctrine.' *Journal of Buddhist Ethics* 24 (2017): 170–223.
Nissan, E. 'History in the Making: Anuradhapura and the Sinhala Buddhist Nation.' *Social Analysis Adelaide* 25 (1989): 55–78.
Nitalavē Siri Gñāṇissara. *Adhikaraṇa Viniścaya* [*The Adjudication of Legal Cases*]. Colombo: U.P. ekanāyaka saha samāgamē mudraṇālaya, 1954.
Nolot, Édith. 'Studies in Vinaya Technical Terms I–III.' *Journal of the Pali Text Society* 22 (1996): 73–150.
'Studies in Vinaya Technical Terms IV–X.' *Journal of the Pali Text Society* 25 (1999): 1–113.
Norman, K. R., Petra Kieffer-Pülz, and William Pruitt, eds. *Overcoming Doubts (Kaṅkhāvitaraṇī): Vol. I The Bhikkhu-Pātimokkha Commentary*. Bristol, UK: Pali Text Society, 2018.
Obeyesekere, Gananath. *The Doomed King: A Requiem for Sri Vikrama Rajasinha*. Colombo: Sailfish, 2017.
Oldenberg, Hermann. *The Vinaya Piṭakaṃ*. 5 vols. London: Williams and Norgate, 1879–1883.
Vinaya Texts (Sacred Books of the East Vols. 13, 17, 20), edited by T. W. Rhys Davids. 3 vols. Oxford: Clarendon Press, 1881–1885.
Oraby, Mona, and Winnifred Fallers Sullivan. 'Law and Religion: Reimagining the Entanglement of Two Universals.' *Annual Review of Law and Social Science* 16, no. 1 (2020).
Ortega, Miguel Álvarez. 'Gihi, Sangha, Raja: Role-based Normativity in Early Buddhism.' *Rivista di filosofia del diritto* 2 (2013): 423–46.
Pamunuva, Chatura. '*Saṅgaruvanaṭa Nīti Dānna Rajayaṭa Balayak Næ* [Government Has No Power to Impose Laws on the Sanghas].' *Divayina*, 1 January 2016. www.divaina.com/2016/01/14/news06.html.
'*Theravādī Bhikṣu Katikāvat Panata Saṅgha Samājayaṭat Behevit Hitakara Vevi* [The Theravādī Bhikṣu Katikāvat Bill Will Be Very Beneficial to Monastic Society].' *Divayina*, 2 February 2016.
n.a. '*Panat Keṭumpata Desa Paṭu Paramārthayen Nobalanna* [When Looking at the Bill, Don't Look [Only] at the Narrow Purpose].' *Lakbima*, 24 January 2016.

Peletz, Michael G. 'Malaysia's Syariah Judiciary as Global Assemblage: Islamization, Corporatization, and Other Transformations in Context.' *Comparative Studies in Society and History* 55, no. 3 (2013): 603–33.

Pereira, Walter, and Chas. M. Fernando, eds. *The Supreme Court Reports: Being Reports of Cases Decided by the Supreme Court of Ceylon, with a Digest, Volume I, 1892–1893*. Colombo: Ceylon Indepenent Press, 1893.

Peters, Anne von. 'Die Birmanischen Kammavācā-Sammlungen Mit Neun Abschnitten.' In *Untersuchungen Zur Buddhistischen Literatur*, edited by Heinz Bechert, Sven Bretfeld, and Petra Kieffer-Pülz, 273–84. Göttingen, Germany: Vandenhoeck & Ruprecht, 1997.

Phadnis, Urmila. *Religion and Politics in Sri Lanka*. New Delhi: Manohar, 1976.

Pieris, P. E. *Tri Sinhala: The Last Phase, 1796–1815*. Delhi: Asian Educational Services, 2001.

Pieris, Udula. '*Mahā Saṅgharatnayaṭa Erehi Naḍu Vibhāgayaṭa Venama Adhikaraṇayak Pihiṭuvanna* [Set up a Separate Court for Litigation against Monks].' *Dinamina*, 31 August 2018.

Pirie, Fernanda. 'Law before Government: Ideology and Aspiration.' *Oxford Journal of Legal Studies* 30, no. 2 (2010): 207–28.

'Legal Autonomy as Political Engagement: The Ladakhi Village in the Wider World.' *Law & Society Review* 40, no. 1 (2006): 77–104.

The Anthropology of Law. London: Oxford University Press, 2013.

Poceski, Mario. 'The Creation of Monastic Codes and the Gradual Transformation of Medieval Chinese Buddhist Monasticism.' In *Rules of Engagement: Medieval Traditions of Buddhist Monastic Regulation*, edited by Susan Andrews, Jinhua Chen, and Cuilan Liu, 163–96. Bochum: Projekt Verlag, 2017.

Polvattē, Buddhadatta, ed. *Buddhadatta's Manuals*. 2 vols. London: Pali text society, 1915.

Prebish, Charles S. *A Survey of Vinaya Literature*. New York: Routledge, 2013.

'The Vinaya'. In *Oxford Handbook of Buddhist Ethics*, edited by Daniel Cozort and James Mark Shields, 96–114. Oxford University Press, 2018.

Premo, Bianca, and Yanna Yannakakis. 'A Court of Sticks and Branches: Indian Jurisdiction in Colonial Mexico and Beyond.' *The American Historical Review* 124, no. 1 (2019): 28–55.

Presler, Franklin A. *Religion under Bureaucracy: Policy and Administration for Hindu Temples in South India*. New York: Cambridge University Press, 2008.

Prothero, Steven. 'Henry Steel Olcott, Anagarika Dharmapala and the Maha Bodhi Society.' *Theosophical History* 6 (1996): 96–106.

Rajasingham, David Sanjayan. 'Dilemmas of Defense and Deference: Buddhism and Constitutions in Sri Lanka and Thailand.' SJD, Yale University, 2023.

Rāmañña Mahā Nikāya Pālaka Saṅgha Sabhā. *Śrī Laṅkā Rāmañña Mahā Nikāya Katikāvata [The Katikāvata for the Sri Lankan Rāmañña Fraternity]*. Colombo: śrī laṅkā rajayē mudraṇa depārtamēntuva, 2015.

Rāmañña Mahā Nikāya Pālaka Saṅgha Sabhā. *Śrī Laṅkā Rāmañña Nikāya Vyavasthā Saṅgrahaya [The Constitional Code of the Rāmañña Fraternity of Sri Lanka]*. n.p.: n.p., 1973.

Rāmañña Nikāya. *Rāmaññanikāyē Katikāvata [The Katikāvata of the Rāmañña Nikāya]*. n.p.: Samarakōn Mudaligē Vijayaratna Appuhāmi, 1901.

Rāmañña Nikāya. *Śrī Laṅkā Rāmañña Mahā Nikāya Katikāvatta*. Colombo: śrī laṅkā rajayē mudraṇa depārtamēntuva [Sri Lanka Government Printing Department], 2014.

Śri Rāmañña Nikāyē Katikāvata [The Sri Rāmañña Nikāya Katikāvata]. Colombo: W.I. Baesṭiyan saha Samāgame, 1925.

Rambukwella, Harshana. *The Politics and Poetics of Authenticity*. London: UCL Press, 2018.

Ratnapala, Nandasena. *The Katikāvatas: Laws of the Buddhist Order of Ceylon from the Twelfth to the Eighteenth Century (Critically Edited, Translated and Annotated)*. Münchener Studien Zur Sprachwissenschaft, Beiheft N. München: R. Kitzinger, 1971.

Redding, Jeffrey A. *A Secular Need: Islamic Law and State Governance in Contemporary India*. Seattle: University of Washington Press, 2020.

Rērukānē Candavimala. *Vinaya Karma Pota [Book of Vinaya Acts]*. Colombo: Śri Candavimala Dharma Pustaka Saṅrakṣaṇa Maṇḍalaya, 2015.

Richland, Justin B. 'Jurisdiction: Grounding Law in Language.' *Annual Review of Anthropology* 42, no. 1 (2013): 209–26.

Roberts, Simon. 'After Government? On Representing Law Without the State.' *The Modern Law Review* 68, no. 1 (2005): 1–24.

Rocher, Rosane. 'The Creation of Anglo-Hindu Law.' In *Hinduism and Law: An Introduction*, edited by Donald R. Davis Jr, Jayanth K. Krishnan, and Timothy Lubin, 78–88. Cambridge: Cambridge University Press, 2010.

Rogers, John D. 'Religious Belief, Economic Interest and Social Policy: Temple Endowments in Sri Lanka during the Governorship of William Gregory, 1872–77.' *Modern Asian Studies* 21 (1987): 349–69.

Rudolph, L. I., and S. H. Rudolph. 'Barristers and Brahmans in India: Legal Cultures and Social Change.' *Comparative Studies in Society and History* 8 (1965): 24–49.

Salgado, Nirmala S. 'Religious Identities of Buddhist Nuns: Training Precepts, Renunciant Attire, and Nomenclature in Theravada Buddhism.' *Journal of the American Academy of Religion* 72, no. 4 (2004): 935–53.

Buddhist Nuns and Gendered Practice: In Search of the Female Renunciant. New York: Oxford, 2013.

'On the Question of 'Discipline' (Vinaya) and Nuns in Theravāda Buddhism.' *Religions* 10, no. 2 (2019): 1–23.

'Tradition Power and Community among Buddhist Nuns in Sri Lanka.' *Journal of Buddhist Ethics* 24 (2017): 369–399.

Samuels, Jeffrey. *Attracting the Heart: Social Relations and the Aesthetics of Emotion in Sri Lankan Monastic Culture*. Honolulu: University of Hawai'i Press, 2010.

'Toward an Action-Oriented Pedagogy: Buddhist Texts and Monastic Education in Contemporary Sri Lanka.' *Journal of the American Academy of Religion* 72 (2004): 955–71.

Saṅghādikaraṇaya [The Sangha Court], Youtube video, 19 July 2016. https://www.youtube.com/watch?v=w4EI2iFtU2M (in four parts).

Santos, Boaventura de Sousa. 'Law: A Map of Misreading. Toward a Postmodern Conception of Law.' *Journal of Law and Society* 14, no. 3 (1987): 279–302.

Schalk, P. 'Unity and Sovereignty: Key Concepts of a Militant Buddhist Organization in Sri Lanka MSV, Movement for the Protection of the Motherland.' *Temenos* 24 (1988): 55–87.

Schedneck, Brooke. 'The Lay Buddhist Gaze and Femininity in Thai Male Monasticism.' *South East Asia Research* 29, no. 4 (2021): 417–33.

Schonthal, Benjamin. *Buddhism, Politics and Limits of Law: The Pyrrhic Constitutionalism of Sri Lanka.* New York: Cambridge University Press, 2016.

'Buddhist Law against the State? Representing Religion, Law, and Conflict.' *Journal of the American Academy of Religion* 87, no. 3 (2019): 662–92.

'Buddhist Law beyond the Vinaya: Monastic Constitutions (Katikāvatas) and Their Transformations in Colonial Sri Lanka.' *History of Religions* 60, no. 4 (2021): 287–324.

'Buddhist Perspectives on Freedom of Religion or Belief.' In *Routledge Handbook of Freedom of Religion or Belief*, edited by Silvio Ferrari, Mark Hill QC, Arif A. Jamal, and Rossella Bottoni, 73–87. New York: Routledge, 2020.

'Buddhist Rules about Rules: Procedure and Process in the (Theravāda) Buddhist Legal System.' *The American Journal of Comparative Law* 69, no. 3 (2021): 539–73.

'Environments of Law: Islam, Buddhism, and the State in Contemporary Sri Lanka.' *The Journal of Asian Studies* 75, no. 1 (2016): 137–56.

'Securing the Sasana through Law: Buddhist Constitutionalism and Buddhist-Interest Litigation in Sri Lanka.' *Modern Asian Studies* 50, no. 6 (2016): 1966–2008.

'The Impossibility of a Buddhist State.' *Asian Journal of Law and Society* 3, no. 1 (2016): 29–48.

Schonthal, Benjamin, and Tom Ginsburg. 'Breaking the Saffron Wave?: Sangha Capture in South and Southeast Asia.' *Journal of Asian Studies* 83, no. 3 (2024): 646–71.

Schonthal, Benjamin, and Matthew J. Walton. 'The (New) Buddhist Nationalisms? Symmetries and Specificities in Sri Lanka and Myanmar.' *Contemporary Buddhism* 17 (2016): 1–35.

Schopen, Gregory. *Buddhist Monks and Business Matters: Still More Papers on Monastic Buddhism in India*. Honolulu: University of Hawai'i Press, 2004.

'Monastic Law Meets the Real World: A Monk's Continuing Right to Inherit Family Property in Classical India.' *History of Religions* 35, no. 2 (1995): 101–23.

'On the Legal and Economic Activities of Buddhist Nuns.' In *Buddhism and Law*, edited by Rebecca French and Mark A. Nathan, 91–114. New York: Cambridge University Press, 2014.

'Vinaya.' In *Encyclopedia of Buddhism*, edited by Robert E. Buswell, 885–89. New York: Macmillan Reference, USA, 2004.

Scott, David. 'Religion in Colonial Civil Society: Buddhism and Modernity in Nineteenth-Century Sri Lanka.' *Cultural Dynamics* 8 (1996): 723.

Seeger, Martin. 'The Bhikkhunī-Ordination Controversy in Thailand.' *Journal of the International Association of Buddhist Studies* 29, no. 1 (2008): 155–83.

Seneviratne, H. L. *The Work of Kings: The New Buddhism in Sri Lanka*. Chicago: University of Chicago Press, 1999.

Seneviratne, Kalinga. 'Sri Lanka Buddhists Divided over Bill to Control Monks.' *IDN News*, 20 February 2016.

Shapiro, Martin M. *Courts: A Comparative and Political Analysis*. Chicago: University of Chicago Press, 1986.

Shirley, Bruno M. 'Constructing Buddhist Sovereignties: Text and Landscape in a Medieval Lankan Kingdom.' Ph.D. Dissertation, Cornell University, 2024.

Silk, Jonathan A. *Managing Monks: Administrators and Administrative Roles in Indian Buddhist Monasticism*. New York: Oxford University Press, 2008.

Silva, Kalinga Tudor. 'Gossip, Rumor, and Propaganda in Anti-Muslim Campaigns of Bodu Bala Sena.' In *Buddhist Extremists and Muslim Minorities: Religious Conflict in Contemporary Sri Lanka*, edited by John Clifford Holt, 119–39. Oxford: Oxford University Press, 2016.

Silva, Sepalika de. 'Cultural Practice of Human Rights: An Anthropological Study of Human Rights in Sri Lanka.' Ph.D. Dissertation, University of California-St. Barbara, 2006.

Sivasundaram, Sujit. *Islanded: Britain, Sri Lanka, and the Bounds of an Indian Ocean Colony*. Chicago: University of Chicago Press, 2013.

Skilling, Peter. 'Nine Recitations and the Inclusive Tripiṭaka: Canon Formation in Pre-Modern Thailand.' In *Evolution of Scriptures, Formation of Canons: The Buddhist Case*, edited by Orna Almogi, 273–350. Indian and Tibetan Studies. Hamburg: Department of Indian and Tibetan Studies, Universität Hamburg, 2022.

Solomons, F. C., ed. *Decisions of the Supreme Court on Appeals from Courts of Requests, 1861–67*. Kandy: n.p., 1871.

Sōmadāsa, K. D. *Catalogue of the Hugh Nevill Collection of Sinhalese Manuscripts in the British Library*. London: Pali Text Society, 1990.

Śrī Kalyāṇī Sāmagrīdharma Mahāsaṅghasabhāva. *Syāmopālinikāyika Śrī Kalyāṇī Sāmagrīdharma Mahāsaṅghasabhāyanta Katikāvata* [*The Katikāvata of the Śrī Kālyāṇī Sāmagrīdharma Sangha Committee of the Siyam Nikāya*]. n.p.: n.p., 1926.

Srikantan, Geetanjali. *Identifying and Regulating Religion in India: Law, History and the Place of Worship*: Cambridge: Cambridge University Press, 2020.

Stephens, Julia. *Governing Islam: Law, Empire, and Secularism in Modern South Asia*. Cambridge: Cambridge University Press, 2018. https://doi.org/10.1017/9781316795477.

Stilt, Kristen. 'Contextualizing Constitutional Islam: The Malayan Experience.' *International Journal of Constitutional Law* 13 (2015): 407–33.

Strauch, Ingo. 'Lost in Translation? Canonical Languages and Linguistic Diversity of Early Versions of the Prātimokṣasūtra.' In *Evolution of Scriptures, Formation of Canons: The Buddhist Case*, edited by Orna Almogi, 5–41. Indian and Tibetan Studies Series 13. Hamburg: Department of Indian and Tibetan Studies, 2022.

Sturman, Rachel. 'Marriage and Family in Colonial Hindu Law.' In *Hinduism and Law: An Introduction*, edited by Donald R. Davis Jr, Jayanth K. Krishnan, and Timothy Lubin, 89–104. Cambridge: Cambridge University Press, 2010.

Sullivan, Brenton. 'Monastic Customaries and the Promotion of Dge Lugs Scholasticism in Amdo and Beydon.' *Asian Highlands Perspectives* 36 (2015): 84–105.

Sullivan, Winnifred Fallers. *Church State Corporation: Construing Religion in US Law*. Chicago: University of Chicago Press, 2020.

Supreme Court of Ceylon. *The Supreme Court Circular: Containing Reports of Cases Decided, and of Orders & Minutes Issued, by the Supreme Court. With Digest*, edited by William Henry Herbert. Government Printer, 1879.

Suraweera, A. V. *Siṅhala Katikāvat Hā Bhikṣu Samājaya [Sinhala Katikāvatas and Monastic Society]*. Colombo: M.D. Guṇasēna, 1971.

Taekema, Sanne. 'Between or beyond Legal Orders: Questioning the Concept of Legal Order.' In *The Challenge of Inter-Legality*, edited by Jan Klabbers and Gianluigi Palombella, 69–88. New York: Cambridge University Press, 2019.

Takakusu, J., and M. Nagai, eds. *Samantapāsādikā: Buddhaghosa's Commentary on the Vinaya Piṭaka*. 5 Vols. London: Pali Text Society, 1966.

Tamanaha, Brian Z. 'A Non-Essentialist Version of Legal Pluralism.' *Journal of Law and Society* 27, no. 2 (2000): 296–321.

'A Reconstruction of Transnational Legal Pluralism and Law's Foundations.' In *Entangled Legalities Beyond the State*, edited by Nico Krisch, 449–77. Global Law Series. Cambridge: Cambridge University Press, 2021.

Tambiah, Stanley Jeyaraja. 'King Mahasammata: The First King in the Buddist Story of Creation, and His Persisting Relevance.' *Journal, Anthropological Society of Oxford* 20 (1989): 101–22.

Than, Tun. *The Royal Orders of Burma, AD 1598–1885*. Kyoto: Centre for Southeast Asian Studies, 1984.

Ṭhānissaro, Bhikkhu. *The Buddhist Monastic Code*. 2 vols. Valley Center, CA: Metta Forest Monastery, 2013.

'*Theravādī Bauddha Saṅghādhikaraṇaya [The Monastic Court in Theravāda Buddhism]*,' Youtube video, 25 August 2018. https://youtu.be/8pHiCruE51U?si=qJqRANmpI6qYOxpH.

Turner, Alicia. *New Book*, Forthcoming.

Rhys Davids, T. W., and Carpenter, J., eds. *The Sumaṅgala-Vilāsini: Buddhaghosa's Commentary on the Dīgha Nikāya*. 3 vols. 1886–1932. Reprint, London: Pali Text Society, 1968.

Vanaratna, Ranjit. *Theravādī Sāmaṇera Baṇadaham Pota* [*Preaching and Dharma Book for Theravāda Novice Monks*]. 1980. Reprint, Colombo: Samaya Books, 2010.

Vanderstraaten, J. W., ed. *The Decisions of the Supreme Court of Ceylon Sitting in Appeal: From 1869 to 1871*. London: Catholic Orphan Press, 1871.

Vijitananda, Kāligama. *Heraṇasikha hā Heraṇasikha-vinisa* [*The Heraṇasikha and Heraṇasikha-vinisa*]. Dehivala: Śrīdēvi Prinṭiṃvarks, 1985.

Vimalananda, Tennakoon *The State and Religion in Ceylon since 1815: With an Introduction Explaining the Culture and Civilization of the People, Together with the Findings of the Parliamentary Select Committee*. Colombo: M.D. Gunasena, 1970.

Visser, Maartje De, and Andrew Harding. 'Monarchical Constitutional Guardianship and Legal Métissage in Asia.' *Asian Journal of Law and Society* 9, no. 3 (October 2022): 345–62.

Voyce, Malcolm. 'Ideas of Transgression and Buddhist Monks.' *Law and Critique* 21, no. 2 (July 2010): 183–98.

'The Communal Discipline of the Buddhist Order of Monks: The Sanction of the Vinaya Pitaka.' *American Journal of Jurisprudence* 29 no. 1 (1984): 123–50.

Walpola Rāhula. *Bhikṣuvagē Urumaya [Heritage of the Bhikkhu]*. 1946. Reprint, Colombo: S. Godagē saha Sahōdarayō, 2012.

Walters, Jonathan S. 'Buddhist History: The Sri Lankan Pāli Vamsas and Their Commentary.' In *Querying the Medieval: Texts and the History of Practices in South Asia*, edited by Ronald B. Inden, Daud Ali, Jonathan Walters, and Jonathan Walters, 90–164. New York: Oxford University Press, 2000.

Watson, Alan. *Legal Transplants: An Approach to Comparative Law*. Athens, GA: University of Georgia Press, 1993.

Weber, Max. *Max Weber on Charisma and Institution Building, Selected Papers*, edited by S. N. Eisenstadt. Chicago: University of Chicago Press, 1968.

Weerasooria, W. S. *Buddhist Ecclesiastical Law*. Colombo: Postgraduate Institute of Management, 2011.

Weerasooriya, Sahan. '180,458 Monks Registered with Department of Buddhist Affairs since 1930s.' *The Island*, 1 August 2024.

Wheatley, Natasha. *The Life and Death of States: Central Europe and the Transformation of Modern Sovereignty*. Princeton: Princeton University Press, 2023.

Whitaker, Mark P. *Amiable Incoherence: Manipulating Histories and Modernities in a Batticaloa Tamil Hindu Temple*. Amsterdam: VU University Press, 1999.

Whitman, James Q. *The Origins of Reasonable Doubt: Theological Roots of the Criminal Trial*. New Haven: Yale University Press, 2008.

Wickramasinghe, Nira. *Sri Lanka in the Modern Age: A History*. Oxford: Oxford University Press, 2015.

Wijetunga, W. M. K. 'Sārōvāda Dīpaniya: A Katikāvata of the 19th Century.' *Vidvodaya: Journal of Arts, Science, Letters* 3, no. 1 (1970): 1–14.

Wilson, A. J. 'Buddhism in Ceylon Politics.' In *South Asian Politics and Religion*, edited by D. E. Smith, 510–30. Princeton: Princeton University Press, 1966.

Wimalasurendre, Cyril. 'Malwatte, Asgiriya Oppose Laws to Control Monks.' *The Island*, 14 January 2016.

Winn, Peter A. 'Legal Ritual.' *Law and Critique* 2 (1991): 207–32.

Woodhouse, G. W. 'Sissiyanu Sissiya Paramparawa and Other Laws Relating to the Buddhist Priesthood (Part I).' *The Ceylon Antiquary and Literary Register* 3, no. 3 (1918/1917): 174–86.

'Sissiyanu Sissiya Paramparawa and Other Laws Relating to the Buddhist Priesthood (Part II).' *The Ceylon Antiquary and Literary Register* 3, no. 3 (1918/1917): 281–90.

Yifa. *The Origins of Buddhist Monastic Codes in China: An Annotated Translation and Study of the Chanyuan Qinggui*. Honolulu: University of Hawai'i Press, 2002.

Young, Jonathan A. 'Adornments of Virtue: The Production of Lay Buddhist Virtuosity in the Upāsakajanālaṅkāra.' Ph.D. Dissertation, Cornell University, 2011.

Young, Richard Fox, and G. P. V. Somaratna. *Vain Debates: Buddhist-Christian Controversies of Nineteenth-Century Ceylon*. Vienna: Institut für Indologie der Universität Wien, 1996.

Zimmerman, Michael. 'Only a Fool Becomes a King: Buddhist Stances on Punishment.' In *Buddhism and Violence*, edited by Michael Zimmermann, Chiew Hui Ho, and Philip Pierce, 213–42. LIRI Seimar Proceedings Series, Vol. 2. Lumbini: Lumbini International Research Institute, 2006.

INDEX

CAMBRIDGE STUDIES IN LAW AND SOCIETY

Books in the Series

Diseases of the Will: Alcohol and the Dilemmas of Freedom
Mariana Valverde

The Politics of Truth and Reconciliation in South Africa: Legitimizing the Post-Apartheid State
Richard A. Wilson

Modernism and the Grounds of Law
Peter Fitzpatrick

Unemployment and Government: Genealogies of the Social
William Walters

Autonomy and Ethnicity: Negotiating Competing Claims in Multi-Ethnic States
Yash Ghai

Constituting Democracy: Law, Globalism and South Africa's Political Reconstruction
Heinz Klug

The Ritual of Rights in Japan: Law, Society, and Health Policy
Eric A. Feldman

Governing Morals: A Social History of Moral Regulation
Alan Hunt

The Colonies of Law: Colonialism, Zionism and Law in Early Mandate Palestine
Ronen Shamir

Law and Nature
David Delaney

Social Citizenship and Workfare in the United States and Western Europe: The Paradox of Inclusion
Joel F. Handler

Law, Anthropology, and the Constitution of the Social: Making Persons and Things
Edited by Alain Pottage and Martha Mundy

Judicial Review and Bureaucratic Impact: International and Interdisciplinary Perspectives
Edited by Marc Hertogh and Simon Halliday

Immigrants at the Margins: Law, Race, and Exclusion in Southern Europe
Kitty Calavita

Lawyers and Regulation: The Politics of the Administrative Process
Patrick Schmidt

Law and Globalization from Below: Towards a Cosmopolitan Legality
Edited by Boaventura de Sousa Santos and César A. Rodríguez-Garavito

Public Accountability: Designs, Dilemmas and Experiences
Edited by Michael W. Dowdle

Law, Violence and Sovereignty among West Bank Palestinians
Tobias Kelly

Legal Reform and Administrative Detention Powers in China
Sarah Biddulph

The Practice of Human Rights: Tracking Law between the Global and the Local
Edited by Mark Goodale and Sally Engle Merry

Judges beyond Politics in Democracy and Dictatorship: Lessons from Chile
Lisa Hilbink

Paths to International Justice: Social and Legal Perspectives
Edited by Marie-Bénédicte Dembour and Tobias Kelly

Law and Society in Vietnam: The Transition from Socialism in Comparative Perspective
Mark Sidel

Constitutionalizing Economic Globalization: Investment Rules and Democracy's Promise
David Schneiderman

The New World Trade Organization Knowledge Agreements: Second Edition
Christopher Arup

Justice and Reconciliation in Post-Apartheid South Africa
Edited by François du Bois and Antje du Bois-Pedain

Militarization and Violence against Women in Conflict Zones in the Middle East: A Palestinian Case-Study
Nadera Shalhoub-Kevorkian

Child Pornography and Sexual Grooming: Legal and Societal Responses
Suzanne Ost

Darfur and the Crime of Genocide
John Hagan and Wenona Rymond-Richmond

Fictions of Justice: The International Criminal Court and the Challenge of Legal Pluralism in Sub-Saharan Africa
Kamari Maxine Clarke

Conducting Law and Society Research: Reflections on Methods and Practices
Simon Halliday and Patrick Schmidt

Planted Flags: Trees, Land, and Law in Israel/Palestine
Irus Braverman

Culture under Cross-Examination: International Justice and the Special Court for Sierra Leone
Tim Kelsall

Cultures of Legality: Judicialization and Political Activism in Latin America
Javier Couso, Alexandra Huneeus, and Rachel Sieder

Courting Democracy in Bosnia and Herzegovina: The Hague Tribunal's Impact in a Postwar State
Lara J. Nettelfield

The Gacaca Courts, Post-Genocide Justice and Reconciliation in Rwanda: Justice without Lawyers
Phil Clark

Law, Society, and History: Themes in the Legal Sociology and Legal History of Lawrence M. Friedman
Edited by Robert W. Gordon and Morton J. Horwitz

After Abu Ghraib: Exploring Human Rights in America and the Middle East
Shadi Mokhtari

Adjudication in Religious Family Laws: Cultural Accommodation, Legal Pluralism, and Gender Equality in India
Gopika Solanki

Water on Tap: Rights and Regulation in the Transnational Governance of Urban Water Services
Bronwen Morgan

Elements of Moral Cognition: Rawls' Linguistic Analogy and the Cognitive Science of Moral and Legal Judgment
John Mikhail

Mitigation and Aggravation at Sentencing
Edited by Julian V. Roberts

Institutional Inequality and the Mobilization of the Family and Medical Leave Act: Rights on Leave
Catherine R. Albiston

Authoritarian Rule of Law: Legislation, Discourse and Legitimacy in Singapore
Jothie Rajah

Law and Development and the Global Discourses of Legal Transfers
Edited by John Gillespie and Pip Nicholson

Law against the State: Ethnographic Forays into Law's Transformations
Edited by Julia Eckert, Brian Donahoe, Christian Strümpell and Zerrin Özlem Biner

Transnational Legal Ordering and State Change
Edited by Gregory C. Shaffer

Legal Mobilization under Authoritarianism: The Case of Post-Colonial Hong Kong
Waikeung Tam

Complementarity in the Line of Fire: The Catalysing Effect of the International Criminal Court in Uganda and Sudan
Sarah M. H. Nouwen

Political and Legal Transformations of an Indonesian Polity: The Nagari from Colonisation to Decentralisation
Franz von Benda-Beckmann and Keebet von Benda-Beckmann

Pakistan's Experience with Formal Law: An Alien Justice
Osama Siddique

Human Rights under State-Enforced Religious Family Laws in Israel, Egypt, and India
Yüksel Sezgin

Why Prison?
Edited by David Scott

Law's Fragile State: Colonial, Authoritarian, and Humanitarian Legacies in Sudan
Mark Fathi Massoud

Rights for Others: The Slow Home-Coming of Human Rights in the Netherlands
Barbara Oomen

European States and Their Muslim Citizens: The Impact of Institutions on Perceptions and Boundaries
Edited by John R. Bowen, Christophe Bertossi, Jan Willem Duyvendak, and Mona Lena Krook

Environmental Litigation in China: A Study in Political Ambivalence
Rachel E. Stern

Indigeneity and Legal Pluralism in India: Claims, Histories, Meanings
Pooja Parmar

Paper Tiger: Law, Bureaucracy and the Developmental State in Himalayan India
Nayanika Mathur

Religion, Law and Society
Russell Sandberg

The Experiences of Face Veil Wearers in Europe and the Law
Edited by Eva Brems

The Contentious History of the International Bill of Human Rights
Christopher N. J. Roberts

Transnational Legal Orders
Edited by Terence C. Halliday and Gregory Shaffer

Lost in China? Law, Culture and Society in Post-1997 Hong Kong
Carol A. G. Jones

Security Theology, Surveillance and the Politics of Fear
Nadera Shalhoub-Kevorkian

Opposing the Rule of Law: How Myanmar's Courts Make Law and Order
Nick Cheesman

Ironies of Colonial Governance: Law, Custom and Justice in Colonial India
James Jaffe

The Clinic and the Court: Law, Medicine and Anthropology
Edited by Ian Harper, Tobias Kelly, and Akshay Khanna

The World of Indicators: The Making of Government Knowledge through Quantification

Edited by Richard Rottenburg, Sally E. Merry, Sung-Joon Park, and Johanna Mugler

Contesting Immigration Policy in Court: Legal Activism and Its Radiating Effects in the United States and France
Leila Kawar

The Quiet Power of Indicators: Measuring Governance, Corruption, and Rule of Law
Edited by Sally Engle Merry, Kevin E. Davis, and Benedict Kingsbury

Investing in Authoritarian Rule: Punishment and Patronage in Rwanda's Gacaca Courts for Genocide Crimes
Anuradha Chakravarty

Contractual Knowledge: One Hundred Years of Legal Experimentation in Global Markets
Edited by Grégoire Mallard and Jérôme Sgard

Iraq and the Crimes of Aggressive War: The Legal Cynicism of Criminal Militarism
John Hagan, Joshua Kaiser, and Anna Hanson

Culture in the Domains of Law
Edited by René Provost

China and Islam: The Prophet, the Party, and Law
Matthew S. Erie

Diversity in Practice: Race, Gender, and Class in Legal and Professional Careers
Edited by Spencer Headworth, Robert L. Nelson, Ronit Dinovitzer, and David B. Wilkins

A Sociology of Constitutions: Constitutions and State Legitimacy in Historical-Sociological Perspective
Chris Thornhill

A Sociology of Transnational Constitutions: Social Foundations of the Post-National Legal Structure
Chris Thornhill

Genocide Never Sleeps: Living Law at the International Criminal Tribunal for Rwanda
Nigel Eltringham

Shifting Legal Visions: Judicial Change and Human Rights Trials in Latin America
Ezequiel A. González-Ocantos

The Demographic Transformations of Citizenship
Heli Askola

Criminal Defense in China: The Politics of Lawyers at Work
Sida Liu and Terence C. Halliday

Contesting Economic and Social Rights in Ireland: Constitution, State and Society, 1848–2016
Thomas Murray

Buried in the Heart: Women, Complex Victimhood and the War in Northern Uganda
Erin Baines

Palaces of Hope: The Anthropology of Global Organizations
Edited by Ronald Niezen and Maria Sapignoli

The Politics of Bureaucratic Corruption in Post-Transitional Eastern Europe
Marina Zaloznaya

Revisiting the Law and Governance of Trafficking, Forced Labor and Modern Slavery
Edited by Prabha Kotiswaran

Incitement on Trial: Prosecuting International Speech Crimes
Richard Ashby Wilson

Criminalizing Children: Welfare and the State in Australia
David McCallum

Global Lawmakers: International Organizations in the Crafting of World Markets
Susan Block-Lieb and Terence C. Halliday

Duties to Care: Dementia, Relationality and Law
Rosie Harding

Insiders, Outsiders, Injuries, and Law: Revisiting "The Oven Bird's Song"
Edited by Mary Nell Trautner

Hunting Justice: Displacement, Law, and Activism in the Kalahari
Maria Sapignoli

Injury and Injustice: The Cultural Politics of Harm and Redress
Edited by Anne Bloom, David M. Engel, and Michael McCann

Ruling Before the Law: The Politics of Legal Regimes in China and Indonesia
William Hurst

The Powers of Law: A Comparative Analysis of Sociopolitical Legal Studies
Mauricio García-Villegas

A Sociology of Justice in Russia
Edited by Marina Kurkchiyan and Agnieszka Kubal

Constituting Religion: Islam, Liberal Rights, and the Malaysian State
Tamir Moustafa

The Invention of the Passport: Surveillance, Citizenship and the State, Second Edition
John C. Torpey

Law's Trials: The Performance of Legal Institutions in the US "War on Terror"
Richard L. Abel

Law's Wars: The Fate of the Rule of Law in the US "War on Terror"
Richard L. Abel

Transforming Gender Citizenship: The Irresistible Rise of Gender Quotas in Europe
Edited by Eléonore Lépinard and Ruth Rubio-Marín

Muslim Women's Quest for Justice: Gender, Law and Activism in India
Mengia Hong Tschalaer

Children as 'Risk': Sexual Exploitation and Abuse by Children and Young People
Anne-Marie McAlinden

The Legal Process and the Promise of Justice: Studies Inspired by the Work of Malcolm Feeley
Jonathan Simon, Rosann Greenspan, Hadar Aviram

Gift Exchanges: The Transnational History of a Political Idea
Grégoire Mallard

Measuring Justice: Quantitative Accountability and the National Prosecuting Authority in South Africa
Johanna Mugler

Negotiating the Power of NGOs: Women's Legal Rights in South Africa
Reem Wael

Indigenous Water Rights in Law and Regulation: Lessons from Comparative Experience
Elizabeth Jane Macpherson

The Edge of Law: Legal Geographies of a War Crimes Court
Alex Jeffrey

Everyday Justice: Law, Ethnography, and Injustice
Sandra Brunnegger

The Uncounted: Politics of Data in Global Health
Sara L. M. Davis

Transnational Legal Ordering of Criminal Justice
Gregory Shaffer and Ely Aaronson

Five Republics and One Tradition
Pablo Ruiz-Tagle

The Law Multiple: Judgment and Knowledge in Practice
Irene van Oorschot

Health as a Human Right: The Politics and Judicialisation of Health in Brazil
Octávio Luiz Motta Ferraz

Shari'a, Inshallah: Finding God in Somali Legal Politics
Mark Fathi Massoud

Policing for Peace: Institutions, Expectations, and Security in Divided Societies
Matthew Nanes

Rule of Law Intermediaries: Brokering Influence in Myanmar
Kristina Simion

Lactation at Work: Expressed Milk, Expressing Beliefs, and the Expressive Value of Law
Elizabeth A. Hoffmann

The Archival Politics of International Courts
Henry Redwood

Global Pro Bono: Causes, Context, and Contestation
Edited by Scott L. Cummings, Fabio de Sa e Silva and Louise G. Trubek

The Practice and Problems of Transnational Counter-Terrorism
Fiona de Londras

Decoupling: Gender Injustice in China's Divorce Courts
Ethan Michelson

Anti-Constitutional Populism
Martin Krygier, Adam Czarnota and Wojciech Sadurski

Lawyers in Conflict and Transition
Kieran McEvoy, Louse Mallinder and Anna Bryson

The Ghostwriters: Lawyers and the Politics behind the Judicial Construction of Europe
Tommaso Pavone

The Sentimental Court: The Affective Life of International Criminal Justice
Jonas Bens

Practices of Reparations in International Criminal Justice
Christoph Sperfeldt

Seeking Supremacy: The Pursuit of Judicial Power in Pakistan
Yasser Kureshi

The Power of the Jury: Transforming Citizens into Jurors
Nancy S. Marder

Undue Process: Persecution and Punishment in Autocratic Courts
Fiona Feiang Shen-Bayh

Discounting Life: Necropolitical Law, Culture, and the Long War on Terror
Jothie Rajah

Clean Air at What Cost? The Rise of Blunt Force Regulation in China
Denise Sienli van der Kamp

Law and Precarity: Legal Consciousness and Daily Survival in Vietnam
Tu Phuong Nguyen

Prosecutors, Voters and The Criminalization of Corruption in Latin America: The Case of Lava Jato
Ezequiel A. Gonzalez-Ocantos and Paula Muñoz Chirinos

Entangled Domains: Empire, Law and Religion in Northern Nigeria
Rabiat Akande

The Social Constitution: Embedding Social Rights Through Legal Mobilization
Whitney K. Taylor

Out of Place: Fieldwork and Positionality in Law and Society
Edited by Lynette J. Chua and Mark Fathi Massoud

Negotiating Legality: Chinese Companies in the U.S. Legal System
Ji Li

Law and Jewish Difference: Ambivalent Encounters
Mareike Riedel

A Sociology of Post-Imperial Constitutions: Suppressed Civil War and Colonized Citizens
Chris Thornhill

The Regulation of Prostitution in China: Law in the Everyday Lives of Sex Workers, Police Officers, and Public Health Officials
Margaret L. Boittin

Immoral Traffic: An Ethnography of Law, NGOs, and the Governance of Prostitution in India
Vibhuti Ramachandran

From Manners to Rules: Advocating for Legalism in South Korea and Japan
Celeste L. Arrington

Risk and Resistance: How Feminists Transformed the Law and Science of AIDS
Aziza Ahmed

Moral Autopsy: Truths, Secrets, and the Judicial Afterlives of Communist Secret Service Archives
Saygun Gökarıksel

Courts, Constitutions and Karma: Buddhism, Law and the Practices of Legal Pluralism in Sri Lanka
Benjamin Schonthal

For EU product safety concerns, contact us at Calle de José Abascal, 56–1°, 28003 Madrid, Spain or eugpsr@cambridge.org.

www.ingramcontent.com/pod-product-compliance
Ingram Content Group UK Ltd.
Pitfield, Milton Keynes, MK11 3LW, UK
UKHW022006220926
475880UK00004B/274
* 9 7 8 1 0 0 9 7 0 6 9 1 9 *